Fine WoodWorking
TECHNIQUES 7

Fine WoodWorking
TECHNIQUES 7

Selected by the Editors
of *Fine Woodworking* magazine

The Taunton Press
Newtown, Connecticut

Typeface: Garamond and Univers
Paper: Warrenflo, 65 lb., Neutral pH

The Taunton Press, Inc.
63 South Main Street
Box 355
Newtown, Connecticut 06470

A FINE WOODWORKING Book

International Standard Book Number 0-918804-42-6
Library of Congress Catalog Card Number 78-58221
Printed in the United States of America

CONTENTS

Continued...

INTRODUCTION

Anything made of wood, be it a complicated piece of furniture or a humble turned bowl, begins as an idea. The woodworker's job is to turn that idea into a finished object, which he or she does by applying the right technique to saw, shape, join and finish the wood. *Fine Woodworking Techniques* books tell how. This series of reprints compiles all of the technical articles from *Fine Woodworking* magazine and preserves them in durable, convenient volumes. This latest volume is based upon articles published in 1983, issues No. 38 through 43. In it, you'll also find a section on plans and projects plus selections from the magazine's Methods of Work and Questions and Answers columns.

Each article in *Techniques 7* is reprinted in its entirety. Where necessary, corrections have been made and information on prices and sources of supply has been updated. The book is arranged into eight subject categories and indexed for handy reference.

WOOD

Dockside at Hamburg, a jumble of cranes, rigging and sheds, is one of many stops for exotic woods on their way to market.

The Trade in Exotic Hardwoods
How wood gets from the tropics to your shop

by Irving Sloane

History records that the demand for exotic hardwoods has always been brisk and, occasionally, voracious. The ebony forests of Mauritius were cut down by the Dutch in the 17th century, and West Indian mahogany (*Swietenia mahagoni*) was so heavily cut for Spanish shipbuilders and 18th-century furnituremakers that by the mid-19th century it had disappeared from commerce. A measure of the ancient esteem for rare woods is the name Brazil, taken from brazil-wood (*Caesalpinia echinata*), an important item in the European trade of the Middle Ages, centuries before Brazil was discovered. Originally, brazilwood came from Sri Lanka, but it also grows in Brazil. It was used for dye extraction before being sought for violin bow making. It is more commonly known today as pernambuco.

Working with exotic woods—rosewood, ebony, boxwood—is one of the great pleasures of being a musical instrument maker. My search for such woods has led me and many other musical instrument makers to Theodor Nagel & Co., of Hamburg, West Germany. A family-owned firm established in 1837, Nagel is the world's foremost timber trader special-izing in exotic hardwoods. An order for 200,000 ebony fret-boards is not unusual, but neither is an order for just one.

Home base for Nagel is a ten-acre tract in the industrial Billbrook section of Hamburg. The firm's timber-sawing and grading operations, dry-kilns and storage sheds spread along both sides of the Billstrasse, the district's main road. Here trucks deposit logs and square-edged timbers from all over the world, brought from dockside at the ports of Hamburg and Bremen. The wood is resawn into boards, and custom-sized billets or scantlings for grading, the ends are waxed to retard checking, and finally it is shipped. Nagel employs al-most 100 people here in Hamburg and another 500 world-wide, with sawmills in Brazil, Indonesia, India, Sri Lanka, Africa, Mexico, the United States and Austria. Their Indian sawmills in Kerala and Mysore cut and shape rosewood and ebony into parts for violins and guitars. The firm's customers include the world's major manufacturers of guitars, pianos, organs, harpsichords, violins and woodwinds. Nagel also sup-plies furniture manufacturers in Europe and Scandinavia.

The export manager in charge of sales to the musical instrument trade is Peter Wiese, a wiry, intense native of Hamburg with almost 30 years of experience in the timber business. Buying and selling rare woods in the international market requires shrewd judgments about world supply and demand, a profound knowledge of these woods and large amounts of capital. Wiese works hard at his job—buying wood and seeing customers—all the while preoccupied with shipping costs, fluctuating exchange rates, and customers trying to preserve liquidity by shrinking their wood inventories. His sales domain is the world except for France, Scandinavia and the Iron Curtain countries. At 7:15 each morning he is in his office, reading telexes from distant places. He is a born trader, forthright and voluble.

"It's tough today, and very competitive," Wiese says. "We're buying and selling a product which is gradually growing scarcer in a world market where economic conditions are changing every day." He explains that dealers used to ship logs to Europe for sawing, but in recent years many developing countries have embargoed the shipment of logs. In such countries as India, Sri Lanka and Brazil, logs must be sawn into dimensioned lumber before export, the idea being to create local jobs. This trend has changed the import business. "Some of our big saws here are closed down," Wiese says, "although we still handle many logs from Africa, Burma and North America. But today you cannot export a board from Brazil thicker than three inches."

This saddens Wiese; cutting open a log felled in some wilderness outpost and freighted halfway around the world is part of the romance of the timber trade.

The stiffest competition Nagel faces these days comes from the ubiquitous Japanese. Their buyers will spend as long as three months in one area buying wood. Nagel, though, requires buyers to return home after a maximum of three weeks—by which time a buyer's aggressiveness, sharpness and resistance to bad deals will start wearing down. Life at the company's tropical sawmills is difficult, Wiese says. "Often we send a person out, and after a few months he starts going bush. His attitudes change, he sleeps late, he drinks, and when he comes home to report we can see that he is changed. It's definitely not for people who are upset by insects and lizards. I myself have been sick twice with malaria."

Still, Wiese declares, "I am a timber man. Timber is a business you have to have a certain feeling for—a gift, you might say. I wouldn't trade my job for any other."

Wiese joined Nagel in 1960. His first overseas assignment was to comb the backwoods of Florida, Georgia and the Carolinas to find hickory logs for European ski makers. It was a hard lesson in how money can be lost in the timber business: "Finally I had accumulated a load dockside in Jacksonville for shipment to Hamburg. That same day the Teamsters went on strike and nobody would move my logs. Day by day I watched them split under that baking sun, and I had to get rid of them for half their value."

He chuckles over the memory while leading me into the yard, a complex of sheds dominated by a large kiln. A corner of one shed is used as a sales display for offcuts of a variety of rare woods. These are stacked on shelves and sold by weight to craftspeople for a nominal price.

We pause in front of one of many big storage sheds piled high with logs: "That balsa lumber from Ecuador and Venezuela will go to the model-making trade. The teak will go mainly for furniture and flooring. This is lignum vitae from Mexico and Central America, one of the heaviest woods." Lignum (*Guaiacum spp.*) contains a natural lubricating oil, guyacan, which makes it suitable for lining ship propeller shaft tubes and for other mechanical applications. The lignum logs are short, 3 ft. to 4 ft., with yellow sapwood and greenish heart. I suggest that this species is also used for the soles of fine wooden planes, but Wiese says no, that's vera wood (*Bulnesia arborea*) from South America. It's not as oily as lignum and a bit lighter in color, but it has the same hardness and weight.

Wiese feels strongly that woods should be sold by their correct names so people know exactly what they are buying. "There are many close substitutes for different woods. Take mahogany—even experts are at a loss sometimes to explain what can be considered a genuine—*Swietenia*—mahogany. Another example is rosewood. The Brazilians call rosewood—*Dalbergia nigra*—jacaranda. The English cutlery makers call it Bahia wood. In India, rosewood—*Dalbergia latifolia*—is called palisander. In Germany it is known by both names regardless of where it comes from, and some Germans have translated the English word rosewood into *rosenholz*. But this is wrong because *rosenholz* is actually tulipwood—*Dalbergia variabilis*." Wiese has a diploma from Hamburg University's School of Forestry and Wood Research; botanical Latin comes easily to him.

Brazilian rosewood is a favorite of mine, so I pursue discussion of its availability with Wiese and his associate, Belsemeyer, who has just returned from Brazil. "All gone," Wiese says, explaining that only veneer cutters can afford to buy the few logs still reaching market. I wonder whether undiscovered rosewood might grow deep in the jungle, but Belsemeyer replies, "Rosewood doesn't grow in the jungle, it grows in the central coastal regions," where it's often planted as shade for cocoa trees. Unfortunately, fertilizer for cocoa spoils the wood. So does prolonged storage of the logs. Unwilling to give up, I ask if logs are ever smuggled out in defiance of the government embargo. Belsemeyer doubts it: "The customs people wouldn't jeopardize their jobs for one log or even for a large bribe. It just wouldn't be worth it to them."

In some countries, India for example, logs are gathered at government depots, then auctioned in parcels of up to fifteen logs each. Half the annual supply of East Indian rosewood is auctioned during September in Mysore, with bidding conducted through native go-betweens. Wiese himself usually attends. "You have to go there many days in advance to study the parcels, make notes, and decide how much you will be willing to pay. Bidding is done in Hindi, but you quickly learn what is one, two, three and so on."

Burmese teak (*Tectona grandis*) is also sold at central depots, but at prices fixed by the government. The Burmese, like the Indians, use elephants for dragging logs because they can work in narrow places where tractors won't fit. In inaccessible areas, teak trees are girdled and left to dry for a couple of years before felling. Then they can be floated downstream; green teak is so heavy it sinks.

We are walking through the yard and a big zebrano log from Africa catches Wiese's eye. He's brought along his timberman's gouge, with which he takes a short, glancing swipe at the end grain, leaving a shallow groove. "When logs stand in storage they get covered over with a coating that hides the true color and grain," Wiese explains. "Here where I've made the cut you can see the color and grain, which look very good

Peter Wiese, above, uses a timber gouge to inspect a bubinga log. Scooping into the log's end grain reveals the wood's color and texture. Behind him is lumber 'sawn in the boule.' Wood is more commonly sawn in this manner in Europe and is stacked in the order it comes from the log, thus preserving the relationship of color and figure from board to board. Theodor Nagel & Co. is a principal supplier of musical instrument woods and provides its customers with custom-sized blanks and billets. At right, a worker dips the end grain of billets in wax to guard against checking during drying and shipping.

on this log. When I go to buy logs, I take the gouge so I can see what I'm buying." Near the edge of the log he points to a dark stain, a resinous suffusion which probably goes right through the wood and will have to be cut away.

Nearby a stack of bubinga logs have just come in, 109 tons Wiese recently bought. On one of them he shows me another defect that can diminish the lumber yield: a large, circular split in the annual rings. "This is bad, a ring shake that may run through the entire log." He hurries to the other end of the log to check. "No, it doesn't show on this end. We can determine approximately where the shake ends by tapping the log with a hammer. You go along tapping, with your ear close to the log, listening carefully to the sound. It will change when you reach the shake. We have to know so that we can cut the log in the right place."

We pass to another shed where a 10-ft. log provokes a cry of pleasure: "This is the finest grenadilla log I have ever seen—East African blackwood. In the size, the grain, the color, an incredible log. It's in the rosewood family, *Dalbergia melanoxylon,* and will be used for making woodwinds and bagpipes. I wish they were all like this one—on some logs we're lucky to get out 20% of usable wood."

Wiese interrupts our yard tour to chew out a man for improperly stickering a log sawn through-and-through. "It really gets me to see that sort of thing," he says. "You bring a log 5,000 miles and then they sticker it the wrong way. Nobody does it, but ideally the end sticks should protrude a bit so they shade the end grain of the board underneath."

There are many woods of great beauty that never find their way to the sawmill. "It's the old story of supply and demand. We sometimes try to introduce new woods, but people who buy wood are very conservative, especially musical instrument

makers, who don't like to experiment." As substitutes for Brazilian rosewood, Nagel now sells amazonas and Santos palisander (*Machaerium scleroxylum*), "a beautiful wood but with the same drawback that cocobolo has, it may cause skin irritation in some people. Gaining acceptance for these woods is going to take time."

Another problem with introducing rare species, says Wiese, is that "they have to have a certain diameter or else there is no profit in it. Many are too small, and others—the top-quality logs of large diameter—will be bought by veneer cutters who will pay big prices." Then there is ocean freight: "I could buy woods in South America for very little, but the freight will cost $200 a ton. I can bring logs into Europe from Africa for $150 a ton including the price of the logs."

Some woods are disappearing from the market not because they no longer can be found in the forest, but because demand is just too low. Satinwood (*Chloroxylon swietenia*), for example, once was sought for making hairbrush handles, but now they're made of plastic. Cocus (*Brya ebenus*) from Jamaica is a beautiful brown wood, but likewise in limited demand and difficult to get out, so there's no incentive to go after it. Pernambuco, the Brazilian wood used for violin bows, is also increasingly hard to find. Snakewood or letterwood (*Piratinera guianensis*), a hard South American wood used for canes, umbrella handles and flutes, has almost disappeared from the market—Wiese estimates the entire annual demand at not more than three tons. "Even if you were willing to pay $3,000 a ton for it you would still buy only $10,000 or $15,000 worth, small stuff for an established timber trader. Labor is expensive today. When people were hunting for bucks, you found men who would go into the forest, cut the trees and carry them out. Nobody seems interested in doing this kind of work today."

On the other hand, boxwood (*Buxus sempervirens*), a favorite of wind instrument makers, is still valuable enough for Nagel to send men into the mountains of France or Turkey to cut it from the high, rocky places where it grows. Ebony is another species that normally grows as isolated trees, the best of it (*Diospyros ebenum*) coming from Sri Lanka. The wood is so heavy that it's usually cut into manageable chunks on the spot, then packed out.

The world's finest ebony was supposed to have come from Mauritius, but Wiese says he has seen a small piece only recently, for the first time. "The best African ebony (*Diospyros crassiflora*) is from Gaboon but very difficult to get. Cameroon is where most African ebony comes from. Gaboon is harder and blacker. Quality can vary greatly in ebony even within a two-mile area, depending on soil conditions. The best stuff grows in the mountains."

We pass a man loading the trunk of a Mercedes with bags of wood. "Those are offcuts of grenadilla," Wiese says. "We bag and sell it for firewood. It makes a fine fire, long-burning, good heat, and slight, pleasant smell. Lignum vitae is even better—it burns with a green flame." As if sensing some concern of mine for the depletion of the earth's forests, he notes that "90% of world wood consumption is for firewood and burning down forests to clear land for agriculture."

•   •   •

In the future, it's clear that technological advances, labor and freight costs, and political upheaval will have more to do with the availability of rare hardwoods than the extinction of individual species. Timber traders are drawn to countries where conditions favor investment: political stability, abundant supply of desirable species, a minimum of red tape. Volatile politics in South and Central America, parts of Africa and the West Indies have wiped out some traders.

If the price of a rare hardwood rises above what buyers are willing to pay, they will turn to substitutes—cheaper woods, plywood or plastics. And as demand dwindles, timber traders will drop those species in favor of the ones that sell well. Many manufacturers have switched to plastics for their labor-saving benefits, or to improve product performance. Composition bowling balls, for example, are far superior to their forerunners which were turned from lignum vitae. Woods from which dyes were extracted have been supplanted by chemical dyestuffs.

For the professional woodworker using rare hardwoods, the future looks expensive rather than bleak. Amateurs may have to switch to domestic hardwoods unless they can afford the escalating prices due to rising labor and shipping costs. For Americans, some of these costs are offset by the dollar's current high exchange rate. Shops using large quantities of rare woods might even find it worthwhile to import their own wood, rather than buying it on the domestic market. □

Irving Sloane is a musical instrument maker and an author of books, including Making Musical Instruments, *published by E.P. Dutton, 2 Park Ave., New York, N.Y. 10016. He lives in Brussels, Belgium. Theodor Nagel G.M.B.H. accepts mail orders for wood and has no minimum price or weight restrictions. Small orders are shipped via parcel post; orders in excess of 50 lb. are shipped by sea freight. Nagel's address is Postfach 28 02 66, D2 Hamburg 28, Germany. Photos by the author.*

Whither Rosewood?
A supply outlook for exotics

by Paul McClure

As conditions in the world market shift, woodworkers who enjoy exotic hardwoods need to know the current status of the different species. Why are some, such as teak and rosewood, becoming difficult to obtain? Are these shortages temporary, or are they harbingers of disappearance? Are available substitutes worth considering? Are new woods emerging in attractive supply?

Some woodworkers feel that we should not import wood from Third World countries, in order to protect our own economy and to not participate in the depletion of the tropical rain forests. But I feel that these are isolationist views which ignore the interdependence of the world economy, and which forget the fact that most land clearing has been done for agriculture, not timber. In fact, increased demand for wood is likely to lead to sound forestry policies in developing countries that don't yet know the value of their forests.

These days, the supply of exotic woods is primarily influenced by political decisions in Third World countries. For instance, most of the teak (*Tectonia grandis*) that is sold on the export market originates in Thailand, India, Sri Lanka, Indonesia, Burma and China. Only the last three are presently exporting teak in log form. Thailand, India and Sri Lanka have banned the export of logs and roughsawn lumber. Their economists believe that the teak stands have been overcut, and that there's more money in milling and exporting small pieces of dimensioned lumber. Consequently, teak exports from these countries have fallen off, because such pieces are of less value to the average cabinetmaker and boatbuilder. Burma, China and Indonesia have picked up supplying the world's demand for larger pieces. The export of ebony (*Diospyros spp.*) and satinwood (*Chloroxylon swietenia*) is similarly constrained because these woods also originate in India and Sri Lanka.

Shortages are not new in the business of importing and exporting wood. They are cyclical and have recurred for as long as records have been kept. Most woods whose availability is now restricted politically, geographically or economically will probably return to the marketplace in two or three years. At present, most woods reaching the American market come from Central and South America. Wood export from the Orient has dramatically decreased and the supply from Africa has become unpredictable.

Brazilian rosewood (*Dalbergia nigra*), however, a prize South American wood, is liable to remain scarce. The tree is peculiar in that it has to be quite old (around 200 years) to be of value. The wood's beautiful figure and fragrance are the result of the tree's gradual deterioration from the center out. Young trees have drab brown heartwood and no scent. There are few saleable rosewood trees left, hence the Brazilian government no longer allows rosewood to be cut and exported in log or lumber form.

Cocobolo (*Dalbergia retusa*), which is yellow, red, brown,

Cost Chart for Imported Woods

Comparative retail costs (per board foot)

Bocote	$11 to $16
Brazilian rosewood	$35 and up
Caviuna	$11 to $16
Cocobolo	$11 to $16
Ebony	$20 and up
Goncalo alves	$4 to $7
Kingwood	$16 and up
Mahogany (true and pseudo)	$2 to $4
Obeche	$2 to $4
Padauk	$4 to $7
Paldao	$4 to $7
Pernambuco	$16 and up
Purpleheart	$4 to $7
Putumuju	$7 to $11
Ramin	$2 to $4
Satinwood	$7 to $11
Teak	$7 to $11
Tulipwood	$16 and up
Zebrawood	$7 to $11

Note: It is difficult to quote prices because they are subject to daily fluctuations in the value of the U.S. dollar on the foreign market.

violet and black when freshly cut, darkens with age to reds and blacks that resemble Brazilian rosewood, for which it's been a popular substitute. Unfortunately, many of the areas where cocobolo grows are in political turmoil, and it can now be purchased only sporadically from a government-approved agent or party. Most of the best cocobolo comes from Nicaragua, but since the ouster of President Somoza, wood has been hard to get. Currency problems in Costa Rica have had a similar effect on supplies from that country. Panama, where cocobolo was first exploited in 1911, has had continuing production problems. With the United States decreasing its involvement in Panama, the situation is not likely to improve. Southern Mexico and Guatemala remain the only dependable sources, but they can supply merely half of what we once received, and then only sporadically.

Paldao (*Dracontemelum dao*), which grows in the Philippines, is a beautiful, light-brown wood, variegated by black streaks. It is in limited supply because the Philippine government stipulates that it can be cut only when it impedes construction. This wood was quite abundant on the market until the 1970s, but concern about its overexploitation led to the current severe limitation on cutting.

Zebrawood (*Brachystegia leonensis*), from western and equatorial Africa, is also becoming hard to get. With the decolonization of Africa, and subsequent withdrawal of European technicians, the newly independent countries are having difficulty with their production methods. Wood buyers can no longer be assured that zebrawood logs will be quartersawn, a procedure essential for proper kiln-drying, and are consequently reluctant to commit their company's funds. Thus zebrawood has doubled in price in the past year.

On the other hand, Brazilian kingwood or violetwood (*Dalbergia cearensis*), which had disappeared for about 20 years, is again available in limited quantities. This wood has a fine violet-and-black color and is truly a wood for the

connoisseur of fine cabinets. Kingwood is a small tree, however, 3 in. to 8 in. in diameter, and prone to considerable degrade. The yield is therefore minimal.

Tulipwood (*Dalbergia frutescens*), beautiful with its red and yellow variegations, is presently available from Brazil in limited quantities. The log is small, the yield minimal, and the piece usually contains the pith of the tree, which results in some checking.

Pernambuco (*Guilandina echinata*), the violin-bow wood, is native to Brazil, but it grows only in the states of Bahia and Pernambuco. This wood is scarce mainly because of its remote geographic location, not because of overexploitation or government embargo.

The supply of some long-popular exotics has been more reliable. Padauk (*Pterocarpus soyaxii*) is a bright orange color when freshly cut, turning to rich maroon when exposed to sunlight. This wood comes from western Africa and is one of the most stable, durable woods available. It makes excellent flooring in high-traffic areas, and it is also good for exterior use. African padauk is quite abundant, and no shortages are foreseen in the near future. Another member of the genus, Andaman padauk (*P. dalbergoides*), also known as vermilion, comes from the Bay of Bengal's Andaman Islands, where it is logged by convict labor. These stands have been exploited since the mid-1800s, so now very little vermilion is available for import into this country. Andaman padauk is pink to red and maintains its color well. A third member of the padauk genus, narra (*P. indicus*), known as amboyna when in burl form, is indigenous to the South Pacific islands and is either red or yellow, depending on growth conditions. This species has been logged since the early 1700s and exported to Europe from the Philippines. There's currently a moratorium on cutting these trees where we have been used to getting them; however, stands of narra have been discovered in Papua New Guinea, and are being marketed as PNG rosewood, though narra is not related to the rosewoods.

Obeche (*Triplochiton scleroxylon*), from western Africa, and ramin (*Gonystylus spp.*), from Malaysia and Indonesia, have been abundant for many years and are in great demand in Europe and Japan, respectively. Both woods are relatively bland, good for carving and molding. Obeche is cream-colored, lightweight and soft (too soft for most furniture), and must be worked with very sharp tools. Ramin is straw-colored, heavier and easier to machine.

What of new woods and substitutes? First, the word "substitute" is inappropriate. No wood will be exactly like another wood. Each is unique, and though one wood will be similar in some respects to another, it will never perfectly replace it. Each wood should be recognized for its own characteristics and used accordingly. On the other hand, many jobs can be done by any of several woods.

The extent to which species are interchangeable can be illustrated with the mahoganies. During the 18th century, true mahogany was highly esteemed—dark reddish-brown in color, it was stable, easy to work and beautiful when polished. This was Cuban mahogany (*Swietenia mahagoni*), procured from the Caribbean islands. Around 1920, as supplies of this wood diminished, inroads were being made into Honduras. This country and its neighbors are the source for Honduras mahogany (*Swietenia macrophylla*), the wood that most cabinetmakers have been using to make fine furniture for decades. It is close in color and figure to the Cuban species, but coarser. Recent political turmoil, currency instability and over-grazing of livestock in Central America have decreased the supply of Honduras mahogany, so a number of other woods are being sold as substitutes. Brazilian mahogany (*Cariniana legalis*) is not related to the *Swietenia* genus but is similar in appearance, and it is becoming more competitive in price and availability. It is lighter in color than the true mahoganies. Another stand-in is African mahogany (*Khaya ivorensis*), whose color varies from light brown to deep reddish-brown and whose texture is coarser than that of the South American mahoganies. This wood was quite popular during the 1960s, but higher prices now make it less attractive. Lauan (*Shorea spp.*), known as Philippine mahogany, has been marketed since the early 1920s as a mahogany substitute, although lauan varies considerably in weight and color, and its texture is coarse and difficult to finish. Lauan is popular in public-school industrial arts programs, as it is relatively inexpensive. Much of it is also made into plywood in Japan.

Caviuna (*Machaerium actufolium*), native to Bolivia, looks like Indian rosewood, but is richer in grain and color, does not have the fragrance and is usually cut on the quarter. It sands and polishes very well and comes in medium sizes. Flat cut, it has a most impressive figure of intermingled browns and purples. It costs less than Indian rosewood, and therefore could replace it in the marketplace. As with rosewood, however, some people develop a skin rash from handling it.

Goncalo alves (*Astronium graveolens*) is a beautiful wood that can be used in many furniture applications. It is golden in color, aging to dark red, with broad black stripes. Unlike most foreign woods, it comes in wide widths and long lengths. It grows in Brazil, and is plentiful at present.

Putumuju or arariba (*Centrolobium robustum*), also from Brazil, is a newly available, moderately priced wood. It is yellow, red and black, with some tinges of green. It seems to be abundant.

Purpleheart (*Peltogyne densiflora*), another Brazilian wood, is still quite abundant, compared with other exotics. The tree is usually large and yields wide, long, clear lumber. Purpleheart has a large amount of silica-oxide, as does teak, and the two woods are of similar density. The silica rapidly dulls cutting tools. Purpleheart is used mostly for accents (inlays and borders), rather than in large pieces, because of its weight and brilliant purple color.

Bocote (*Cordia spp.*) is the color of tobacco and has irregular dark brown or blackish streaks. It is hard and waxy in texture and comes from a tree that reaches heights of 100 ft. Bocote grows in Central America and Mexico, and still can be obtained with relative ease at a moderate price. It makes beautiful turnings and small cabinets.

These and other woods, mainly from South America, are filling the need for exotic woods in contemporary woodworking. While some historically popular species are now hard to get, other less familiar species are becoming available. And while the general quality of wood, both domestic and imported, seems to be declining, a sharp eye can still find choice stock, whether in the forest or at the lumberyard. □

Paul McClure is a wood technologist who has worked in the lumber trade for 12 years. He has recently opened a hardwood retail outlet, a branch of Wood World, in Tempe, Ariz.

Storing precious scraps

by Tom Dewey

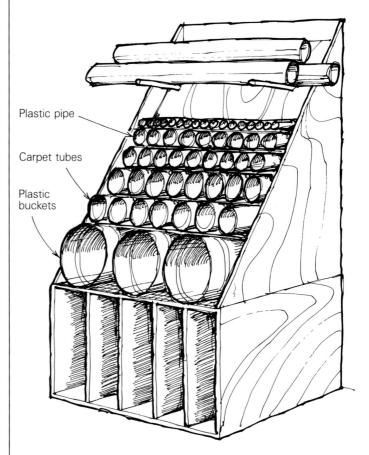

Plastic pipe

Carpet tubes

Plastic buckets

. . . And then there was the deceased frugal widow who, friends found, had very carefully labeled shoe boxes "pieces of string too short to save" and had, of course, just as carefully stowed them away. Like her, I had a scrap box into which I tossed little pieces of wood I didn't really need but couldn't bring myself to burn. I'd paw through the jumble, wasting time trying to locate that dandy piece of ebony I remembered being there. Most of the time I ended up cutting a new piece anyway, creating yet more scrap and an even thicker clutter.

It finally came to the point where it was either me or the scrap, and I was forced to deal with the problem. My solution occupies no more floor space than the original scrap box, holds a lot more, and keeps wood out where it sort of winks at me as I pass by.

I turned the original box on its side, made a sloping rack out of plywood and nailed this to the wall. I fashioned bins from 5-gal. paint buckets, sections of plastic drain pipe, carpet tubes and, for small pieces of wood, lengths of 1½-in. plastic pipe. Two broomstick braces—inserted through the rack into holes in the studs behind—hold more carpet tubes across the top of the main rack. I store longer pieces of molding, splines and shim stock in these. Plywood, wider boards, and odds and ends go in the bottom.

The rack has turned out to be so accessible that I find myself storing cutoffs as I work, instead of letting them pile up until I'm done. When I'm looking for a small turning square, I can invariably find just what I need. □

Tom Dewey makes custom cabinetry in Coudersport, Pa.

As Dries the Air, So Shrinks the Wood
Why woodworkers keep a weather eye on relative humidity

by R. Bruce Hoadley

Most woodworkers realize that wood moves, shrinking and swelling according to its moisture content. Accordingly, we use joints and constructions that allow for a moderate amount of wood movement, and many of us now use moisture meters to ensure that our wood has been dried to a safe level. But a one-time check of moisture content isn't enough. Here in the northeast, you can take delivery of wood kiln-dried to 7% moisture content, but if you then store it in an unheated garage, it will gradually adsorb moisture from the air and increase to a new level of up to 14%, which, if unanticipated, would come as an unpleasant surprise.

The amount of moisture in wood balances and adjusts to the relative humidity of the air around it. Assessing the humidity of the air in shop or storage areas, therefore, is as important as working with wood that has been properly dried in the first place. An extremely dry or damp period may not last long enough to cause much dimensional change in a board, but moisture exchange in the board's surface layer, which takes place immediately, can cause disheartening problems with glues and finishes.

Equilibrium moisture content—One sometimes comes across wood that has been sitting in a well-ventilated, unheated barn for thirty or forty years. It probably reached its lowest moisture content within the first two or three years, and it is not any drier or more stable today than it was then. In wood, *moisture content* (MC) is the ratio (expressed as a percent) of the weight of water in a piece of wood to the weight of the wood if it were completely dry. Green wood may start off with more than 100% moisture content (the sapwood of green sugar pine is actually more than twice as much water as wood, averaging 219% MC), but it will commonly be dried to about 7% to 9% MC for woodworking purposes. Water is held in the wood in two ways: *free water,* held in the cell

---

Weather, temperature and humidity

Weather systems bring air masses having a certain *absolute humidity,* the actual amount of moisture in the air at a given time, expressed in grains per cubic foot (there are 7,000 grains in a pound). Because the maximum amount of water the air can hold depends on the temperature of the air, temperature determines the upper limit of absolute humidity.

As shown at right, at 70°F the air can hold 8 gr./cu. ft., whereas at 41°F the air can hold only 3 gr./cu. ft. We naturally associate cold weather with low absolute humidity and hot weather with high absolute humidity. It isn't absolute humidity, however, that causes the problems for woodworkers but relative humidity. And where relative humidity is concerned, the generalization does not always hold true. A hot summer day can be dry; winters can be cold and damp.

Relative humidity (RH) is the ratio (expressed as a percent) of the amount of water in the air at a given temperature to the amount it could hold at that temperature. Since air at 70°F could hold 8 gr./cu. ft., if it actually held only 4 gr./cu. ft., the RH would be 50%; if it held 2 gr./cu. ft., the RH would be 25%, and so forth.

Dew point is the temperature at which air of a given absolute humidity becomes saturated. As an example, air that contains 4 gr./cu. ft. has a dew point of 49.3°F. That is, when cooled to 49.3°F the air will be saturated and therefore will be at 100% RH. If it gets any colder, moisture will condense out. —*R.B.H.*

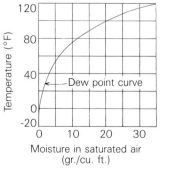

Dew point curve

Temperature (°F) / Moisture in saturated air (gr./cu. ft.)

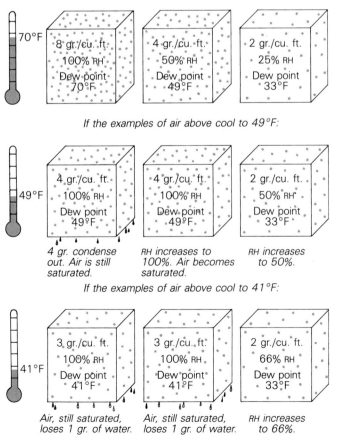

Humidity   *Boxes represent a cubic foot of air.*

70°F — 8 gr./cu. ft. 100% RH Dew point 70°F | 4 gr./cu. ft. 50% RH Dew point 49°F | 2 gr./cu. ft. 25% RH Dew point 33°F

If the examples of air above cool to 49°F:

49°F — 4 gr./cu. ft. 100% RH Dew point 49°F | 4 gr./cu. ft. 100% RH Dew point 49°F | 2 gr./cu. ft. 50% RH Dew point 33°F

4 gr. condense out. Air is still saturated. | RH increases to 100%. Air becomes saturated. | RH increases to 50%.

If the examples of air above cool to 41°F:

41°F — 3 gr./cu. ft. 100% RH Dew point 41°F | 3 gr./cu. ft. 100% RH Dew point 41°F | 2 gr./cu. ft. 66% RH Dew point 33°F

Air, still saturated, loses 1 gr. of water. | Air, still saturated, loses 1 gr. of water. | RH increases to 66%.

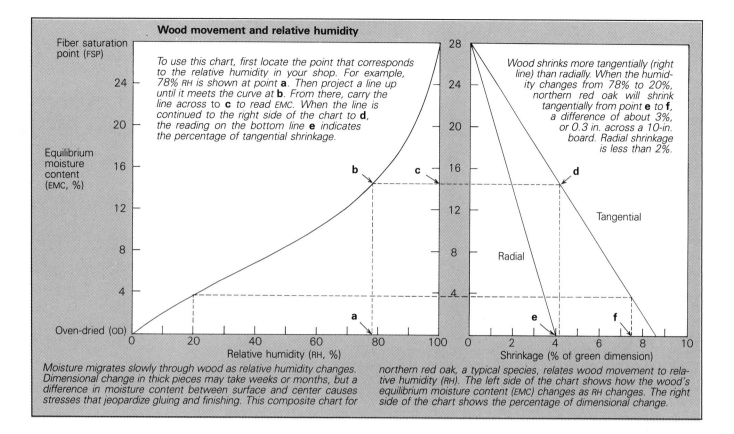

Wood movement and relative humidity

*To use this chart, first locate the point that corresponds to the relative humidity in your shop. For example, 78% RH is shown at point **a**. Then project a line up until it meets the curve at **b**. From there, carry the line across to **c** to read EMC. When the line is continued to the right side of the chart to **d**, the reading on the bottom line **e** indicates the percentage of tangential shrinkage.*

*Wood shrinks more tangentially (right line) than radially. When the humidity changes from 78% to 20%, northern red oak will shrink tangentially from point **e** to **f**, a difference of about 3%, or 0.3 in. across a 10-in. board. Radial shrinkage is less than 2%.*

Fiber saturation point (FSP)

Equilibrium moisture content (EMC, %)

Oven-dried (OD)

Relative humidity (RH, %)

Shrinkage (% of green dimension)

Tangential

Radial

Moisture migrates slowly through wood as relative humidity changes. Dimensional change in thick pieces may take weeks or months, but a difference in moisture content between surface and center causes stresses that jeopardize gluing and finishing. This composite chart for

northern red oak, a typical species, relates wood movement to relative humidity (RH). The left side of the chart shows how the wood's equilibrium moisture content (EMC) changes as RH changes. The right side of the chart shows the percentage of dimensional change.

cavities, and *bound water,* held within the cell walls themselves. When wood dries, it loses free water until the moisture content drops to about 30%; from then on it loses bound water. As the cells lose bound water they shrink, creating stresses that can lead to checking and warping.

Even after kiln-drying, wood cells continue to lose and gain moisture until there is an equilibrium between the amount of bound water and the surrounding air's *relative humidity* (RH, explained in the box on the facing page). When this balance with RH is reached, the MC of the wood is called the *equilibrium moisture content* (EMC). Note the left side of the chart above, which is based on red oak, a typical species; other species differ only slightly. Generally the EMC can vary from 0% (when oven-dried, in effect at 0% RH) to a maximum of about 30% (in an atmosphere where the air is saturated with moisture, in effect at 100% RH). A 30% moisture content is all the bound water the cells can hold, the *fiber saturation point* (FSP). The wood will not adsorb more moisture from the air than this, although if rained on or soaked it would absorb some free water again at the surface layers.

Left outdoors (as in a typical drying pile), the wood will arrive at an average equilibrium moisture content depending on the average relative humidity of the area. This is called its *air-dried moisture content,* and once the wood reaches this point it will more or less stay there, varying slightly with environmental fluctuations. Air-dried moisture content can vary widely from region to region—wood reaches a different EMC in southwestern deserts than it does in the northwest's rain forests. EMC can vary depending on local conditions within an area; the windward side of a lake, for instance, is measurably drier than the leeward. As I mentioned earlier, air-dried wood reaches an equilibrium at about 14% EMC in the northeast. This is because the relative humidity here averages about 75%. In your own part of the country, you can determine the EMC for air-dried wood if you know the average RH.

Some people define EMC as *surface moisture content,* an appropriate reminder that the wood cells at the surface attain an immediate equilibrium with the surrounding air. When we put a finish on a wooden object, it slows down moisture exchange, giving some protection from sudden changes in relative humidity. And even raw wood takes time to adjust fully—the rate of moisture migration into wood is quite slow, and one or two days of high humidity are not enough to cause much dimensional change in thick pieces. But even temporary change in a raw-wood surface layer can have critical consequences, and abrupt changes in relative humidity, particularly in the workshop, can cause serious problems: drawers that will never work right, faulty glue joints, finishes that won't shine or, at worst, won't adhere at all. These problems can come as a surprise because human beings are relatively insensitive to changes in relative humidity. While the average person can estimate indoor temperatures within a few degrees, sensitivity to relative humidity is quite another matter. We become acclimated to gradual seasonal changes, and our sense of "normal" adjusts to summer humidity and winter dryness.

I'm frequently reminded of this in my daily work. Our laboratory has an experimental room closely controlled at 72°F and 50% RH. When I enter it in winter it seems oppressively muggy and damp, while in summer it seems cool and dry. We cannot trust our senses, but must rely on instruments such as those shown on p. 11 to tell us of conditions that to us may feel only moderately uncomfortable, but to a woodworking project may spell disaster.

Effects of changes in RH—The chart above correlates dimensional change in wood to EMC and RH. My basement, surrounded by bedrock, is also my workshop, and its RH can swing from more than 90% in August (relative humidity rises when hot, muggy air is cooled by the basement) to 5% in midwinter when I have been using the woodstove. Extremes of this magnitude can cause as much as a ½-in. variation in the width of a 10-in., flatsawn red oak board. Wood exchanges moisture with the air fastest on the surface and through the end grain. Abrupt changes in RH mean that the inside of a piece of wood is at an EMC (and size) different from the surface. A sudden dry day can cause microscopic surface checking that will interfere with the quality or adhesion of finishes. Wood has a certain elasticity that allows it to absorb stresses caused by moisture changes, but this elasticity can be lost. A sudden damp day can have somewhat the same effect as a dry one—the surface, restrained from swelling by the center, becomes *compression set* (*FWW* #14, pp. 80-81). When the surface redries, checks result.

EMC can interfere with gluing. Silicone adhesives will not bond properly if the EMC of the wood surface is too high, and plastic resin glues (urea-formaldehyde) will not bond well if the wood is *drier* than about 7% MC. As the left side of the chart on p. 9 shows, one might encounter problems with urea-formaldehyde glues when the shop RH drops below 40%.

While thick pieces of wood may take days, weeks or even months to completely adjust to a new RH, thin veneers can reach equilibrium within an hour or less. Thus they don't surface-check, but they may quickly undergo the maximum overall change in size. I would not work veneer in my basement when its RH is approaching either extreme.

With the RH in my basement so unstable, even moderate-size pieces of wood, drawer parts for instance, can move enough from one weekend to the next to make precision cuts meaningless. Although I manage to store my wood someplace else, upstairs usually, in a closet, under the bed, in the mudroom or wherever, it still leaves me with the problem of what to do with projects that are half-done. I routinely wrap wood sculptures in plastic between work sessions to protect them, because changes in RH can cause extreme stress between the center and the surface of a thick block. Plastic film or bags have the same effect as a coat of finish—while they can't maintain the moisture content of a piece of wood indefinitely, they can isolate the wood against drastic responses to temporary swings by making changes slow and uniform.

Controlling RH

—The ideal moisture content for wood is not necessarily the numerical mean between the highest and lowest extremes, but depends on the yearlong seasonal variation. Indoors, the average RH in the northeast averages close to 40%, mostly due to heating in winter, which commonly lowers levels to 20% for weeks at a time. Red oak furniture, therefore, will eventually reach an average EMC indoors of about 7% to 8%. This is the reason woodworkers in the northeast start out with wood dried to this level. Our workshops, then, should be maintained at a humidity level of about 35% to 40% in order to keep our stock at a 7% to 8% EMC. One would do well to think: "My lumber should be at an equilibrium with 40% relative humidity," rather than thinking only about the wood's 7.5% moisture content. This approach has the advantage of automatically accommodating the different EMCs of various wood species and of wood products such as particleboard, fiberboard and hardboard.

Without its being our intent, many of our daily activities affect indoor RH. In our homes and workshops, we routinely modify temperature by heating and cooling the air. If we increase the temperature while the absolute humidity remains unchanged, the relative humidity will be lowered. If we cool the air, such as happens when I ventilate my cool basement with warmer air from outside, the relative humidity will rise. Routine activities such as cooking and washing may release surprising amounts of water. Mopping a kitchen floor and allowing it to dry, for instance, may add several *pounds* of water to the indoor air. So will moving a quantity of green wood into a storage area filled with wood that has been carefully dried. On the other hand, air conditioners and dehumidifiers cool the air below its dew point. The water condenses out and drips away. Muggy summer air can lose so much moisture as it passes through an air conditioner that it will be comfortably dry when it mingles with the warmer air inside the room. The principles involved above are the basic ways we can control humidity. Some of the methods are expensive, and corrective methods are, in the end, based on economics.

One key factor in deliberately controlling humidity is the size of the area—the smaller and better insulated, the more isolated from volumes of outdoor air, the easier (and cheaper) the job. It is probably futile to try to control RH in a drafty area with leaky doors and windows. Where an entire workshop is too large to be brought under control at a reasonable cost, part of it can be sealed with polyethylene sheet, and small heaters or dehumidifiers can be used to lower RH. If RH must be raised, a humidifier such as the vaporizers sold in drugstores for respiratory relief (about $15 and up) will suffice. In a tight shop, even a pan of water placed on a heater outlet may be enough.

The individual woodworker must decide how much variation he can stand. Rough drawshaving of green-wood chair parts can be done at just about any RH. A marquetarian, however, should monitor humidity very carefully, in both workshop and storage area.

One way to keep an eye on RH is to listen to weather reports, and perhaps to arrange a visit with a local meteorologist (television, radio or university) to get information about local high and low periods and the times of year when drastic change is most likely. This, combined with good instruments, will give you a jump on the most dangerous periods.

In winter, with my woodstove drawing in and heating large amounts of already dry winter air, there is a practical limit to the RH that I can maintain in my basement shop. As it gets to a reasonable level, water condenses on cold walls and windows. In summer the outdoor temperature may reach into the 90s, with RH levels above 85% for days at a time. Letting this air into my basement is disastrous. It is frustrating to get ready to spend a weekend on a project, only to discover that low or high humidity makes it unwise to work. For many of us, woodworking is a periodic or a sporadic activity. We can, perhaps, choose our work times to coincide with suitable shop conditions. Someday, when I get to it, I'll partition and insulate part of my basement, at least enough for storage, and I'll use a small heater, dehumidifier and humidifier to get me through the extremes. In the meantime, I'll watch my instruments, exercise restraint, and keep exhorting woodworkers to pay attention to humidity. □

R. Bruce Hoadley is professor of wood technology at the University of Massachusetts at Amherst, and author of Understanding Wood, *published by The Taunton Press. See also "Drying Wood,"* FWW #5, pp. 40-43; and "Measuring Moisture," FWW #8, pp. 78-79.

Measuring relative humidity

Perhaps the most familiar instrument for measuring relative humidity is the dial-type hygrometer commonly found in home weather stations. This type uses a hygroscopic material, such as animal skin or hair, connected to the pointer on the dial. It has the distinct advantage of providing continuous readings at a glance. But it is subject to inaccuracy for several reasons: the sensing element may react differently to rising humidity than it does to falling, it may lose accuracy after being exposed to extremes, and it can be quickly contaminated by sawdust. These dial instruments are cheap ($15 and up) and convenient, but most of them come with inadequate directions. If you use one, keep it clean, mount it where there will be good air circulation around it, and check its calibration regularly.

The instrument most frequently used to calibrate other hygrometers is the sling psychrometer (about $35). It consists of two thermometers mounted side by side. One thermometer bulb is covered with a dampened wick. As water evaporates from the wick, it lowers the temperature of the wet-bulb thermometer. The difference is called the *wet-bulb depression*. On dry days, the water evaporates more rapidly than it does on damp days, so the drier the day, the greater the wet-bulb depression. Wet-bulb depression can be converted (by consulting a chart such as the one below) to relative humidity. To ensure that the air around the wet bulb does not become saturated with evaporating moisture, the instrument is swung in vertical circles (by means of its swiveled handle) until the wet-bulb temperature no longer drops.

A variation of the sling psychrometer is the stationary dual-bulb hygrometer ($10 and up). You can easily make one from a pair of matched thermometers. Wicks can be made from stretchy cotton slipped tightly over one bulb with the free end dangling in a small reservoir. It's best to use distilled water so that mineral deposits don't accumulate in the wick. Keep a good airflow (fan it until the wet-bulb temperature no longer drops), avoid mounting the instrument where conditions such as direct sunlight would affect the dry-bulb reading, and keep the wick clean.—*R.B.H.*

Sources—Here are some suppliers who carry instruments for monitoring RH:
Abbeon Cal. Inc., 123-78A Gray St., Santa Barbara, Calif. 93101 (805) 966-0810
The Ben Meadows Co., PO Box 80549, Atlanta, Ga. 30366 (800) 241-6401
Edmund Scientific Co., 5975 Edscorp Bldg., Barrington, N.J. 08007 (609) 547-3488
Fisher Scientific Co., 711 Forbes Ave., Pittsburgh, Pa. 15219 (412) 562-8300
Fine Tool & Wood Store, 724 West Britton Rd., Oklahoma City, Okla. 73114, Tel: (800) 255-9800
TSI Company, PO Box 151, Flanders, N.J. 07836, Tel: (201) 584-3417
Sporty's Tool Shop, Clermont County Airport, Batavia, Ohio 45103 (513) 732-2411

Part of a dry-kiln control system, this cellulose wafer (left) reacts almost instantly to changing RH levels to yield EMC readings directly, without reference to conversion charts. Available from Lignomat USA (14345 NE Morris Court, Portland, Ore. 97230), the device currently costs $80 without the meter, mostly due to the cost of the kiln-proof holder—the wafers themselves, which are replaced every three weeks, are only about 35¢.

Reading a psychrometer

Wet-bulb depression (°F)

Relative humidity (%) vs Dry-bulb temperature (°F)

Find the dry-bulb temperature (the room temperature) on the bottom line; read up to meet the curved line that indicates wet-bulb depression (the difference between wet-bulb and dry-bulb readings), and then read the RH, as indicated by the lines numbered at the left.

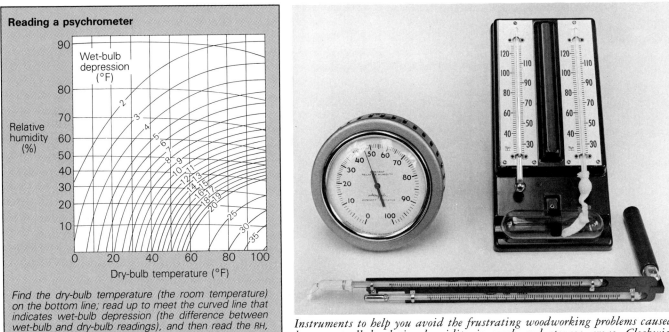

Instruments to help you avoid the frustrating woodworking problems caused by uncontrolled relative humidity in work and storage areas. Clockwise from upper left: dial hygrometer, dual-bulb hygrometer, sling psychrometer.

Keeping the "Poplars" Straight
Many woods, good for many different things

by Jon W. Arno

To be told at the lumberyard that the board you are about to buy is poplar may be only slightly more helpful than to be assured that it is wood. The name poplar and the backwoods corruption of this term, popple, are applied to many different kinds of lumber in various regions of the country. Embroiled in the confusion are some dozen or more species belonging to four genera in two totally separate botanical families: the magnolia family, *Magnoliaceae,* and the willow family, *Salicaceae,* as shown in the chart on p. 14. Your lumber dealer probably doesn't know which species he has—to some extent he's at the mercy of the mill from which he buys his wood. The best clue to the wood's identity may be the part of the country it came from.

My first exposure to poplar came several years ago when I purchased a few board feet from a mail-order house. It was absolutely beautiful stock, arriving in nice wide boards with almost pure white sapwood and an olive-green heartwood streaked with chocolate brown. Some time later I ran across poplar advertised at an unbelievably low price from another mail-order house and I bought in quantity. Alas, it was a completely different wood. Both the sapwood and heartwood were creamy white in color, with a lot of tension wood, and the boards were no wider than 8 in. It even smelled different, reminding me of stale aspirin.

Both woods ultimately proved useful for totally different purposes and I'd gladly buy both again, but this experience launched me on a determined quest to learn what I could about the poplars, so I would at least know what had arrived when I got my future mail-orders.

The magnolia family—My first purchase turned out to have been **yellow-poplar** or tuliptree, *Liriodendron tulipifera,* a member of the magnolia family native to the lower midwest, mid-Atlantic and southern states. Poplar shipped from mills in this region or referred to as tulip-poplar probably is this species. The tuliptree is a fast grower, and under the right conditions it produces a tall, clear trunk, so that boards up to 12 in. wide are fairly common. The tuliptree and sycamore vie for distinction as the largest of the deciduous trees east of the Mississippi. Tuliptree's huge size was once put to use by some Indian tribes for making dugout canoes. Although truly giant specimens are now rare, young stands are more common than ever. One reason that tuliptree is so plentiful is that it occupies the same ecological niche as the chestnut, and it has taken over many sites where chestnut once predominated.

Although the price of yellow-poplar seems to be increasing faster than other woods, it is a cabinet wood in its own right and still a good buy. According to the U.S. Department of Agriculture's *Wood Handbook,* the correct commercial name is yellow-poplar, but unfortunately it is neither yellow in color nor, as we shall see, a true poplar.

Yellow-poplar is a soft, diffuse-porous, fine-textured

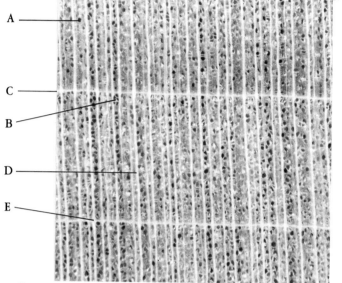

Yellow-poplar (Liriodendron tulipifera)*: Moderately soft and moderately light (average specific gravity 0.42). Heartwood commonly green or greenish brown, occasionally shaded with purple, blue, black or yellow, or with streaks of various colors. Sapwood flat creamy or grayish white ('whitewood'). Diffuse-porous, pores small, solitary (A) and in multiples (B). Growth ring distinct due to whitish or pale-yellow line of terminal parenchyma (C), clearly visible to the naked eye. Rays (D) also visible to the naked eye (about as distinct as terminal parenchyma), often swollen (noded) at the growth-ring boundary (E).*

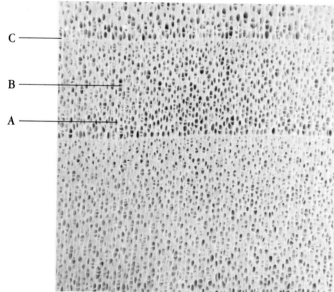

Cottonwood, typical of Populus *species: Relatively soft and light to moderately light (average specific gravity P. balsamifera 0.34, P. deltoides 0.40). Heartwood light brown to light grayish brown. Green wood often has a sour, unpleasant odor. Wood generally diffuse-porous, sometimes semi-diffuse-porous. Pores numerous, densely but uniformly distributed, solitary (A) or in radial multiples (B). Largest pores barely visible to unaided eye. Terminal parenchyma form a fine, light line along the growth-ring boundary (C). Rays very fine, indistinct even with hand lens.*

Black willow

Cottonwood

Tuliptree

Bigtooth aspen

Quaking aspen

Leaves shown half-size.

Leaves allow quick identification of living trees, but the woodworker must rely on subtle differences in the boards to tell these species apart.

wood. It's easy to work and stable, and it takes a good finish. It has a very subdued figure, much like birch except for its noticeably green color (sometimes streaked with brown, black or purple), which in time may turn deep brown.

Tuliptree was a new species to the European colonists. Wiped out in Europe by the Ice Age, it is native now only to the United States, with one very similar species found in southern China. In Colonial times the massive logs were often sawn so as to segregate the dark heartwood from the sapwood. The sapwood was referred to as whitewood, and was used in furniture as a secondary wood for drawer sides and interior parts. This same technique can still be used by the frugal cabinetmaker to create a piece of furniture that is solid yellow-poplar, yet appears to be made of two different woods.

Another member of the magnolia family, *Magnolia acuminata,* or cucumbertree, is sometimes mistakenly marketed with tuliptree as yellow-poplar. They are botanically close relatives and their wood is almost identical. A sharp-eyed timber grader looks for a lighter-colored sapwood in cucumbertree. The woodworker can distinguish both from the true poplars by their greenish heartwood. Under a 10x hand lens, as shown on the facing page, look for a fine whitish line separating the annual rings in the end grain. This line is formed by a row of small cells called parenchyma. When these cells appear as a line separating the annual rings, they are called terminal parenchyma. The line is clearly defined in both tuliptree and cucumbertree, while in the true poplars it is indistinct.

The willows and true poplars—These belong to the *Salicaceae* family, a broad grouping that includes many species, some of which are mistakenly sold as poplar. When freshly cut or slightly damp, most species in this family have a characteristic odor, an acidic, vinegary smell similar to damp aspirin. In fact, the willows are a natural source for the salicylic acid used in aspirin. When the wood is thoroughly dry, the odor disappears, but it may return under humid conditions.

The willows and their cousins the true poplars are far more similar to each other than any of them are to yellow-poplar, and are difficult to tell apart in photomacrographs. Yet each wood has subtle visual clues to its identity, and there are significant differences in their workability.

One branch of the family, the genus *Populus,* contains the aspens, the poplars and the cottonwoods, and virtually all of them have so many local and regional names that each tree ends up having more aliases than a con-man.

My second purchase of "poplar" was actually **aspen,** and should have been sold as such—the wood from the two aspens, quaking aspen and bigtooth aspen, is potentially troublesome because it's loaded with tension wood. This is not always easy to spot in the unfinished board, but the minute it is stained the surface becomes fuzzy or blotchy in appearance, and usually ends up looking like a very amateurish staining job. All of the true poplars have this problem to some degree, but the aspens are the worst. If the surface chips in planing or becomes fuzzy while sanding, you can expect it to stain unevenly, even after you think you've sanded all the fuzziness out.

The aspens have the finest texture of all the woods in the genus *Populus*. The wood is a very light cream color, almost white, with little contrast between sapwood and heartwood. The heartwood may have a slight gray cast and show streaks of a rusty or reddish-brown color around knots or where the wood has been damaged, but no greenish cast. It is soft and rather bland in figure, and for pieces that will be either painted or left unfinished, it is a reasonable choice as the primary wood. You can put on a clear finish, but plan to do a lot of sanding between coats.

Aspen shrinks fairly uniformly in drying, and is quite stable compared to other woods and even other members of the willow family. This makes it a good secondary wood for drawer sides and panels where any appreciable swelling can pose a problem. With an average specific gravity (SG) of 0.35 (oven dry), aspen is softer than yellow-poplar, 0.42 SG, and it compares to white pine, 0.34 SG, in being easy to work, but it is far superior in resistance to splitting when being nailed. It is a wood that will not splinter, making it a prime choice for children's toys—and sauna seats, too.

Also in the genus *Populus* of the willow family are the **cottonwoods.** Several trees have such similar wood that they can all be considered together. Unlike the aspens, the cottonwoods have a tendency to be semi-ring-porous. To be sure, they are not as large-pored as the oaks and the ashes, but they have enough variation in the size of the earlywood and latewood pores to produce a distinct figure when stained. The semi-ring-porous nature of cottonwood is easy to spot on the unfinished surface of a board by holding the board up to a bright light in the same way you would examine a freshly

Photos from *Understanding Wood,* The Taunton Press; drawings: Christopher Clapp

Family	Genus	Species	Common name	Lumber	Lumber characteristics
Magnolia (**Magnoliaceae** spp.)	*Liriodendron*	*tulipifera*	Tuliptree	Yellow-poplar	Close-grain/diffuse-porous, white sapwood, greenish heartwood. Soft, but slightly harder than other "poplars."
	Magnolia	*acuminata*	Cucumbertree		
Willow (**Salicaceae** spp.)	*Salix*	*nigra* (and others)	Black willow (other willows)	Willow	Semi-ring-porous/open-grain, very similar to the cottonwoods. Black willow has dark-colored heartwood.
	Populus	*balsamifera*	Balsam poplar (balm-of-Gilead)	Cottonwood	Semi-ring-porous, very soft, cream-colored sapwood, light grayish heartwood. Can make an attractive primary wood if tension wood is avoided. Nice figure when stained.
		deltoides	Eastern cottonwood ("eastern poplar")		
		heterophylla	Swamp cottonwood		
		trichocarpa	Black cottonwood		
		grandidentata	Bigtooth aspen ("popple")	Aspen	Close-grain/diffuse-porous, white color with rust-brown streaks around knots and blemishes. Tension wood very common. Soft, easy to work. Stable, makes good secondary wood.
		tremuloides	Quaking aspen ("popple")		

varnished surface for dust spots. As a result of its coarser texture, the wood is not as lustrous as that of the aspens. Cottonwood is also not as stark white in color as aspen, and generally produces a cream-colored sapwood and slightly gray heartwood, which often has a very slight greenish cast.

While the cottonwoods are similar, they are not identical. Some balsam poplar I recently bought from a mill in the Upper Peninsula of Michigan was darker in color and more open-grained than cottonwoods I had purchased from other sources. So far it's my favorite "poplar," and I'd like more of it. I wouldn't buy it green, though—it's hard to dry.

One final group of species should be thrown into the confusion: the *willows,* of which there are many. While not members of the genus *Populus,* the willows are more closely related to the aspens and the cottonwoods than is the tuliptree. At least they belong to the same family. Technically they should never be marketed as poplar, but occasionally they are. From the user's standpoint, little harm is done, since the woods of willow and cottonwood are very similar. Normally, willow will be darker in color. This is because black willow, *Salix nigra,* is the most important of the willows in commerce: it's the largest and most plentiful. If you've been shipped black willow instead of cottonwood, don't complain. Black willow, while soft like all of the woods described here, makes a very nice primary wood. Its dark, brown-gray color is sometimes dark enough to not require staining, and its semi-ring-porous grain gives it a soft-spoken figure.

Price and availability

Price and availability—Virtually all of the so-called poplars are moderate to low in price, ranging from less than $.50 a board foot to more than $1.50. As with any lumber, the price depends on the grade, the amount of processing that has gone into it, and the quantity you purchase.

Yellow-poplar (*Liriodendron tulipifera,* i.e., tulip-poplar) is rising in price. It's still sold by several mail-order sources at $1.00 to $1.50 a board foot, but if you don't live in its native range, shipping costs will likely make it no cheaper than the common local hardwoods in your area. One of the advantages of yellow-poplar is that you can get wide boards with especially attractive heartwood color. For such stuff a price of $2.00 or more a board foot is not unreasonable.

Aspen and, in some areas, cottonwood are the most plentiful and least expensive of the true poplars. The aspens are "camp-followers of disaster" in that their favorite habitat is prepared for them when a forest is cut over or burned. In this sense they have benefited mightily from the arrival of European man and are now more common in pure stands than they probably have ever been. Although the aspens are relatively short-lived and eventually overtaken by the conifers and hardwoods which form the climax forest, they are fast-growing and a valuable resource for today's cabinetmaker.

Quaking aspen is native to most of Canada from coast to coast, and to the northern United States, while bigtooth aspen is an eastern tree, but their ranges overlap in the Great Lakes region and the St. Lawrence basin. Woodworkers who live in a region where aspen is common can save money by using it in place of the typical No. 2 ponderosa pine. Bought "run-of-mill," ungraded and green, directly from a local sawmill in reasonably large quantities—say, 100 to 500 board feet—aspen can be had for $.40 a board foot or less. In fact, on orders for more than a couple of thousand board feet, half that price would be a good place to start bargaining.

If kiln-dried and surfaced, aspen and cottonwood in the better grades—No. 1 and better—should sell by mail-order for between $1.00 and $1.50 per board foot. If you shop around, buy in fairly large quantities and haul it yourself, you'll be able to do better.

The genus *Populus* includes some of the fastest-growing cold-tolerant trees in the world, and hybridizing them for still faster growth has become a high-priority project among tree geneticists. There is real promise that from this work may come the "super tree" of the future.

It's important not to let one experience with a wood called poplar create a fixed opinion about what poplar is and what it's good for. The truth is, it's good for many things, because it's many woods. Discovering them and learning the unique qualities of each is not only challenging, it is enjoyable. □

Jon W. Arno, of Brookfield, Wis., is an amateur woodworker. He wrote about elm in FWW #25, *pp. 86-89.*

Q & A

Desert woodworking—*We live in the Nevada desert near Death Valley and our humidity is zero for most of the year. We buy kiln-dried hardwood and find that the wood splits and shrinks after it has been here a matter of days. Some of the furniture I've made has split apart at the joints. I'm thinking of putting a humidifier in the shop, but that won't do someone who buys my furniture any good. I'd appreciate any advice you can give.*

—*Evan W. Thompson, Beatty, Nev.*

R. BRUCE HOADLEY REPLIES: I don't think I'd try to humidify the shop if your work will go outside it, as it obviously will. Instead, I'd concentrate on letting the wood slowly reach equilibrium moisture content (EMC) with the desert environment before working it. Because you are faced with moisture contents as low as 1% to 3%, resistance-type moisture meters won't help you measure EMC, since they function down to only about 6% or 7%. Instead, you can keep weight records on representative pieces of lumber. For example, out of a given shipment, pick out three or four boards that together weigh 80 lb. to 100 lb. Weigh them on a bathroom scale weekly, or perhaps daily, and plot the weights on a chart against time. When the boards reach EMC, they will hold a constant weight. Keep the data thus collected as a guide for judging how long you'll need to let each species adjust to EMC at various times of the year.

Rapid loss of moisture may cause end checking or other defects, so you may have to slow down drying. End-coating valuable lumber with glue or latex paint usually pays for the effort in reduced checking. If your lumber is fairly moist when it arrives, slow the drying rate by stacking the lumber tightly without stickers, or if you do sticker it, cover it with a loose wrap of kraft paper or plastic. Weights placed atop a stickered stack will help keep the more troublesome species from warping and cupping too badly, though you should expect some degradation in your harsh climate. But better to get it over with before you use the lumber.

Once you've built a piece, a final coat of a film finish such as shellac, lacquer or varnish will slow down moisture exchange and minimize sudden dimensional changes, although your pieces should be designed to allow for the eventual expansion if you expect that your customers will move them to a more normal environment.

[R. BRUCE HOADLEY teaches wood technology at the University of Massachusetts at Amherst.]

Slicing a burl—*I recently acquired a piece of white oak burl, about 4 ft. in diameter, which weighs at least 1500 lb. How should it be cut? Should I keep it outside for a year or two, or should it be sawn, stacked and cured in my basement? I have a piece of plastic over the top, to keep the rain off, and I have oiled the ends.*

—*Robert S. Wattles, Arlington, Va.*

DAVID HOLZAPFEL REPLIES: Yours is the job of the diamond cutter. How you cut your burl depends on what you intend to make. A turner will see turning stock in a burl, a furniture-maker will see boards and a carver will see what needs to be removed. The burl itself, its shape, seams and end checks, will also determine how it should be cut.

I would recommend that you ripsaw "through and through," from top to bottom as the tree grows. Leave the natural edge complete with bark. Don't crosscut, else the oak will check terribly and you will lose a lot. Slice the burl as soon as you can. The wood won't really begin to dry until you do. Immediately coat the end of each board with white glue, paint or tree surgeons' pruning tar. Since you will be air-drying the wood, keep it stacked outside off the ground,

and cover it with a sheet of plywood or roofing tin to keep it out of the sun and rain for a year or more. Then store it in a heated room for another year. Use a moisture meter to be sure that the wood is at 10% to 12% moisture content before you use it. Good luck. Go slowly.

[DAVID HOLZAPFEL makes whole-tree furniture in Marlboro, Vt.]

Finding doussié—*As I read James Krenov's books, I am puzzled by the apparent nonexistence of his favorite wood, doussié. I've researched wood books from A to Z, but this beautiful wood still eludes me. Can it still be found, or has it been, as Krenov says of other woods, hunted down to extinction?* —*Dave Kolanek, Wolcott, Conn.*

JAMES KRENOV REPLIES: No, doussié is not extinct. Not yet. An *afzelia*, it can be found in West Africa, where it is rather common. Some is exported. In fact, during a recent trip to Sweden, at the firm that has supplied me with wood for many years, I saw three fine logs. I bought and we quarter-sawed one log, 1700 bd. ft. of it—clear and beautiful, with beige and tan colors, open pores, and end grain typically bamboo-like. The wood in this log was only slightly rowed, and it responded well to a fine hand plane. I have seen doussié dark brown and quite smooth. It can be definitely rowed, though, with ripples of reddish hues running through the tan.

Doussié is a stable, reliable wood, more heavy than hard. It has a solid ring, what I call a quality sound. But it is not a tough wood; it does not flex or bend well, and in joinery such as mortise-and-tenon it has to be properly dimensioned so as not to fracture under strain. Also, it tends to split if carelessly worked.

Most doussié is not really difficult to glue. Sanded, it may feel "fat" and resist glue or finish more than when cleanly cut. Doussié works well with very sharp cutting tools, though on rowed areas it is safest to use a cabinet scraper.

Like people, woods age differently. Doussié ages with dignity, deepening to a medium or dark brown, usually with a reddish undertone, depending on exposure and finish. What kind of finish? I can only answer in the light of my own experiences with, and feelings for, this fine wood. So I'll say don't smear anything on doussié. Enjoy it as it is. If you want another color, use another wood. Doussié wears well with an oil finish, however. A doussié table—or any interior work—treated with fine oil will look good for many years. If you want a dry finish that is less apparent, a coat or two of polish followed by a little Renaissance wax, or even polish alone, will do. Goddard's or any such oil-based wax will give an in-between finish. Tung oil, used carefully, is also good.

You may wonder whether this wood is expensive. I'm tempted to say it should be. Actually, it is not, at least not everywhere. Strange things happen in the wood market, though. On the one hand, good, reliable woods are being neglected, misrepresented and misused. We craftspeople contribute to some of this. Elsewhere, amid blasting, bulldozing and burning, species of wood are found and marketed. And again we craftspeople are there, attracted by the flash of bright colors and new names. Many, though not all, of these woods are an expensive disappointment. They check and twist and spring, leave sandy sawdust on our dulled bandsaws, play havoc with hand tools, are difficult to glue, and later, in the piece, take their final revenge as the seasons change. True, some fine old exotics, even classics, can be found, but you or I might have to sell our machines in order to afford them.

[JAMES KRENOV teaches woodworking at the College of the Redwoods in Ft. Bragg, Calif.]

EDITOR'S NOTE: Theodor Nagel G.M.B.H, Postfach 28 02 66, D2 Hamburg 28, Germany, will ship small quantities of doussié.

HAND TOOLS

The Backsaw
How to buy, use and sharpen this basic tool

by Ian J. Kirby

Skill with the backsaw comes easily if you learn how to hold the tool and how to stand comfortably. Sawing is primarily an arm movement and it's encouraged by the stance illustrated above. Kirby saws right-handed, so he places his right foot farther back and bends slightly at the knees. You should modify this stance to your own comfort. He grips the saw much like a pistol; the pointed index finger is important, as it spreads and strengthens the grip, and helps you keep the saw vertical.

Backsaw is the generic name for any handsaw with a metal stiffening strip along its top edge, opposite the teeth. A backsaw works like any handsaw that cuts on the push stroke, but a finer cut is possible because the saw's reinforcing strip allows a thinner blade. This saw shouldn't be overlooked by the machine woodworker—it's a versatile tool for cutting tenons, dovetails and other joints, and for clean crosscuts.

Of the better-quality saws now manufactured, there are two main types—the tenon saw and the dovetail saw. The tenon saw is the larger of the two, and it is commonly sold in three lengths: 10-in., 12-in. and 14-in. Selecting the length is really a matter of personal preference. The 12-in. length is probably the most useful; the 14-in. is heavier and therefore more difficult to use. Tenon-saw blades are about 4 in. wide and usually have 13 or 15 points per inch. The dovetail saw looks like a miniature version of the tenon saw. It is commonly 8 in. long and about 3½ in. wide, with 20 points to the inch. Dovetail saws with blades 2 in. wide are sold. These usually have a turned rather than a pistol-grip handle.

The dovetail saw's finer teeth leave a smoother surface than does a tenon saw, inviting its use for cutting tenons. Don't yield to the temptation, because dovetail saws are quite delicate and should be reserved for sawing thin wood. A good rule of thumb is that the dovetail saw will keep an accurate cut 1 in. deep in 1-in. thick maple, maximum.

The best-quality backsaws available in North America are brass-backed and English-made, though steel-backed saws of good quality are sold. If you order a saw through the mail, inspect it carefully before you accept it. First, hold the saw end-on at arm's length with the handle away from you and sight down the blade. The sides of the brass back should be parallel to the sides of the blade. Misalignment doesn't affect the way the saw cuts, but sighting along the back is the easiest way to keep the saw upright, and learning to compensate for one that is askew is a skill you can do without.

Next, turn the saw teeth up and sight along them for straightness. A slight curve at one end or the other can be gently bent out of the blade, but an S-curve should be rejected. Rotate the saw 90° and view it again to check the blade for wind or twist. A slight twist can be corrected by bending it the other way. An inaccurately mounted handle may make the blade appear twisted, a difficult condition to adjust.

Finally, sight the back for straightness. This isn't easy, because the metal is folded and distorted during manufacture, but you can at least gain an impression.

Using the backsaw—The backsaw can cut along the grain, as when sawing tenon cheeks or dovetails, or across the grain,

---

Ian J. Kirby is an educator, designer and cabinetmaker. For more on the backsaw and the joints it will cut, see FWW #2, p. 28, and #15, p. 46.

as in cutting boards to finished length or sawing tenon shoulders. For each type of cutting, there are refinements of technique, but the basic operation of the saw is the same.

Grip the saw with three fingers wrapped around its handle, the index finger pointed alongside the handle toward the saw tip. Extending your index finger is important: it spreads and strengthens your grip, and it helps you keep the saw vertical. Wrap your thumb around the back of the handle so that it just touches your middle or ring finger.

From your grip to your shoulder, the saw, wrist, forearm and upper arm should be in a straight line when viewed from above. From a side view, the forearm should be in a line that if extended would intersect the saw at about the center of its length. Work to be sawn should be positioned on the bench at a comfortable height (which obviously varies with the individual) that gets you closest to this alignment. The rest of the body doesn't do anything when you're sawing—the action is entirely an arm movement—but you must position yourself so that you can easily move your arm like a piston. If you are off to the left or right of the line of sawing, your wrist will turn and the saw will jam.

Stand comfortably away from the workpiece and lower your body to a crouch by placing your right foot (if you are sawing right-handed) farther back and bending your knees slightly. Standing with your feet too close together bunches up the whole flow of movement and is an almost universal fault among beginners. You'll never get your foot back far enough by inching it back, so put your rear foot ridiculously far back, then inch it forward.

Before you actually begin to saw, you will have to learn to position the saw correctly on the work. This is best done by sighting down the saw back and developing a feel for where the saw is, relative to the work. You want to hold the blade vertical, at right angles to the surface you are cutting, and at the same time learn to sense the angle at which the line of teeth strike the wood. To sense verticality, you could have a friend stand in front of you and simply tell you when you are tilting the saw—a warm gesture but pretty much a waste of time for your friend. A better method is to prop a mirror in front of you on the bench and make the observation solo. You could also set a small square next to the saw for reference, but I think that this method is less accurate than the mirror.

Learning to control the angle at which the teeth strike the board is just as important, otherwise you may pitch the front of the saw—which is at the opposite side of the workpiece and difficult to see—so it cuts deeper than you intend, past your marks when making tenons or dovetails. The sense of angle comes with practice. Start by holding the saw with all the teeth flat on the bench. Memorize this feel and you'll be able to tell precisely where the saw's cutting edge is, and you won't be surprised by an overcut.

Before you begin, boards to be crosscut, tenons, and dovetail pins and tails should be marked out with a knife, gauge or pencil. You must, of course, decide whether you will split the line or cut to one side of it. In most instances, it doesn't really matter which you choose as long as you are consistent. When crosscutting a board or sawing a tenon shoulder, however, it is advisable to cut to the waste side of the line and then trim to it with a chisel or a plane.

Boards must be held firmly and at a height that will encourage a comfortable stance. For crosscutting, a bench hook or sawing board (for a bench hook, see *FWW* #13, p. 54) is helpful; it gives you a way to grip the board, while protecting the bench from a wayward blade. For tenons or dovetails, mount the work in the vise.

Whether you are sawing along the grain or crosscutting, the cut is started in the same manner. Place the saw's forward-most teeth on your mark at the far edge of the board, with the saw pitched up 10° or so at the handle end. Using your thumb and/or index finger to position and guide the blade, make your initial cut about ⅛ in. deep, then gradually pivot the saw down and carry the kerf over to the near side of the board. If you are crosscutting a board to length, complete the cut with the saw held flat in the kerf. Don't force the saw by bearing down on it. A steady hand and a light touch will give the best results.

To saw tenon cheeks, start the cut as before, but once you've carried the kerf over, pivot the saw down farther at the handle end and saw down the tenon cheek line facing you to the shoulder line. Don't lift the saw out of the kerf when you pivot it. Reverse the workpiece and saw down the other cheek line. Then hold the saw flat in the kerf and saw almost to the shoulder line. Complete a tenon by crosscutting the shoulders.

For dovetails, after starting the cut, keep the saw flat in the kerf, and saw to the knife line at the base of the pins or tails. Finish the joint by sawing the waste with a coping saw and

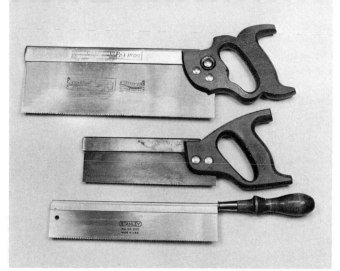

The fine teeth and thin blade stiffened by a brass or steel back make the backsaw an ideal joint-cutting tool. Backsaws are of two types: the larger are called tenon saws, the smaller are dovetail saws. Shown above are a 12-in. English-made brass-backed tenon saw, a 7-in. dovetail saw, and an 8-in. dovetail saw with the straight turned handle preferred by some craftsmen.

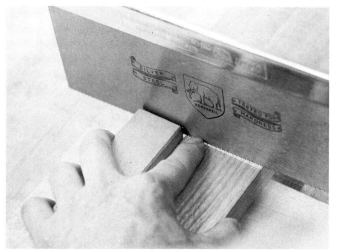

Kirby grips a board in a bench hook to demonstrate a crosscut. Start the cut by placing the saw's forward-most teeth on the mark at the board's far edge. Then tilt the saw up about 10° from the handle end and begin the cut with a slow, firm thrust. Use your index finger (not the bench hook's block) to guide the blade. Make the initial cut about ⅛ in. deep, then carry the kerf across the board to guide the saw and complete the cut.

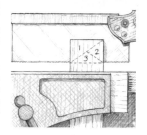

To saw tenon cheeks, mount the workpiece in the vise at about a 60° angle as shown above and start the cut at the edge of the piece opposite you. Carry the kerf over, and without lifting the saw out of the cut, pivot it toward you and saw down the cheek line until you reach the shoulder. Reverse the workpiece in the vise and saw down to the other shoulder line.

paring to the line with a chisel (*FWW* #27, pp. 74-75). Some woodworkers clamp the work in the vise at an angle so they can hold the saw vertical, but I think it's better to clamp the work upright and learn to control the angle of the saw.

A couple of recurring problems plague novices learning backsaw use. One is holding the saw at too great an angle to the wood when starting the cut and forcing it on the first stroke or two. Keep the angle about 10° and hold the saw with no more than its own weight on the wood, less than its own weight if starting problems persist. Another problem is learning just the right arm movement so that all but the three or four teeth at each end of the blade are used. Using only the middle four inches of the saw is inefficient, but burying the ends of the saw in the cut frequently jams the blade. Try sawing in slow motion to get a sense of where you should be taking the saw for optimum results.

As with any tool, practice is essential. A common fallacy is that you should make finished joints to practice with tools. The end results, of course, bear all the scars of bad workmanship. So practice first, and soon enough you will have the skills to use the backsaw to its fullest advantage. □

To saw dovetails, clamp the workpiece upright in the vise, and hold the saw to match the tail and pin angle. Guide the cut with your thumb and, keeping the saw flat in the kerf, saw down to the line marking the base of pins and tails.

Sharpening the backsaw

Many woodworkers send their saws out to be sharpened. Yet sharpening a saw is as easy as grinding and sharpening a plane iron or a chisel, and we don't send either of them out.

Half the battle is won by having the correct tools: a saw vise, a setting tool and the right files. Vises are available from several mail-order tool outlets, or you can make your own out of wood (*FWW* #22, p. 63, and #38, p. 18). You can buy a saw set or make the simple anvil described in figure 2, a particularly good one for setting dovetail saws, whose teeth are usually too fine for commercially made sets. The Tool Works, 111 Eighth Ave., New York, N.Y. 10011, is one source for saw-sharpening files.

Tenon saws and dovetail saws have more teeth than regular handsaws, but they are sharpened in much the same way. Sharpening itself consists of four separate steps: topping, shaping, setting and sharpening.

Topping is essentially getting the teeth in a straight line so that none projects above its mates and all cut evenly. Use a straightedge to see if the teeth are of uneven height. If so, clamp the saw in the vise and file the teeth into line with an 8-in. or a 10-in. mill file held flat.

Shaping will restore the proper profile to any teeth flattened by topping. You are aiming both for uniform gullet depth and for the approximate profile of the other teeth on the saw or for the profile shown in figure 1. To shape the teeth, use a slim or extra-slim, 4-in.-taper triangular file held horizontally and at right angles to the blade's length. Remove metal from both the front and back of the teeth.

To keep the saw from binding, the kerf must be about 1½ times as wide as the blade itself. This is done by setting the saw—bending the outer half of each alternate tooth outward. Using the setting anvil shown in figure 2, place the

Fig. 1: Tooth profile and sharpness angles

60°

15° rake angle

Mount saw with gullets just beyond vise jaws.

Fig. 2: Saw setting

Set alternate teeth with punch or screwdriver, flip saw end for end and repeat.

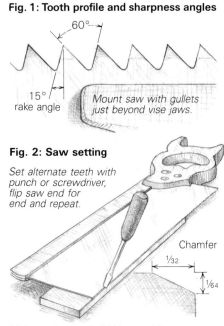

Chamfer

1/32

1/64

Make setting anvil of ¼-in. steel bar stock. 2x10. Grind or file 1/64-in. chamfer.

saw teeth on it so that their upper halves project just beyond the edge of the chamfer. Then, with a screwdriver (grind the blade down if necessary), set every other tooth, flip the saw end for end and set the rest of the teeth.

Sharpening is the final step. Before you begin, rub a piece of chalk over the teeth so you can keep track of which ones have been filed. Put the saw in the vise and, starting at the saw tip, work toward the handle. You can sharpen your backsaw as a ripsaw, with the front and back of each tooth filed at 90° to the saw's length, or as a crosscut saw, with the fronts and backs alternately beveled. If you bevel the teeth, make the angle slight—less than 15°—or you'll remove too much metal and weaken the tooth. Whether you bevel or not, position the file in the gullets so you are filing the front of one tooth and the back of the adjacent tooth at the same time. Four to six light file strokes per tooth should do it.

Test your sharpening job on a scrap of wood. The saw should start easily and cut quickly and smoothly. If it grabs or catches, one or more teeth may be overset and should be dressed into line with a benchstone rubbed lightly along the side of the blade. If you get in the habit of sharpening your saws before they become too blunt, you shouldn't have to do anything but set and file the teeth. Topping and shaping won't be necessary. *—I.J.K.*

Centerfinders—three variations on a theme

An old organ-builder friend showed me this handy home-made guide for center-drilling holes in the edges of boards to be doweled and edge-glued. The device consists of five sticks of hardwood screwed together in the configuration shown.

The sticks should pivot so that the device collapses like a parallelogram. For the drill guide, fit the center strip with a bolt ⅛ in. larger than the bit size. Then, using a drill press for

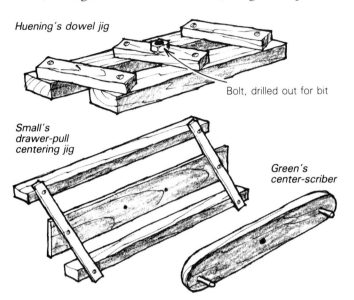

Huening's dowel jig

Bolt, drilled out for bit

Small's drawer-pull centering jig

Green's center-scriber

accuracy, drill a pilot hole through the bolt using a bit one number larger than the bit you intend to use for doweling. To use, first align the edges of the boards and mark off the dowel locations with a square. To center the dowels, set the device to straddle each board's edge and squeeze the parallelogram shut. Then slide the device to each mark, and drill.

—*John Huening, Seffner, Fla.*

Here's a self-centering jig for boring drawer-pull holes. The pivoting sticks should be made long enough to span your widest drawer. The center plate may be fitted with drill-bit guide bushings or just small holes for marking with an awl.

—*J.B. Small, Newville, Pa.*

This old-time gadget is handy for center-scribing boards. Install dowel pegs at the ends of the device and drill a hole in the center for a pencil point. —*Larry Green, Bethel, Conn.*

Hand drill

I made this tool ten years ago for holding cut-off Allen wrenches. Since then I've found several other uses for it and I use it often in my workshop. I haven't seen a hand drill this size available commercially, but it is easy to make. Smaller versions are available as pin vises. Some uses are:

—as a holder for sharpening small drill bits
—as a handle for needle files
—as a leather or scratch awl (chuck a sharpened nail)
—as a handle for hex screwdriver bits
—for deburring wood or metal holes (chuck a countersink).

And, in its primary use as a hand drill, for a few shallow holes it is easier to use than a power drill.

—*Robert J. Harrigan, Cincinnati, Ohio*

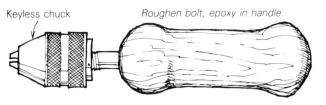

Keyless chuck   *Roughen bolt, epoxy in handle.*

Handsaw storage rack

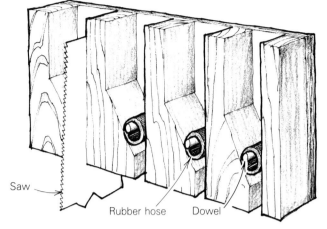

Saw

Rubber hose   Dowel

This shopbuilt saw holder provides a convenient place to store handsaws and straightedges. To use it, slip the saw in from the bottom and give it a tug down to wedge it in place. I used ½-in. plywood for the back of the rack and 2-in. material for the partitions. I found that rubber hose from an automobile heater works better for the grippers than plastic garden hose, which is too smooth. The dimensions aren't critical, but if the dowels are too high, the hose won't pinch the sawblade. If they are too low, the hose jumps to the floor when you remove a saw. —*Kim Anderson, Loyalton, Calif.*

Regrinding plane irons

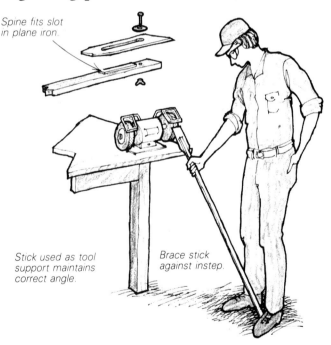

Spine fits slot in plane iron.

Stick used as tool support maintains correct angle.

Brace stick against instep.

With the simple stick jig shown here, you can quickly, easily and accurately regrind plane irons on a bench grinder. Select a good, stiff hardwood stick—mine is 44 in. long. Add a short wooden spine and a stove-bolt/washer arrangement to hold the iron in place. Now brace the stick against the inside of your foot and lightly arc the iron across the wheel. The stick can be picked up to check the progress of the grind, then returned to the same spot against your shoe. The resulting grind won't be perfectly straight but crowned ever so slightly. This convex profile will prove superior to a straight profile for most hand-planing applications, and is tricky to achieve any other way. —*Paul D. Frank, Fond du Lac, Wis.*

21

Spoon Bits
Putting 17th-century high technology to work

by David Sawyer

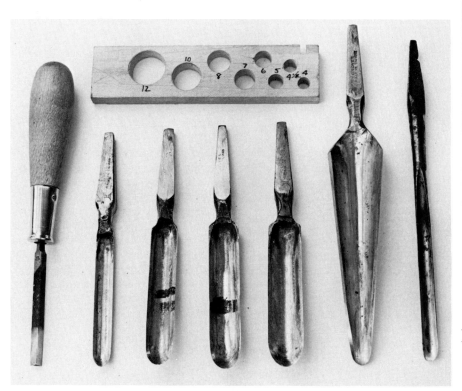

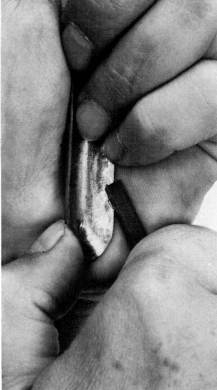

At left, a Windsor chairmaker's toolkit. The hardwood hole gauge provides references when sharpening. Lined up from left to right are the sharpening scraper, four spoon bits for mortises, a tapered reamer for leg-to-seat joints, and an old shell bit for back spindles. As shown above, bits are soft enough that you can sharpen them easily by scraping with an old file honed to a keen edge. They are tough enough to remain sharp for a few dozen holes.

For the last couple of years, Conover Tools has been selling a set of eight spoon bits and a tapered reamer in a neat canvas roll. They are copies, made in Taiwan, of a fine old set in Michael Dunbar's Windsor chairmaking toolkit. The bit sizes are six, seven, eight, nine, ten, eleven, twelve and sixteen sixteenths, with spoons about 2¾ in. long. The reamer tapers a hole at a 10° included angle, quite useful for chair leg-to-seat joints—although I'd prefer 8°, since 10° barely "sticks."

As bought, these spoons are straight-sided doweling bits, which were a mainstay for many craftsmen, such as coopers and brushmakers. Chairmakers either used the bits straight, as in Dunbar's set, or modified them into duckbill bits for boring the large-bottomed mortises found in so many old green-wood chairs. John Alexander, author of *Make a Chair from a Tree* (Taunton Press), explains the advantages of this joint on p. 24. Old-timers also used open-end spoon bits, called shell bits, which look almost like "ladyfinger" gouges. They are easier to sharpen than spoons, and cut nearly as well, even in dry hardwood chair backs. This is fortunate, since a used-up spoon bit will become a shell bit.

When you first unroll Conover's bits, they're beautiful. Upon closer inspection, they're kind of lumpy and bumpy, apparently finished in a hurry with a belt sander. Fear not—with a little tinkering and sharpening, they will work just fine. A lot of folks object to having to tune up new tools, but I find that this is a great way to learn all about the tools and make them truly your own.

How a spoon bit cuts—The spoon bit cuts on only one side of its semicircular lip. No other part needs sharpening. The cylindrical portion guides on its outside, clears chips on its inside, and must not have a diameter greater than the cutting edge, to avoid binding or reaming a tapered hole.

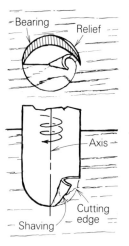

Any cutting edge must have some relief on its underside. What I call the "lead" of a cutting tool would be the progress per revolution in a drill or a reamer, or the thickness of the shaving a plane takes. For a plane, lead is regulated by how far the blade projects beneath the sole; for an auger bit, it is regulated by the leadscrew. A machinists' twist drill is like a spoon bit with a straight cutting edge, and if you can visualize how it cuts and how it is sharpened, this will help you understand the spoon. Try to imagine the spiraling development of the hole and the bit following it. In a spoon bit, lead depends entirely on how much relief you grind into it—if too much, the bit gets too hungry. The relief space shown above is exaggerated for clarity. It will be gradually used up as the bit is resharpened, and then the outside must be re-shaped. The bearing surface gives stability in the hole.

As we all know, you can force a dull twist bit, or one that

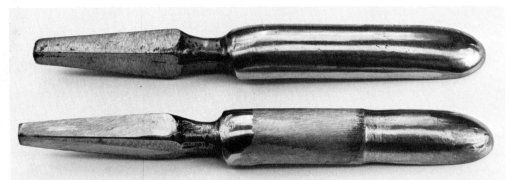

The spoon bit at top is as it comes from the manufacturer. The one below it has been modified into a duckbill for boring the chairmakers' mortise, shown at right. When shaping the bit, maintain full diameter just behind the cutting lip, but relieve the sides so that the bit can pivot in the hole to enlarge the bottom without enlarging the opening. The mark on the bit is a depth gauge.

has lost its relief, to drill a hole if you press hard and compress the material. No doubt you can also do the same with a spoon bit, but it's more pleasurable to sharpen correctly and let the bit follow itself through the hole.

Tinkering

Tinkering—To avoid slop when boring, the axis of the bit must be right in line with the brace handle. At least one of my bits came with a misaligned tang, easily corrected with some vigorous taps on the anvil. Flattening the surfaces of the tang and some grinding at its base will improve the fit in the chuck. I use a Spofford (split-chuck) brace, and try various bit orientations to cancel errors. Then I mark the tang so that it goes in the same way every time.

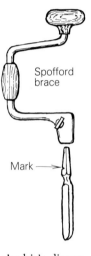

Conover's bits are hardened to Rockwell C45-50, which is soft enough to cut with a file but hard enough to drill numerous holes between sharpenings. A 10-in. mill smooth file is fine for truing up bits. You can eyeball the bit's diameter with a ruler, but vernier calipers are better. As an additional aid, make a hole gauge as shown in the photo on the facing page, or use draftsmen's circle templates, which come in $\frac{1}{32}$-in. and $\frac{1}{16}$-in. increments. By testing the bit in a series of round holes, you can judge its roundness and relief. A metal-cutting scraper sharpens the inside of the cutting edge by removing shavings like a one-tooth file. My scraper is an old broken-off triangular saw file, with teeth ground off two sides to yield a 60° straight cutting edge, which is then honed sharp.

First make the cylindrical portion of the spoon bit truly straight and round. Don't worry about maintaining diameter, because tenons can be made to fit. Then shape the outside of the point for relief and bearing, checking by eye with various diameters in the hole gauge. I would normally aim for clockwise rotation. My $\frac{9}{16}$-in. bit has an imperfect left lip, which would have shortened its working life, so I sharpened it to turn counterclockwise. Now do some scraping on the inside and light stoning on the outside to remove the burr, and try some boring. After you've got the bit working well, you can convert it to a duckbill if you like. I relieved my $\frac{5}{8}$-in. bit back about $1\frac{3}{8}$ in., as shown at right, to accommodate inch-long tenons.

The reamer

The reamer—At first glance I thought the reamer was a disaster, since the tang is not cranked over to the centerline as on the spoon bits. But Michael Dunbar said no, just put it in the brace and ream holes, and sure enough it works fine. You just have to gently bend the tang until the reamer's axis aims dead on the brace handle. Don't even look at the chuck! The tang has a tiny waist and I noticed some twist in Dunbar's. So less brute force and more sharpening.

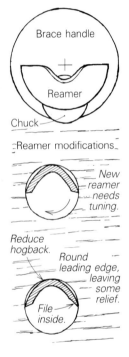

The reamer's cross section has a lot of hogback, which makes for too much lead and encourages a scraping rather than a paring action. It's also somewhat barrel-shaped. All this is easily fixed by filing or grinding. There's plenty of metal, but you can check with calipers if you get nervous. After shaping, you can sharpen with stones and do some scraping at the point. If the point is sharp, the reamer works like a shell bit, and you need no pre-boring in softwood seats. It does a neat job of breaking through on the other side, too. You can bore and ream seats like mad, in one operation.

Making chairs

Making chairs—I worked up a kit for Windsor chairs and proceeded to put together two Federal period chairs using 17th-century high technology. After another dozen chairs I may see no need for Forstners, augers or brad points. I have a $\frac{5}{8}$-in. duckbill for stretchers, $\frac{7}{16}$-in. and $\frac{1}{2}$-in. spoon bits and the reamer for seats, and a $\frac{5}{16}$-in. shell and $\frac{3}{8}$-in. spoon for spindles.

With a little practice, the bits start easily. To bore at an acute angle, it's best to start straight and change direction after the full cutting edge is in the wood. The chips are marvelous, tightly cupped spirals, like pearly-everlasting flowers. On through holes, you will be pleasantly surprised by the neatness of the break-through. Stretcher mortises can be enlarged at the bottom by canting the duckbill bit. You can do this nearly as well with a straight (doweling) bit. In either case, you will have to sharpen part of the side of the bit as well as the round point, to help the side-reaming action.

Tenons can be turned green, oversize, and dried in hot sand—a wonderful method I learned from Dunbar. This way, you can have green mortises and bone-dry tenons in the same piece. Drying takes four to eight hours (depending on size) at 200°F. Over 200°F causes too much internal checking; at 400°F you get charcoal. Check dryness by rotating the tenon between your fingers: when it won't get any more oval, it's dry. With a little experience, you can turn just oversize enough so that joints will pop together (with a large hammer) with no further fitting. The larger diameter fits *tight* against the mortise end-grain; the smaller diameter is just snug on the sides. For ⅝-in. tenons, I allow 3/64 in. oversize (7½%). You can start there, and adjust for your woods and bits.

For an angled joint, you can chamfer the shoulder of the tenon and one side of the mortise. Make the mortise extra deep so that the shoulder will seat. Shrinkage may open the joint a little, but it will still look good.

The same process of green-turning and sand-drying works with tapered leg-to-seat joints. I ream the hole in an air-dried pine seat, then fit the tenon with a cabinetmakers' rasp. With the leg properly oriented (major diameter against end grain), I rotate it back and forth a little. Then I file off the shiny spots, just like lapping the valves in a car. Repeat this until the leg feels really solid in the seat and is at the proper depth. Some angular correction is possible, and often needed. □

Dave Sawyer, the green-wood chairmaker featured in FWW #33, was trained as a mechanical engineer and now makes Windsor chairs. You can get spoon bits from Conover Woodcraft Specialties, Inc., 18125 Madison Rd., Parkman, Ohio 44080.

The incredible duckbill spoon bit joint
by John D. Alexander

There is no one way to drill round holes in round sticks. I have used auger bits, Forstner bits, Power Bore bits, multispur bits and spade bits to make chair joints, and I have a few more ideas. Modern bits, however, have drawbacks. You don't want a leadscrew or a point projecting ahead of the cutting edge, where it will poke through the other side of the chair leg before the mortise is deep enough. You don't want a flat-bottomed hole—because its bottom profile limits the size of the tenon, as explained below. Nor do you even want the hole to be truly round, because an oval hole conforms better to the tenon. Chairmakers traditionally used the duckbill spoon bit, and its peculiar quirks combine to make the ideal mortise for green-wood chairs. The duckbill even turns the spoon bit's main shortcoming, boring slop, into a virtue.

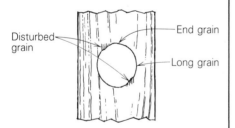

Spoon bits cut deeper in end grain than in long grain, producing an oval hole with characteristic tearout where the cutting edge makes the transition from a paring cut to a scraping cut.

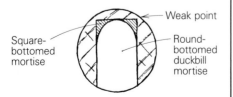

Rounded corners in round stock make for a stronger chair. If the mortise were square-bottomed, both mortise and tenon would have to be smaller.

By canting the duckbill bit during boring, you can cut the lower and upper walls of the mortise deeper, into a dovetail shape, without enlarging the opening or the sides.

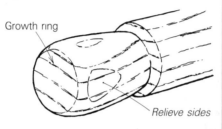

Tenons are turned green, then dried. The tenon shrinks to an oval cross-section during drying, which automatically helps it conform to the oval mortise. In side view, the tenon should be shaped to conform to the mortise's dovetail profile, so that it will bear tightly against the end grain in the leg. The end of the tenon is larger than the mortise opening, but the green wood in the chair leg is compressible enough that the tenon can be pounded home. The sides of the tenon are relieved, so as not to split the chair leg as it dries and shrinks.

If a joint does not split when a tenon is pounded home, or very shortly thereafter, it is most unlikely to split later, unless the mortise is near the end of the stick. In a test piece, drive home a series of increasingly larger tenons until the leg splits, listening to the difference in sound as the peg seats. When it comes time to make the chair, drive home the size tenon just smaller than the one that split the mortise. One caution: Immediately after assembly, the dry tenon absorbs moisture from the green leg and swells, while the chair leg shrinks tighter against the sides until the leg is fully dry—if the sides of the tenon have not been relieved enough, the leg will split, starting in the areas of disturbed grain left by the spoon bit.

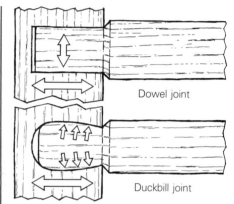

With cyclical changes in humidity, the mortise depth lengthens and shortens as the leg shrinks and expands. The length of the tenon, however, does not change. In the ordinary dowel joint, this creeping mortise eventually breaks the glue joint. In the duckbill joint, because of its dovetail shape, as the mortise changes, the tenon tends to remain wedged tight because it swells and shrinks in height. The duckbill joint does not rely on a glue bond, although glue doesn't hurt.

The joint, once assembled, can't be easily taken apart. If something goes wrong during assembly, the only solution is to saw off the tenon at the mouth of the mortise, bore it out and start again.

In extremely dry weather, the tenon may rattle in the mortise, but its shape prevents it from coming out. Because of all its virtues, you might think this joint would last forever, but if the joints are too dried-out, the chair will be wobbly, and the leverage effect at and within the mortise will eventually break the joints down. In a similar manner, extremes of humidity, such as in outdoor use, will sooner or later destroy the chair—there is opposing wood movement built into chair joints, and wood, once its compressible limit has been exceeded, cannot recover to normal size. □

Souping Up the Block Plane

It's a matter of geometry, plus perception

by Richard S. Newman

This tuned block plane easily smooths a curly maple strip that showed severe tearout after a pass over the jointer.

Imagine trying to hand-plane a strip of curly maple sawn to one-sixteenth inch thick, or a one millimeter ebony veneer. This is daily work for luthier Robert Meadow, who creates exquisite lutes of exotic and highly figured woods. As every musician knows, some instruments must be forced to make sound, while others sing at the slightest touch. So it is with tools. Meadow's planes consistently take shavings you can see through, the full width of the iron and the full length of the board.

This is not just extraordinary skill at work. Meadow has spent years investigating how edge tools work. His desire to share his experiences has led to the formation of a school providing intensive instruction in hand-tool work, and to frequent workshops across the country where he impresses audiences with his ability to plane the nastiest wood. I visited Meadow at his school and workshop in Saugerties, N.Y., and discovered that he has evolved to almost exclusive use of Japanese edge tools, both in his own work and at his school. He is convinced that these tools are the ultimate solution to cutting wood. I wasn't ready to take that plunge, so I asked him to share his earlier work with metal planes. In this article I'll describe how Meadow would turn an ordinary block plane into a fine finishing tool.

To begin with, Meadow claims that for fine work, hand tools are a practical, even superior, alternative to machines and abrasives. Planes remove wood a lot faster—and cheaper—than sandpaper. The surface is clearer, feels better and is far more beautiful than an abraded one. Of this last I have no doubt, as Meadow later planed half of a $\frac{1}{16}$-in. curly cherry veneered tabletop for me on a visit to my own shop, in order to relax after a trying workshop. His surface was so much better than the adjacent sanded surface that I was in-

spired to tune up my own planes in order to complete the job. You can test this by applying a coat of oil to a wood surface sanded as smooth as you can get it. The oil will soak into the minute scratches that were left by sanding, leaving a dull surface that will require many coats of oil to improve. Apply oil to a planed surface and even the first coat will gleam.

Meadow says, "Tools, hand and power, are really only kits as they come from the manufacturer." Getting the most from a tool means not only mastering its use, but understanding how its design works and tuning it, or even reworking it, to do its job. A razor-sharp edge won't take a good shaving if the plane's bed is warped, nor will a perfectly lapped sole help a plane if its blade is sharpened at an inefficient angle. All the components must be balanced.

In order to soup up a plane, we must try to understand what happens between the cutting edge and the wood. Textbooks contain complex formulas on the subject, but Meadow bypasses the mathematics and goes directly to the results, talking in terms that craftspeople can understand.

A balance of forces—There is a complex balance of forces and resistances when you plane wood. *Back pressure* is the sum of all forces acting to keep the cutter out of the work. Some back pressure is due to the resistance of the wood to being cut, and some comes from friction generated by the plane's sole. Too much back pressure requires excessive effort. *Cutting pressure* is the force the blade exerts as it cuts the wood. A sharp blade working at the correct angle exerts only a small amount of cutting pressure, just enough to sever the wood fibers right at the cutting edge. If the pressure at the edge overcomes the fiber strength of the wood very far ahead

Fig. 1: Plane geometry

A secondary microbevel deliberately honed onto the face or back of the plane iron will increase its cutting angle (**A**) or reduce its clearance angle (**B**). This can help you in dealing with ornery woods, reduce deflection and chatter, and prolong the life of the edge.

Honing the iron with a soft strop or a buffing wheel is liable to add an unwanted, rounded microbevel. On the face of the iron (**C**), a rounded bevel will increase the cutting angle. On the back of the iron (**D**), it may so reduce the clearance angle that the iron can't cut at all. Bearing down too hard while sharpening is liable to reduce the sharpening angle and leave a fragile edge (**E**).

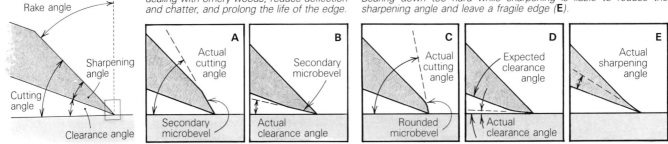

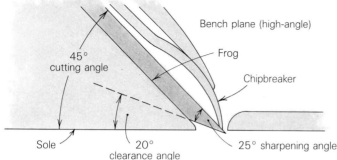

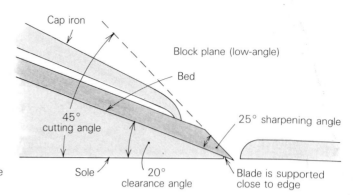

A high-angle plane and a low-angle plane can both have the same clearance angle, the same sharpening angle and the same cutting angle. But the low-angle plane suffers less from deflection and chatter because its blade is better supported at the cutting edge.

The block plane's cutting angle can be adjusted by honing a secondary microbevel on the face of its iron, and this change does not affect its clearance angle. But a secondary bevel on the bench plane's iron reduces only its clearance angle, without affecting the cutting angle.

of the blade, hardwoods will tear out, and softwoods will compress and crush. *Leverage* refers to the tendency of the cutting pressure to bend or deflect the blade at the cutting edge. Leverage varies according to the bed angle, the cutting force and how well the plane body supports the blade.

Edge geometry—The geometry of the cutting edge—its cutting angle, sharpening angle and clearance angle—are familiar concepts, but they can be deceptive (figure 1, p. 25). Slight changes in the angles right at the cutting edge, made by microbeveling or stropping, can yield actual working angles that are very different from those built into the plane. These angles can easily be varied and balanced to suit particular jobs.

The *cutting angle* affects the amount of cutting pressure and the way it is applied to the wood fibers. Softwoods generally require a lower cutting angle than hardwoods, otherwise the wood can crush ahead of the blade. On highly figured hardwoods, a low angle introduces a riving action that causes tearing out. Western planes have a variety of cutting angles ranging from bench planes at 40° to special scraping planes at 115° or more. For a block plane, the cutting angle is actually determined by the *sharpening angle,* as shown in the comparison between the bench plane and the block plane in figure 2. By varying the bevel angle or by adding a microbevel not much wider than the shaving is thick, you can, in effect, change the design of the plane. On a bench plane, the sharpening angle is a compromise. The lower it is, the sharper the edge (but thinner, more fragile and more subject to deflection); the higher the angle, the sturdier the edge, but increasing the sharpening angle simultaneously reduces the *clearance angle.*

Clearance reduces back pressure. The cutting edge must press downward, thus compressing the wood as it works, but the wood springs back immediately after the cut. The clearance angle makes space for this expansion. Harder woods require less clearance, while softer, more compressible woods require more, but all woods require some. Insufficient clearance causes friction that heats the cutter, dulling it quickly. A plane iron loses clearance as it dulls. This tends to hold the blade out of the cut, so that the plane skids without cutting.

Why choose a block plane?—Metal planes can be divided into two basic types: bench planes (high bed angle, bevel down) and block planes (low bed angle, bevel up). These planes can look very different yet have essentially the same clearance angle and cutting angle. The ubiquitous Stanley and

Record bench planes are a good example of high-angle design. The cutting angle is set at 45° by the frog, and the clearance angle varies according to the sharpening angle. These planes suffer badly from leverage problems and blade deflection, causing chatter and torn wood, because the blade is not supported close to its edge. This weakness is compensated for by the chipbreaker, a misnomer, as its function is more to pre-stress the cutting edge than to break the chip.

In a block plane, clearance is built into the design by the plane's bed angle. This angle is usually either 20° (Stanley No. 9½) or 12° (Stanley No. 60 or 65). Because the block plane's iron is mounted bevel up, clearance can be modified only by adding a microbevel to the back of the blade, or by stropping. The bed supports the blade right up to the edge, effectively eliminating leverage problems. The cutting angle is variable, determined by the sharpening angle. Meadow says that most woodworkers will find a low-angle block plane to be the best bet for tuning up as a fine finishing plane.

Tuning a plane—For this article, we modified an old No. 9½ block plane. Start by making sure that the back of the blade is perfectly flat, by truing it on a series of stones, on plate glass with carborundum powder, or on diamond-coated steel plates (EZE-Lap-Diamond Sharpening Products, Box 2229, Westminster, Calif. 92683). Then check the mating of the blade to the bed, especially right at the throat. Coat the back of the iron with machinists' layout dye or artists' oil paint (phthalo blue works well) and position it on the bed. When you remove the iron, blue dye on the bed will mark high spots that need to be filed down. If there is any space at all between the iron and the bed, it will fill with dust as you work, deflect the edge, and cause uneven shavings. Remove the burr left by hand-filing, then square up the front edge of the bed by filing a narrow land, just wide enough to see.

Now flatten the bottom of the plane, with the blade tightened in place so the plane body will be stressed as in use. Lap the sole flat or have it ground flat by a machine shop (*FWW* #35, p. 87). This cures the common problem of a store-bought plane that bears down most at its ends, leaving the plane body unsupported at the cutting edge and inviting chatter. The plane actually needs to bear only at its throat and at both ends of its sole. Meadow speeds the flattening process by using a ball mill in a Dremel tool to hollow out parts of the sole, much as the Japanese relieve the soles of their wooden planes. This looks terrible, but it reduces friction and back pressure without affecting the tool's stability.

Its sole relieved with a ball mill to cut friction, the plane bears only at its ends and its throat, and leaves a smooth surface.

Now the iron must be properly sharpened. Meadow shapes his bevels flat, not hollow-ground, in order to limit deflection. He shapes the primary bevel to about 25° and then hones the secondary microbevel to whatever angle works best. Steels vary. For any blade, if the sharpening angle is too small, the blade will tend to chip. If the angle is too large, the blade will get dull a little more quickly. It's a lot easier to hone a blade sharp again than it is to reshape a chipped edge. So each time he hones a particular blade, Meadow gradually makes the sharpening angle smaller until the blade starts to chip, then he retreats. The ordinary alloy-steel iron in the No. 9½ plane is prone to chipping even when sharpened at 25°, so we thickened it up by putting a few degrees of microbevel onto its flat back side. This simultaneously reduced the plane's clearance angle, which is generally not a good idea. But the 20° clearance angle built into the No. 9½ is several degrees more than necessary for planing hardwoods anyway.

The edge of the plane iron should not really be straight but slightly convex, so that a full-width shaving will feather out to nothing at its edges. Meadow makes this curve by bearing down more at a corner as he sharpens. The amount of curvature is greatest on a roughing plane and least on a fine plane: it should approximate the thickness of the shaving.

Meadow cautions that too much pressure when sharpening distorts the metal at the cutting edge. When the metal springs back, the blade has an actual sharpening angle smaller than anticipated. This results in too thin an edge which, although sharp, will quickly break down.

Meadow does not use a leather strop because its surface is too soft. It rounds over the edge, changing the plane's geometry. Instead he makes a hard strop from fine-textured wood—cherry, pearwood, poplar or basswood—planed even and smooth, not sanded. He then rubs a little wet mud from his waterstones onto the wood. When the abrasive mud dries, the strop is ready. Meadow recommends the same procedure for honing carving gouges. Take a pass with the tool on a piece of scrap, and you've made a wooden slip-strop that matches its curvature. After stropping, Meadow washes the blade and his hands in clean water to remove abrasive particles, and then wipes the blade dry and laps it on the palm of his hand.

Adjusting the throat opening is the last step before making a shaving. The throat should be narrow enough to compress the wood ahead of the blade, but when the blade is sharp, the throat opening isn't critical—tearout will be prevented mostly by the geometry of the cutting angle. As the blade dulls, narrowing the throat will eliminate some tearout, but friction and heat will increase the rate at which the blade dulls, and may even draw the steel's temper. Again, a balance is necessary.

Now the plane should work perfectly. If he encounters problems with a plane, Meadow doesn't automatically blame the cutting edge, but rather looks to see if the planing action is imbalanced. The tightness of the cap iron, for instance, affects both the plane body and the blade. When your plane is set up perfectly, you will find that you can vary the thickness of the shaving just by tightening or loosening the cap iron.

Meadow quotes the Japanese saying, "A master is the person who sharpens least and has the sharpest tools." The real enemies of a sharp edge are friction and impact. Dragging a plane backwards across the work, between strokes for instance, dulls the blade, as does too narrow a throat or insufficient clearance. The most dulling part of the cut is the impact of forcing the edge into the wood in the first place. As long as the edge is firmly in the cut, and doesn't chatter, it dulls relatively slowly. A well-tuned plane helps keep edges sharp. Meadow adds that oiling the cutting edge reduces friction. A thin film wiped on with the fingers is enough, but it must stick to the blade and not be wiped off. Meadow uses camellia oil, but olive oil also works well.

The next step in tuning up a plane, Meadow says, would be to replace the standard blade with one made of laminated steel. Japanese plane irons are laminated, but practically impossible to fit into a metal-bodied plane. Another possibility is to use an old iron from an antique wooden-bodied plane. These heavy, tapered cutters are made of mild steel with a forge-welded edge of high-carbon steel. The qualities of the carbon steel and the forging process create an iron that is capable of taking and holding a much keener edge than the alloy steel used in modern irons, which compromise cutting qualities for ease of manufacture. It would probably be easiest to adapt a laminated iron to a bench plane rather than to a block plane; some ingenuity would be required, but in the long run it might be well worth the trouble.

In woodworking, as in any discipline, the best work can be done only when our tools inspire us. Whether they are antique or modern, Western or Japanese, the challenge is to use them to their fullest potential. But in the end, says Meadow, a craftsperson's most valuable tools are his or her own perception and understanding.   □

Richard Newman is a furnituremaker in Rochester, N.Y. Robert Meadow's school is The Luthierie, 2449 West Saugerties Rd., Saugerties, N.Y. 12477.

Sharpening to a Polished Edge
A cool, easy grind and a hard felt buff

by Charles F. Riordan

I've heard so many craftsmen complain about the length of time (and the expenditures for equipment) involved in bringing tools to a razor-sharp edge that I feel I must pass on the sharpening method I've evolved in the fifty-odd years I've been making shavings and sawdust.

My first mentor taught me to do it all by hand, using three grades of oilstones, with the final edge honed on a waterstone like those used to prepare a straight razor for the final stropping. After all these years I can still hear him saying, "If you can't shave with it, don't try to carve with it." While I can't disagree with his goal, his process was, at best, tedious. I began to search for methods that would let me spend more

time using my tools than I was spending sharpening them.

An interest in gunsmithing led me to take courses in machine-shop practice, patternmaking and toolmaking. This, coupled with several years of machine-shop experience during World War II, taught me that there was a great deal more to sharpening a tool than scrubbing it back and forth on a flat stone, oil or otherwise.

I learned, to my surprise, that a coarse-grit grinding wheel properly dressed with a diamond dresser could remove metal faster than a fine-grit wheel, and leave a very good finish, with less chance of burning. And I found that using mist to cool the edge while grinding practically eliminates burning.

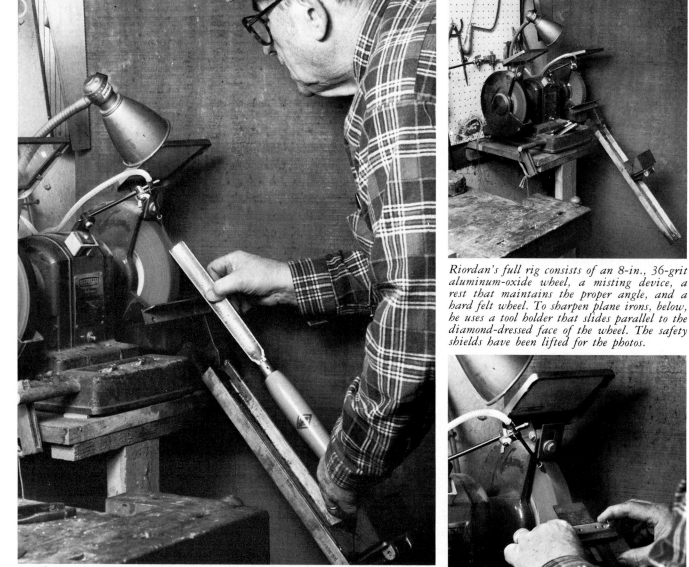

Riordan's full rig consists of an 8-in., 36-grit aluminum-oxide wheel, a misting device, a rest that maintains the proper angle, and a hard felt wheel. To sharpen plane irons, below, he uses a tool holder that slides parallel to the diamond-dressed face of the wheel. The safety shields have been lifted for the photos.

Riordan rotates a gouge, supported by an adjustable V-block, until the bevel is evenly ground. A misting nozzle directs its spray at the cutting edge. Mist, together with a light touch, keeps things so cool that there are hardly any sparks.

Then I discovered that buffing the ground edge on a hard felt wheel charged with gray compound would leave a razor edge. I also learned that to produce a good, even bevel on a tool, a positive rest (for gouges and small chisels) and a holding jig (for plane blades and wide chisels or skews) are absolute necessities. I have seen the results of freehand grinding by craftsmen who really thought that they were getting good results, until they tried sharpening with my rig.

The grinder I use is an old model Craftsman (Sears) ¾-HP with an 8-in., 36-grit wheel. The wheel is 1 in. wide and leaves a hollow grind that is neither too shallow nor too deep. You can adapt my system to whatever grinder you have. I removed the tool rest that came with the machine and fitted a 20-in. long arm that extends down in front of the grinding wheel. It is made from two pieces of 1-in. angle iron (preferably stainless steel) welded or bolted together by means of separators at each end so that there is a ⁵⁄₁₆-in. slot running its whole length. I bolted the arm to the clamp that came with the grinder, which allows the arm to pivot up and down. It can be clamped at whatever angle is necessary. As a socket for tool handles, I made a wooden V-block about 4 in. long and attached it to the arm by means of some strap iron and a carriage bolt extending through the slot. It can be secured at any point by tightening a wing nut. These two adjustments make it easy to get just the right bevel, whether the tool is a long-and-strong turning gouge or a small carving gouge.

For sharpening plane blades, skew chisels, skew turning tools and chisels that are wider than the wheel, I use a tool holder that rides on a 1-in. wide, 7-in. long piece of strap iron that can be adjusted parallel to the axis of the wheel. I wax the tool rest—it makes the jig slide much more easily. The strap iron can remain in place, as it will not get in the way when you are using the V-block.

I use the strap-iron rest in dressing the wheel with the diamond dresser—a small diamond chip mounted on the end of a handle. When the diamond contacts the spinning wheel, it removes glaze and trims off any high spots. You won't get a good edge unless your wheel is free of glaze, perfectly round and vibration-free. The ideal way to diamond-dress a wheel, of course, is to have the dresser mounted in a fixture that has a micrometer adjustment into the face of the wheel and a screw-feed across it. However, a little practice with the dresser, moving it slowly across the face of the wheel with very light, even pressure, can make you very adept at it. Diamond dressers can be obtained from any machine-tool dealer who handles grinding machines. A good one costs about $60, but it will last a long time—I've had mine for 25 years.

I use a compressed-air-driven misting device to cool the cutting edge while I grind. I won't go so far as to say that you can't burn an edge using mist, but it sure makes it a whale of a lot more difficult. The mist also keeps the wheel cleaner and thus minimizes dressing. I usually use plain water in the misting device, but coolant concentrates are available from mill suppliers and I would especially recommend the use of one with a good rust inhibitor if the water in your area tends to be acidic. The misting device I use is manufactured by Kool Mist Corp., 13141 Molette St., Santa Fe Springs, Calif. 90670; it costs about $22, and works fine at 40-lb. air pressure. If you do not have a compressor and do not wish to invest in one, you might try using plant sprayers or some other source of sprayed water instead. But mist, generated by high pressure, is a much more efficient coolant than water

After grinding, Riordan buffs a secondary bevel onto his tool edges, using a hard felt wheel charged with gray compound. He holds the tool so rotation is away from the edge, otherwise the wheel might catch the edge and hurl the tool.

droplets—people who use water come close to drowning.

Once I have ground the edge to the point where some people would accept it as sharp, I turn to the felt wheel, buffing the tool as shown in the photo above. This leaves a secondary bevel that has the strength to make many cuts before needing a touch-up. As shown in the drawing at left, a felt wheel as large as, or larger than, the grindstone can leave a fairly flat bevel (A), whereas the usual kind of polishing wheel, sewn-cloth, would undesirably round the edge (B). You can get a ⅝-in. wide, 8-in. hard felt wheel for about $50 from Paul H. Gesswein and Co., 255-A Hancock Ave., Bridgeport, Conn. 06605.

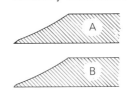

When I buff, I hold the heel of the bevel slightly away from the wheel, which results in a secondary bevel about ¹⁄₁₆ in. wide across the cutting edge. Use very little pressure—too much and the cutting edge will be burned, and you will have to start over. In fact, most of the time I shut off the motor and get a good edge as the motor runs down.

For touching up the tool while working, I make three or four passes over a smooth leather strop, leading with the heel of the bevel. The strop is simply a piece of leather belting stretched over a heavy hardwood block and soaked with a light mineral oil. I charge the strop by vigorously rubbing gray compound into it. One application lasts a long time. This strop restores the cutting edge amazingly well and cuts down on the number of trips to the buffing wheel.

No doubt, there will be those who will read this article and not be moved to try the method. For those who do decide to give it a whirl, however, I can guarantee that you will have no regrets—and very sharp tools, quickly and efficiently. □

Charles Riordan makes reproductions of period furniture and repairs antiques in Dansville, N.Y.

The Legendary Norris Plane
A hard-to-find tool that's worth the search

by Edward C. Smith

The London firm of Thomas Norris and Sons made exceptionally fine woodworking planes from about 1860 to 1940. Their products, especially the smooth plane which is the subject of this article, are arguably the finest planes ever manufactured. Although expensive, they are prized by cabinetmakers and tool collectors. For the worker who handplanes regularly, and who appreciates fine tools, the Norrises are worth knowing about.

I have owned a Norris smooth plane for about three years, and have used it on timbers ranging from docile cherry to hard, contrary ebony, cocobolo and bird's-eye maple. It invariably performs better than other metal or wooden planes I've used, producing a fine finish even against the grain and adjusting easily for the finest shavings.

In concept the Norris is simple. It's a metal box—mild steel plates dovetailed together, or a single-piece iron or bronze casting—stuffed with rosewood, beech or occasionally ebony. The plane's virtues accrue from this construction. Any Norris is about 1½ times heavier than the equivalent Stanley, so it hugs the work with an inertial force that makes planing easier. The cutter is twice as thick (³⁄₁₆ in.) as that in a comparable Stanley-type plane and is firmly bedded on a large wooden frog, a combination that virtually eliminates chatter. The adjuster is precise, moving the iron horizontally and vertically with little of the play that plagues other planes.

The Norris has a further virtue: it's beautiful, particularly the early, rosewood-filled versions. Most models are graceful and fit the hand well, and the contrasting colors of steel, bronze and rosewood attract the eye. Since few of us would regularly work a Norris to the limits of its capability, the ultimate justification for ownership must be somewhat subjective, the feeling that comes from owning the best. One more reason for owning a Norris is as an investment. Demand from workmen and collectors has pushed Norris prices steadily upward, and this trend shows no sign of change.

If you buy a Norris, there are important caveats to note. The Norris was produced in four product lines, each with a range of models. Only some of these are worth considering. The costliest Norris planes were made of bronze with steel soles and rosewood or ebony infill. They are heavier than other Norris planes and striking in appearance. But the slight advantage of their greater weight is counterbalanced by their extreme rarity and high price, about double that of the comparable steel or iron versions.

The dovetailed steel models filled with rosewood are much more common. These are the "classic" Norris planes most prized by workmen, and the ones generally thought of when the marque is mentioned. These were made with either curved or straight sides, with open or closed handles, and in a curved-sided version without a handle.

Next in price were some annealed cast-iron planes, cheaper because they required less skilled handwork and preferred by

The Norris adjuster mechanism consists of a steel eyelet with an attached rod threaded into the adjuster shaft. The eyelet engages the cap-iron screw to raise or lower the iron. To align the cutting edge, the shaft pivots on a cylindrical knuckle.

some because they are heavier than the joined steel planes. Except for the model A15, which I own and consider quite attractive, I find most of these planes a bit homely.

There is a subgroup of cast-iron planes worth noting. During its later decades, Norris made iron planes in a curved-sided model similar in appearance to the steel planes and filled with stained beechwood. Though not as attractive as the classic-period planes, they retain all the practical virtues of the Norris, including—except as noted below—the adjuster. These planes are relatively common and often available in good condition at half or two-thirds the price of a rosewood model. Unfortunately, some of these later planes have a cheapened version of the adjuster. The better adjuster consists of a threaded rod within a threaded sleeve, permitting precise turning. The cheaper model has no sleeve, resulting in an adjuster with more play. There's generally no difference in price so avoid those with the poorer adjuster.

Least expensive in the Norris line were cast-iron planes with model numbers 49 to 61. These are of much lower quality than the general line, and were meant to compete with Stanley-type planes, which were becoming very popular by the turn of the century. They are Norris in name only, like a downsized Cadillac, and may be of interest only to collectors.

My choice of planes today would be the curved-sided models A2 (open handle), A5 (closed handle) and A4 (no handle), which are all of the classic dovetailed steel type; the cast-iron A15; and, only if available at a much lower price, the beech-filled iron model.

With model numbers in mind, check the following points when examining a plane for purchase, or when instructing a dealer regarding a mail-order purchase.

The plane body: This is crucial. I know of no way to repair a cracked casting or battered and bent steel plates. Such damage has likely forced the sole out of truth. Rust, if superficial,

Where to look for a Norris

Besides smoothers, Norris made panel and jointer planes; shoulder planes; miter, rabbet and bullnose rabbet planes; and chariot and thumb planes. For a survey that includes two Norris catalog reprints ($6), write Ken Roberts Publishing Inc., Box 151, Fitzwilliam, N.H. 03447. Below is a list of dealers who may have Norris planes for sale, or who will accept a standing order.

> The Mechanick's Workbench
> PO Box 544, Front St.
> Marion, Mass. 02738.
> Iron Horse Antiques, RD 2
> Poultney, Vt. 05764.
> Tom Witte, Box 35
> Mattawan, Mich. 49071.
> Roy Arnold, 77 High St., Needham
> Market, Suffolk IP6 8AN, England.
> Philip Walker, Beck Barn
> The Causeway, Needham Market
> Suffolk IP6 8BD, England.

Sources for Norris cutters:

> Henley Plane Company, 13 New Rd.,
> Reading, Berkshire, England, will
> make irons to fit pre-war Norrises in
> the 2⅛-in. to 2⅜-in. sizes (£34 ppd.).
> London Auction House occasionally has
> second-hand irons: Tyrone Roberts,
> Watton Rd., Swaffham, Norfolk, England.

The Norris plane is considered by many to be the Rolls-Royce of hand edge-tools. This model A15 smoother has a one-piece cast-iron body and rosewood infill and handle, a construction that makes it 1½ times heavier than an equivalent Stanley-type plane.

can be removed with steel wool or fine emery. If the metal is pitted, the plane's market value may be lowered, as will its utility if the sole is scarred. Offer a lower price for a plane with pitting on the sides. The sole can be resurfaced by a machine shop or by laborious hand-lapping.

Wood parts: The condition of the wood parts is more important in fixing price than in determining utility. In fact, some look-alike Norris competitors sold just the plane body, leaving the customer to make his own infill and handle. The workman willing to repair or replace damaged or missing wood parts may be able to acquire a perfectly serviceable plane well below the usual price.

The adjuster: This mechanism is simple, quite heavily constructed and not likely to be damaged. And a damaged or missing adjuster can be reproduced by any competent machinist. Many adjusters are fastened to the plane frog with special screws requiring a custom-made screwdriver. Further, it appears that the screws were driven home before the lever cap was installed, so their removal requires a right-angle driver even if the screw heads are common.

The cutter: The back of the cutter, opposite the bevel, must be free of all but the mildest rust. It should be perfectly flat and highly polished. Pitting will require grinding and lapping, or machine-shop services. Remember, the Norris has no provision for frog adjustment; making the cutter thinner by surface-grinding may open the mouth more than you want. The frog can be shimmed, but this isn't good practice because the iron's firm bedding is at the heart of the Norris' performance.

Plane irons, of course, wear away as they are sharpened, so most Norrises are likely to have partly used-up irons. When new, a typical Norris cutter would have had about 2¼ in. of usable blade below the cap-iron screw cutout. I would try to get a cutter with at least 1 in. of usable blade. When I needed replacement irons a couple of years ago, I discovered that

they are scarce and quite expensive. I purchased mine from Roy Arnold for £15 (about $22) each plus shipping from England. Except for collectors, it is not important that the cutter be stamped with the Norris name, but it should be the right width and it must be a "gauged" or "parallel" iron. This means that it is the same thickness throughout its length rather than tapered like irons in most wooden planes. In a pinch, a tapered iron can serve, but as the iron wears through sharpening, the mouth of the plane will widen. The cap iron should be original, since the adjuster works by receiving the cap-iron screw. Check that the cap iron mates properly with the iron—no light should show between it and the cutter when they are tightly fitted.

Against this background, the question is: where to find a Norris and how much to pay? Norris planes were imported to America, but they aren't likely to be found at a garage sale, an antiques shop, or even an old-tool shop. American buyers should contact dealers who specialize in British tools. I know of only two, both mail-order, who have had more than one or two Norris planes over the past three years (see box). You may need to place a standing order with a dealer for a specific model. Specify the condition of the plane you want, including what sort of damage you consider acceptable.

Prices for antique tools are fairly volatile, but you can make an educated guess after perusing a recent auction catalog. I would expect to pay about $300 to $350 for a rosewood-filled smoother in one of the desirable models, and about $200 to $225 for a beech-filled model. Though expensive compared with other hand planes, Norrises are a bargain measured against the labor it costs to buy one: about a week's pay, both in the 1920s and today. □

Edward C. Smith lives in Marshfield, Vt., where he makes furniture and tools.

Making Ax Handles
A good handle fits at both ends

by Delbert Greear

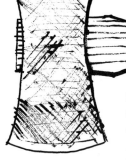

The ax has been around since civilization began and is likely to be with us for the duration. In a popular witticism, an old-timer claims to have had the same ax for forty years, only it's had twelve new handles and four new heads. This joke actually harks back to the frugal days when the ax head was regularly reforged and retempered after it had become blunt and misshapen from much use and sharpening. The old-timer's ax head could be made "new" by reforging, but a new handle, then as now, is a new handle.

While good manufactured handles are readily available at the hardware store, many woodsmen prefer a handle custom-made to suit the type of ax and the job to be done. A good ax handle will fit the ax head at one end and the ax wielder at the other.

The handle is an extension of the arm, and its main purpose is to give leverage. Too long an ax is unwieldy; one too short can result in extra work, bent posture and danger from a short stroke. Full-size axes average just under 3 ft. long. A hatchet handle may be as short as 1 ft. A camp ax, balanced for either one-handed or two-handed use, is usually about 2 ft. long, as are the small double-bit cruising ax and the light Hudson's Bay ax.

Parts of a handle—Except for broad-hatchets and broad-axes, which call for offset handles to protect the wielder's knuckles (see "Hewing," *FWW* #21, pp. 64-67), the ax handle, from top view, needs to be straight in line with the head so that the blade will strike true. An initial drop, as shown in the drawing below, puts the center of weight of the ax head a little behind the line of the handle. This helps aim the blow, reduces the tendency of the ax to twist when it strikes the wood, and somewhat reduces shock.

In side view, single-bit handles frequently have a slight S shape, and often there is a pronounced recurve and a fat knob at the end, sometimes resembling a deer's foot. The deer's-foot pattern is a good one for short handles. It provides a firm grip for the hand, and the recurve lets the wrist work at a comfortable angle, especially in one-handed work, where the elbow is held close to the body for control and the arm is never fully extended.

Parts of an ax handle

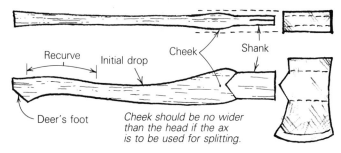

Recurve | Initial drop | Cheek | Shank

Deer's foot

Cheek should be no wider than the head if the ax is to be used for splitting.

Full-length axes—As the handle length increases and you go to two-handed use, a strong recurve with a deer's foot becomes less practical (though the initial drop is still a good design). Most experienced woodchoppers say the deer's-foot pattern interferes with their aim and presents the blade at the wrong angle to the work when their arms are fully outstretched.

Deer's foot or no, it is good practice to extend the handle back beyond the grip for a few inches and to end it with a flare or a knob. Many axmen of the old school rely on a pull at the end of their stroke to shorten the radius of the ax head's arc, thus increasing its final velocity. A flare or a knob gives the hand a stopping place, and also dampens shock. Most people when using an ax, a hammer or any such striking tool for very long tend to choke up a little on the handle because with every blow a shock wave travels down the handle, focuses at the very butt, and transfers itself to the hand and arm. A few inches up the handle this shock is less.

Special cases—A double-bit ax needs a straight handle, usually more oval in cross section than a single-bit handle. As with the single-bit ax, the cheek needs to be deep and strong—it takes the most abuse from overshooting and other mislicks. It shouldn't be thicker than the head, however, or it is liable to fray and splinter, especially when the ax is used for splitting. Also, for a splitting ax, the main length of the handle should be as skinny as is commensurate with strength and a good grip. This gives the ax more whip and speed. A wood splitter accommodates the increased vibration by relaxing his grip as the blade meets the wood. A hewing ax needs a stiffer handle, since whip and vibration can quickly tire the hewer. And it also needs a flare or a knob. Axes and hatchets used for carving and trimming call for a comfortable handle shape for special one-handed grips, such as right behind the head, or where the ax balances best for short chopping strokes.

Handle wood—Oak, ash, maple and birch are often used, but where it is available, hickory is the woodsman's choice. All the hickories I've tried have made good handles: pignut, bitternut, mockernut, shellbark and shagbark. The shagbark enjoys a reputation for exceptional strength and good grain.

Unless a marked offset is needed, as for a broadax handle, straight, clear wood is best. A tree about 9 in. in diameter is likely to be nearly all sapwood, better than heartwood for a handle. And even for a long ax handle, the bolt needs to be only about 42 in. long, to allow for seasoning checks and waste. Thus a tree that might be culled in a managed timber lot may produce six or eight handle blanks.

Quarter the log right away, and if it's large enough, take it to eighths. This will relieve much of the stress in the wood and prevent deep seasoning checks. Blanks that won't be used immediately should be leaned up in a sheltered place to season. Leave the bark and heartwood on to slow seasoning and prevent, to some extent, the blanks from bowing as they dry. If you orient the blank as in the drawing at right, a slight bow will actually work to your advantage.

Removing the old handle—Drilling the old handle out can be a chore if the handle is full of metal wedges. I usually burn the old handle out. This won't damage the blade if you bury the cutting edge in dirt (both edges on a double-bit ax) and keep the fire very small. You need to char the handle stub just enough so that you can punch it out. Keep the fire close around the eye, and don't remove the ax head from the dirt too soon, or residual heat may run out to the edge and spoil its temper.

Roughing out and shaping—Green hickory splits fairly easily, and it splits straight with the

grain. Once it has been seasoned, however, it becomes difficult to split and is prone to run out.

Before the blank dries completely, I like to rough out a handle with a hatchet, then go to a shaving horse and a drawknife to skinny it down and refine its shape. I do most of the finish work with a knife, making the final touches after the head has been mounted. One difficulty in carving hickory is unwanted riving of the grain. Reverse directions before the riving gets out of control, work slightly across the grain, and keep the knife sharp.

A rasp works well when the wood gets hard from seasoning and the knife no longer cuts freely. The rasp leaves a rough surface that can be smoothed by scraping with broken glass or by sanding.

Sometimes when an ax is needed right away, you can make the handle and install it green, but it is almost sure to need resetting within a week or two. For a more lasting fit, allow the handle to season until it is dry and hard, and "sounds" when struck with another piece of wood.

Fitting the shank—Be sure that the shank of the handle completely fills the eye of the head in length, depth and thickness. Slip the ax head gently on the handle to check the fit, remove it, and cut away the tight spots with a knife or a rasp until the handle beds firmly in the eye of the head and protrudes a little beyond. After the handle has been wedged,

the extra length should be trimmed off flush with the head.

Sometimes the handle needs to be tapped in and the head knocked back off to find the thick spots on the shank. The best way to drive the handle into the eye is to hang the ax by its handle in one hand and strike its grip end with a maul. The handle is thus driven against the inertia of the head. Don't get the head stuck on too tight before you are ready to wedge it—it can be a real bear to remove.

Before final-fitting and wedging, woodsmen of the old school heat the end of the handle in an open flame until it is nearly smoking, but not charred. This drives out the moisture through the end grain, and shrinks and hardens the hickory. The wood later swells a little as it absorbs moisture again, tightening the fit.

Wedging—I used to saw the slot for the wedge, but an old-timer set me straight. It's easier to split the shank. Both the wedge and the split should be about two-thirds the depth of the eye. With care, the split won't run down the handle and ruin it.

A fat wedge will loosen from compression due to moisture changes, thus it tends to work out easily. The slimmer the wedge the better. In fact, if the handle fits the eye of the blade to perfection, the wedge can be dispensed with. Needless to say, this is not usually the case.

A soft but tough wood makes the best wedge—pine, spruce, cedar and gum are often used. A fibrous wood, such as honey locust, grips well. A hard wood such as oak or maple is a poor choice, as such wedges work loose. Some people apply white glue to the wedge first. This lubricates the wedge as it is driven in, and sets it firmly in place.

Laying a flat piece of steel on the end of the wedge while hammering will keep the wedge from breaking into pieces. Metal wedges are best saved for tightening up later, should the ax head start working loose. Don't hesitate to drive in a metal wedge at the first sign of movement—once an ax head begins to rock, it's surely on its way off.

Finishing—Final-sanding and finishing are best done after the handle has been fit onto the head. I like to use mutton tallow or similar heavy grease to seal the wood. Rub the grease in well and polish it dry with a cloth, for initially it makes the handle too slick to use safely. Tallow is good protection for the wood, and, incidentally, for the steel. Linseed oil will also do nicely. Many commercial handles are varnished, but varnish tends to blister the hands and soon wears off, whereas grease or oil wears in, and is gentle on the hands.

Keep any frayed wood at the cheek trimmed off, to reduce splintering. If a handle splinters badly, a roll of tape may get you through the day's work, but the handle is starting to go. The tape merely hides the extent of the damage and traps moisture, accelerating decay. A failing handle is dangerous. Before your ax handle gives out completely, go look for a hickory tree and treat yourself to some peace of mind. □

Delbert Greear, a country woodworker from Sautee, Ga., wrote on making dough trays in FWW #35.

Plane-iron honing tool

Mecklin's horse

Here's a simple, inexpensive jig for honing slotted plane irons. Just attach a 4-in. long, ⅜-in. or ⁷⁄₁₆-in. carriage bolt to the iron, as shown in the sketch above. The round head of the bolt slides easily on the bench, maintaining a constant honing angle. For honing microbevels, you can twist the bolt up or down a hair. —*Paul Weissman, Centerville, Ohio*

Gripping thin wood

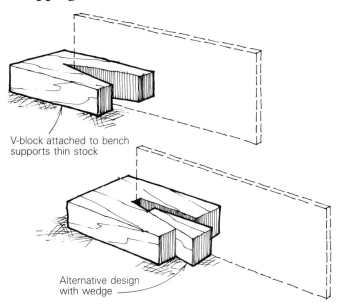

V-block attached to bench supports thin stock

Alternative design with wedge

When I hand-plane thin wood on edge, it often gets away from me. This V-cut support block is like having an extra hand. I screw the block to the bench or fit it with dowels that mate with holes in the benchtop. You should arrange the dowels near the mouth of the V and angle them back slightly so the block won't shift as you plane.

You might try a variation by cutting one side of the V parallel to the work and using a wedge for a positive grip. A pull on the workpiece releases the wedge.

—*Percy W. Blandford, Stratford-Upon-Avon, England*

Shaving horse

To make a shaving horse quickly with a chainsaw and broad-ax, select a 6-ft. long hardwood log, 8 in. to 10 in. at the butt. Snap parallel lines down the log, halving the circumference. Saw kerfs down to the snap lines every 3 in. or 4 in., stopping 2 ft. from the butt end. Hew the chips out with the broadax. Next hew out the remaining 2 ft. to act as a stage, angling it and tapering it as shown—the front of the work area should be less than 6 in. wide, to clear the drawknife handles. Make three 2-ft. long legs, and mortise them into the bench at an angle for stability. Now you have the basic work area

shaped. It can be smoothed with adze or plane. Spend time on the work area to ensure that it is flat and true.

Traditionally, the head extends through a mortise in the work area. However, I prefer the "ladder-rung" head shown. With this setup you can work a long piece of wood unencumbered by the neck of the traditional head. Also, the ladder-rung head holds larger pieces of wood. Make the head out of two 2-ft. long 1x3s and two 1-in. dowels glued and wedged in the 1x3s. The head pivots on a ⅝-in. linchpin through the bench. Drill additional holes in the 1x3s as you experiment with the horse. If you wish, add a more elaborate pedal to the bottom of the head frame. Now you're ready to make excellent kindling. —*John Mecklin, Cherryfield, Maine*

All-wood benchdogs

Here's a simple, inexpensive way to make benchdogs of wood, including the spring. First cut the dog to shape, as shown in the drawing at right. Then saw a kerf at the lower end of the dog and insert a wooden tongue of the same thickness as the sawcut. Simply press the tongue into place, don't glue it. When it breaks, it will be easy to replace.

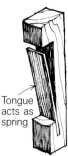
Tongue acts as spring

—*Michel Petrin, Ste-Marie Salome, Que.*

Spur dogs for clamping miters

Here is a method that allows you to clamp up mitered edges. The method is based on a spur dog, a device that provides a perch for C-clamps and spreads clamping pressure evenly over the joint. To make the dogs, cut several pairs of 3-in. sections from a length of 1-in. angle iron. In each section, hacksaw two ⁵⁄₁₆-in. deep slots about ½ in. from each end of one side. Bend the two tabs down about ³⁄₃₂ in. and file the spurs sharp.

To use, spread glue on both faces of the miter and press them together for a light tack. Tap the two (or more) dogs into place and clamp. The spurs enter the wood grain about ⅛ in. and therefore leave small scars on the wood. These scars can be removed by rounding over the corner, or they can be closed up some by steaming. You might decide to simply tolerate them. —*Peter Bird, Midhurst, Ont.*

Spur dog

The Stanley #55
Understanding an ingenious workhorse

by Gregory Schipa

The Stanley #55 Universal Combination Plane, because of its apparent complexity, is often relegated to the collector's shelf. But you can put it back to work.

Most people, when they first set eyes upon a Stanley #55 Universal Combination Plane, are sure they've discovered the ultimate contraption, though one undoubtedly too crazy to work. That's what I first thought, yet many years later the #55 has grown to be a part of me. As the Stanley Tool Company modestly described it in their 1897 catalog:

> Combining as it does all the so-called 'Fancy' Planes, its scope of work is practically unlimited, making the Stanley #55 literally 'A planing mill within itself.'

I have my reservations about that sweeping claim, but there is no doubt that for the cabinetmaker, house joiner or restorationist, the #55 is a most useful and even addictive tool. With a little patience, you can set it up to do the job of any one of a hundred specialty planes, and it will duplicate period moldings you simply cannot find in the lumberyards, nor even mill with a spindle shaper.

History—Although the #55 seems to have landed from space, it is actually the product of a gradual, rational evolution. In the 19th century, single-purpose wooden planes, basically the same design as had been used in ancient Egypt and Rome, had multiplied until a cabinetmaker or housewright might have needed a hundred of them to fashion all the moldings in style, an expensive and weighty collection to store and transport. These beautiful wooden planes were also un-

stable, liable to check and warp.

The Industrial Revolution provided a metal technology that avoided wood's drawbacks. In 1871, after successfully marketing a series of cast-iron bench planes, Stanley introduced the "Miller Combination Plane" as a replacement for the carpenters' plow—it employed metal screw threads instead of wood, and a sole that "would not warp or swell." Within a few years Stanley came out with the #45, which replaced a boxful of plows, fillisters and beaders. Meanwhile, improvements in machinery resulted in abundant, newly available mill-run moldings, which reduced the need for handwork and hastened the decline of the wooden molding planes. It was only a matter of time until the #55 came along and claimed to be able to take over all molding functions.

My crew and I have four of the contraptions, and they are invaluable for the restoration work we do. It's curious how we came to discover them. I had been using old wooden planes to duplicate moldings, and had even had a few new ones made for me by Norman Vandal (*FWW* #37, p. 72). I'd picked up some old metal planes, too, including a Stanley #45 with interchangeable cutters. I remember musing to myself that the #45 would be able to do just about anything if only it had sole runners that could be adjusted vertically as well as horizontally. And then I discovered the #55, which has exactly this feature. In my own day-to-day work, I'd gone through the same evolution as had a generation of 19th-century housewrights.

The Stanley #55 Universal Combination Plane was developed by Justus A. Traut and Edmund A. Schade, who patented it in 1895. It was first marketed by the Stanley Tool Company in 1897, with 52 cutters (the number gradually climbed to 55), and remained relatively unchanged until it went out of production in 1962. There were 41 optional cutters as well, which are now quite rare. In addition, a craftsman could grind cutters of his own design out of flat tool stock. The catalog listed it as a "molding, match, sash, beading, reeding, fluting, hollow, round, plow, rabbet and filletster, dado, slitting, and chamfer plane." It is 10 in. long and weighs 15¾ lb., including all parts and cutters. The body is nickel-plated, and the fences and handles are rosewood. As much as the following description (quoted from the 1897 Stanley catalog) is a tangle of terminology, to a craftsman who could use this versatility in his daily work it must have been engaging reading:

> This plane consists of: A Main Stock (A) with transverse sliding arms (H), a Depth Gauge (F) adjusted by a screw, and a slitting cutter with stop. A Sliding Section (B) with a vertically adjustable bottom. The auxiliary Center Bottom (C) is to be placed in front of the cutter as an extra support, or stop, when needed. This bottom is adjustable both vertically and laterally. Fences (D) and (E). Fence (D) has a lateral adjustment

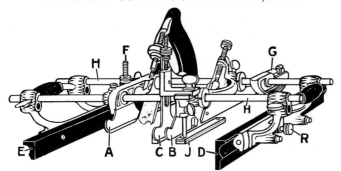

> by means of a screw, for extra fine work. The Fences can be used on either side of the plane, and the rosewood guides can be tilted to any desired angle up to 45°, by loosening the screws on the face. Fence (E) can be reversed for center beading wide boards. An adjustable stop (J) to be used in beading the edges of matched boards is inserted on left hand side of sliding section (B). A cam rest (G) aids stability.

The #55 with all its cutters fits in a case the size of a shoebox, and it will produce handmade moldings of considerable depth and classic shape. It was never intended that the combination plane should outperform all individual molding planes, but rather that it should allow the craftsman at the job site to match whatever profile he might need. A #55, trimmed for work, weighs at least 3½ awkward pounds, whereas a small beading or molding plane weighs a balanced and comfortable 10 oz. to 14 oz. Over the course of a day, the difference is significant.

Also, even though the #55 is more straightforward than it at first looks, setting it up takes time. After setting three runners, the blade, two fences, spurs and perhaps the cam rest, you would certainly hesitate before disassembling everything to cut a plain rabbet. You'd grab the nearest rabbet plane—or an electric router—instead.

Despite its complexity, the Stanley #55 becomes easy to understand when you examine its relationship to some of the

planes it replaces. In the drawing on the facing page, for instance, we see three old planes. The first, one of a pair, is a single-purpose plane that makes a groove on the edge of a ⅞-in. thick board (the other plane in the set makes a tongue). The next, a more versatile plow plane, has an adjustable depth stop and a fence on adjustable arms. The fillister plane has features that allow it to cut cross-grain rabbets. Both the grooving plane and the plow plane, instead of requiring a broad, flat sole like a bench plane, have a single, thin metal runner that limits the depth of cut on each pass. The main stock of the #55 has a similar runner. With one of its fences attached to the metal arms, the main stock of the #55 would closely resemble a plow plane, as shown at **A**, and, with none of its other parts attached, could be used to plow a narrow groove. A wider iron, however, such as cutter no. 15 in the small drawing below, would be difficult to use with a single runner, because if the plane tilted at all, the cutter would dig in. The #55 therefore has a second runner that can support the other side of the iron, as shown at **B** on the facing page. These two runners suffice for most of the #55's cutters. By designing this sliding-section runner to be vertically adjustable, Stanley made the plane capable of reproducing wide flutes (cutter no. 55) and thumbnails (no. 64), as shown at **C**. An auxiliary half-runner is used to support the middle of the wider cutters when necessary.

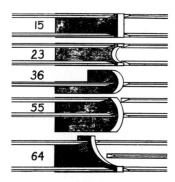

How it works—Setting the heights and locations of the runners is the key to setting up the plane. Two pairs of arms

Stanley's 52 (later 55) standard cutters were originally packed in flat wooden boxes. There were 41 additional cutters available, wider and narrower versions of the basic shapes.

Fig. 1: Evolution of the #55

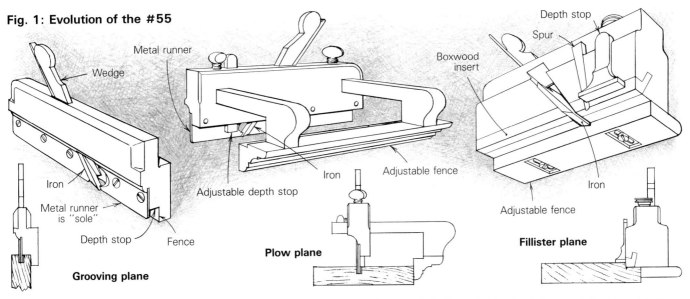

Grooving plane

Grooving plane has only one function, hence no adjustments except for the wedge that locks the iron at the correct depth. The metal runner acts as the sole, preventing the iron from digging in. Fence and depth stop are built-in.

Plow plane

Plow plane, with adjustable fence and depth stop, makes grooves on the face of a board. Some plows have assorted blades of different widths; with others you plow grooves side by side if you need one wider than the iron.

Fillister plane

Fillister plane's fence and depth stop are adjustable. A sharp spur severs the wood fibers ahead of the iron, allowing the plane to work cross-grain. For efficiency, the iron is wider than the cut; the fence adjusts beneath it.

The "main stock" of the #55 has features derived from the wooden planes shown above. Instead of having a single, broad sole like a bench plane, it has metal runners that slide on the arms and adjust to an assortment of cutters, as shown in the drawings at right.

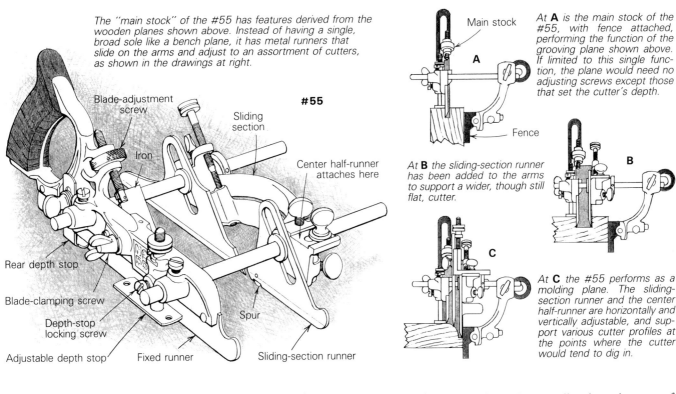

At **A** is the main stock of the #55, with fence attached, performing the function of the grooving plane shown above. If limited to this single function, the plane would need no adjusting screws except those that set the cutter's depth.

At **B** the sliding-section runner has been added to the arms to support a wider, though still flat, cutter.

At **C** the #55 performs as a molding plane. The sliding-section runner and the center half-runner are horizontally and vertically adjustable, and support various cutter profiles at the points where the cutter would tend to dig in.

come with the #55: one set is 4½ in. long, the other is 8¼ in. long. To adjust the plane for different cutters, you simply slide the runner sections you need onto the arms, then clamp them in place by tightening the wing nuts. Runners, when you are using them at the outside edges of a cutter, should be set as close inside each edge as possible, so that they can bear against the sides of the groove being cut. To set the proper exposure of the cutter, I find it simplest to set all the runners exactly flush with the cutting edge, then to lower the cutter. This is easily done by turning a single, knurled nut—it tracks the iron up and down with almost no play.

The cutters: The 96 factory-made cutters, shown in the photo at the bottom of the facing page, are used one at a time in the #55. When a combination molding must be made, a series of shapes can be planed next to each other until the profile is complete. You usually plane the part of the profile farthest from the fence first, working progressively toward the edge of the stock on which the fence rides. Also, you must plane each shape on all your sticks before you

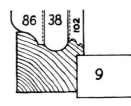

change the cutter for the next part of the profile. It is tricky to maintain consistency, and a slip in any one of the operations means that you've ruined your molding. You need to plan for a lot of wasted sticks. I find that the moldings created this way are the least effective use of the #55 plane. Stanley liked to think that there were virtually unlimited options and combinations, and technically there are. Most combinations of cutters on a single piece, however, take considerable sawing and rabbeting in combination with the actual molding cuts. This is extremely time-consuming. Combined moldings usually come out a bit inconsistent as well. Instead, it is more practical to make a series of separate moldings, then combine them, such as by nailing on a cove-and-bead below a reverse ogee to form a nice cornice molding.

The fences: The #55's fences can be adjusted up and down—by means of alternative holes for the arms—as well as in and out. They also tilt to 45° for making chamfers. There are two major fences that come with the #55. The larger one has adjustment screws that help in setting the fence vertically parallel to the side of the cutter. Keeping the fence flat against the work is the best way to keep the plane perpendicular. If the fence is not parallel to the side of the cutter, the plane will run either into or away from the work, binding and cutting poorly. Stanley suggests using both fences whenever possible (one on each edge of the stock), but I find that this causes the plane to bind, and mostly I just use the smaller one.

When you use the plane, keep pressure toward the work, so the fence won't ride off (especially on coves and thumbnail moldings). Also, to keep the plane running straight, push the #55 with your right hand only—use your left hand to keep inward pressure on the fence.

Depth stops: The main depth stop adjusts with a single knurled nut. It works the same as the depth stop on the fillister plane in the drawing on p. 37, eventually contacting the top surface of the work and preventing the plane from cutting too deeply. There is another depth stop, located on the main stock behind the blade, which should be used whenever it can make contact. When you use the front depth stop alone, the plane tends to tip back. In addition, some of the cutters accept a little, built-in depth stop that can be adjusted with a screwdriver (note cutter no. 1 in the photo on p. 36).

The spurs: The main-stock runner and the sliding-section runner both have adjustable spurs located just in front of the blade. As in the fillister plane, these sever the fibers ahead of the iron for a cleaner cut, and they must be kept sharp.

The slitting cutter: A knife-blade-like cutter can be set into a holder located behind the usual blade location. It is used to split strips off the edge of boards—similar to the Japanese splitting gauge in *FWW* #34, p. 52—and works faster and more neatly than a saw on thin stock.

Primary functions—Perhaps the function for which the #55 is best suited (or at least most easily applied) is beading, the creation of a small half-round with a groove (called a quirk) on the edge of a board, or occasionally in the middle. A bead was most often applied to embellish the joint (and to disguise wood movement) between two matched boards, or as the inside edge of window and door casings. If the cutter, depth gauge and fence are set properly, the bead will be perfectly shaped. A flat-topped bead means the depth is set too shallow; a flat-sided bead means the fence is too close to the blade. If there is a flat on the outside of the bead, the fence is too far from the cutter (you have created an astragal). The most common mistake in beading is letting the fence ride away from the work, which results in an enlarged quirk, and a shrinking bead.

Rabbets and grooves are simple with the #55. It is always easiest when rabbeting to use a cutter wider than the rabbet.

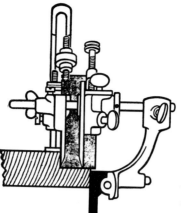

The smaller fence can be adjusted so it bears on the edge of the stock below the blade, as shown at left. The plow function is accomplished very handily as well, although the narrower cutters are best.

Of the "fancier" moldings, the #55 cuts some well, but it makes others only with difficulty. The Grecian ogees (cutters no. 102-106) seem to work most easily, because the plane has less tendency to ride off the piece. On these and all fancy moldings, however, you must take care not to roll the plane out, or the moldings will be uneven and impossible to join on the same work without carving. Profiles that drop off away from the work tend to encourage this riding-off. Coves, Roman ogees and reverse ogees fall into this category, and the simple "thumbnail" or ovolo cut on the edge of a stile is the most difficult (the cutter is referred to as a quarter hollow). These cuts all call for a

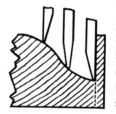

very shallow blade setting, and strong pressure toward the work. On many, Stanley recommends that you leave some stock uncut on the outside edge, as shown at left, to be trimmed off later. This traps the bottom runner and prevents it from sliding off the work.

Availability—Stanley's "miracle" tool is out of production. The combination planes that are on the market (the best two I've seen are the Record #405 Multi-plane and Stanley's #13-050 Combination) do not have the vertically adjustable fence and thus lose most of the functions that made the #55 so versatile. With the resurgent interest in hand-tool work, the popularity of the #55 is again growing. Unfortunately, these planes are usually found at the antique tool dealer's, where demand from the tool collectors, the nemesis of the joiner and cabinetmaker, has driven up the price. The planes seem to be harder to find each year, but the major dealers can usually come through with one for about $200 to $350, a price comparable to a new combination plane.

The number of cutters will vary according to the year that the plane was manufactured, but check to see that most of them are there and in good condition. Check the rest of the parts against a complete list (available from Stanley), and examine the castings for small hairline stress cracks, especially on the depth-gauge housing. Also check that the runners are not bent, but perfectly parallel. A hint: never put a #55 where it can fall from the bench—the results are disastrous. When you get your new/old plane home, keep it well oiled against rust, and spend some time sharpening and honing your cutters—they have to be perfectly sharp. □

Gregory Schipa, of Waitsfield, Vt., is president of Weather Hill Restoration Co., which takes apart period houses and refurbishes them. The Stanley Tool Co. will supply instruction booklets to owners of the #55 (write R. West, Manager, Product Research Standards, Stanley Tool Co., 600 Myrtle St., New Britain, Conn. 06050). A 1980 reprint, The Complete Woodworker, *edited by Bernard Jones (Ten Speed Press, PO Box 7123, Berkeley, Calif. 94707; $7.95), has 16 pages on the fine points of the #55.*

Putting an old #55 to work

by T.D. Culver

If you decide to buy a Stanley #55, first examine the plane body and all the parts for broken castings, bent runners and chipped cutters. A plane with bent or broken castings has been dropped and will be cranky. A "bargain" on a #55 may be no bargain. I would not buy one sight unseen.

If the plane is okay, check the cutters. Ideally, the bevels should still have the grind marks from the factory. If any of them have been badly honed, their profiles will be wrong. Count the cutters. My #55 came with 52 of the 55 regular cutters, including two sash cutters, and none of the 41 special cutters. I have yet to find a molding I cannot duplicate.

There are two positions for setting up the stock to be molded: on edge in the vise or flat on the bench. It is difficult to hold a piece narrower than about 2 in., so glue it temporarily to a waste piece. After molding the shape, saw it free.

If you are starting with a wide board and making narrow moldings, plane one edge, flip the board (paying attention to grain direction), and plane the other edge. Rip these moldings off, joint the edges and begin again. You can turn out a surprising amount of molding in a fairly short time.

The position of the stock determines how the fences will be set on the #55. When the stock is on edge, it is extremely useful to set up both fences, because then there is no worry of tilting the plane and spoiling the molding. Set the left-hand fence, place the #55 on the stock, and tighten the wing nuts

as you squeeze the fences together hard. When you begin planing, there will be quite a bit of resistance, but it soon eases.

When you're planing work flat on the bench, the dogs and vise may not hold it against the considerable side pressure you need to exert. Or the board may not be wide enough to be clamped in the dogs and still overhang the benchtop. A few finish nails through the work and into the bench will hold and will not foul the fence arms. You can support the ends of long stock on sawhorses.

Usually only one fence can be set when the work is laid flat, which allows the #55 to tip and ruin the molding. After five years of struggling, I finally acquired a cam rest and it is worth every penny I paid. Contra the instruction manual, I set it opposite the fence on the front arm. By adjusting the screw so that the cam rotates stiffly around the fence arm, I can set the bottom of the cam even with the edge of the cutter. Now the #55 rides on two points instead of one. As the cut progresses, the cam pivots and continues to hold up its end of the plane. Be sure to twist the cam back to its original position when you start to plane another stick.

The cutter should protrude beyond the runners at the sides, just as it must at the bottom. Otherwise the runners will foul the molding. The depth of cut should be set very light for molding and slightly heavier for plowing. The runner on the sliding section may creep, causing the cutter to dig in, unless the thimble check-nuts are tightened. These are round, knurled nuts located on the out-

side of the sliding section through which the fence arms pass. Finger-tight is usually enough, though there are holes for a tommy bar. If the plane throat jams with shavings, you are taking too heavy a cut. Check that the sliding section hasn't crept up, or reset the cutter higher in the plane body.

You will find vernier calipers a great help in setting up the #55. Once the cutter is fixed, set the depth stop with the calipers, measuring to the cutter edge, not the runner. Then set the fence, measuring at both the front and the back, so that it is parallel to the runner. Be sure to square the bearing face of the fence to the fence arms.

It is especially important to plane through the work in one continuous stroke. Choppy strokes will choke the plane and damage the molding. Clear a space in front of the bench and walk through each stroke with firm pressure against the fence. Shavings will curl out like excelsior and wind around your wrist. Clean out the throat when you're walking back for the next stroke, so the plane won't jam.

Clear wood is best, although very small, tight knots can be molded, with luck, in an easily worked wood such as walnut. Straight grain is helpful but not essential on many shapes.

The #55 is surprisingly effective in rabbeting and plowing plywood. Some split-out can be expected, but a heavy knife cut on the layout lines will minimize this. In desperate straits, costly hardwood plywood can be jointed, plowed and splined just like solid wood. The #55's no. 12 cutter makes a nice groove for ¼-in. fir-plywood splines.

The major problem with any antique plane is finding parts, although some parts for the Record No. 405 Multiplane do fit the #55. Cutters for the Multi-plane fit both the #45 and #55, but the selection is not as vast as the original Stanley cutters. The fence arms are the easiest to replace—pieces of ⅜-in. mild steel rod work just fine.

I've had my #55 for six years, and every year it seems to work better and better. It is a complex tool, and it takes some time to learn well. That time will be amply rewarded one day, when you stand ankle deep in shavings and hold up to the light a crisp molding fresh from the plane. □

T.D. Culver is a carpenter and cabinetmaker living in Cleveland, Ohio.

Gregory Schipa

The #55 in full array, geared up to plane a quirked bead on a pine board.

Tools Are Where You Find Them

Luthier borrows lots of help from other trades and crafts

by Michael Dresdner

My shop, where I repair and restore musical instruments, is filled with paraphernalia that you won't find in the average woodworking catalog. Over the years I've confronted innumerable jobs that required some special tool that didn't seem to exist in my field, and often I've had to invent a tool to do the job. But it's easy to forget that what may be a rare and unlikely job for one craftsman is another's bread and butter. I am reminded of a luthier who painstakingly made a small aluminum riser for a guitar repair job. Upon showing off his invention, he was told that he had made a piano string jack, a 3-in. high tool readily available in piano repair shops. I've had enough similar experiences that I now check out other trades' tool catalogs before I set about to reinvent the wheel.

STRING JACK

Local specialty stores, such as jewelry suppliers and medical and dental suppliers, are often very helpful. They not only have access to scores of wholesale outlets and manufacturers who don't want to bother with small retail sales, but they also have a good idea of the range of tools and possibilities, and they give good, pithy advice. Look in the Yellow Pages, and scan the ads in specialty magazines. The Tool Works, 111 Eighth Ave., New York, N.Y. 10011, has a good catalog, but the place is even more valuable for the tools the catalog has no room to list. Owner Bart Slutsky has steered me in the right direction more than once. Among other things, he turned me on to a set of machinists' round-edged joint files, such as those drawn below. If you ever need to make round-bottomed grooves of specific widths, such as for guitar strings, these are just perfect.

Catalogs I rely on because of their broad range include Techni-Tool, 5 Apollo Rd., Box 368, Plymouth Meeting, Pa. 19462; William Dixon Company, Division of Grobet File Co. of America, Carlstadt, N.J. 07072; and Brownells, Inc., Rt. 2, Box 1, Montezuma, Iowa 50171 (gunsmithing). Also, affiliated local hardware stores usually have a monster catalog of things they can't stock but will order. My neighborhood store isn't very big, but their catalog has almost 2,000 pages, lists over 30 manufacturers, and has illustrations—a great help if you don't know what something is called, but have a good idea of what it should look like.

The cleverest suggestions, however, always seem to come from mechanics. I had been complaining to my friend Barry about the inadequacy of the available turntable mechanisms to provide me with a portable, heavy-duty, spray-booth turntable. A few days later, he handed me a 20-lb. chunk of metal that turned out to be a transmission bearing from a junked Pontiac. It consisted of two plates, already drilled with four evenly spaced holes, connected by a *very* heavy-duty bearing. It took only minutes to attach a board on the top plate and set the mechanism on a base, and I was spraying with a smooth, sure turntable that is, so far, impervious (due to the protected, greased bearing) to clogging by spray dust.

Here's another tip from the automotive field: Sometimes I have to steam open old glue joints, and one of my favorite aids is a small cappucino maker, a steam generator that produces very hot, dry steam under a good deal of pressure. It has a built-in safety valve and a cut-off valve. To get into tight spots, I extended the output stem by adding a length of surgical tubing, with a basketball air-fill pin as the tip, and secured both with hose clamps. As I was using it one day, I watched in horror as the tubing suddenly ballooned out. As I made a grab for the cut-off valve, the bubble burst, spewing steam and pieces of rubber all over me and the shop. The oven mitts on my hands prevented injury, but the incident shook me up. I set out to the nearest auto supply store, and came back with some reinforced heat-resistant fuel line hose. It's been holding like a trooper for more than two years now.

Although surgical tubing was a "bust" as a steam hose, it's still indispensable. It's no secret that random lengths make fine tie-offs for holding things, and that this tubing can act as a rubber-band clamp. But it has other uses as well. I keep a split length handy to protect the soundhole of a guitar from being marred by metal clamps, and I usually slip a strip onto a bar clamp to protect the wood from the bar. The hose comes in various diameters and, because it's latex, it will not mar or react with lacquer finishes. Strips of tubing can be slipped over metal hangers that are to hold finished wood, and the larger diameters attached to the fingers of a drying rack make a cushiony support. A loop thrown onto a rough tabletop will allow you to float a finished board on it while the other side is being worked on.

Don't walk out of the medical equipment store yet. Surgical gloves are more sensitive and less clumsy than grocery store rubber gloves, especially for aniline staining and French polishing, when you need to feel the pad. Various surgical clamps and hemostats make fine extra hands and mini-clamps for small or delicate parts. Even the humble petroleum jelly (Vaseline) is handy as tapeless masking for lacquer, as well as being a must for lubricating spray guns. Vaseline won't mess up a finish if a drop of it migrates, as will some oils. Surgical jelly has similar properties and is water-soluble as well.

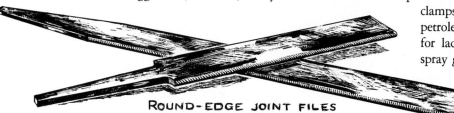

ROUND-EDGE JOINT FILES

There is a versatile gunstock vise, such as shown at right, on just about every luthier's workbench. It rotates 360° and its jaws pivot to grip non-parallel stock. Most luthiers pad the jaws with leather or suede, and a

GUNSTOCK VISE

rubber band draped between the jaws will protect the stock from dropping onto the metal guides. While you are checking out gunstock vises, take a look at checkering tools too. They make a whole range of handy little chisels of odd shapes and sizes, great for getting into tiny spots to clean up intricate carvings. And for the backgrounds of those carvings, remember that leather stamps work just as well on wood. Leather punches are also very handy. They'll make clean circular holes in veneer or plastic, or else cleanly cut-out dots, whichever you happen to need. Don't overlook leather workers' files and rasps either. They work superbly on wood, are generally finer-cutting than woodworking ones, and often come in different, handy profiles. Machinists' files add to the arsenal. Many of them cut on the pull stroke rather than the push stroke, which is great for tight spots. Speaking of fine cutting and versatility, dental bits and burs can't be beat. The burs will fit a Dremel, and come in an astonishing array of sizes and shapes—far more than the motor tool companies offer. Catalogs of jewelers' tools usually list them.

For pearl inlay work, you need something that draws a constant, narrow line, unlike a regular pencil whose point gets thicker and thicker as it dulls. I used to curse my way through six or seven pencil points while drawing on pearl, and one day I finally stomped out and steamed my way over to the local art supply store. There I saw a heartwarming display of mechanical drafting pencils. They take leads of a dozen different diameters and all degrees of hardness. I chose a 0.3mm pencil and a medium-hard lead, and I now use it for all marking and drawing where scribing is impossible or the scratch line undesirable. On my way out of the store, I asked for a thinner masking tape than was on display, and got accidentally introduced to another worksaver. They sold me a paper tape used in drafting, and I soon found that while it masks every bit as well, it doesn't lift off old, checked finishes the way masking tape invariably does.

Spray adhesive, also from the art supply store, has simplified many temporary holding jobs. It makes working with pearl or other small inlays much easier. I spray-glue the back of the inlay and stick it on the surface where it will go. Then I spray the surrounding area with a contrasting color of tinting lacquer—a mixture of almost pure pigment and solvent that has virtually no binder. After I lift off the inlay, I can rout out the wood within the crisp, colored outline. Mineral spirits loosens the adhesive without affecting the lacquer. Lacquer thinner removes both adhesive and color.

Years ago, I went out to buy a ³/₃₂-in. router bit, for cutting bridge slots. The salesman looked at me as if I were crazy, and sold me an end mill instead. I took it home, set it up in my slower drill press (rigged up like an overarm router), and found that its spiral cutting edges made a clean, burn-free cut. It works especially well in hard woods such as ebony and rosewood, causes less chipping, and, because it's made to cut metal, has outlasted every router bit in my shop.

My friend Barry, the bearer of clutch bearings, has been my main guide to metalworking tools. One frequent job I'm asked to do, installing a larger set of guitar tuners, involves enlarging all or part of a hole already drilled. My old method had me plugging the hole, finding the center, and drilling a new hole. It was time-consuming and inaccurate. Then Barry introduced me to the counterbore, shown at right, a metal bit with a removable pilot in its center. Any size pilot (with a standard shaft) will fit in any size bit, so you can enlarge or partially bore any hole from any other one, and the pilot ensures that the hole center remains the same. In addition, the bit makes a clean, uniform hole, with no chipping.

COUNTERBORE

Don't overlook the trash can. I make a regular practice of raiding the local glass cutter's rubbish for scraps of clear plastic sheet. It shows up in several thicknesses, and I tote them all back to my shop. As clamping cauls, they let you see how the seam underneath is lining up, saving many repeat jobs, and wood glue will not stick to them. But it is the larger pieces that are really indispensable—they become my instrumentmaking templates. The plastic lets you see through to line up the grain the way you want it, or to include the prettiest figure.

Having borrowed so much from other trades, perhaps I can give something back. We've all learned that lining a jig with face-up sandpaper stops things from sliding around, but a common item from my own trade, violin rosin, works just as well and does less damage to the piece. It crushes into a fine, sticky powder which will cling to

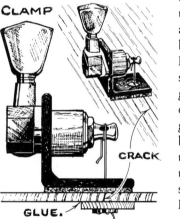

CLAMP

CRACK

GLUE.

the jig and provide just the right tack. Mineral spirits cleans away any residue. Also from my workbench is a small clamp, shown at left, used for repairing cracks in soundboards. The objective is to glue a tapered cleat beneath the crack. The clamp, made from a guitar tuner and angle iron, works by pulling up on the cleat, leveling the crack at the same time. When the glue is dry, the guitar string is simply clipped off and pulled out, leaving a tiny hole.

One final word of warning when accumulating what seems to be free for the taking. I have several sandbags in my shop that I use for bedding curved or rounded objects on the drill-press table. One day I asked my wife to fill one for me, as she was on her way to the beach—living on the Jersey shore, with its over 100 miles of beachfront, I assumed there would be ample sand to spare for my small bag. But the bag came back empty. After mutely watching my wife fill the bag and lug it to the car, a policeman had stepped up and ordered her to take it back and dump it on the beach. Apparently, in New Jersey, you can take home only as much sand as you can unwittingly carry in your shoes and bathing suit. □

Michael Dresdner, of Red Bank, N.J., came to instrument repair via an apprenticeship in antique restoration.

JOINERY

Quick and Tricky Little Boxes
How I bookmatch scrap wood into Christmas gifts

by Jim Cummins

I'm an impatient putterer with thrifty inclinations. Over the past year I've gotten a big kick out of converting my scrap pile into a bunch of Christmas presents. Inspired by Sam Bush's matched-grain box from *FWW* #32 (figure 1, facing page), I began exploring variations in the design and construction of small boxes, aiming to have fun while not making the same box twice. I ended up with a dozen variations, most of them figure-matched in one way or another, with different designs for lids and bottoms, and different joinery details. Some required a little thoughtful planning, some were last-minute adaptations based on chance, and a couple of my favorite details grew out of my efforts to fix mistakes. The elements can be combined in lots of ways, and there isn't a box here that can't be made in an hour or two, not counting the finishing, of course.

The first variation—Sam Bush's box in figure 1 comes out of a board, but my first bookmatched box, shown in figure 2, came from a walnut turning scrap about 2 in. square by 9 in. long. First I bandsawed it into four strips, and planed them smooth on both sides. On one pair of strips, I laid out the

box sides and ends the same way Bush did. The other pair of strips I edge-glued, using masking tape to clamp the joint (p. 46). This bookmatched piece was as wide as the ends of the box, and long enough to cut in half to become the bottom and lid. While the strips dried, I rabbeted the top and bottom edges of the sides and ends as shown in figure 2A, then I mitered and glued them, again with tape, adding rubber bands for more pressure. While the sides cured, I rabbeted the lid and the bottom to fit into the rabbets in the sides. I glued the bottom in, using tape clamps, put the lid on and sanded the edges flush.

When I was done, I realized that I'd made three dumb mistakes. First, I hadn't examined the direction of the grain in the turning square. Bookmatching, because of the sawkerf, is never perfect, but if you arrange the grain as shown in figure 2B, it will be close. I had sawn the blank at an intermediate angle to the annual rings, which gave me pretty wood, but a poor match. My second mistake was in jointing and thicknessing the stock before I joined the sides. Bookmatched figure matches best right at the sawkerf, so you want to remove minimum wood from the show surfaces. I should

Square pegs in round holes pin these lapped corners.

Splined boxes of red maple, spalted hackberry, and cherry.

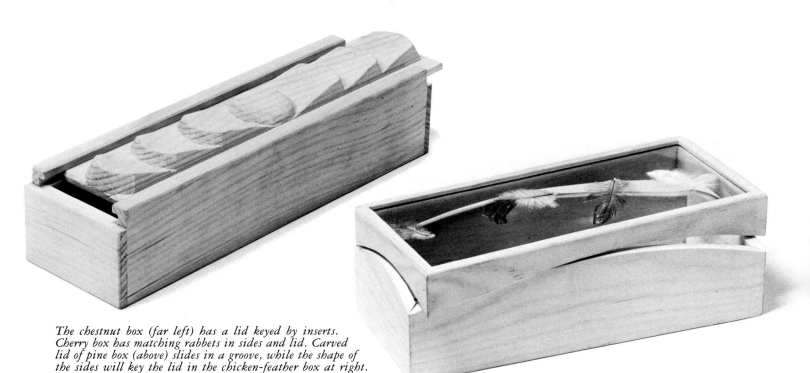

The chestnut box (far left) has a lid keyed by inserts. Cherry box has matching rabbets in sides and lid. Carved lid of pine box (above) slides in a groove, while the shape of the sides will key the lid in the chicken-feather box at right.

have smoothed the inside surfaces only, and waited until the box was joined before sanding the bandsaw marks off the outside surfaces. A more careful workman than I might plane both sides of the stock smooth before bandsawing, and might be sure to resaw exactly in the middle of the thickness. Then he could skim off the sawmarks before gluing up. Others might just tablesaw the stock to thickness in the first place. Since people argue about which resawing procedure wastes the most wood, I tested several tablesaw blades against my bandsaw. I found that by the time I'd planed away the bandsaw marks, I'd lost more wood than to an ordinary ripping blade. Two carbide blades—the Freud thin-kerf and the Forrest/Mr. Sawdust—left surfaces clean enough to sand.

The third mistake was the rabbet for the top and bottom: it left no allowance for wood movement. Even in this small box, the width of the top and bottom could drift $\frac{1}{16}$ in. from summer to winter, and sooner or later the glue joint would break, or the lid would stop fitting, or both. I knew all this, but I'd been too interested in the figure match to bother about it. Anyway, it is humid summer as I write, and nothing untoward has happened to my walnut box yet.

(continued on p. 47)

Fig. 1: How it all began

This simple bookmatching technique yields a box with perfectly matched grain at all four corners. The rough lumber need be only as long as one side and one end of the box, but thick enough to resaw. First resaw. The inside surfaces match, so reverse them to become the outside of the box. Cut the sides and ends sequentially, keeping all the waste to one end. To assemble, I prefer the dramatic matched effect of mitered corners, with spline reinforcements. —*Sam Bush, Portland, Ore.*

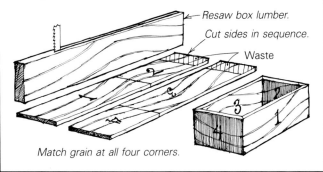

— Resaw box lumber.

Cut sides in sequence.

Waste

Match grain at all four corners.

Fig. 2: First attempt

2A: Bottom in rabbet

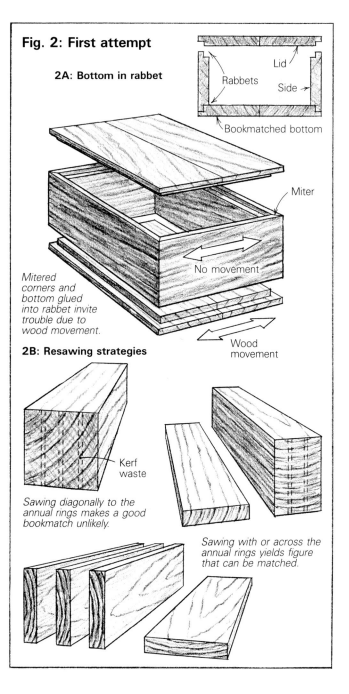

Lid

Rabbets

Side

Bookmatched bottom

Miter

Mitered corners and bottom glued into rabbet invite trouble due to wood movement.

No movement

Wood movement

2B: Resawing strategies

Kerf waste

Sawing diagonally to the annual rings makes a good bookmatch unlikely.

Sawing with or across the annual rings yields figure that can be matched.

Miters, tape and glue

I use ordinary masking tape to clamp up a bookmatched panel for the lid or bottom of one of my little boxes. To glue up a box's mitered corners, I supplement the tape with rubber bands.

Before gluing up a matched panel, sand, plane or joint the good side of both pieces so that you can see the final figure. Then hold the pieces together in front of a window or a bright light, to make sure the gluing surfaces meet exactly. If they don't, plane them until no light shows through anywhere. You don't have to fret about square edges if you fold the bookmatch good-side-in, clamp the pair of boards in the vise and plane both edges at the same time. If you machine-joint, you'll get the cleanest glueline by skimming off the mill marks with a pass of the hand plane.

Both pieces of wood ought to end up the same thickness, but if at this stage they aren't, you'll have to take care that the good side glues up flat, with the irregularities on the back side only. To do so, lay the pieces on the bench good-side-up, and line up the figure. Run a piece of masking tape across the joint line to keep the figure from shifting. Next, lightly apply a strip of tape along the full length of the joint and flip the assembly over. From the back, press along the joint to stick the tape down firmly.

Bend the joint open and apply glue. Yellow Titebond, as it comes from the jug, is formulated for filling gaps and thus is thicker than it needs to be for long-grain gluing. If your joint is light-tight, such a thick glue will leave a visible glueline. If you thin a tablespoonful of the glue by adding a few drops of water, it will hold better, and the joint will be invisible. To clamp the joint, run a short piece of tape opposite the first one, then similarly tape every 2 in. or so across the joint, taking care to balance the tension on both sides of the panel as you go, else it will curl. You should not need to weight the panel flat.

Miters for box sides are best cut with the wood flat on the saw table, with the blade tilted to 45° and the gauge set at 90° to the blade. I used to set the miter gauge with the aid of a carpenters' square, but a reader, Dustin Davis of Frostburg, Md., sent in a simple device (figure A) that makes the job much easier. It's a shim of ¼-in. plastic that allows you to register the face of the miter gauge against the front edge of the saw table, which on most saws is accurately machined at 90° to the slots in the table. Just drop the shim over the miter-gauge guide bar, push the gauge against the saw table, and tighten the knob. Some saws don't need a shim—you can just turn the gauge upside down for squaring against the table's edge.

The 45° setting is almost as easy. First, tilt the blade to a nominal 45°. To check the angle, take a straight, squared-up length of wood about 2 ft. long, and miter-crosscut it near its middle (figure B). Then recut the miter on the offcut end. Butt the mitered surfaces together and see if the wood lies straight. If it doesn't, the angle is not 45°, and the saw's adjustment wheel needs a twist one way or the other. On my saw, this trick will tell me if I'm as little as a sixteenth of a turn off. Save the test pieces. You can miter them quite a few times before they get too short.

To tape up a box, lay the sides and ends on the bench, outside up, with the points of the miters touching. Run wide tape along the length of each joint (figure C). Press down hard, but don't try to stress the tape so that it will exert pressure across the joint. Just keep the corners touching. When you roll up the box to check the fit of the top and bottom, the tape takes the long way around, automatically pulling taut.

The glued miter is strong enough for most small boxes, except when the sides are so thick that wood movement in the thickness can force the joint to open up, or so thin that there's just not enough gluing surface. To reinforce the corners, I insert a couple of cross-splines in table-sawn kerfs. I saw the slots with my sharpest rip blade (because its kerf has a flat bottom), supporting the box in a simple jig made from a scrap of 2x4, as shown in figure D. The jig runs against the saw's rip fence, and the clamping tape on the box corners is usually enough to prevent chipping.

If the miter angle is correct, you can use tape and rubber bands to clamp almost any number of sides during glue-up—one of my boxes has 15 sides. A possible pitfall: On my first hexagonal box (how I hate to admit this), I unrolled the box and put glue in all the joints, but I forgot to glue the miters at each end, leaving me one joint completely unglued when the tape came off. There might be a plus in that experience some day: If I'd left two joints unglued, the box would still have gone together fine, but later I would have been able to remove one side, and I probably could have figured out some way to make a sideways lid out of it. —J.C.

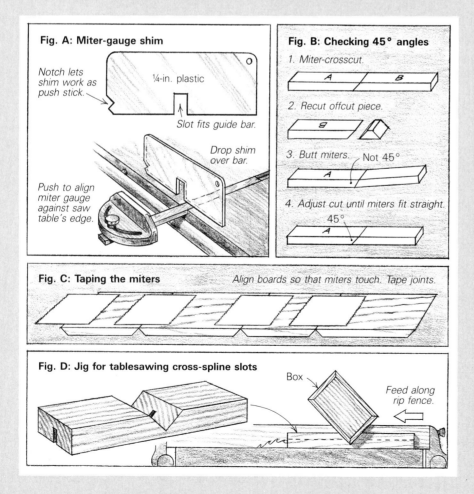

Fig. A: Miter-gauge shim
Notch lets shim work as push stick.
¼-in. plastic
Slot fits guide bar.
Drop shim over bar.
Push to align miter gauge against saw table's edge.

Fig. B: Checking 45° angles
1. Miter-crosscut.
A   B
2. Recut offcut piece.
B
3. Butt miters.   Not 45°
A
4. Adjust cut until miters fit straight.
45°
A

Fig. C: Taping the miters   Align boards so that miters touch. Tape joints.

Fig. D: Jig for tablesawing cross-spline slots
Box
Feed along rip fence.

Coping with movement—In the next box, I made room for both the lid and the bottom to move (figure 3). I used some bird's-eye maple picture-frame molding, which was barely thick enough to yield ³⁄₁₆-in. thick strips for the sides. I ran the rabbet for the lid and the groove for the bottom, cut the miters, and taped the corners together without glue. Then I cut the bottom and top to fit. I removed the tape from one corner of the box and unfolded the box flat on the bench. I applied glue to the miters, fit the bottom into its groove without glue, and rolled the box up tight, taping the last corner.

Because the sides were so thin, I felt I should reinforce the glue joint at the corners. So while the glue was setting, I grabbed a 2x4 scrap and made a jig (facing page) for sawing a couple of slots for cross-splines through each corner. Then I puzzled over what to do about the lid. As things stood, there was no way of getting it out of its rabbet, short of turning the box upside down.

I debated drilling a finger hole through it, but then remembered that Desmond Ryan (*FWW* #33, pp. 59-65) had worked out a lever-action lid with a built-in fulcrum. If you pressed one corner of the lid down, the other end would rise out of its rabbet. I used the same idea, and the relief cuts turned out to be decorative as well. To make them, I raised the tablesaw blade ⅜ in. above the table, and clamped a stop to the fence at about the location of the arbor. Feeding with the stock faced against the fence produced the curved shape, which is simply the profile of a 10-in. sawblade. I cut the detail on both ends and both sides of the lid, so it fits and works no matter which way around it's put (figure 3A).

Two other variations of the lever-action lid are also shown in figure 3. In 3B, the fulcrum is built into the rabbet instead of the lid. Make the relief cuts on the tablesaw before the box is joined, and be sure to relieve the ends as well. In 3C, the fulcrum is in the lid, but it isn't obvious. The lid is symmetrically tapered on both faces of both ends, so that it fits either way, and the projecting lip of the rabbet is shaped to conform to the lid's curve.

It can be perilous to tablesaw box-sized pieces of wood, if you don't take precautions. When you're resawing or making relief cuts, the stock might slither down beside the sawblade, which you can prevent by making a new, tightly fitting table insert. Bandsaw the outline from ¾-in. plywood, file or sand it to a good fit in the saw's throat, shim it (or relieve it) so that it sits flush with the table, then raise the blade through it to cut a snug slot. When ripping small pieces to width, be sure that the bottom of the fence is tight to the saw table, otherwise the work can slide under it and bind. Small pieces are notoriously prone to catch and kick back, so push sticks are essential. My favorite is a sharp ice-pick. With it you can hold the work tight on the table at the same time as you feed it forward. Strive to keep the work moving steadily through the blade, to avoid blade-marks and burns.

Frame-and-panel lids—Another type of lid that accommodates wood movement is the frame-and-panel assembly, essentially what I used for the bottom of the box in figure 3. Here are a couple of ways to secure such a lid without hardware. The little cherry box shown at the top of p. 44 has a rabbet in the lid that fits over a matching rabbet in the box. In a large box, it's easy enough to cut the rabbet in the lid before it is joined up around its panel, but in a small box the lid pieces are tricky to handle. It's better to glue up the whole

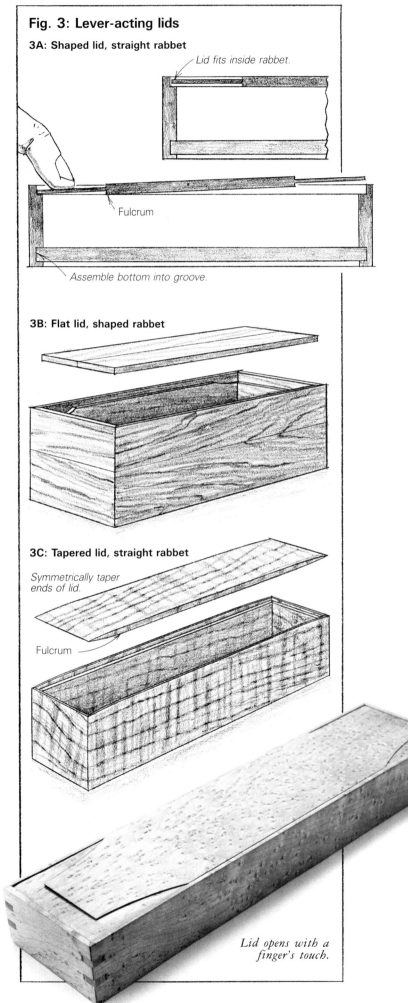

Fig. 3: Lever-acting lids

3A: Shaped lid, straight rabbet

Lid fits inside rabbet.

Fulcrum

Assemble bottom into groove.

3B: Flat lid, shaped rabbet

3C: Tapered lid, straight rabbet

Symmetrically taper ends of lid.

Fulcrum

Lid opens with a finger's touch.

box, then cut the lid off later, complete with rabbet.

The procedure, as shown in figure 4, is to groove the inside of the box at three places—top (for the panel in the lid), bottom (for the box bottom), and along the lid's rabbet line. Join up the box, then after the glue has set, cut the box open to leave the rabbet in the lid. Finally, run the box part over the tablesaw to make the exterior rabbet that receives the lid. By varying the width and depth of the cuts, this method can be generalized up to blanket-chest size, where it ensures that box and lid are not only figure-matched but also the same size. Some people find it most efficient to saw the groove for the exterior rabbet in the box sides before glue-up, while the square-bottom grooving blade is on the arbor. This saves a blade change, and also leaves no doubt about where the lid begins and ends when you saw the box open. Allow for the box-opening kerf when you lay out the grooves. If you use the tablesaw to separate the two pieces, cut one side at a time, and shim each kerf open before cutting the next, to keep the box

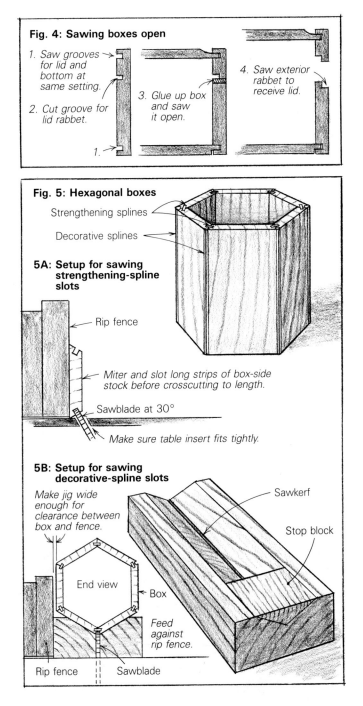

Fig. 4: Sawing boxes open

1. Saw grooves for lid and bottom at same setting.

2. Cut groove for lid rabbet.

1.

3. Glue up box and saw it open.

4. Saw exterior rabbet to receive lid.

Fig. 5: Hexagonal boxes

Strengthening splines

Decorative splines

5A: Setup for sawing strengthening-spline slots

Rip fence

Miter and slot long strips of box-side stock before crosscutting to length.

Sawblade at 30°

Make sure table insert fits tightly.

5B: Setup for sawing decorative-spline slots

Make jig wide enough for clearance between box and fence.

End view

Box

Sawkerf

Stop block

Feed against rip fence.

Rip fence   Sawblade

from closing and pinching the sawblade. If you handsaw, first scribe a line all around the box with a sharp marking gauge.

Frame-and-panel lids don't have to be straight. The chestnut box shown on p. 44 was cut open in a curve on the bandsaw. To form the lip that secures the lid, I inserted false sides in the box, then trimmed them to conform to the curve. Of course, false sides work just as well in a box that's been sawn open on a straight line.

In any frame-and-panel design, whether for a box lid or a piece of furniture, the way the edge of the panel is shaped affects, even determines, the look of the piece. Some of the options are considered on the facing page.

Hexagonal boxes—A dead hackberry tree yielded such strikingly spalted wood that I thought I'd try matching the corners all around a hexagonal box (p. 44). The method works just like Bush's, except that you lay out the box to get three equal sides from each half of the resawn blank's length. In my box, because the pattern in the wood ran at an angle, each sawcut threw off the match a little bit. As I taped up the sides, I found that I could accommodate the loss by shifting each side upward in order to align the figure. This trick finally caught up with me at the last corner, which ended up being not a good match at all.

When the box's top and bottom edges had been trimmed straight on the bandsaw, I removed the tape at one corner, unrolled the box flat, and tablesawed a groove for the bottom. I had no hackberry left, so I made a glass bottom instead: I rolled up the box dry, traced its outline, laid a piece of glass on the tracing, and cut out a hexagon, allowing for the depth of the groove. The glass hasn't broken, even though this box does daily work holding pens and pencils. I've since added cross-splines to each miter joint, because spalted wood cut ¼ in. thick needs all the help it can get.

In another box, shown in figure 5 and on p. 44, I planned to put lengthwise splines in the miter joints, both for strength and to make a pretty detail at the top rim. The box went together dry, but when I added glue, the splines swelled and forced open the joints at the outside corners. As I strained to get the joints tight, I became covered with slippery glue squeeze-out, masking tape and rubber bands, but I knew that if I tried to retreat, the mess would be even worse. I clamped up as well as I could and hoped for the best.

The corners dried open, but the splines were holding the box sturdy and tight. I rescued it by making another 2x4 jig (figure 5B), this one oriented to run a sawkerf the length of each corner. With the second round of splines in place, the box looks as if I'd planned it that way. For thin splines, such as in the little cherry box shown on p. 44, you can kerf the corners on the bandsaw—no jig necessary.

A self-keying lid—While I was making the chestnut box with the false sides, I noticed that the top automatically aligned itself in one direction because of the crown in the bandsaw cut. I reasoned that if I could get the crown on both the long sides and the short sides (pine chicken-feather box, p. 45), the top would align without my having to insert false sides. This meant that I would have to make the bandsaw cuts before the box was joined.

I resawed a piece of #2 common pine, about 3 in. wide and 14 in. long, then cut the sides to length, matching the grain the way Bush did. Then I ran a groove for the top and bottom. Next I bandsawed a curve on each side, taking care that adjoining cuts would meet at the box's corners.

The marks from the bandsaw blade were very obvious, but planing or sanding the edges would have altered the fit of the lid. Instead I ripped thin slivers of pine (half the thickness of the bandsaw kerf) to mask the rough edges on both the lid and the box. I glued the edge-banding in place before I mitered the corners, using tape for alignment and a vise for pressure. Because all four sides were the same height, I could glue up the first side, clamp it in the vise, then simply add the other sides to the stack as I got them ready.

While the stack was in the vise, I cut a mirror for the bottom and a piece of old picture glass for the top. The picture glass was so thin that it rattled, but, luckily, two pieces filled the kerf perfectly. To add some decoration, I stuck a few chicken feathers between the panes.

If I were making this box again, I'd do a couple of things differently. It is almost impossible to match the figure around the corners and match the bandsaw cuts as well. I'd forget about the figure, and concentrate on matching the bandsaw cuts—they're more important. Also, I'd seal the edges of the double glass with clear tape before I slid it in. When I sanded the resaw marks off the outside of the box, dust worked between the pieces of glass and muddied the clarity. I'd also take the time to catch a clean chicken, rather than just picking up any old feathers off the floor. □

Jim Cummins is an associate editor at Fine Woodworking.

Panels for lids

The simplest way to fit a panel into a frame is to make the groove the full thickness of the panel (**A**). In large-scale work, this has the drawback of requiring that the panel be very thin, or that the frame be weakened by a wide groove. So, usually, a panel is made thick enough to be stable, and then its edges are thinned down so that it fits a narrow groove in the frame. This process is called "raising" the panel, and it leaves a raised "field" in the center.

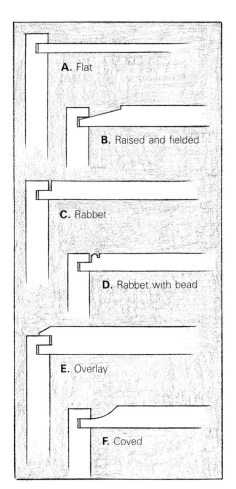

A. Flat

B. Raised and fielded

C. Rabbet

D. Rabbet with bead

E. Overlay

F. Coved

There are innumerable ways to raise panels, each with a different look.

For the little boxes in this article, treatment **A** succeeds because the pieces are so small that strength and stability aren't a factor. Also, the plain, flat panel doesn't interfere with your efforts to bookmatch the wood's figure.

In **B,** the edge has been tapered down and the center field defined by a little vertical shoulder, the traditional form of the frame-and-panel. In **C** it has been rabbeted, so seasonal wood movement will show up as variation in the width of the space between frame and field. The bead at **D** is an elegant touch that tends to conceal seasonal movement in the panel's width. It can be routed, but is easily hand-worked with a homemade tool called a scratch-beader (*FWW* #11, p. 60). The overlay panel at **E** conceals any evidence of wood movement. You can run the cove at **F** against an angled fence, cautiously raising the tablesaw blade a little on each pass until you reach the depth you want.

Where you make the groove affects how much the panel is raised. The top groove, if near the edge, can raise the panel higher than its frame (**F**), which looks fine on the lid. But if the same spacing were used for the bottom, it would cause the panel to project too far—you want the box to rest on the edges of its sides, not on the panel's raised field. You can also shape the edges of the frame to complement the treatment on the panel itself. Such details can be delicate on the lid, but shouldn't be too fragile if on the bottom or they may break off.

All these variables are easy to work into the design if you plan ahead for them—many require just a single pass over the tablesaw. If you wait until the box is glued up, however, trying to add even a simple detail may very well tax your patience. —*J.C.*

Starting and finishing— thoughts on design

by John Kelsey

A box is only a box. Still, there is an infinite variety of rectangular wooden boxes. What makes one simple box different from another? Three general considerations are the size and proportions of the overall form, the way the surfaces are decorated, and the detailing at corners and edges. These outline a rich universe of design possibilities.

The size and proportions of the boxy form often grow logically from function: what has to fit inside? Just as often, however, the box is being made simply to have a box, perhaps for a gift, and because *here's* a good-looking piece of wood. Some people have an eye for proportional harmony and somehow know when the components are long enough, wide enough, high enough. Other people prefer to devise some proportional scheme, instead of choosing dimensions at random or defaulting to the largest pieces possible within the given plank.

I like to think of proportion as the visual analog of rhythm in music. We see harmony in dimensions that interrelate. Perhaps we subliminally measure, by subconsciously comparing the time it takes the eye to traverse adjacent edges. As in music, simple proportional schemes are usually pleasant (figure 1, p. 50). But the very simplest, the cube, is dull as drumming until you embellish it. The double cube and the root-of-two cuboid are interesting; so is the 1:2:3 proportion. Whole volumes have been written on the intricacies of the golden

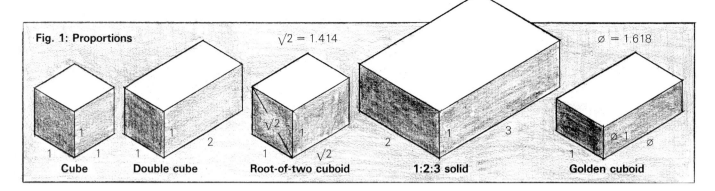

Fig. 1: Proportions

$\sqrt{2} = 1.414$ $\varnothing = 1.618$

Cube   Double cube   Root-of-two cuboid   1:2:3 solid   Golden cuboid

section: the division of a line into two parts such that the smaller part is to the larger as the larger is to the whole. It gives rise to the "golden cuboid." Many people think this looks just right, and its proportions are often rediscovered by artisans working entirely by eye.

"Surface decoration" usually means a design imposed on the form, worked out in paint, carving or inlay. But bookmatched wood figure is also surface decoration. The woodworker perceives and enhances what grew in the tree, instead of laying on what's seen in the mind's eye. A featureless corner joint, such as the splined miter, doesn't compete with the main attraction.

With woods that don't have flashy figure, we can play up corner joinery and tooled edges. Even people who shudder at glued-on gee-gaws can usually accept the decoration of careful joinery, because the joint isn't an afterthought, it holds the box together. The half-lap with square pegs shown in figure 2 requires only the ability to saw on a line. The pegs are split out square and whittled round for half their length, then driven with glue into round holes. Decorative nails would do instead. The cleanest edge treatment is probably a bold chamfer, straight off chisel and plane.

The dovetail isn't the most difficult joint, but non-woodworkers don't know that, so it can make a small box into a real show-off. Dovetailed boxes with

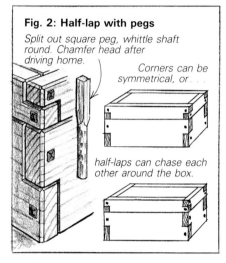

Fig. 2: Half-lap with pegs

Split out square peg, whittle shaft round. Chamfer head after driving home.

Corners can be symmetrical, or . . .

half-laps can chase each other around the box.

paneled lids are customarily made closed and then sawn open, as shown in figure 3A. The grooves for lid and bottom usually exit through the sockets of the pins pieces, but they must be shaped in mid-tails, else a hole will show. Grooves are easy to stop when routed; if you tablesaw or hand-plane the groove, you can't make it stop, but you can whittle a peg to fill the hole. If your eye sticks on pegs and half-pins, chisel neat endmiters instead (figure 3B).

Antique dealers sometimes import veneered boxes from England. The best ones are dovetailed hardwood under the veneer, although most are made of pine joined by miters or rabbets, glued and nailed. Some boxes might even have se-

cret mitered dovetails, who can say?

When a box's reason for existence is its pretty wood, the quality of the finished surface is important. Varnish is too coarse and plasticky for little things. Bookmatched wood that's been planed smooth shows best under a glossy penetrating oil finish such as Minwax natural oil, a thin formula you have to build up and rub out hard. But it is an unforgiving finish, emphasizing flaws as much as beauty, and a waste of time if you've sanded your boxes, as grit and dust just muddy the oil's clarity. Watco Danish oil, McCloskey Tung-Seal and Minwax Antique oil complement sanded wood. They dry to a satin gloss when rubbed, and two coats are usually enough. Avoid linseed oil unless you want to smell it every time you lift the lid.

Oil finishes are no good for soft, absorbent wood or any wood that has spalted, because the oil soaks in, it takes forever to dry, and you have to apply so much to build up the finish that you'll bury the figure. One answer is a brushing lacquer such as Deft. Dense woods such as rosewood can take a high-gloss oil, but for best results you ought to fill the open grain. An alternative is a single coat of paste wax, buffed.

Finally, there's always no finish. Like a tool handle, small boxes acquire a nice patina from use. If what I'm calling "patina" looks like dirt to you, a light sanding will renew the wood.   □

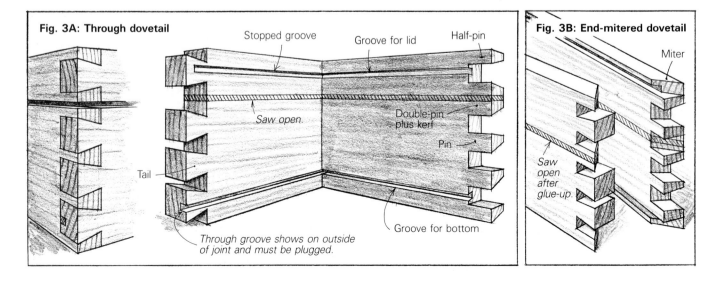

Fig. 3A: Through dovetail

Stopped groove   Groove for lid   Half-pin

Saw open.

Double-pin plus kerf

Pin

Tail

Through groove shows on outside of joint and must be plugged.

Groove for bottom

Fig. 3B: End-mitered dovetail

Miter

Saw open after glue-up.

The Laminated Wood Ribbon
A built-up joint with sculptural possibilities

by James Rannefeld

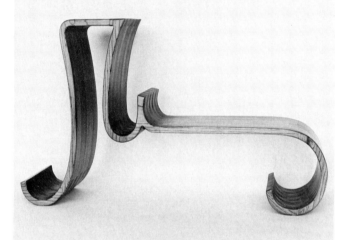

Visual lightness and the illusion of mass without weight make the laminated wood ribbon a compelling method for sculptural furniture. 'Inspiration Bench' (top of page) is made of 33 pieces of oak accented with padauk. 'Signature' (above) illustrates another application of this method. The drawing (facing page) shows how short-grain is cross-laminated for strength.

A great deal has been said about the vanishing line between sculpture and furniture, part of a larger dialogue about the indistinction between art and craft. The stack lamination techniques pioneered by Wendell Castle have contributed substantially to this discussion, resulting in forms more closely related to sculpture than to traditional furniture.

The laminated joint I'll describe here (actually a finger or box joint) is a natural outgrowth of Castle's early bricklay lamination techniques. It differs from traditional joinery in that the joint is made *during* the lamination process, rather than being cut into prepared stock. This joint makes the solid wood ribbon possible, freeing the contemporary woodworker from many of the constraints imposed by traditional rectilinear furniture construction.

The laminated wood ribbon has the assets of mass, without being massive—a common criticism of stack-laminated furniture. It can also be light and delicate, without seeming weak or fragile. As an alternative to bent plywood, the laminated-joint technique requires less initial setup time, with little or no specialized tooling or forms, and allows better use of lower grades of wood. And it's truly versatile—as easily used to wrap a set of drawers, doors or tambours as to define a spare, flowing table form or a bench.

The laminated ribbon is made by face-gluing many individual strips of wood that have been roughly bandsawn to shape. It's not unusual for a small, relatively simple bench to involve 33 or more bandsawn pieces, and a complicated project such as the "Signature" bench/console (above) might require more than a hundred.

Construction begins with two templates—one for each alternating layer. I make my templates out of Masonite from a full-size sketch of the profile, taking care to fair their shape as close to the finished profile of the piece as I can, to conserve wood and to minimize shaping work later. For a recurved foot, such as that of "Inspiration Bench" (top of page), I make a series of templates, one for each layer, from a full-size drawing of the parabola.

Bandsawing curves from flat, straight-grained boards (usually 1 in. or 1¼ in. thick) inevitably leaves weak, short-grain areas. Templates must be arranged so that any short grain is cross-laminated by long grain in the next layer. This usually

Hardly a surface goes unclamped when a wood ribbon is glued up. Rannefeld assembles at a pace that allows the glue's natural tack to keep parts from sliding. Particleboard cauls spread clamping pressure and align the faces of the outermost laminae. Once the ribbon has cured, Rannefeld works it over with body grinders, sculpting by hand and eye to the final shape. He uses a small drum sander to get inside the tight spots.

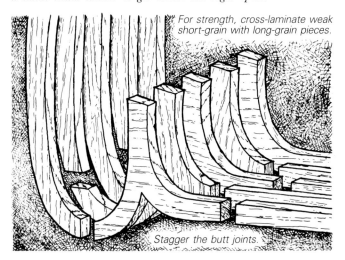

For strength, cross-laminate weak short-grain with long-grain pieces.

Stagger the butt joints.

results in an odd number of laminations in the finished piece, much as a sheet of plywood is made up of an odd number of veneers. In New Mexico's arid climate, such cross-grain constructions have held up well, but in areas where the seasonal moisture gradient is higher, they might crack. To avoid this problem, orient the layers so that the grain runs at a slight bias instead of at right angles.

When laying out pieces to be bandsawn, the shapes can be nested and ganged on individual boards to best utilize random width and length stock. Often I am able to use lower grades of lumber, at considerable savings, by working around natural flaws in the wood. Wood for lamination must be of uniform thickness, and should be free from obvious ridges from the planer. Flat surfaces, where the laminae butt together, for example, or where a table's legs meet the floor, are best cut square on a radial-arm saw.

Before laminating, it's a good idea to make cauls the shape of the finished project. This speeds glue-up and aligns the layers. Wax or varnish the cauls so that they won't stick to

the work. Obviously, glue-up is the most critical operation, and the most difficult, since the glue (I use Titebond) acts as a lubricant, encouraging the laminae to slip out of alignment. You could use dowels or tacks to hold the layers in place, but I prefer to lay up the stack one by one, working as quickly as possible but at a rate that allows the glue to grab, holding one layer in place before the next one goes on. Timing is important here. As the glue slowly cures, it becomes increasingly tacky, and with a little bit of care you get a feel for the speed at which layers can be stacked without causing lower layers to slip. In cold weather I sometimes bring in a small electric heater to expedite things.

Spare no clamps—especially in complex, staggered layering. Spacing clamps closely will straighten out slightly bowed or wound pieces and will flatten minute irregularities between boards.

When the clamps are removed 24 hours later, the piece can be attacked with a variety of sculpting and sanding tools to shape it to the desired form and surface. My favorite tools for removing wood quickly are 7-in. and 4-in. body grinders. I also have a pneumatic sculptors' gouge that comes in handy for wasting large amounts of wood quickly.

I use a drum sander on a flexible shaft to give shape and clarity to the form, followed by electric and pneumatic finish sanders, and then a smaller drum sander for hard-to-reach places such as tight inside curves.

I finish my laminated work with a 3:1 mixture of Watco exterior Danish oil and polyurethane. This mixture gives a satiny finish, looks and repairs like an oil finish, yet resists water and alcohol like polyurethane.

My most recent explorations of the ribbon have shown me that these forms have even wider applications than I had first imagined. It is the laminated joint that gives us the ability to realize complex, even convoluted forms in solid wood, without the intimidating technology associated with laminated veneer construction. And it is the ribbon that sets our imaginations free. □

James Rannefeld sculpts fanciful ribbons and contemporary furniture in Taos, New Mexico. Photos by the author.

Bandsawn Dovetails

Tilt, saw and chop

by Tage Frid

Routers and tablesaws aren't the only way to make through dovetails with a machine. I use my bandsaw to cut the pins and tails, and the results aren't much different from cutting the joint by hand. Start by using a marking gauge to scribe the baselines of pins and tails on both boards. Cut the pins first. Tilt the bandsaw table 10° (or whatever angle you wish your pins to be) to the right, and clamp a fence parallel to the blade and slightly farther away from it than half the width of the stock, as in drawing **A**. (If your table won't tilt in both directions, see *FWW* #17, p. 15, for a jig to solve this problem.) Clamp a stop to the fence so that the blade will cut just to the baseline. All the cuts for this method should be made with the inside face of the board up. Mark your stock so that you won't lose track. Make the first cut, which will be one side of a center pin, then turn the stock end-for-end and make the second cut, one side of the other center pin.

Between the stock and the fence, place a spacer equal in width to the pin spacing. For this example, you'll cut one center pin and two half-pins at each edge. Cut the half-pin on one end of the stock, then turn the board end-for-end and cut the other half-pin (**B**).

Now tilt the table 10° to the left, move the fence to the opposite side of the table, and use the spacer to cut the other two half-pins (**C**). Then remove the spacer and cut the other side of the two center pins (**D**). Chisel out the waste in the pin boards, just as you would in making hand dovetails.

With the pins chiseled out, scribe their location directly on the tail board (**E**). Return the bandsaw to the horizontal position and saw freehand to the waste side of the lines that mark the tails. To remove the waste where the center pins will fit, saw up to the baseline repeatedly (**F**), shifting the stock sideways each time, before cleaning to the line with a chisel. To waste the area where the half-pins will fit, saw right up the baseline (**G**). Try the joint and adjust its fit with a chisel where necessary. This method will work with wider boards, but you'll need more spacers to locate the other pins. □

Tage Frid is a cabinetmaker, author, and professor emeritus at the Rhode Island School of Design.

Bandsawn dovetails

A

To cut one side of the center pins, tilt the bandsaw to 10°. Clamp a fence to the saw table slightly more than half the stock width from the blade. Make one pin cut; turn the board end-for-end for the other.

B

To cut the half-pins, put a spacer block between the fence and stock, and cut one half-pin. Turn end-for-end and repeat. Make the width of the spacer block equal to the pin spacing.

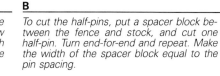

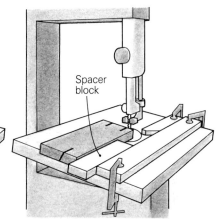

C

Tilt the table to the opposite angle and move the fence to the opposite side; using the spacer block, cut the other two half-pins.

D

Remove the spacer block and cut the other side of the center pins. Chisel out the waste, as with hand-dovetailing.

E

To cut the tails, mark them out directly from the pins.

F

With the saw table horizontal, saw the outer edges of the tails, then nibble out the waste with repeated cuts.

G

Saw the half-pin shoulders, then pare with a chisel until the joint fits correctly.

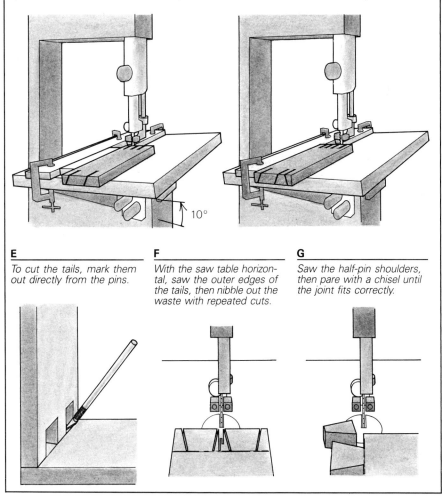

Cutting Dovetails With the Tablesaw
A versatile way to join a stack of drawers

by Mark Duginske

For joining such basic casework as small boxes, chests and drawers, I've always felt that there was a missing link between the tedium of hand-cutting dozens of dovetails and the faster method of producing monotonous-looking joints with a router jig. With that in mind, I developed this table-saw dovetail method which combines hand-tool flexibility with power-tool speed and accuracy.

With this technique, you can vary both the width and the spacing of the pins and tails for practically any aesthetic effect. The blocks that set the spacing are self-centering and will produce perfect-fitting, interchangeable joints, eliminating the need to mark boards so that individual joints will fit, as with hand-dovetailing. Besides a good combination sawblade and dado head for your tablesaw, you'll need a marking gauge, a bevel gauge and a couple of sharp bench chisels. Before proceeding, screw a wooden fence to the saw's miter gauge. A 3-in. by 20-in. fence will safely support most work.

Begin by squaring the ends of the boards to be joined. Take your time with this step—inaccurately prepared stock virtually guarantees sloppy results. I spaced the pins equally for the 4¼-in. wide drawer parts I'm joining in the photos. You can mark the pin centers directly on the pin boards, or, as I did here, you can just cut the spacer blocks to create whatever spacing you want the pins to have. In any case, the width of the blocks should equal the distance between pin centers. You'll need one block for each full pin, plus one.

The pin size is also controlled by the blocks. When they're lined up edge-to-edge, the total width of all the blocks should be less than the width of the stock by an amount equal to the width of the narrow part of each pin, that is, on the outside face of the pin board. I chose ¼-in. pins for the drawer sides shown in figure 1; if you want finer pins, decrease this dimension. The blocks must be of consistent width, so I crosscut them from the same ripping, then sandpaper off any fuzzy corners so that they'll line up with no gaps. To mark the depth of the pin and tail cuts, set your marking gauge to the stock thickness, and scribe a line on the faces of the pin board and on the face and edges of the tail board.

Cut the tails first with the saw arbor (or table) tilted to 80°, an angle that I've found produces the best combination of appearance and strength. A bevel gauge set at 80° can be used to set both the sawblade for the tails and, later, the miter gauge for the pins. As shown in figure 2, position and clamp a stop block to the miter-gauge fence so that when all the blocks are in place, a half-pin space of the correct size will be cut. At its narrowest width, the half-pin space should equal the narrow width of a pin. Raise the sawblade until it cuts right to the gauge line, then, with all the blocks in place, begin cutting the tails, flipping the board edge-for-edge and end-for-end (photo, right). Continue this process, removing a spacer block each time, until all the tails are cut.

A good-quality carbide-tipped blade will saw crisp pins

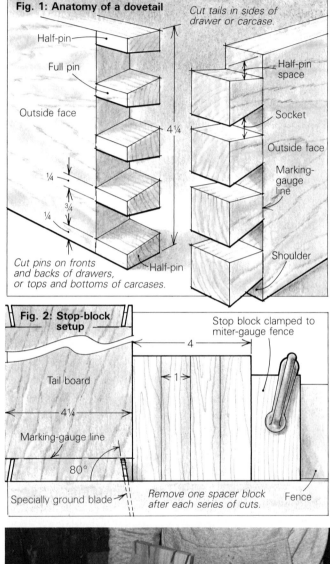

Fig. 1: Anatomy of a dovetail

Cut tails in sides of drawer or carcase.

Half-pin

Full pin

Outside face

4¼

¼

¾

¼

Cut pins on fronts and backs of drawers, or tops and bottoms of carcases.

Half-pin

Half-pin space

Socket

Outside face

Marking-gauge line

Shoulder

Fig. 2: Stop-block setup

Tail board

4¼

Marking-gauge line

80°

Specially ground blade

Stop block clamped to miter-gauge fence

4

1

Remove one spacer block after each series of cuts.

Fence

In Duginske's tablesaw dovetail method, the tails are made first in a series of cuts with the table or arbor set at 80°. After each series, a spacer block is removed and the cuts are repeated for the next tail. The last tail is made with one block in place.

Photos: Bill Stankus; drawings: David Dann

Machine-cut dovetails don't have to have the stiff, predictable look dictated by many router jigs. Using your imagination and the author's tablesaw technique, you can vary the width and spacing of pins and tails for infinite visual variety.

and tails, but set at an angle it leaves a small triangle of waste at the bottom of the cut that must be chiseled out later. To minimize handwork, I had the tops of the teeth on a carbide blade ground to 80°. The grinding cost $12 and the blade can still be used for other work. If you have a blade ground, make sure that all the teeth point in the same direction, and when you tilt your saw, match the tooth angle.

To cut the pins, clamp the boards together and scribe either of the outermost tails onto the pin board with a knife, as in the photo at right. Mark the wood to be wasted with an X. Only one pin need be marked; the spacer blocks will automatically take care of the others. The pins will be formed in the series of three cuts illustrated in figure 3.

First, return the arbor or table to 90° and install a ¼-in. dado blade raised to cut right to the gauge line. Adjust the miter gauge to 80°, and with all the spacer blocks in place, reset the stop block so that, with the outside face of the board positioned away from you, the first dado cut will be made just to the inside of the knife line. Make sure that the board is positioned correctly, or else you'll end up cutting the pin angle in the wrong direction. Make the first cut, flip the board end-for-end and cut only the opposite corner. Then remove the first block and repeat until one side of each pin is cut.

For the second series of cuts, set the miter gauge to 90° and waste the material between the pins. You'll have to remove a lot of wood in several passes to form widely spaced pins, in which case it's handier to judge the cuts by eye rather than relying on the spacer blocks. Don't waste too much material, else you'll nip off the opposite side of the pins. While the miter gauge is at 90°, use the dado blade to waste the wedge of wood remaining in the sockets of the tail board. If the sockets are narrower than ¼ in., nibble out the wedges on the bandsaw or with a coping saw and a chisel. Use a backsaw or the tablesaw to trim the shoulders where the half-pins fit.

Next set the miter gauge to 80° in the opposite direction, and reset the stop block so that the dado blade cuts just inside the other knife line. Make the third series of cuts like the first, but before proceeding, slip three or four strips of paper between the last spacer block and the stop block. Complete the cuts and try the joint. It should slip together by hand or with light mallet taps. If the joint is too tight, remove one or more paper shims, repeat the cuts and try again. Smooth the space between the pins and the tails, pare any tight spots with a chisel, and you're ready to glue up. □

Mark Duginske is a cabinetmaker in Wausau, Wis.

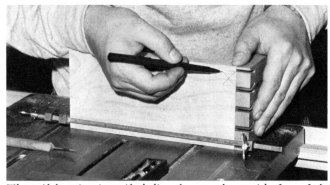

The tail location is scribed directly onto the outside face of the pin board with a knife. A bold X marks the material that will be wasted to form the pins.

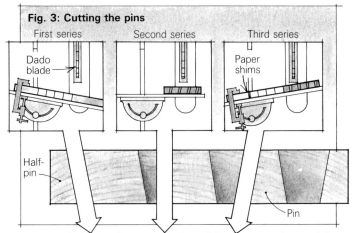

Fig. 3: Cutting the pins
First series   Second series   Third series
Dado blade
Paper shims
Half-pin
Pin

Once marked out, the pins are formed by wasting the wood between with dado-blade cuts. In the photo below, Duginske completes the second series of pin cuts.

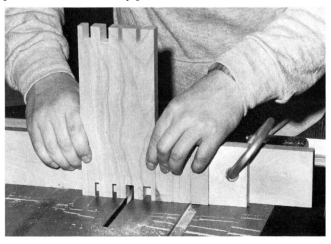

Radial-Arm Raised Panels
You can even make them out of plywood

by William D. Lego

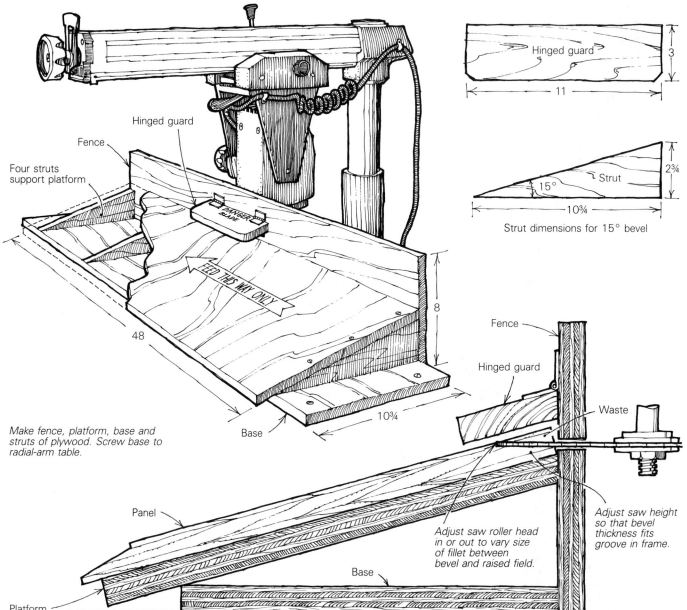

Hinged guard

11

3

15°

Strut

2¾

10¾

Strut dimensions for 15° bevel

Hinged guard

Fence

Four struts
support platform

Fence

Hinged guard

Waste

8

48

10¾

Base

*Make fence, platform, base and
struts of plywood. Screw base to
radial-arm table.*

*Adjust saw height
so that bevel
thickness fits
groove in frame.*

Panel

*Adjust saw roller head
in or out to vary size
of fillet between
bevel and raised field.*

Base

Platform

I use raised panels in much of the cabinetry I build, but like
many small-shop woodworkers, I can't justify the expense
of buying a large shaper just for this purpose. I probably
couldn't shoehorn one into my shop anyway. Instead, I designed this jig that allows me to cut all sizes of raised panels
with my radial-arm saw. As shop aids go, this one is practically bullet-proof—you can make it out of scrap, set it up in
no time and, when it's not in use, hang it up on the shop
wall, out of the way.

I built this jig two years ago, and I've found that it has two
advantages over a shaper: it's safer to operate and the panels
have smoother, splinter-free bevels. This last point is important to me because I make my raised panels out of hardwood

plywood and then cover the exposed edges of the plies with
veneer backed by a thermosetting adhesive. This veneer,
which I buy in rolls and sheets from Allied International Inc.,
PO Box 56, Charlestown, Mass. 02129, can be applied with
a hot iron. The technique may not delight the purist, but
with all the crooked, twisted lumber we seem to get these
days, using plywood saves the time and frustration of gluing
up solid stock and then milling it flat. This method seems
best for panels that will be painted, but if you apply the
veneer carefully, you can get decent results with clear finishes.
Of course, the jig works just as well with solid wood panels.

As the drawing shows, my jig consists of an inclined platform mounted on a base that can then be screwed or clamped

Drawings: Jim Richey

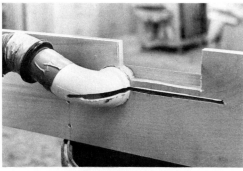

A 2-in. PVC elbow, left, mounted behind the fence and connected to a shop vacuum collects the dust from Lego's panel-raising jig. He glued the elbow in place before slowly sawing its blade slot. Fence cutout accommodates saw motor when sanding bevels. The photo below illustrates safe hand position for feeding a plywood panel past the sawblade. Hinges attach the guard to the fence, allowing it to pivot up slightly, so offcuts won't jam.

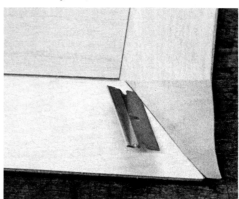

Exposed plies on the bevels of a plywood panel won't do, but once they are covered with adhesive-backed veneer tape, above, they look fine and they will take an excellent paint finish. The veneer tape is applied with a hot iron. Where it meets at the corners, Lego razors a neat miter joint, below.

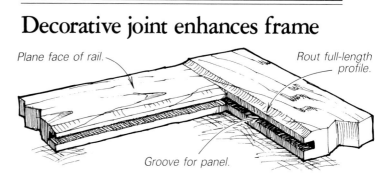

to the radial-arm table. You can experiment with the platform angle, but 15° is a good starting place. I'm kind of a safety nut, so I installed a hinged guard above the point where the blade projects through a slot in the jig's fence. The guard has to pivot only slightly, but don't use a rigid guard—the panel offcuts might jam between the blade and the guard. To collect dust and chips, I used construction adhesive and a few brads to mount a 2-in. PVC elbow in the fence behind the blade, then connected the elbow to my shop vacuum, as in the photo at top left.

Once you've built and positioned the jig, make some test cuts and adjust the height of the saw until the panel bevel tapers to a perfect fit in the grooves of the frame it will go into, as shown in the drawing at left. To vary the size of the fillet between the bevel and the panel's raised field, move the saw roller head in or out. Steel combination blades work well for panel-raising, but because they dull quickly, I find that I have to install a sharp blade after raising a half-dozen panels or so. A carbide-tipped blade would last longer. If I'm using solid wood, I sand the sawmarks off the bevels using a Sears 8-in. sanding disc with a 2° taper (catalog number 9 GT 2274). This tapered disc contacts the wood with a small, conical-shaped section instead of the wide, swirling arc of a flat sanding disc, thus leaving fewer sanding marks. You don't have to sand the bevels of plywood panels, since they'll be covered by veneer tape anyway. □

William Lego owns and operates a six-man cabinet shop in Springfield, Va. Photos by the author.

Decorative joint enhances frame

Plane face of rail.

Rout full-length profile.

Groove for panel.

For my cabinet doors I use a simple frame-and-panel construction with mortise-and-tenon joints. The method described here allows me to add a decorative molded profile to the inside edge of the frame, without having to cope the molding joint at the corners or to go to the trouble of making a masons' miter.

First I mill all my stock to the same thickness, cut the frame members, mortise the stiles and tenon the rails. After the joints have been fitted, I plane 1/16 in. or so off the face of each rail. This step puts the face of the rail on a different plane than the face of the stile. Now you can rout a shallow (no deeper than 1/16 in.) profile on the inside edges of both stiles and rails. Of course, the decorative molding runs the length of the stiles rather than stopping at the inside edge of the frame. The effect, though not traditional, is handsome, and the resulting doors are strong and light.

—Pat Warner, Escondido, Calif.

FURNITURE, PROJECTS

Building a Secretaire-Bookcase

Lots to learn from this 18th-century case study

text and drawings by Victor J. Taylor

It's not often that you come across a piece of English antique furniture that can be dated precisely, but glued to one of the drawer linings of this handsome secretaire-bookcase is the following receipt: "B. Milward [the purchaser]. Jan 25. 1787. Bought of Mr. Evans, Broadmead, Bristol. Price £15.15."

Today the piece stands in the Withdrawing Room of the Georgian House, Bristol, which is a real treasure store of late 18th-century household goods ranging from fine furniture and priceless paintings down to kitchen utensils. It is officially described as Hepplewhite style, but it seems to me that the date is too early for Hepplewhite, and that the piece is more likely late Adam. In drawing this complex piece, I was struck

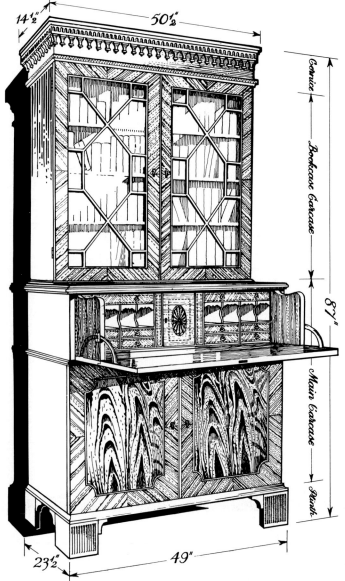

by how instructive it can be of various features common to much simpler furniture. Rather than follow a strict (and probably oppressive) how-to-do-it formula, I have attempted to present the piece as a tour of period construction practices, with side-trips into alternatives for the present-day craftsman.

As can be seen in the drawing on this page, the piece is composed of five sections: from the floor upwards these are the plinth, the cupboard (containing cutlery and linen drawers, and two butler's trays), the secretaire, the bookcase and the cornice. These sections were usually made as complete, separate units, then fitted together, although in this piece the bookcase and cornice are combined as one unit.

Often the sections merely rested on each other so that they could easily be dismantled if they had to be moved—indeed, quite often the main cupboard section had handles fitted to it to make lifting easier. Usually the weight of each section kept it in place, with various sorts of blocks and keys serving to keep things from shifting.

Mahogany is used for all show-wood parts, with oak and pine for the hidden parts and groundwork, normal practice for the time. The mahogany is almost certainly Cuban, and the superb "Spanish Feather" veneer is virtually unobtainable these days. All veneer is laid on without benefit of counter-veneer, which would be risky with today's central heating.

In the following drawings, each part of the secretaire-bookcase is illustrated and its construction explained, beginning with the plinth and working upwards, which is not necessarily the order in which it would be built. All pieces are numbered to correspond to the listing in the bill of materials on p. 66. In each figure, there is a small diagram of the full cabinet—the shaded part of the diagram is shown exploded in the drawing.

In drawing the piece, where it was impossible to see the joints, I have followed orthodox cabinetmaking practice. Doweling, incidentally, was a very common method in the old days. Craftsmen made their own dowels by trimming down a suitable piece of scrap wood, and then hammering it through a dowel plate, a piece of ⅛-in. thick metal in which holes of various sizes had been drilled—¼-in., ⅜-in. and ½-in. were usual. Dowels were often shaped from offcuts from the parts they were intended to join, minimizing uneven shrinkage. Willow was also used; its stems could be made into dowels with hardly any trimming.

At the time this piece was made, French polishing had not been invented (it did not become widespread in England until about 1820), so the piece was probably originally finished with linseed oil and wax, then French polished at a later date.

Victor Taylor, of Bath, England, spent many years in the furniture industry. He has written seven books, and was editor of the British magazine Woodworker.

Figure 1: Plinth. The basic members of this subassembly are the four corner posts *(1)*, which are connected at the front and back by rails *(2 & 3)*, and at each end by a rail *(4)*. The cupboard rests on this base and is almost certainly keyed to it with blocks screwed beneath the cupboard bottom *(5)*, though I couldn't see them.

The feet *(8)* are not weight-bearing, but are merely glued as decoration around the corner posts. The ear pieces *(9)* are glued and doweled to the feet, then the moldings *(10)* are pinned and glued on. Brackets are glued and screwed into each corner to strengthen the whole framework. Screws (hand-made) were first introduced in the late 17th century and by 1720 were common. Nails and pins (brads), of course, have been used for centuries, and there is even a reference from 1343 on using an adze to smooth "old timber" full of nails. On the arris of the foot there is a staff bead, whose profile makes any opening of the joint less obvious. A central frame rail *(11)* is mortised flush into the front and back rails. Following the usual practice of the time, the main carcase ends *(7)* are lap-dovetailed to the cupboard bottom *(5)*. There is a filler strip *(6)* beneath the cupboard doors, and this is shown in section at *A*.

Figure 2: Cupboard and drawer framing. The doors overlap the upright ends of the carcase, therefore the carcase ends have to be stepped back by ¾ in. below the point where the front secretaire separation rail *(15)* meets them.

The front and back drawer rails *(12)* are tenoned into the main carcase ends *(7)*, as are the top separation rails *15* and *38* (visible in figure 4, overleaf). Muntins *(14)*, drawer bearers *(13)* and a central bearer *(16)* connect these four rails. The two upper drawers are supported by this conventional framing, while the lower single drawers run on bearers *(30)* glued to the cabinet ends. This ignores wood movement, but the bearers are still secure. The drawer construction is orthodox, with lapped dovetails on the fronts and through dovetails on the backs. The bottoms are solid wood, grooved into the sides and fronts without being glued in, so that they can expand and contract. You could, of course, use plywood for the bottoms instead. The handles on the drawers are solid brass and match those on the fall front; they are shown at *A* in figure 10.

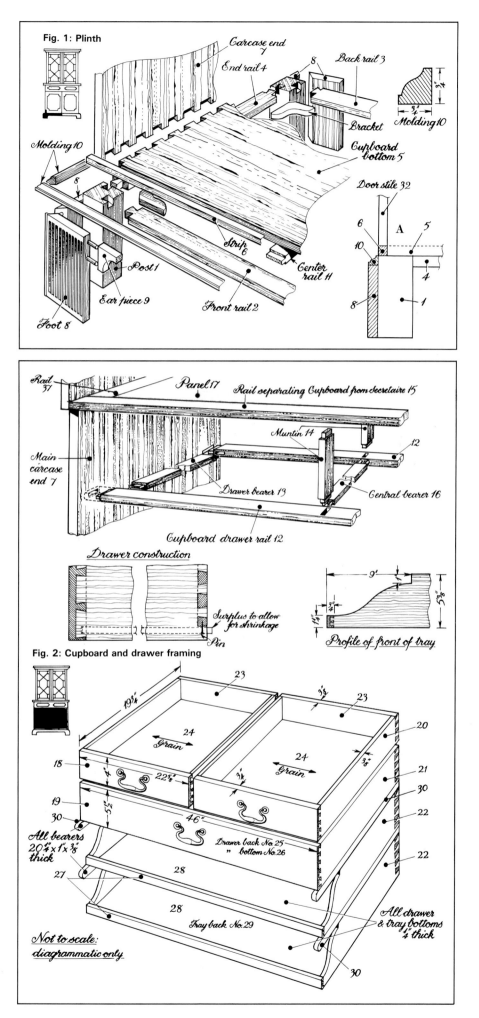

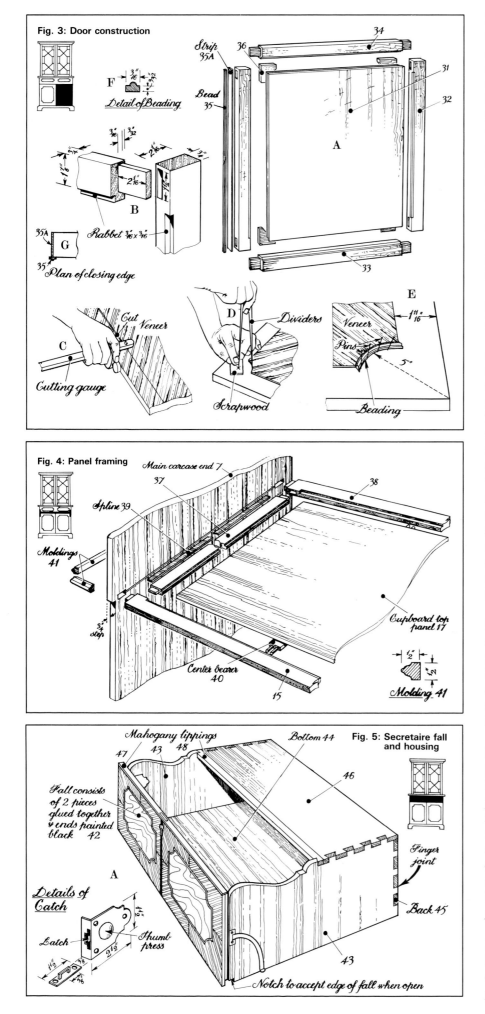

Fig. 3: Door construction

Strip 35A

Detail of Beading F

Bead 35

Rabbet 3/16 x 3/16 B

Plan of closing edge 35 35A G

36 34 31 32

A

33

Cut Veneer C *Cutting gauge*

Dividers D *Scrapwood*

Veneer E *Pins* *Beading*

Fig. 4: Panel framing

Main carcase end 7

37

Spline 39

Moldings 41

38

Cupboard top panel 17

Molding 41

Center bearer 40

15

Notch to accept edge of fall when open

Mahogany tippings 47 43 48

Bottom 44 **Fig. 5: Secretaire fall and housing**

46

Fall consists of 2 pieces glued together & ends painted black 42

A

Finger joint

Back 45

Details of Catch

Latch *Thumb press*

43

Figure 3: Door construction. The doors are hung by pairs of brass hinges. As you can see at *A,* the frame is a straightforward mortise-and-tenon job with a rabbet for the panel, which lies flush, glued and pinned. The rabbets on the rail run the full shoulder length, while those on the stiles are stopped, as at *B.* The tenons on rails *33* and *34* go right through the stiles, and their ends can be seen on the outside edges. On the closing edges, however, a thin strip *(35A)* has been glued to the edge to mask them. Blind tenons would do just as well here, and the cover strips could thus be omitted. A thin astragal beading *(35)* is fixed as shown at *G.*

The corner brackets *(36)* appear to have been glued behind the panel merely to add rigidity.

The doors were constructed entirely of oak, with no veneer on the inside. At the time the piece was made, veneers were sawn and consequently were much thicker than our present-day veneers. The central part of the veneered panel would have been laid in a press, while a veneering hammer would have been employed to put down the border. Workmen trimmed the edges of the veneer, after laying, with a cutting gauge *(C),* simply a marking gauge with a small, sharp blade instead of the usual marking pin. A pair of dividers, with one point sharpened, was used to scribe the corners, as at *D,* and the cut was finished off with a knife.

Detail *E* shows the small ovolo beading being glued—almost certainly, it was steamed first. Both this and beading *(35)* are a blond color and could be birch, sycamore or holly. The left-hand door has brass bolts top and bottom, and a false escutcheon that matches the lock on the other door.

Figure 4: Panel framing. This panel *(17)* appears to be 3/8-in. thick pine, but I'd suggest birch plywood instead. It is pinned and glued into 3/8-in. by 3/8-in. rabbets worked on the edges of rails *15, 37* and *38.* Although the frame lines up at the front with the front edge of the carcase end *(7),* it falls 3/4 in. short of the back edge, to leave room for the back framing. The moldings *(41)* are glued and pinned on, corners mitered.

Figure 5: Secretaire fall and housing. The pigeon-hole section has a clever feature that I have not seen on other pieces from this period. It is contained within a fall-front drawer, shown at right and at the bottom of the previous page, that pulls out to provide knee room for writing. The fall front *(42)* is made up of two pieces face-glued together to form a lip that fits into a notch cut into the side *(43)* when the fall is down (see *B* and *D*). The fall has three hinges, and is fitted with two brass handles, shown at *A* in figure 10. Two mahogany lippings *(47 & 48)* mask the drawer front's top edge and the exposed pine edge of the drawer top.

The quadrant stay was made from solid brass, with a small fixing flange brazed on. Cut out a $\frac{3}{16}$-in. channel in the drawer side for the stay to run in. You might wish to install a lock in the fall front and catches fitted into the sides (see *A* and *B*).

The fall front is veneered similarly to the cupboard doors, with the addition of a black inlaid line running from top to bottom in the center. Lippings are applied after veneering so that the top edge of the veneer is protected. The ends of the fall are painted black—not an attractive feature—and you may wish to substitute another thin lipping.

Figure 6: Secretaire unit. This is a real work of art, as all the parts are only $\frac{1}{8}$ in. thick, except for the drawer fronts, which are $\frac{1}{2}$ in. thick (including the veneer). All parts are mahogany. With such thin partitions, a practical joint is the interlocking joint shown at *C*.

The main structure comprises the bottom *(50)* and the two ends *(49)*, which can be butted together and glued to the "drawer" side and bottom *(43 & 44)*. The remaining partitions *(51, 52, 53, 54, 55 & 68)* can be connected with interlocking joints. Construction of the drawers is shown at *D*.

The veneer is enlivened by black and white stringing about $\frac{3}{32}$ in. wide, and the cupboard door is further embellished with an inlaid fan.

Now we come to an intriguing item: the secret compartments *(B)*. Frankly, they are rather obvious and clumsy compared to some I have seen, and you may wish to elaborate upon them. They are built in behind the two pilasters (see *A*). Once you have opened the door, the two inner walls can be pulled inward and taken out completely. I had to pry them out with the point of a penknife, but probably a leaf spring had originally been fitted behind the tray to help push it out.

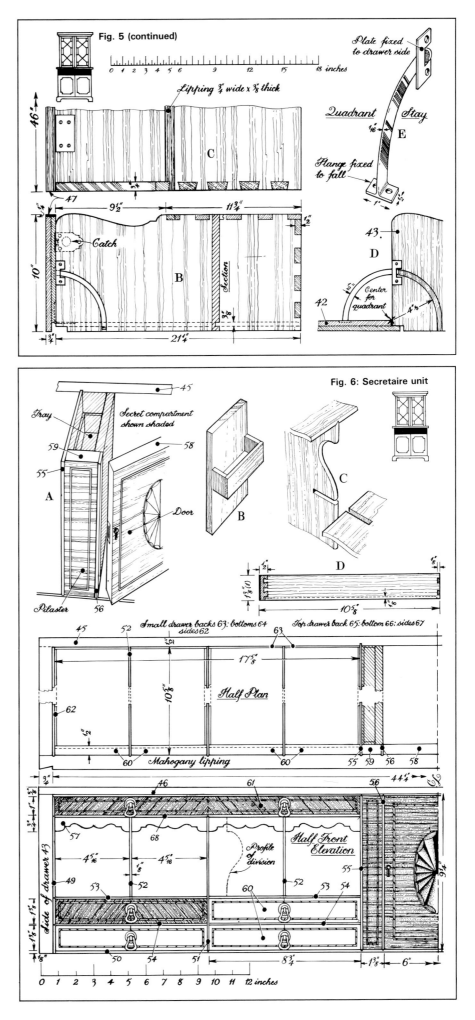

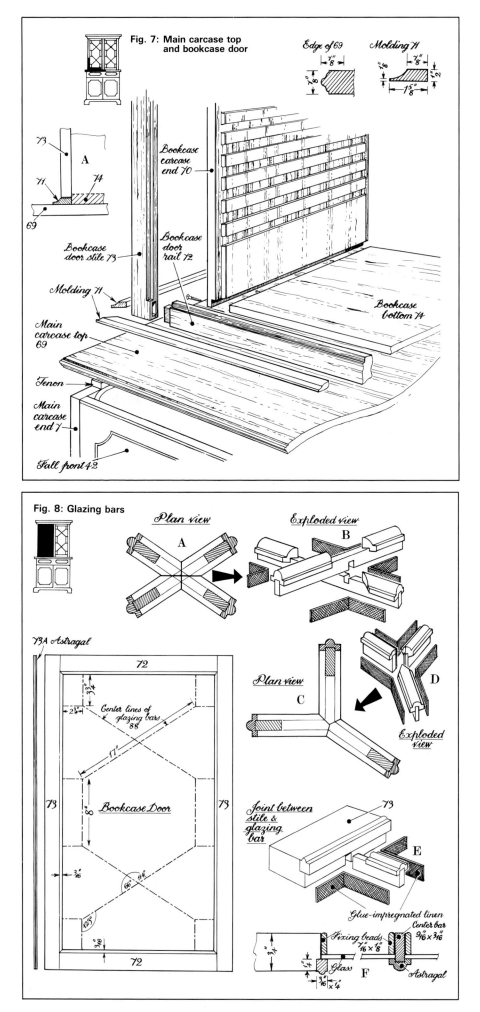

Fig. 7: Main carcase top and bookcase door

Edge of 69

Molding 71

73

A

71

74

Bookcase carcase end 70

Bookcase door stile 73

Bookcase door rail 72

Molding 71

Main carcase top 69

Tenon

Main carcase end 7

Fall front 42

Bookcase bottom 74

69

Fig. 8: Glazing bars

Plan view

Exploded view

A

B

73A Astragal

72

Center lines of glazing bars 88

Plan view

C

D

Exploded view

73

Bookcase Door

73

66° 114°

123°

Joint between stile & glazing bar

73

E

72

Glue-impregnated linen

Center bar 9/16 x 3/16

Fixing beads 7/16 x 1/8

Glass

F

Astragal

Figure 7: Main carcase top and bookcase door. The top of the main carcase (69) is fixed to the carcase ends by means of blind tenons on the main carcase end (7). Moldings (71) are attached to the top (shown in section at A) so that the removable bookcase section does not shift. The bookcase is made up of the two ends (70), the bottom (74), and the top. The ends extend up to include the cornice, and we shall be dealing with the upper part, including the top (76), in figure 9.

The bottom (74) is housed in a rabbet formed at the foot of the end. The joint is glued and then strengthened with wood screws driven in from the outside—the surrounding molding (71) will conceal the screw heads. The shelf supports (70A) are glued and pinned to the carcase end—these supports are made from a piece of 5/16 in. stock which first has a small thumb molding worked on its front edge, and is then sawn into separate strips. Note that their back ends must stand 3/4 in. away from the rear edge of the bookcase end to allow for the fitting of the back frame.

On the actual piece, the corners of the bookcase doors have through tenons, but I have drawn blind tenons, on the assumption that you will prefer them.

Figure 8: Glazing bars. Once the bookcase door frames are made, lay them on a flat board so that you can pencil the centerlines for the glazing bars on it, following the pattern and measurements shown. Leave off the astragal beadings until you have gotten the center bars fitted. Delicate joints such as these (A–E) can be reinforced with strips of linen soaked in glue.

In the original piece, the glass is fixed in place with putty instead of the fixing beads shown at F. I cannot recommend putty, as it has no resiliency, and consequently the glass will crack easily if the wood swells or shrinks—in fact, several of the panes have done so.

The last step is to hang the doors with three 2-in. hinges per door, and if you wish, you can fix a closing bead on to the right-hand door to match the one on the cupboard door. Door stops can be fitted beneath the top, where they will be out of the way.

As with the cupboard doors, the right-hand door has a lock and an escutcheon, while the left-hand door has just an escutcheon plus a brass bolt at top and bottom.

Figure 9: The cornice and top. The cornice *(75)* consists of a piece of mahogany lap-mitered to the top of the bookcase end *(70)*. It is rabbeted along its lower edge to house the bookcase top. Note the dado for the top in the bookcase end, as shown at *A*.

The carcase top *(77)* laps over the back framing (shown in figure 10), and it also laps over the bookcase ends *(70)* and the cornice *(75)*. In the original, it is screwed down all around, which does not allow for wood movement.

The piece will look best if you reproduce the original moldings instead of substituting lumberyard patterns.

The top molding *(78)* is quite straightforward, but the one below it *(79)*, which comprises the dentil motif with a cavetto beneath it, is not so easy. Probably the best way to tackle it is to run off the outline profile first on a spindle shaper, and then use a router to take out the slots for the dentils. Then you will need to chop out the rounded end of each slot with a small scribing (in-cannel) gouge.

Now for the bracket molding *(80)*. On many designs of the period this was a straight run of molding with the brackets joined together at the top. In our model, however, they will need to be sawn out separately with a fretsaw or jigsaw, and the small pieces of beading glued on beneath them. These small pieces were turned on a lathe as "split" turnings—two small blocks were glued together with a sheet of paper between them and then turned; it was easy to split them apart afterward.

Lastly, we have to deal with the Grecian key motif *(81)*, and the best way, again, is to use a router, squaring up with a chisel.

Once the brackets are glued on, it will be difficult to polish into all the nooks and crannies, so you can adopt the method employed by the old-timers. First they would have polished the cornice and the brackets as separate pieces, then they would lay the brackets on the cornice to scribe around them. When they removed the brackets, an outline was left and the polish was scraped away from this. Next they warmed up a metal plate (called a sticking board), so that the glue would not chill when it was spread on it. They would draw the backs of the brackets lightly across the sticking board so that each received a thin coat of glue, enabling them to be fixed with no fear of gummy crevices.

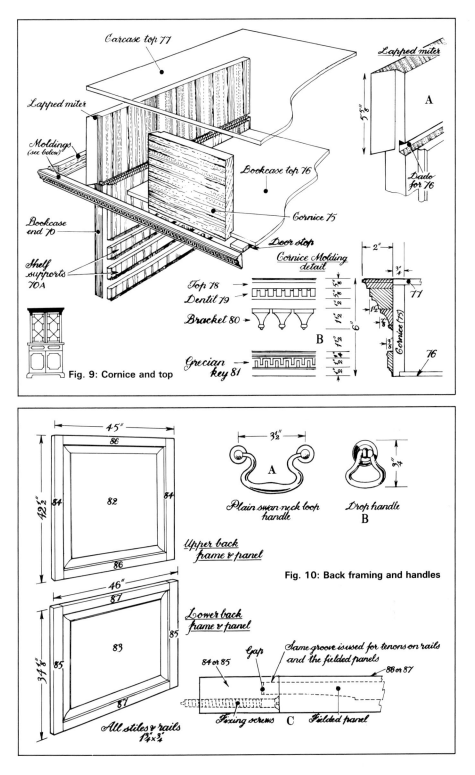

Fig. 9: Cornice and top

Fig. 10: Back framing and handles

Figure 10: Back framing and handles. Chances are that the framed panels in this piece were screwed into place, not glued. This would have allowed their removal, considerably lightening the piece if it had to be moved. It was difficult to see how the back frame was constructed, so I am giving details of typical framings that you can use. Those on the original were of solid oak, although you may wish to use pine. In any case, the frames are made up with conventional mortise and tenon joints. The fielded panels *(82 & 83)* are grooved in all around as shown at *C*—bear in mind that solid panels must not be pinned or glued in place but left loose to shrink or swell—leave some space, too, in the groove.

If you make the groove ¼ in. wide by ⅜ in. deep, you can then use it to accept the tenons as well as the panels. You may stop the grooves on the stiles *(84 & 85)* to avoid their running through the top and bottom edges when the frame is made up, although when everything is in its place, finally, these edges won't show. ▶

Bill of Materials

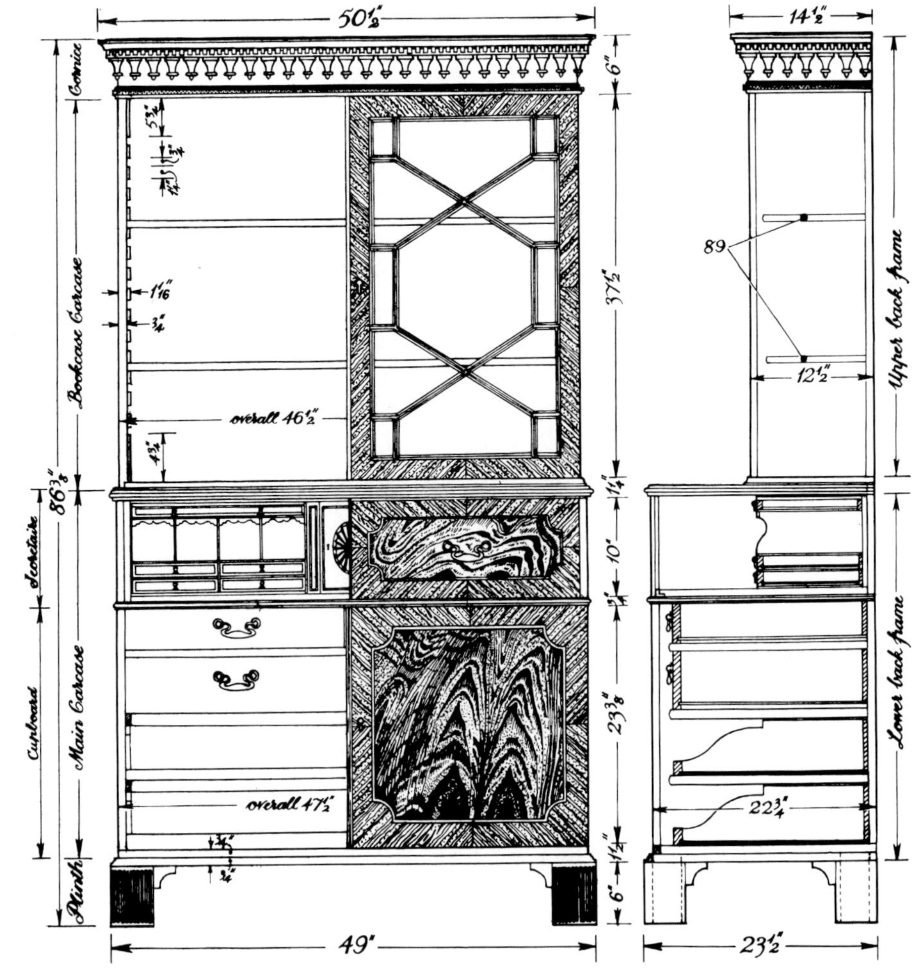

The dimensions given below are net, and you should allow extra for sawing, planing, etc., at the rate of about 1 in. in length, $\frac{1}{4}$ in. to $\frac{1}{2}$ in. in width, and $\frac{1}{8}$ in. in thickness. Where I have shown shoulder lengths you will need to add extra length for tenons. I have left the tenon dimensions mostly up to you, and you may, of course, use whatever joinery you prefer throughout the piece.

I have not included parts for the secret compartments, as no doubt you will wish to design more ingenious (and less publicized) ones of your own.

In measuring a complicated piece like this, one often finds that many of the parts were scribed from other parts or cut to fit, rather than laid out with a ruler. I found I had to adapt some of the measurements in order to get things to add up. Although I have made every effort to ensure accuracy, parts of the cabinet were inaccessible—cooperative as the folks at Georgian House were, no one was about to let me move it, let alone take it apart. I suggest that you temper haste with a bit of caution, and cut to fit as you go along. □

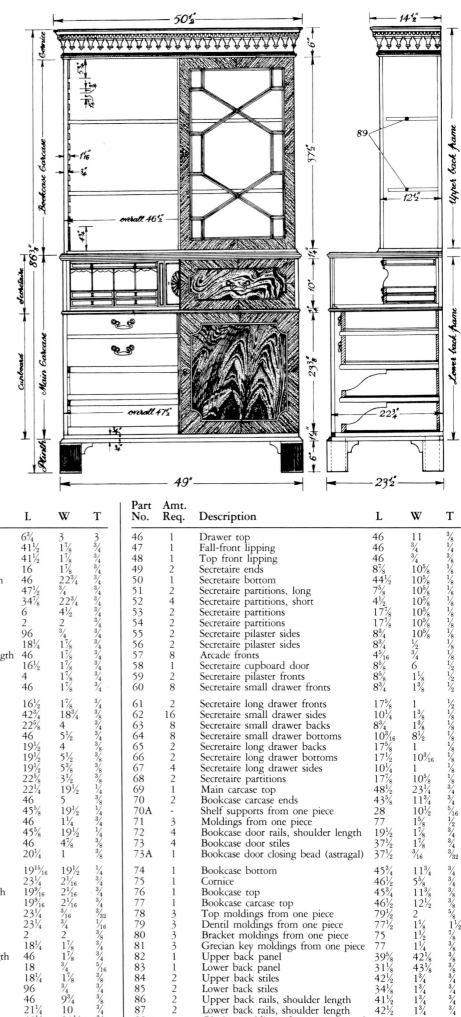

Part No.	Amt. Req.	Description	L	W	T
1	4	Posts	$6\frac{3}{4}$	3	3
2	1	Front rail, shoulder length	$41\frac{1}{2}$	$1\frac{7}{8}$	$\frac{3}{4}$
3	1	Back rail, shoulder length	$41\frac{1}{2}$	$1\frac{7}{8}$	$\frac{3}{4}$
4	2	End rails, shoulder length	16	$1\frac{7}{8}$	$\frac{3}{4}$
5	1	Cupboard bottom, shoulder length	46	$22\frac{3}{4}$	$\frac{3}{4}$
6	1	Strip	$47\frac{1}{2}$	$\frac{3}{4}$	$\frac{3}{4}$
7	2	Carcase ends, shoulder length	$34\frac{7}{8}$	$22\frac{3}{4}$	$\frac{3}{4}$
8	8	Plinth feet	6	$4\frac{1}{2}$	$\frac{3}{4}$
9	8	Ear pieces	2	2	$\frac{3}{4}$
10	3	Moldings from one piece	96	$\frac{3}{4}$	$\frac{3}{4}$
11	1	Center rail, shoulder length	$18\frac{1}{4}$	$1\frac{7}{8}$	$\frac{3}{4}$
12	1	Cupboard drawer rail, shoulder length	46	$1\frac{7}{8}$	$\frac{3}{4}$
13	2	Drawer bearers, shoulder length	$16\frac{1}{2}$	$1\frac{7}{8}$	$\frac{3}{4}$
14	2	Muntins, shoulder length	4	$1\frac{7}{8}$	$\frac{3}{4}$
15	1	Separation rail, shoulder length	46	$1\frac{7}{8}$	$\frac{3}{4}$
16	1	Central bearer	$16\frac{1}{2}$	$1\frac{7}{8}$	$\frac{3}{4}$
17	1	Panel	$42\frac{3}{4}$	$18\frac{3}{4}$	$\frac{3}{8}$
18	2	Upper drawer fronts	$22\frac{5}{8}$	4	$\frac{3}{4}$
19	1	Lower drawer front	46	$5\frac{1}{2}$	$\frac{3}{4}$
20	4	Drawer sides	$19\frac{1}{2}$	4	$\frac{3}{8}$
21	2	Drawer sides	$19\frac{1}{2}$	$5\frac{1}{2}$	$\frac{3}{8}$
22	4	Tray sides	$19\frac{1}{2}$	$5\frac{3}{8}$	$\frac{3}{8}$
23	2	Drawer backs	$22\frac{5}{8}$	$3\frac{1}{2}$	$\frac{3}{8}$
24	2	Drawer bottoms	$22\frac{1}{4}$	$19\frac{1}{2}$	$\frac{1}{4}$
25	1	Drawer back	46	5	$\frac{3}{8}$
26	1	Drawer bottom	$45\frac{5}{8}$	$19\frac{1}{2}$	$\frac{1}{4}$
27	2	Tray fronts	46	$1\frac{1}{4}$	$\frac{3}{4}$
28	2	Tray bottoms	$45\frac{5}{8}$	$19\frac{1}{2}$	$\frac{1}{4}$
29	2	Tray backs	46	$4\frac{7}{8}$	$\frac{3}{8}$
30	4	Bearers	$20\frac{1}{4}$	1	$\frac{3}{8}$
31	2	Door panels	$19\frac{15}{16}$	$19\frac{1}{2}$	$\frac{1}{4}$
32	4	Stiles	$23\frac{1}{4}$	$2\frac{1}{16}$	$\frac{3}{4}$
33	2	Door bottom rails, shoulder length	$19\frac{9}{16}$	$2\frac{1}{16}$	$\frac{3}{4}$
34	2	Door top rails, shoulder length	$19\frac{9}{16}$	$2\frac{1}{16}$	$\frac{3}{4}$
35	1	Closing bead	$23\frac{1}{4}$	$\frac{3}{16}$	$\frac{3}{32}$
35A	2	Strips	$23\frac{1}{4}$	$\frac{3}{4}$	$\frac{1}{16}$
36	8	Corner pieces	2	2	$\frac{3}{8}$
37	2	End rails, shoulder length	$18\frac{1}{4}$	$1\frac{7}{8}$	$\frac{3}{4}$
38	1	Back separation rail, shoulder length	46	$1\frac{7}{8}$	$\frac{3}{4}$
39	2	Splines	18	$\frac{3}{4}$	$\frac{5}{16}$
40	1	Center bearer	$18\frac{1}{4}$	$1\frac{7}{8}$	$\frac{3}{8}$
41	3	Moldings from one piece	96	$\frac{3}{4}$	$\frac{3}{4}$
42	2	Fall-front pieces	46	$9\frac{3}{4}$	$\frac{3}{8}$
43	2	Drawer sides	$21\frac{1}{4}$	10	$\frac{3}{4}$
44	1	Drawer bottom	$45\frac{1}{4}$	$21\frac{1}{16}$	$\frac{3}{8}$
45	1	Drawer back	46	10	$\frac{3}{4}$

Part No.	Amt. Req.	Description	L	W	T
46	1	Drawer top	46	11	$\frac{3}{8}$
47	1	Fall-front lipping	46	$\frac{3}{4}$	$\frac{1}{4}$
48	1	Top front lipping	46	$\frac{3}{4}$	$\frac{3}{8}$
49	2	Secretaire ends	$8\frac{7}{8}$	$10\frac{5}{8}$	$\frac{1}{8}$
50	1	Secretaire bottom	$44\frac{1}{2}$	$10\frac{5}{8}$	$\frac{1}{8}$
51	2	Secretaire partitions, long	$7\frac{5}{8}$	$10\frac{5}{8}$	$\frac{1}{8}$
52	4	Secretaire partitions, short	$4\frac{1}{2}$	$10\frac{5}{8}$	$\frac{1}{8}$
53	2	Secretaire partitions	$17\frac{7}{8}$	$10\frac{5}{8}$	$\frac{1}{8}$
54	2	Secretaire partitions	$17\frac{7}{8}$	$10\frac{5}{8}$	$\frac{1}{8}$
55	2	Secretaire pilaster sides	$8\frac{3}{4}$	$10\frac{5}{8}$	$\frac{1}{8}$
56	2	Secretaire pilaster sides	$8\frac{3}{4}$	$\frac{1}{2}$	$\frac{1}{8}$
57	8	Arcade fronts	$4\frac{5}{16}$	$\frac{3}{4}$	$\frac{1}{8}$
58	1	Secretaire cupboard door	$8\frac{5}{8}$	6	$\frac{1}{2}$
59	2	Secretaire pilaster fronts	$8\frac{5}{8}$	$1\frac{1}{8}$	$\frac{1}{2}$
60	8	Secretaire small drawer fronts	$8\frac{3}{4}$	$1\frac{3}{8}$	$\frac{1}{2}$
61	2	Secretaire long drawer fronts	$17\frac{5}{8}$	1	$\frac{1}{2}$
62	16	Secretaire small drawer sides	$10\frac{1}{4}$	$1\frac{3}{8}$	$\frac{1}{8}$
63	8	Secretaire small drawer backs	$8\frac{3}{4}$	$1\frac{3}{8}$	$\frac{1}{8}$
64	8	Secretaire small drawer bottoms	$10\frac{3}{16}$	$8\frac{1}{2}$	$\frac{1}{8}$
65	2	Secretaire long drawer backs	$17\frac{5}{8}$	1	$\frac{1}{8}$
66	2	Secretaire long drawer bottoms	$17\frac{1}{2}$	$10\frac{3}{16}$	$\frac{1}{8}$
67	4	Secretaire long drawer sides	$10\frac{1}{4}$	1	$\frac{1}{8}$
68	2	Secretaire partitions	$17\frac{7}{8}$	$10\frac{5}{8}$	$\frac{1}{8}$
69	1	Main carcase top	$48\frac{1}{2}$	$23\frac{1}{4}$	$\frac{3}{4}$
70	2	Bookcase carcase ends	$43\frac{5}{8}$	$11\frac{3}{4}$	$\frac{3}{4}$
70A	-	Shelf supports from one piece	28	$10\frac{1}{2}$	$\frac{5}{16}$
71	3	Moldings from one piece	77	$1\frac{5}{8}$	$\frac{1}{2}$
72	4	Bookcase door rails, shoulder length	$19\frac{1}{2}$	$1\frac{7}{8}$	$\frac{3}{4}$
73	4	Bookcase door stiles	$37\frac{1}{2}$	$1\frac{7}{8}$	$\frac{3}{4}$
73A	1	Bookcase door closing bead (astragal)	$37\frac{1}{2}$	$\frac{3}{16}$	$\frac{3}{32}$
74	1	Bookcase bottom	$45\frac{3}{4}$	$11\frac{3}{4}$	$\frac{3}{4}$
75	1	Cornice	$46\frac{1}{2}$	$5\frac{5}{8}$	$\frac{3}{4}$
76	1	Bookcase top	$45\frac{3}{4}$	$11\frac{3}{8}$	$\frac{3}{8}$
77	1	Bookcase carcase top	$46\frac{1}{2}$	$12\frac{1}{2}$	$\frac{3}{8}$
78	3	Top moldings from one piece	$79\frac{1}{2}$	2	$\frac{5}{8}$
79	3	Dentil moldings from one piece	$77\frac{1}{2}$	$1\frac{1}{8}$	$1\frac{1}{2}$
80	3	Bracket moldings from one piece	75	$1\frac{1}{2}$	$\frac{7}{8}$
81	3	Grecian key moldings from one piece	77	$1\frac{1}{4}$	$\frac{3}{8}$
82	1	Upper back panel	$39\frac{5}{8}$	$42\frac{1}{8}$	$\frac{3}{8}$
83	1	Lower back panel	$31\frac{1}{8}$	$43\frac{1}{8}$	$\frac{3}{8}$
84	2	Upper back stiles	$42\frac{1}{2}$	$1\frac{3}{4}$	$\frac{3}{4}$
85	2	Lower back stiles	$34\frac{1}{8}$	$1\frac{3}{4}$	$\frac{3}{4}$
86	2	Upper back rails, shoulder length	$41\frac{1}{2}$	$1\frac{3}{4}$	$\frac{3}{4}$
87	2	Lower back rails, shoulder length	$42\frac{1}{2}$	$1\frac{3}{4}$	$\frac{3}{4}$
88	-	Glazing moldings, from total run of	242		
89	-	Shelves (number optional), each	$44\frac{7}{8}$	$10\frac{1}{4}$	$\frac{7}{8}$

Q & A

Errant router bit—*I recently bought a 3-HP router that will accept ½-in. shank bits. When I set the router to take a deep, hogging cut in oak, the bit slipped down out of the collet, ruining my day and the job. I've already made a mess of two projects. What causes this slippage and what can I do to prevent it?* —*W.B. Lord, New York, N.Y.*
JOHN RUSHMER REPLIES: To clear waste from the cut, some (not all) router bits have cutters brazed on at a slight angle to the bit axis, as shown in the drawing. This angle creates an "upcut" that lifts chips out of the cut much as an auger would. Under the heavy load of hogging, this upcut exerts considerable downward thrust on the bit, actually pulling it out of the collet. The deeper the cut is, the greater the thrust will be. The clearance angle of the bottom of the bit, which is necessary for plunge-cutting, is critical in countering some of this downward thrust. Too great an angle, more than about 7°, results in a bit that plunges too easily and thus offers little resistance to downward thrust. Tests we've done at Milwaukee Electric Power Tool Corp. indicate that 5° seems to be the ideal clearance angle.

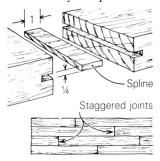

Cutter is angled slightly (1° to 3°) to produce an upcut that clears chips.

Thrust

Ideal clearance angle is about 5°.

The easiest way to avoid slippage is to do your deep routing in several shallow passes instead of one deep one. The bit will stay cooler and you'll get a smoother cut. If you must take deep cuts, try to have the bit's clearance angle reduced at the next sharpening. Don't, however, overtighten the collet nut to counter slippage; you risk stripping it or cracking the collet itself. Dirt or chips in the collet seat will keep the collet from gripping the bit evenly, so keep it and the bit shank clean. When you install the bit, push it into the collet until it bottoms and then back it out about ⅛ in. This will keep the bit from vibrating against the unmachined bottom of the seat.
[JOHN RUSHMER is chief engineer at the Milwaukee Electric Power Tool Corp.]

Dyeing hardwoods—*How can I dye hardwoods, mostly red oak, different colors? I want a deep black finish that allows the grain to show through. I'd also like some bright reds, blues and greens as accent colors.*
—*Kurt Martinson, Coeur d'Alene, Id.*
OTTO HEUER REPLIES: There are three kinds of dyes that can be used to stain oak: water-, oil- and alcohol-soluble aniline dyes. All three should be available in a well-stocked paint store, though you may have to special-order them. Some dyes can be bought mail-order from H. Behlen and Bros., Rt. 30 N., Amsterdam, N.Y. 12010. All of these dyes can be brushed or wiped on, or sprayed on with a pump-type sprayer like that used for insecticides.

Water-soluble aniline stains are the most lightfast. In a plastic or glass container, mix about 4 oz. of dry stain powder in a gallon of hot water, allow it to cool, then strain it through a triple layer of fine cheesecloth or muslin. Vary the application rate to get the color you want. Water-soluble aniline stains should be freshly prepared for each application, and they shouldn't be stored in metal containers.

Alcohol-soluble aniline stains will produce bright colors, but they are likely to be light-fugitive, especially the reds. To mix them, add 2 oz. to 6 oz. of powder to 1 gal. of a mixture composed of 8 parts methanol and 2 parts denatured alcohol.

Oil-soluble aniline-dye mixtures can be made by mixing 2 oz. to 6 oz. of stain powder to 1 gal. of toluol, xylol or any other aromatic petroleum solvent. Agitate the mixture well, let it settle, strain it and apply as above. Avoid breathing the vapors, and don't work around open flames—the solution is extremely flammable. To bring out the colors of any of these dyes, especially the blacks, you may need to add a top coat of semigloss or gloss lacquer, or reduced white shellac.
[OTTO HEUER is a finish chemist and consultant.]

End-to-end gluing up—*I'm planning to build an 11-ft. counter out of 6/4 white oak, but I don't have boards long enough. Is it acceptable to glue up random-length lumber end to end to make a counter that's 11 ft. long, 25 in. wide and 1⅟16 in. thick?*
—*Patrick Warner, Escondido, Calif.*
TAGE FRID REPLIES: Yes, you can glue up your boards end to end to make them long enough. First square the ends of the boards and cut ¼-in. grooves in the end grain with a slotting cutter in a router, if you have one. So the splines will be strong and to keep seasonal movement from cracking the boards at the joint, run the grain in the splines in the same direction as the grain in the boards. Glue your boards lengthwise before you rip them to final width. If you don't have clamps long enough, just nail blocks to the floor at each end of the stock and apply pressure to the joint with wedges against the blocks. When you edge-glue your lengthened boards into the finished counter, stagger the joints to lessen the stress on each one. I'd suggest you use a hard film finish such as polyurethane; otherwise the tannic acids in oak may react with metal that comes in contact with the counter, staining it.
[TAGE FRID is a cabinetmaker, educator and professor emeritus at the Rhode Island School of Design.]

1
¼
Spline
Staggered joints

Camphor hazards—*Camphor tablets are sold as a rust preventive for tools, but a pamphlet I've seen on hazardous chemicals says that this material can irritate the eyes and skin, and cause nausea, vomiting, headaches and other discomforts. Are these symptoms significant enough to rule out camphor? I don't want to expose my students or myself to unnecessary hazards, but neither do I want to see my grandfather's tools rust before my eyes.*
—*C. Roy Blackwood, Hammond, La.*
MICHAEL MCCANN REPLIES: Camphor is mainly a local irritant that affects the eyes, nose, throat and skin. But overexposure can affect the central nervous system, causing the symptoms you mention, and very high levels of camphor vapors can kill the sense of smell.

If the tablets are put in the tool cabinet, the camphor will produce a constant level of vapors in the closed area. When you go to open it, you could inhale the vapors, thus exposing yourself to irritation, though the risk from this level of exposure is probably quite low. If camphor is spread directly on the tools, skin irritation is likely, particularly in the summer when the camphor is dissolved by sweat on the hands. By using machine oil as a rust preventive, you avoid this hazard entirely. Another rust inhibitor available in tablet form is sold by Cortec Corp., 310 Chester St., St. Paul, Minn. 55107. I don't know how well this product works, but the manufacturer claims that it contains no hazardous materials and is FDA-approved.
[MICHAEL MCCANN heads the Center for Occupational Hazards in New York.]

How I Make a Rocker

A master craftsman reveals the details

by Sam Maloof

Of the twelve different basic rocker designs I make, the model with solid wood seat and flat spindles is the most popular, and the most imitated. I don't believe in copying, but if knowing the way I work will help other serious woodworkers develop their own ideas, I'm happy to share my methods. I don't have a formula that I follow, nor do I work out mathematically the way my rocker rocks. Each rocking chair differs somewhat in dimension and also somewhat in the density of its parts, so I just work out its balance along the way. I aim for a rocker that doesn't throw you back or tip you out, and somehow I'm usually right on.

I begin with the seat, cutting from 8/4 stock usually five boards at least 22 in. long and 3 in. to 7 in. wide—enough to add up to a 20-in. width after glue-up. I buy random width and length, common #1 or #2 walnut because its figure is more interesting than that of firsts and seconds. After milling the wood to size, I arrange the boards for the nicest figure match, regardless of whether this happens to be bark-side up or down. I then take the middle board and draw on its long edge the contour of a dished seat, a gentle curve whose maxi-

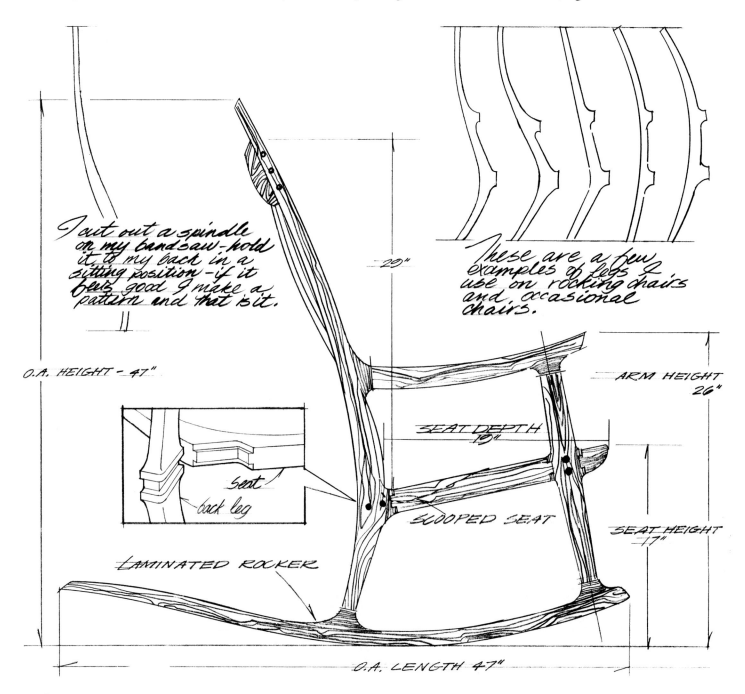

I cut out a spindle on my bandsaw-hold it to my back in a sitting position -if it feels good I make a pattern and that is it.

These are a few examples of legs I use on rocking chairs and occasional chairs.

O.A. HEIGHT - 47"

20"

ARM HEIGHT 26"

SEAT DEPTH 19"

seat
back leg

SCOOPED SEAT

SEAT HEIGHT 17"

LAMINATED ROCKER

O.A. LENGTH 47"

Drawings: Sam Maloof

mum depth leaves ½ in. of thickness about three-quarters of the way back from the front of the seat. I bandsaw this curve, holding the board on edge, then I angle the board through the blade and saw the top of the seat toward the front, to leave a ridge in the middle. I put this middle board back between the two seat boards to which it will be glued, and mark the contour I've just sawn on the edge of each. I bandsaw this contour, and transfer it to the edge of each outer board of the seat. I angle the boards to saw this contour, so that when joined together the five boards form a hollowed-out seat. Before gluing up, I mark and drill for 3-in. long, ½-in. dia. dowels, staggering them about 2 in. apart for ease of assembly, and for strength.

While the seat blank is in the clamps, I lay out both back legs, nesting them on a roughsawn 8/4 board about 7 in. wide and 48 in. long. I look for a curve in the grain to match the curve in the legs. I bandsaw the legs before jointing and thickness-planing them, because flattening the wide blank might result in a leg that is too thin. I get both legs to be the same shape with a 2¼-in. long straight cutter on the spindle shaper, using a template. When I've decided which is the right leg and which the left—by how the grain looks from the back and the front—I saw off the bottom of each leg at a 5° angle. Canted to this degree, each leg will join its rocker properly, giving the chair back a nice splay.

Now I take the clamps off the chair seat and I square up the edges so that the blank is 20 in. wide by 21 in. long. With a 7-in., 16-grit disc on my Milwaukee body grinder, I rough out the bandsawn hollow in the chair seat. I continue shaping and smoothing with 5-in. and then 2-in. discs, up to 150-grit. The top of the seat thus shaped, I cut the notches in the seat to receive the legs. For the back legs, I tablesaw a notch in each rear corner of the seat blank, 3 in. in from the

back and 2½ in. in from the side. For the cuts with the back edge of the seat on the table, I set the miter gauge at 85°, first in one direction, then the other, so that the leg posts will cant outward at their 5° angle. On some chairs I also angle the cuts on the sides, to cant the legs backward or forward, but on the rocker design shown here I make the side cuts at 90°. Now using a router with rabbeting bits—a regular 90° one for the front edges, and custom-made 85° and 95° bits for the side edges—I rabbet the top and bottom edges of these notches, as in the detail of the drawing on the facing page.

The notches for the front legs are less complicated: they're simply dadoed out at 90° and rabbeted, top and bottom, with a regular 90° rabbeting bit. (For a similar joint, see *FWW* #25, p. 54.) Having cut the leg joints in the seat, I bandsaw its outline. Then I round over the underedge of the seat along the back and the two sides, using a 5-in. dia., 2-wing router bit that tapers the seat to about a 1-in. thick-

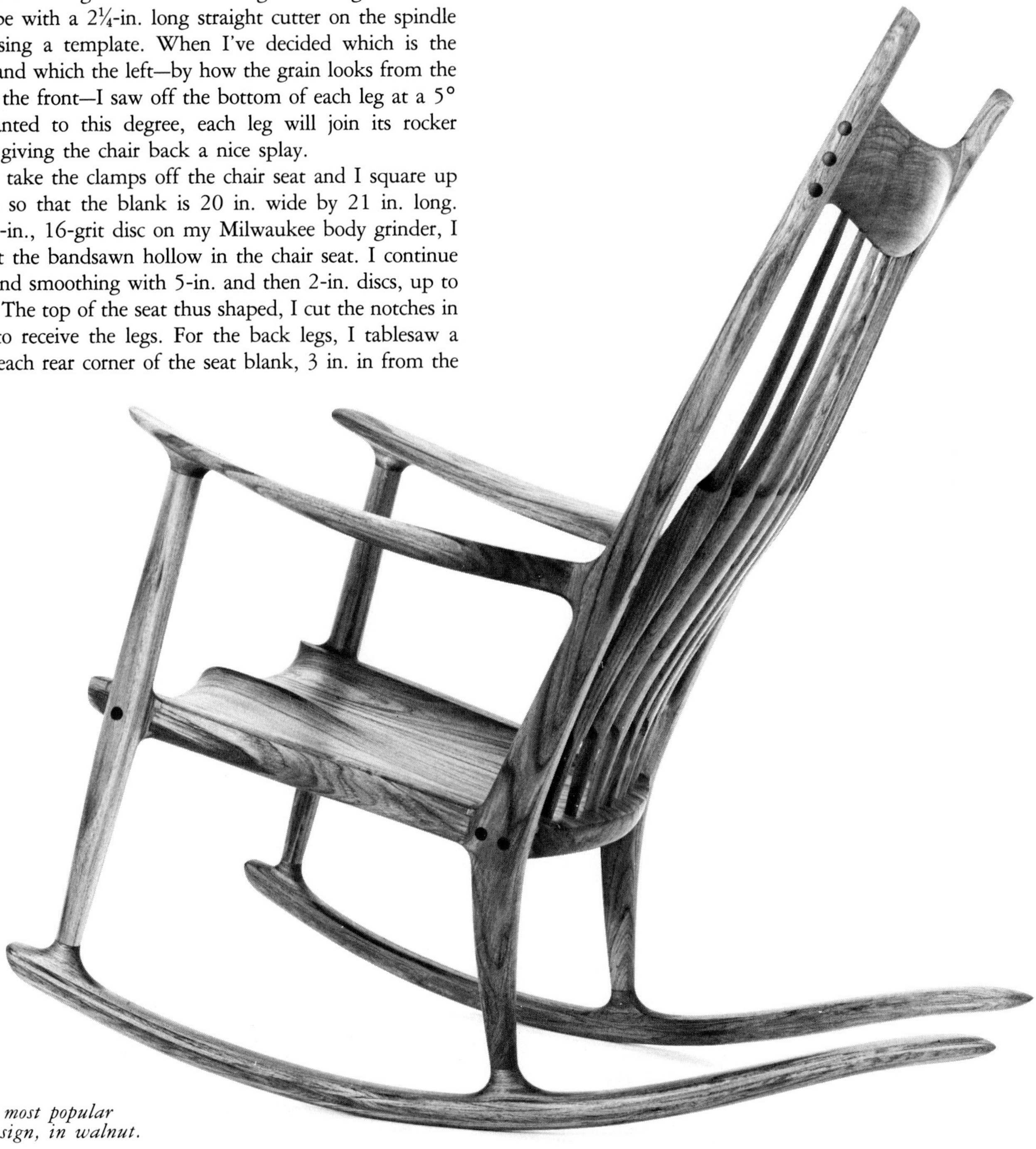

*Maloof's most popular
rocker design, in walnut.*

With assistant Mike Johnson tracing the curve, Maloof demonstrates how he casts the shape of a rocker on the piece of particleboard that will be its gluing form. Also shown is the glued-up blank, with platforms for smoothing the transitions between legs and rocker, ready for shaping.

ness. I leave the area around the joints unshaped, for fairing later. Before fitting the legs, I finish-sand the seat.

With backsaw and chisel I cut the dadoes in the back legs that fit the rabbeted grooves in the seat. I suppose I could jig up and cut these on the tablesaw, but because the back legs are irregularly shaped and because I vary the angles of the back legs in different chair styles, I find the backsaw easier. Next I bandsaw the thickness of the back legs to 1⅜ in., leaving the full 2-in. thickness in the area of the seat joint and the crest-rail joint, for fairing. With the leg still basically rectangular in section, I drill a ½-in. hole in the bottom of the leg to receive the dowel that will connect it to the rocker. To shape the edges of the leg, including the corner that will fit the seat joint, I use a ½-in. roundover bit, but I leave unshaped the area where the arms will attach, and also the outside edges of the leg, because these will be hard-edged. Now I glue the back legs on, clamping across the width of the seat and from back to front.

I make each front leg out of 8/4 stock, 2¾ in. wide and 18 in. long. First I dado it on the tablesaw on three sides to fit the rabbeted notch in the sides of the seat. I then lathe-turn the leg, offsetting the center to the outside of the leg, so that the joint area will be thick enough for fairing into the seat. To complete the leg, I drill a ½-in. hole at each end for attaching the arm and the rocker. I then round over the corners that will fit the rabbet around the seat notch. Now I glue

the front legs on. When the glue is dry, I secure all the leg joints, front and back, to the seat with 4-in. drywall screws, countersunk and plugged with ebony.

At this stage, the chair looks like a seat board with a leg at each corner: no back, no arms, no rockers. I fair the leg joints now, sanding to 150-grit before attaching the arms, so that I have room to work. Each arm requires a piece of 8/4 stock, 6 in. wide and 19 in. long, although I usually cradle two arms on a longer piece. I lay out the arm, locating the dowel hole to attach the arm to the front leg, and saw the flat at the end of the arm to abut the flat on the back leg; this latter joint will be screwed from the back and plugged. Then I freehand-bandsaw the arm, shape it using a Surform, attach it, and fair the joints.

I make the back spindles, seven of them for this rocker, from pieces of 6/4 stock at least 29 in. long. I also use the waste from the back legs, thicknessed to 1⅜ in. I lay out the side profile on the face of the board, being careful to avoid areas where the grain will cross the width or the thickness of the spindle, and bandsaw. I also bandsaw and then spindle-sand the contour of the spindles as seen from the front. I used to shape the spindles, but one day I had two shatter on me, and I said phooey, there must be a safer way. They're just too slender to feed into the shaper, and it doesn't take that much longer to bandsaw them. I round over the back edges of each spindle with a ½-in. roundover bit, and then shape both ends with a rasp. The end that goes into the seat is ½ in. in diameter; the end that goes into the crest rail is ⅜ in. These dimensions are all eyeballed. I shape the slender parts by hand with a patternmakers' file, leaving hard edges along the front. Most of the front of the spindles remains flat.

Next I make the crest rail out of 10/4 stock, 7 in. wide and 26 in. long. I cut the ends to the 5° angle that will accommodate the splay of the back leg posts, then bandsaw the curve of the front and back faces. This gives me an accurate thickness in which to lay out the spindle holes. I space the hole centers evenly across the length of the crest rail, and then do the same across the width of the back of the seat, which will evenly splay the spindles. I use a yardstick now, aligned between corresponding hole centers in the crest rail and seat, to set my bevel gauge for positioning my drill-press table. I bore the crest-rail spindle holes on the drill press, but the seat spindle holes by eye. All holes drilled, I bandsaw the bottom edge of the crest rail and shape it with a Surform. I glue the spindles into the seat, fit the crest rail on the spindles and glue the rail in place between the back leg posts. When the glue is dry, I screw from the leg posts into the crest rail, countersinking and plugging the 2½-in. screws. I then fair the joint and finish-sand.

I laminate the rockers, beginning with 6/4 stock, thicknessing it to 1⅜ in. and then sawing it into ⅛-in. plies. I use a carbide-tipped blade on the tablesaw, and I don't joint the stock between passes—I find the sawn surface smooth enough for laminating. The rocker consists of seven plies about 48 in. long. To make the form for gluing them up, I bend a strip of wood to a shape that looks right, and have a helper trace this curve on a piece of ¾-in. particleboard. I bandsaw three pieces of particleboard along this line and face-glue them into a clamping form. I add seven more short plies to form two platforms for fairing the rocker into the legs. Then I glue up, using white glue. To ensure flatness, I clean up one edge of the rocker blank on my jointer, the other in the thickness planer. I round over the outside corners with a ½-in. bit, except in the area where the legs will connect. The rockers rough-sanded to shape, I put them on the flattest surface in my shop, my tablesaw, and mount the chair on top. The platforms allow for up to 2 in. of adjustment, forward or back, in the placement of the chair. I shift the chair back and forth until the rockers come to rest contacting the ground at about 2 in. in front of the rear legs. I find this looks best, and rocks best. I mount the chair to the rockers with ½-in. dowels, 4 in. long in the back, 3 in. long in the front. Then I fair the joint with a rasp.

I finish-sand the whole chair to 400-grit and apply three coats (at two-day intervals) of a three-part finish: equal parts of polyurethane varnish, raw tung oil and boiled linseed oil, removing all excess oil after each application. I then apply a final coat of a mixture I mix up on a double boiler: a half-gallon each of tung oil and boiled linseed oil, with a couple of handfuls of beeswax grated in. Do this outdoors and be careful—linseed has a low boiling point. The mixture has a long shelf life (stir before using), and leaves a beautiful sheen when buffed with a soft cloth. ☐

Sam Maloof has been making furniture for more than 35 years in Alta Loma, Calif. He is author of the book Sam Maloof: Woodworker, *published by Kodansha International. For more on his work, see* FWW #25.

A Child's Rocker
It's small and straightforward

by William Lavin

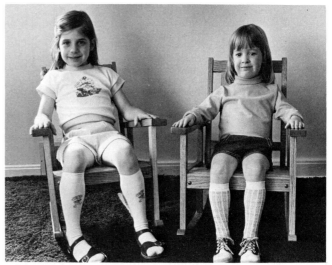

The author's daughters, testing out his project.

Picture an elderly woman knitting, or an old-timer chewing tobacco while playing checkers or whittling, and invariably both are sitting in rocking chairs. The rocking chair stereotypes this age. At the other extreme is the youngster full of unbridled energy that only a rocker can vent. We've all seen it: the elder rocking with gentle, smooth movement in a full-size chair, next to which the child rocks as vigorously as can be in a smaller version. For the average woodworker, a full-size rocker is intimidating to build—too many expectations to fulfill. A child-size chair, however, can inspire freer energies: simple, basic joints and modest proportions demand something reasonable from our abilities.

The idea for this particular chair came from one built more than 50 years ago for my father-in-law by his great uncle, John McCarthy. Originally handcrafted in white oak by a skilled woodworker for an energetic little farm lad, the design yields to simple power tools and a few hand tools. I've toyed with the idea of a short production run, so readily does this design lend itself to a simple router jig for the mortises (compare *FWW* #30, pp. 90-92, and #35, p. 52).

Construction is divided into three subassemblies: the sides, the backrest and the seat. The sides and backrest are joined similarly: horizontals mortised into verticals, except for the arms, which are mortised to receive the tenons on the front posts. Cut this stock, and lay out and cut the joints. Leave the legs a few inches longer than needed so that you can trace the curve of the rocker and then saw the legs later to fit. Note also that for maximum strength the rockers ought to be bandsawn from stock whose grain follows the rocker curve. Dry-assemble, and when everything fits right, take the assemblies apart and sand, finishing up those surfaces that would otherwise be difficult after assembly. All corners should be chamfered. Drill the holes for the screws that will fasten the

Cutting patterns
Scale: 1 square = 1 in.

Rocker (D)

Arm (C)

Inner seat rail (I)

Making a rocker for a child brings a formidable furniture project down to size. Detail, above, shows where backrest is screwed to seat frame and arms.

arms to the backrest posts and the backrest posts to the seat. The backrest assembly is completed in a like manner. Glue, clamp and allow to set overnight. When the side assemblies have cured, center the legs on the rockers, drill and fasten with 2-in. screws.

The seat assembly is a butt-glued and screwed frame with the slats tacked on top. The top edge of the inner seat rails is sawn to a contour that dishes the seat. The seat frame is tapered in plan, and I find it helpful to draw the full-size plan view, showing the thickness of the seat rails and front and rear crosspieces. Then I cut the pieces oversize, and place them directly on the view for final cutting (at an angle of 3°) and assembly. The front crosspiece is assembled directly with glue and screws (countersunk and plugged), while the rear crosspiece is fastened only temporarily by a couple of pins—I use large cotter pins, because their rounded ends make them easy to remove. The pins keep the seat rails in position while the slats are attached. At final assembly, screws attaching the backrest to the seat will replace the pins.

The seat slats are ripped from a wide piece of ¾-in. thick stock. I shape the edge first using a Stanley #45 fitted with a Record 12H nosing attachment. Another way would be to

scribe guidelines about ³⁄₃₂ in. from the edge and block-plane a rounded edge. And, of course, there's always the router with a roundover bit, although you'd only approximate the nosing drawn. Rip a slat (I actually rip two at once, because I use 30-in. long stock and chop the ripping in half), then shape and rip the next slat. Make a couple of extras in case you make a mistake when cutting to the exact length later. I find it easier to finish each strip before assembly, so that finishing material will not fill in the crevices between the slats.

Cut the finished slat lengths individually, scribing directly from the seat frame, and drill a small hole in each end using a jig to ensure that all the holes will be equidistant and aligned. Fasten the slats with glue and brass nails.

Complete the assembly by first gluing and screwing (from the inside) the seat frame to the side crosspieces. Then attach the backrest, screwing from the backrest posts into the seat frame, and through the arm extensions into the backrest posts. Countersink these screws and plug with buttons for a tactile detail. A durable varnish will finish your heirloom chair. □

William Lavin teaches junior high school industrial arts in Camillius, N.Y. Photos by the author.

72

CUTTING LIST

Part	Amt.	Description	Dimensions T x W x L
A	4	Posts	¾ x 1⅛ x 13 s/s
B	2	Side crosspieces	¾ x 2¼ x 10¾ s/s
C	2	Arms, from one piece	¾ x 4 x 15¾
D	2	Rockers, from one piece	1⅛ x 4 x 22
E	2	Backrest posts	¾ x 1⅛ x 18
F	1	Crest rail	¾ x 1¾ x 10¾ s/s
G	1	Lower backrest rail	¾ x 1¼ x 10¾ s/s
H	3	Back slats	⅜ x 1½ x 11⅜
I	2	Inner seat rails, from one piece	1⅛ x 4 x 11½
J	1	Seat crosspiece, front	½ x 1½ x 14
K	1	Seat crosspiece, rear	½ x 1½ x 13
L	15	Seat slats, from one piece	¾ x 8 x 16

s/s = shoulder-to-shoulder. Add at least ⅜ in. to length for each tenon.

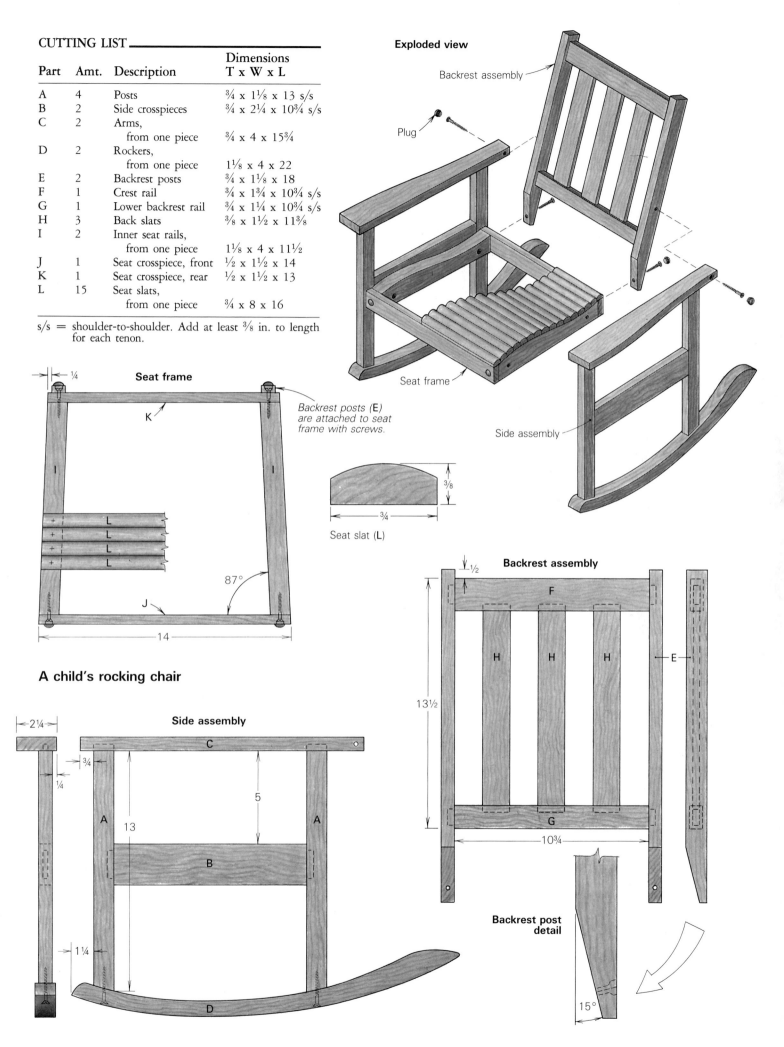

Exploded view

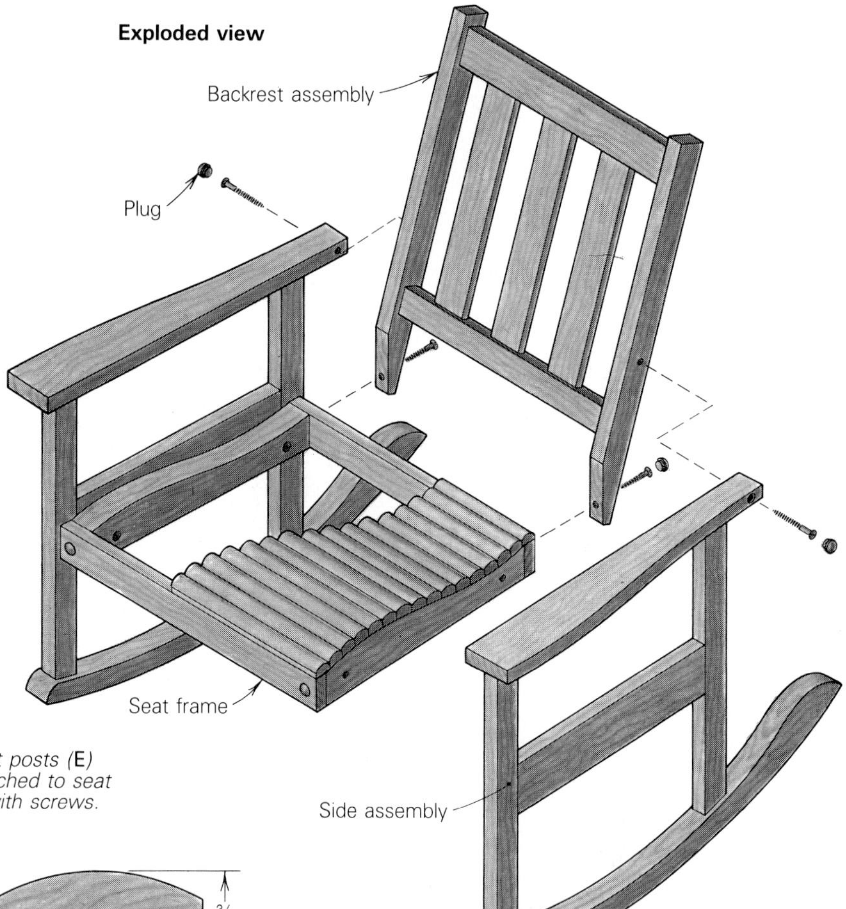

Backrest assembly
Plug
Seat frame
Side assembly

Seat frame

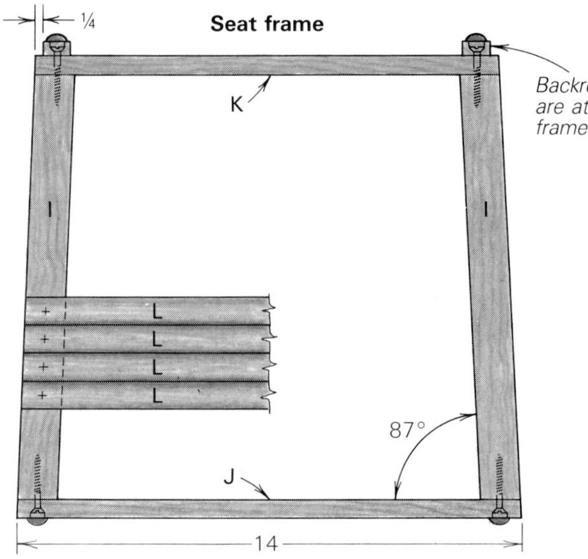

¼
K
I
I
L
L
L
L
87°
J
14
Backrest posts (E) are attached to seat frame with screws.

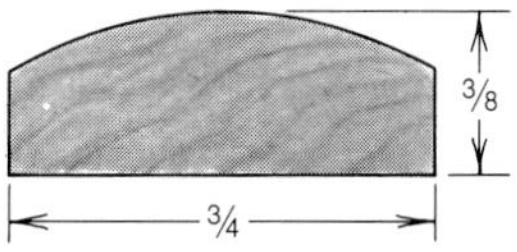

⅜
¾

Seat slat (L)

A child's rocking chair

Side assembly

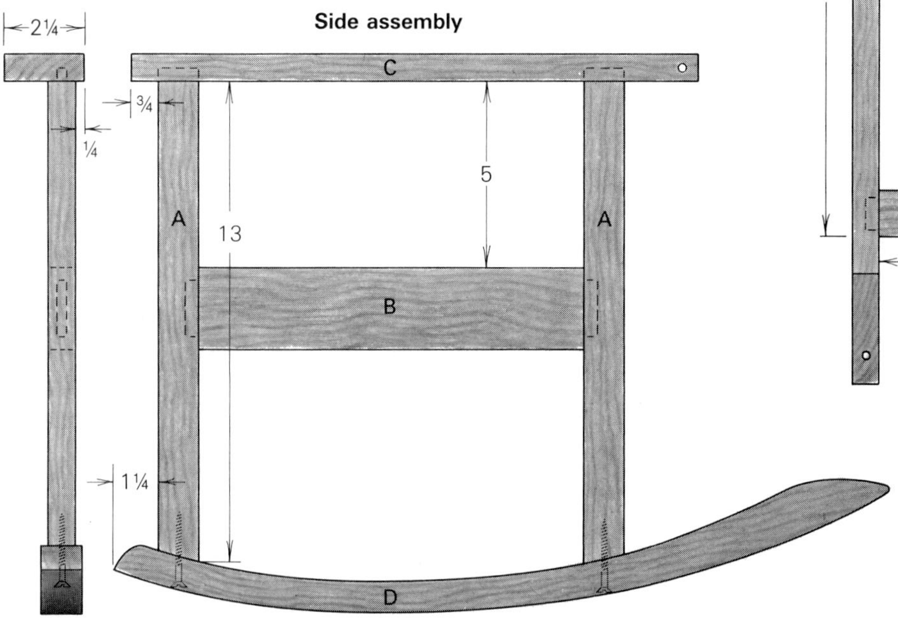

2¼
¾
¼
C
5
A
13
A
B
1¼
D

Backrest assembly

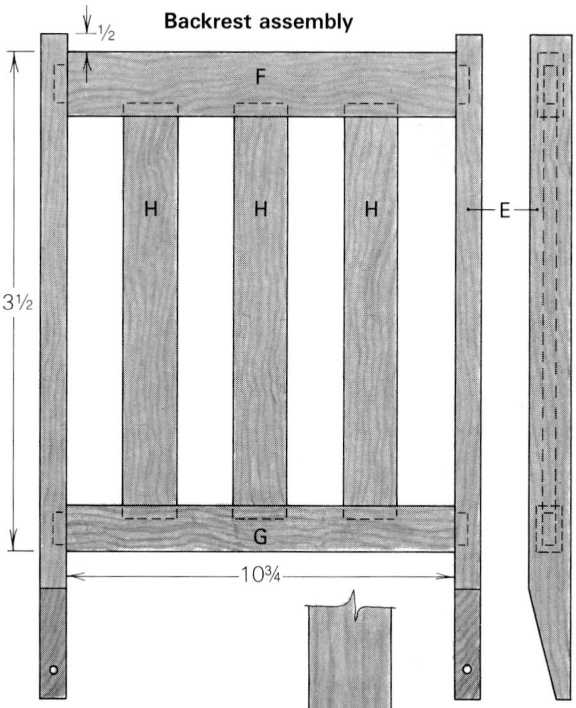

½
F
H
H
H
E
13½
G
10¾

Backrest post detail

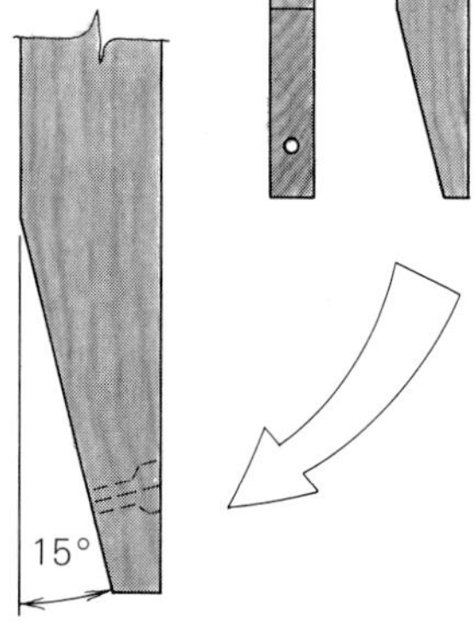

15°

A Southern Huntboard

Cock bead is an elegant touch for doors and drawers

by Carlyle Lynch

"With the Southern forests rich with game and the housewife eager for the results of the day's hunt," wrote Paul Burroughs in *Southern Antiques,* "the sport was engaged in by all classes. The hunting boards around which the owners of Southern plantations gathered before and after the hunt resemble the sideboard. They were often simple in design. . . . As a general rule, they were taller than sideboards . . . and were used chiefly in halls, where members of the hunt could stand and partake of wine and food in the fashion of a buffet lunch." Besides serving as informal hall furniture, huntboards helped keep the muddy hunters off the chairs.

This huntboard is adapted from one that I measured and drew in 1952 while it was on loan to the Museum of Fine Arts in Richmond. It's like most of those illustrated in Burroughs' book in that it has four legs instead of the six usually found on sideboards, and it's of a convenient size. Within reason, the piece can be made longer, deeper or taller without destroying its appearance. When I built the huntboard, I put doors on the two end compartments instead of the deep drawers of the original. The center compartment could be fitted with doors or with two drawers of differing depths.

The edges of the doors and drawer fronts of the original were decorated with a plain, but elegant, molding called cock bead and I recommend retaining this detail. Though cock bead is defined as any beading that stands proud of the surface it is meant to decorate, it is best applied as a strip glued to the edges, as shown in the drawer detail in the drawing, rather than merely stuck on the front. Cock bead is common on drawer fronts and door edges of furniture of the Chippendale, Hepplewhite and Sheraton styles. I see no reason why it couldn't be used to good effect on more contemporary furniture. Because cock bead is an applied molding, it can be of a different wood than that of the drawer or door, giving the maker an opportunity to experiment with colors and textures. I made the cock bead of cherry, which contrasts subtly with the walnut used for the rest of the piece and with the holly inlaid in the doors and drawer fronts.

Building the huntboard is straightforward. The carcase consists of two solid wood sides and a back mortised into the four tapered legs. Openings for the doors and drawers are formed by rails attached to the front legs. Two solid wood partitions, mortised into the front stiles and nailed through the carcase back, divide the case into three compartments. Except for plywood doors veneered with walnut, I built with solid wood throughout. But you could substitute plywood for the drawer bottoms and the carcase bottom.

Start by making the legs. They are rectangular in section, 1½ x 1⅝, as on the original. Lay out and cut the joints to join the sides, back, and front rails to the legs. Then cut and fit the stiles, the center rail, the drawer runners and the two partitions. Dry-clamp the carcase before gluing it up. Before assembly, groove the bottom front rail to accept the bottom; the bottom itself, though, can be fitted later. For added strength, the leg, back and rail tenons should be pinned after assembly.

So they won't warp or swell, the doors should be made of ¾-in. plywood veneered on both sides. Don't forget to allow for the thickness of the cock bead when sizing the doors. If you squeeze the leaves of the hinges a bit in a vise, you can mortise them entirely into the legs instead of into both leg and door edge—this makes a neater appearance.

Drawer construction is conventional. I allow for the cock bead on the top and bottom edge of the drawer fronts by making the fronts narrower than their sides by an amount equal to twice the thickness of the cock bead. Or, you could glue up the drawer and cut down the drawer front after assembly. In either case, cock bead on the drawer sides is let into a 5/16-in. wide, ⅛-in. deep rabbet. The rabbet should be cut after assembly so that the rearmost edge of the bead will just touch the tapered ends of the dovetail pins.

I make cock bead by ripping thin strips and then using a jack plane to remove the sawmarks and shape the small radius on the bead's front edge. Once made, the bead is simply mitered to length and then glued in place so that it projects about 1/16 in. You'll have to cut a stopped miter where the wider bead along the top and bottom edges of the drawer fronts meets the narrower bead on the drawer sides. □

Carlyle Lynch is a retired designer, cabinetmaker and teacher. He lives in Broadway, Va. More of his drawings are available from Garrett Wade or Woodcraft Supply.

Materials List

4 Legs: 1½ x 1⅝ x 38
2 Sides: 13/16 x 12⅛ x 13⅞, shoulder to shoulder (s/s)
1 Top rail: ⅞ x 1½ x 43¾ (s/s)
1 Bottom rail: ⅞ x 1½ x 43¾ (s/s)
1 Back: ¾ x 12⅛ x 43¾ (s/s)
2 Stiles: ⅞ x 1½ x 10⅜ (s/s)
2 Partitions, pine: 13/16 x 11¼ x 14½ (s/s)
1 Center rail: ¾ x 1½ x 16 (s/s)
1 Bottom, pine: ¾ x 14¾ x 46⅛

1 Top: ⅞ x 18¼ x 49
2 Doors: ¾ x 10 5/16 x 12 15/16 plywood, plus veneer of desired species
2 Drawer fronts: 13/16 x 4½ x 15 15/16
2 Drawer backs: ½ x 4⅛ x 15 15/16
4 Drawer sides: ½ x 4¾ x 15⅝
2 Drawer bottoms: ⅜ x 15 7/16 x 15⅜
4 Drawer runners, pine: ⅝ x ¾ x 14¼ (2 are kickers)
15 linear ft.: 1/20 x 1/16 x 36 holly inlay

14 linear ft.: ⅛ x ⅞ cock bead
2 linear ft.: ⅛ x ⅜ cock bead
14 Joint pins, walnut: 3/16 x 3/16 x 1½ (2 in front, 4 each end, 4 in back)

Hardware: 2 pairs brass butt hinges, 1¾ x 1⅜ open; 4 bright brass drawer pulls, 3¼-in. bore; 2 brass thread or inlay escutcheons; 2 cupboard locks, ¾-in. selvage to key pin, with barrel keys.

HUNTBOARD
From a Private Collection

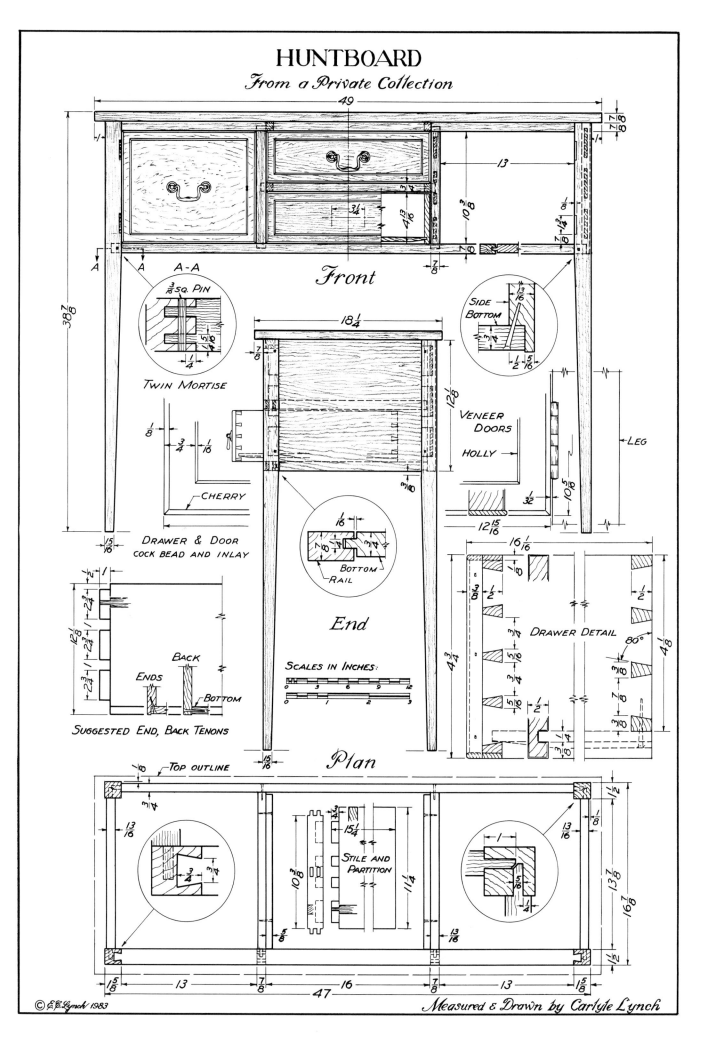

Front

A-A

TWIN MORTISE

$\frac{3}{16}$ SQ. PIN

SIDE BOTTOM

VENEER DOORS

HOLLY

LEG

DRAWER & DOOR
COCK BEAD AND INLAY

CHERRY

End

BOTTOM RAIL

SCALES IN INCHES:

SUGGESTED END, BACK TENONS

ENDS

BACK

BOTTOM

DRAWER DETAIL

TOP OUTLINE

STILE AND PARTITION

Plan

Measured & Drawn by Carlyle Lynch

A Spider-Leg Carriage Table
Turned legs, tray top evoke diminutive elegance

by D. Asher Carmichael

Shortly after I moved to Mobile, Ala., five years ago, Dr. Samuel Eichold asked me to reproduce a table which an antique dealer refused to part with. I met with the dealer, Charles Crane, and coaxed him into letting me make the drawings, measurements and descriptions from which the table shown here eventually developed.

The original table was English, late Georgian (circa 1800), and seemed a tiny cousin to the butlers' tray-on-stand, which was then very popular, primarily for serving wines. The smaller examples—this one is only 21 in. high—were employed in outdoor excursions and were commonly called carriage tables. They are rare today because of their fragility and the rigors of country excursions. The one I copied had probably remained at home most of the time, serving as a chairside table for occasional use.

This table is mahogany with crotch veneer and satinwood veneer border. Like many butlers' tables, it could be made with fancier inlay or even painted and gilded. The top should be veneered rather than made of one piece of solid wood that would likely warp. A butlers' table, of course, has a removable tray, a possible alternative here. Perhaps hinging the top was meant to be insurance against leaving it behind, overlooked at the end of the day beneath some leafy English shrub.

To begin construction, refer to the bill of materials (p. 78) and prepare the rough stock. Dress the stock for the legs, stretchers, cap rails and hinge strip to finished square dimensions, and cut the pieces to length.

Turning the legs—Without a steady rest, legs as thin and long as these tend to whip a good bit on the lathe, but they can, like the original, be turned as one piece. Mount a leg blank in the lathe with just enough pressure to hold it securely—you don't want to introduce any more compression force than necessary, because it will increase the amount of whip. To further reduce whip, start at

the center, work toward the ends and don't remove any more wood than you have to for each step.

Cut the shoulders of the pummels with the long point of a skew chisel, then follow the sequence shown in figure 3, using a small gouge to rough out the legs. Mark the beads. If you are a confident turner, you can round them with the skew. Otherwise, leave them as V-cuts, then shape them with 150-grit sandpaper after you have turned the cylinders to their finished diameters.

An alternative method for making the legs, which decreases whip, is to turn each one as two shorter pieces, then join the pieces with a ½-in. diameter tenon (leg detail, figure 2). Turn the tenon slightly oversize to allow for trimming and fitting. Also, sand the separate leg pieces while they're still on the lathe—it's not likely that the joint will be perfectly centered, and the leg will thus run off-center if you try to sand it on the

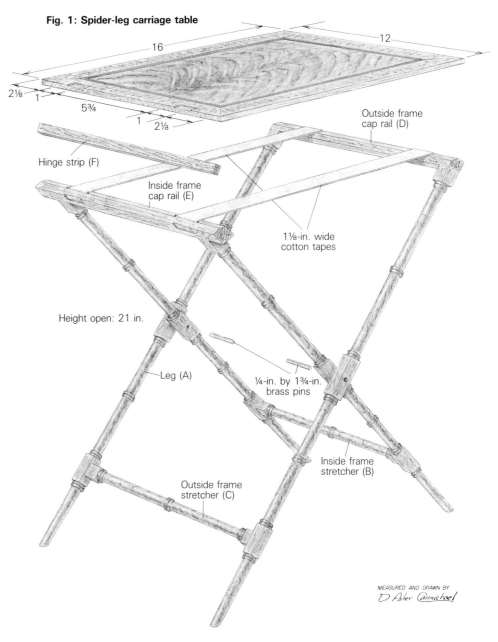

Fig. 1: Spider-leg carriage table

16

12

2⅛

1

5¾

1

2⅛

Outside frame cap rail (D)

Hinge strip (F)

Inside frame cap rail (E)

1⅛-in. wide cotton tapes

Height open: 21 in.

Leg (A)

¼-in. by 1¾-in. brass pins

Inside frame stretcher (B)

Outside frame stretcher (C)

MEASURED AND DRAWN BY
D. Asher Carmichael

lathe after it's been glued up. Bore the ½-in. diameter mortises in the upper legs with a Forstner or a Power Bore bit chucked in a drill press or in your lathe.

Cap rails and frame assembly—

Before you chamfer the cap rails, lay out and cut the leg and tape mortises. Also, lay out the stretcher mortises in the legs. You can cut the square mortises with a ⅜-in. hollow-chisel mortiser, or you can rough them out with a ⁵⁄₁₆-in. brad-point bit and then chisel them square. Take care cutting the leg mortises in the cap rails. If they are too deep, they will show when you cut the chamfer. To cut the slot mortises for the tape, drill adjacent ⅛-in. holes through the stock, then clean up with a thin file.

Now cut the tenons on the legs and stretchers, using your choice of tablesaw, radial-arm saw or hand tools. Also,

bore a ¼-in. diameter hinge-pin hole through the center square of each leg.

I chamfered the cap rails with a hand plane—it's risky to use a tablesaw or a jointer on such small pieces.

When tooling is finished, sand the rails to 120-grit, then glue and clamp the frame assemblies.

Top and final assembly—

You might decide to use ¼-in. plywood for the ground, hiding its edges with a thin band of veneer, but the original table's ground is edge-glued from pieces of quartersawn stock. This choice of grain—along with the maker's care to veneer both sides and apply a good finish—has kept the thin top flat and true.

If you use solid stock, dress the lumber for the ground to ⅜-in. thickness. Watch for tearout as a clue to grain direction, then, to make planing easier,

Fig. 3: Turning the legs

To avoid whip, work from center toward ends, removing only enough wood to allow you to clean up details as you go. As an alternative to turning the beads with a skew, you can leave them V-shaped (as in step 2), then round them with sandpaper after you have turned the legs to finished diameter.

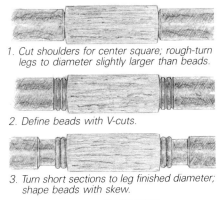

1. Cut shoulders for center square; rough-turn legs to diameter slightly larger than beads.

2. Define beads with V-cuts.

3. Turn short sections to leg finished diameter; shape beads with skew.

4. Turn leg to finished diameter.

Fig. 2: Details and measurements

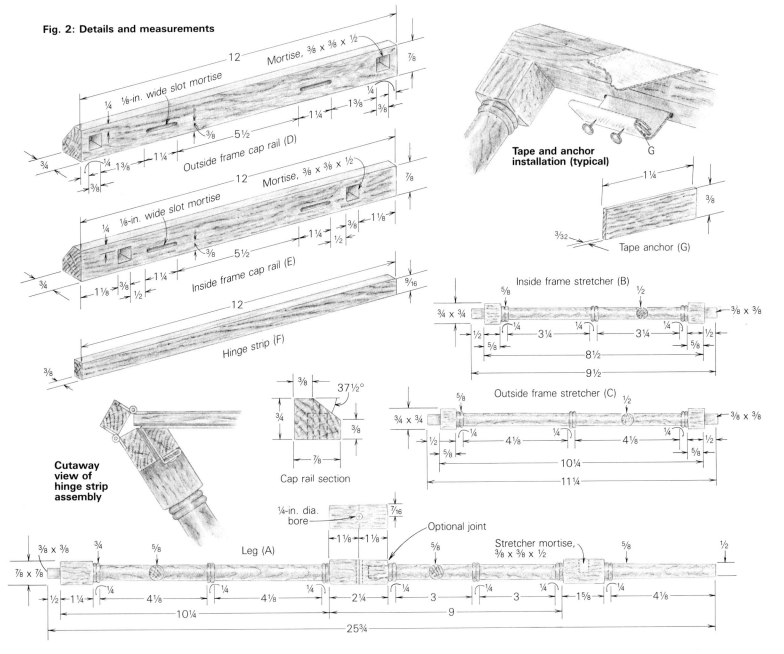

Tape and anchor installation (typical)

Cutaway view of hinge strip assembly

arrange the boards so that all the grain goes the same way. Edge-glue the pieces to make a panel ½ in. oversize. Plane the panel to about ¼ in. thick, and cut it to final size.

Lay out and cut the veneers, allowing 1/32 in. extra on the counter veneer and the border veneer to ensure complete coverage. Using a straightedge and a razor or a veneer knife, cut the miters from the long point toward the inside, to avoid breaking off the long point. Assemble the veneers as shown in figure 4 with some glue between the joints. The tape will be removed with scrapers and sandpaper once the veneers and ground have been laminated.

When the face veneer lay-up is dry, you can glue up the ground and veneers with yellow, plastic-resin, or hide glue (figure 5). Deep-throated handscrews and C-clamps will supply plenty of pressure if they are arranged evenly over the cauls (see p. 82 for another veneer glue-up method). Get everything ready, then apply glue to one side of the ground (not to the veneer) and center the counter veneer, best face showing. Turn the top over, apply glue to the other side, and center the top veneer, taped side out. Press down to remove any air bubbles, then, to keep it from sliding, secure the sandwich with several small strips of tape. Place either

waxed or plain paper over the veneers as a parting agent, and clamp up.

When the top is dry, remove the veneer tape with a freshly sharpened scraper. Then plane the veneer flush with the edge of the ground. Finish-sand, carefully easing the veneer edges.

Cut and sand the hinge strip and attach it to the top with two 1-in. by ¾-in. brass butt hinges. Let in the hinges so that they are flush. You'll have to pre-drill the screw holes and file the screws shorter to keep them from going through the tabletop. Next, hinge the strip to the inside frame assembly.

Finishing up—Remove all the hinges, clean up any blemishes and give the table a final sanding to 150-grit. If you plan to stain the wood, seal the stringing and border veneer with shellac first. To avoid this step, I used a chemical stain, 2 cups of quicklime (calcium oxide) in 1 quart of warm water, which colored the mahogany black-red without darkening the lighter veneer too much.

Any finish will do, but be sure to apply thin coats rather than heavy ones, which would fill in the grooves at the beads and obscure the detail.

Next, reattach the top. To allow the table to fold, pin the legs with brass rod as shown in figure 1. If the pins do not fit snugly, peen one end oval. Resist any temptation to use epoxy, as this would prevent disassembly of the base frames should the need arise.

Now you can attach the cotton tapes (available from upholstery shops) to the cap rails as shown in figure 2. As with the hinges, pilot-drill the tape anchors to keep them from splitting. It will be easier to attach both tapes to the inside frame cap rail first and then use the top as a gauge to determine their final length.

Set the table up and check for level posture, then mark and trim the bottom of the legs to ensure a stable footing. Seal the trimmed leg ends, then apply a thin coat of wax until the table gleams.

Now that you're finished, the people in your life whom you've neglected so long would probably love to use the table for its original purpose—an outing in the country. If your heart isn't quite that strong, it's up to you to convince them that something a mite more substantial would be more appropriate. □

D. Asher Carmichael works for Emperor Clock Co. In his spare time he draws and makes furniture.

Fig. 4: Laying up the face veneer

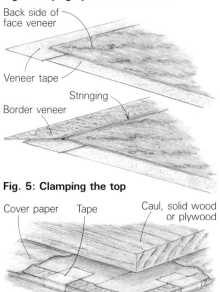

Back side of face veneer

Veneer tape

Stringing

Border veneer

Fig. 5: Clamping the top

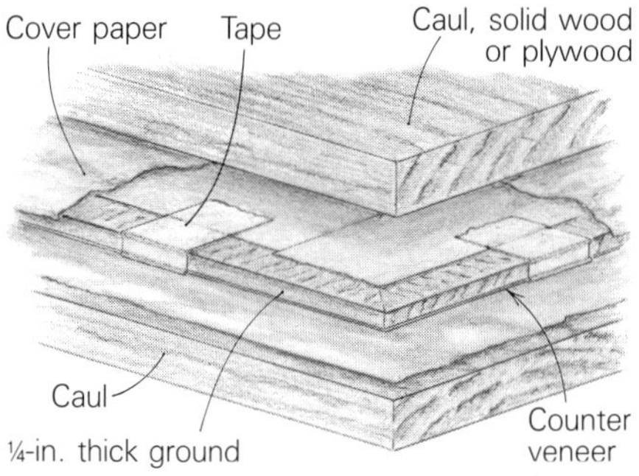

Cover paper   Tape   Caul, solid wood or plywood

Caul

¼-in. thick ground

Counter veneer

Marilyn Tario

The carriage table, even in semi-repose, tells tales of elegant Georgian picnics. It folds up for easy carrying, and the tray is attached with hinges so you won't accidentally leave it behind.

BILL OF MATERIALS

No. of pieces		Description	Dimensions (net) L x W x T
Mahogany:	4	Legs (**A**)	25¾ x ⅞ x ⅞
	1	Inside frame stretcher (**B**)	9½ x ¾ x ¾
	1	Outside frame stretcher (**C**)	11¼ x ¾ x ¾
	1	Outside frame cap rail (**D**)	12 x ⅞ x ¾
	1	Inside frame cap rail (**E**)	12 x ⅞ x ¾
	1	Hinge strip (**F**)	12 x 9/16 x ⅜
	4	Tape anchors (**G**)	1¼ x ⅜ x 3/32
	1	Top (ground), can be plywood	16 x 12 x ¼
Veneer and stringing:	1	Counter veneer	16 x 12 x 1/28
	1	Figured face veneer	14 x 10 x 1/28
	50 in.	Holly-ebony-holly stringing	⅛ in. wide
	60 in.	Satinwood border veneer	⅞ in. wide
Hardware:	2	Cotton tapes	18 x 1⅛
	4	Brass butt hinges	1 x ¾ (open)
	2	Brass pins	1¾ x ¼ dia.
	8	Brass tacks or light upholstery nails	

Marquetry pictures can add visual flourish to furniture of all kinds. For this walnut coffee table, Silas Kopf mounted an 18-in. by 46-in. floral picture with background of Australian laurel on a plywood base let into the table's top.

Marquetry on Furniture
Double-bevel sawing leaves no gaps

by Silas Kopf

Although we really don't have a long tradition of using marquetry in American furniture, applying assemblages of colored veneers to add visual interest to a piece is gaining favor. Veneers, sold in hundreds of colors and textures, are quite workable for making rich designs and pictures. The techniques involved, though not simple, are easily learned; the real challenge is in creating patterns complementary to the furniture being decorated.

One of the beauties of marquetry is that it requires very little equipment. Perfectly satisfactory pictures can be made with a good hand-held fretsaw or a knife, although, as I'll explain later in this article, a power scroll saw has advantages. There are several methods for making a marquetry picture. I favor a technique called the double-bevel cut, as it offers both speed and precision when making just one or a few pictures. With relative ease, many pieces of veneer can be fitted together without gaps between the parts. I mount, or press, my marquetry work onto panels, which can then be applied to small boxes and furniture of all sizes. This double-bevel method is applicable to about 95% of the work I do.

Double-bevel cutting is an additive process. You start with two pieces of veneer, one of which will fit into the other, and you build up the picture around them part by part, taping each piece into position until the picture is complete and ready for mounting. One piece is set on top of the piece it will fit into, and the saw, angled to cut a bevel, cuts through both at once. The waste is set aside and the two pieces are placed together. The gap that is created by the sawblade is taken up by the bevel, so when the piece on top "falls into" the lower one, it will wedge in place with no space or an invisibly small space between, as in figure 1 (p. 80). The angle of the bevel is a function of the thickness of the sawblade and the thickness of the veneer. Using $\frac{1}{28}$-in. thick veneer and 2/0 jewelers' blades, the gap will be filled if you cut a bevel of around 13°.

Designing and making a picture—I try to make the picture the focus of my work and then design the furniture to best display it. This rules out mounting pictures close to the floor; eye-level application on cabinet doors or on tables seems ideal. Surfaces subjected to a lot of abrasion and wear aren't good locations for marquetry, but tabletops will hold up fine if they are protected with a hard surface finish such as polyurethane. Keep in mind that tabletops are horizontal surfaces that are frequently cluttered, so your efforts may be invisible much of the time.

Using marquetry on furniture calls for relatively large pictures that fit the human scale of pieces being decorated. A tiny, detailed rendering, for instance, goes better on a small box than in a tabletop. Attention should be paid to grain texture and figure as well, since this has a great deal to do with the size and scale of a picture. Marquetry pictures of any size are possible, and with a little planning the throat opening of the saw needn't restrict picture size—you can make

Fig. 1: The double-bevel cut

Background and insert veneer are cut together, bevel hides gap

Piece taped in position

Fig. 2: Building a simple leaf

Transfer pattern to one veneer.

Dividing line

A. Position veneers with desired grain orientation.

B. Bevel-cut along dividing line; tape unit together on front side.

C. Retransfer pattern, and place taped unit on background.

D. Bevel-cut outline to fit unit into background.

A marquetry picture begins as a drawing transferred to veneer with tracing and carbon paper. In the top photo, Kopf has traced the leaf and positioned it on the veneer for a pleasing grain orientation. Next, to transfer the pattern, he slips carbon paper between the tracing paper and the veneer. He often skips the transfer, preferring to just draw his picture directly on the veneer. This allows more spontaneity—the successful picture relies as heavily on the wood's figure as it does on a preconceived plan.

several small pictures in sections and put them together later on the finished piece.

Making the picture itself with the double-bevel technique can best be explained by using a leaf pattern consisting of two pieces of the same kind of veneer joined at the middle in the process shown in figure 2. This leaf "unit" is then placed in a background of another color of veneer. When you double-bevel cut two pieces of veneer, you may find it helpful to put a little rubber cement between the pieces to keep them from slipping during cutting. The rubber cement will have to be cleaned off before pressing, so to avoid that step, you can rely on finger pressure to keep the veneer aligned. Transfer the leaf pattern using the method described in the photos above.

To set the leaf into the picture, place it on the background and then drill a $\frac{1}{16}$-in. hole through the taped unit and the background. The hole can go anywhere on the outline of the leaf, although it's more practical to drill where another part, such as a stem, can ultimately cover the hole. Insert the sawblade through the hole and saw around the perimeter of the leaf, again on a bevel. After sawing, the leaf should fit into the background with tight joints.

As you build the picture, hold it together with veneer tape applied to what will eventually be the front or exposed part of the picture. The tape will obscure the face side, so you'll have to transfer your patterns to the back as the work progresses. This will make it possible to see the joints and align your tracings with parts that are already in place. You can

make more complex patterns by transferring then sawing more and more pieces into the package. It is always the same additive process. Occasionally multi-piece units will be added to one another, a flower for example. The individual petals each have three or four parts, which are made up separately. Then they are all added together to make the more complex flower. Experience will show where to make these divisions. Parts that are structural units, such as petals, a face or a tree, work well as single marquetry units.

The actual cutting can be done by hand or with a power scroll saw. If you do it by hand, use a deep-throat fretsaw and a V-notch bird's-mouth saw table made from scrap. With a little practice, you'll be able to hold the saw at the correct angle while manipulating the work over the bird's mouth. When cutting by hand, you should back the veneer with a waste piece to keep work from being splintered by the downward pressure of the saw. Poplar works well as a waste veneer because it saws easily and is inexpensive.

Sawing with a power scroll saw has several distinct advantages over hand-sawing. First, the bevel is maintained at a constant angle by tilting the table of the saw. Second, both hands are free to steer the wood through the sawblade. Third, the work gets better backup support from the narrow opening in the saw table, so no waste veneer is necessary for most cuts. Finally, the throat opening of the stationary saw is often larger, allowing a bigger picture to be made more conveniently. My saw has a 24-in. throat, versus the 12-in. of a deep-

Power scroll saws ease marquetry cutting, but acceptable work can be done with a fretsaw and a bird's-mouth jig, here made of plywood nailed to a box clamped to the bench. Kopf is cutting a leaf pattern, and he is using a waste sheet of veneer as a backing to keep the saw from splintering the back side of the cut.

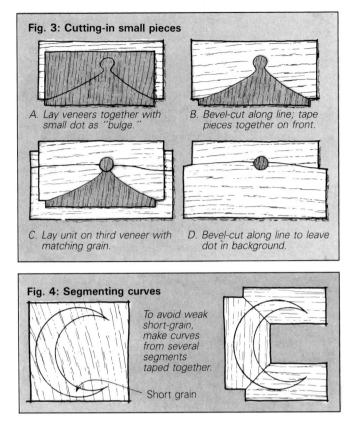

Fig. 3: Cutting-in small pieces

A. Lay veneers together with small dot as "bulge."

B. Bevel-cut along line; tape pieces together on front.

C. Lay unit on third veneer with matching grain.

D. Bevel-cut along line to leave dot in background.

Fig. 4: Segmenting curves

To avoid weak short-grain, make curves from several segments taped together.

Short grain

throat fretsaw (see *FWW* #27, p. 53, for an article on a marquetry-cutting jigsaw).

I have removed the hold-down device from my saw so I can better see the saw line. The blade can easily bind in the narrow kerf, so I have to hold my fingers close to the sawblade to keep the veneer from jumping on the upstroke. This sounds dangerous but really isn't, since the saw's short strokes make it unlikely that your fingers could be dragged into the blade. Even if they are, the blade is so fine that it doesn't cause much more than a nick.

The most difficult maneuver in the double-bevel cut is the nearly complete turn around to make a pointed part. When you reach that stage in the cut, the veneers are pivoted with the saw running. While pivoting, pull back slightly so there is pressure on the rounded back of the blade and you can hear that it is not cutting. When the pieces are swung around to the proper orientation, continue cutting on the line. This will make the parts pointed and not rounded over, giving the whole picture a crisper look.

Breaking sawblades is a constant and annoying problem for the marquetarian. The choice of sawblades is a compromise between a thin sawkerf and strength. With double-bevel cutting, 2/0 blades work well. Standard jewelers' sawblades have teeth spaced closely together for cutting metal. These cause problems with certain woods, particularly when power-sawing. Resinous woods, such as rosewood, clog the teeth, overheating the blades and causing them to snap. Double-tooth (skip-tooth) blades are better for marquetry because they adequately clear away the sawdust.

When a blade does break in the middle of a perimeter cut, I return to the original drill hole to restart the cut because it is difficult to insert a new blade in the kerf. When you change the blade the unit may move, so realign it and the background veneer. Retracing a cut in the kerf is also difficult; it's best to saw the perimeter in the other direction, tilting the saw table the opposite way so the bevel will match where they meet.

It is difficult to double-bevel small pieces, but one way is to start larger and cut back. For instance, to make a ⅛-in. dot of walnut in a maple background, scribe the walnut as a "bulge," as in figure 3. Double-bevel along this line and place the completed unit on a second sheet of maple, taking care to match the grain. The next cut will bevel the two ma-

ple veneers together along the grain for an almost invisible joint, while at the same time leaving the dot in place.

Sometimes it's better to knife-in small parts, using the window method. With this method a hole is cut into the background and the piece to be let in is set underneath. You don't need a double bevel here, because the knife takes no kerf. The hole's outline is scribed with a knife, the piece removed and the cut finished. The piece is then ready to be taped in place. In cutting with the knife, only one piece is cut at a time. When you use the window method, the piece to be let in can be slid around until the grain is oriented to best tell the marquetry story.

Selecting veneer—Certain species of wood work beautifully and look good in a marquetry picture. As a general rule the softer or more closely grained the veneer, the easier it is to saw. An open-grained wood, such as oak, takes a little extra care, as it tends to splinter away, particularly in short-grain situations. A single layer of tape covering these spots before the veneer is cut will often hold the wood fibers together. I occasionally rub a little yellow glue on the surface and let it dry before cutting to help hold the wood together. Backing troublesome parts on the power saw with waste veneer also helps. Experience and a few shattered parts will, in time, identify the problem woods. Parts that do shatter can sometimes be salvaged by gluing or taping them together until they go into the picture and are eventually pressed.

As with all woodworking, you want wherever possible to avoid short grain and its inherent weakness. Thin parts will cut better if the grain is aligned with the long axis. It is often advisable to segment the pieces when forming a thin curve, as with the crescent in figure 4. Tape the segmented pieces together as you go.

At this point a word about veneer tape might be helpful. Every new piece that is cut means the addition of another

Marquetry panels are pressed onto curved tops in this particleboard jig Kopf mounts in his veneer press. The picture is laminated to a subbase of three ⅛-in. lauan plywood sheets. Scrap Masonite and a rubber sheet put between the form and the work spread clamping pressure, and bridge the jig's irregularities.

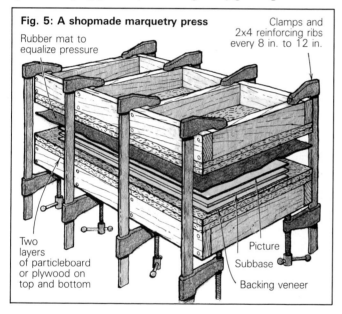

Fig. 5: A shopmade marquetry press

Rubber mat to equalize pressure

Clamps and 2x4 reinforcing ribs every 8 in. to 12 in.

Two layers of particleboard or plywood on top and bottom

Picture

Subbase

Backing veneer

layer of tape. When there are a number of small pieces in a small area, the thickness of the tape can be a factor when the picture is pressed. The thinnest tape I have found is a 30-gram paper tape manufactured by the Ubro company in West Germany and available from Woodcraft and from Welco Machines, PO Box 18877, Memphis, Tenn. 38118. Even using the thinner tape, the buildup may be so heavy that it's best to remove all the built-up tape and then retape, so that one even layer holds all the little pieces together.

It is important to realize that the colors and contrasts you see when you choose veneer will not necessarily be there in the end. Finishing generally changes the wood color, and it is not always an even change in tone from wood to wood. Time will also alter the picture considerably. Light woods tend to darken and dark woods get lighter, giving the marquetry picture a progressively monochromatic look as time passes. This is why old work often seems faded: it is faded. These color changes are unpredictable, so I usually don't try to compensate for them in my designs.

There are tricks for manipulating color. A traditional way

of attaining a three-dimensional illusion in marquetry is to scorch the wood in hot sand to darken it, simulating a shadow. I have a hot plate with a cast-iron skillet heating sand whenever I'm working on a picture. The depth of the sand is about 1½ in. The deeper the veneer is shoved into the sand, the darker the scorching, because the temperature is hottest at the bottom. This yields a gradation of color that is particularly fitting for shadows. Various woods react differently to the treatment. Soft woods scorch more quickly than harder species. Pointed parts have more surface area exposed to the hot sand and therefore burn faster. Dip the piece in and out until the desired shade is reached. Sand-shaded parts should be slightly darker than you would ultimately like, as there is some surface charring that will be scraped and abraded away after the picture is pressed.

Instead of plunging the piece of veneer into the sand, it is sometimes easier to scoop the hottest sand from the bottom of the frying pan and run the wood through it. I use an old gouge for a scoop. By pulling a curved piece, such as the crescent in figure 4, through the hot sand in the scoop I can char the veneer evenly. In the skillet, the thin ends would burn before the center of the arc became dark enough. You can also stain marquetry parts before or after they are assembled, and dyed veneers of various colors and species are sold by marquetry suppliers.

Mounting or pressing—After the parts have been cut, the picture should be checked over to see if all the parts are present and accounted for. Any missing pieces can be knife-cut in. The finished picture can then be mounted to the panel or subbase that will hold it together after the tape is removed. This panel can become a decorative element in a piece of furniture or it can be put in a frame for display. In any case, a marquetry picture should have solid wood around its edges to protect the veneer from damage.

I prefer lauan plywood as a subbase. It's cheap and available and usually free of voids. I apply many of my marquetry pictures to small boxes with curved tops. For these, I use three layers of ⅛-in. plywood laid up in a curved form (see *FWW* #6, p. 35, for an explanation of this method). Other types and thicknesses of plywood and particleboard work fine as marquetry bases, but solid wood panels should be avoided. They move too much during seasonal moisture changes, and this can pop loose small veneer pieces or cause serious cracks. Subbases should get a backing veneer on the side opposite the picture to keep the panel balanced and prevent warping.

Pressing the picture onto the surface is essentially like any other veneering operation. The key in marquetry is to equalize the pressure over the entire surface. With the slight differences in thicknesses of veneers and the buildup of veneer tape in concentrated areas, the potential for uneven pressure is ever present. A veneer press is the best way to ensure even pressure. But it's a bulky and expensive piece of equipment for the occasional maker of marquetry panels. Not owning one needn't stop you from trying marquetry. Thick pieces of particleboard and quick-action clamps can make a suitable press (figure 5). To spread the pressure evenly, I use a hard rubber mat ¹⁄₁₆ in. thick between the picture and the press. The mat, which I bought at a rubber supply house, is similar to tire inner-tube rubber.

A variety of adhesives can be used, but I generally choose urea-formaldehyde glue. It has several advantages: it spreads

Kopf applies his marquetry to furniture, but small jewelry boxes are a more frequent showcase for his art. After the picture has been mounted and let into the tops of these boxes, Kopf trims the joint between frame and picture with a contrasting wood.

easily, allows a long open time, and also fills gaps by curing to a neutral tan color (of course *you* won't have any gaps to worry about). I don't use contact cements at all because they seem to be unreliable for veneer work.

The marquetry picture should be oriented with the grain direction of the majority of its pieces running at 90° to the grain of the subbase. Run the grain of the backing veneer in the same direction as the picture. Spread glue evenly on the subbase, picture and backing veneer, and then press or clamp it up and let the assembly cure in the press for 12 hours.

The pressed picture emerges from the press covered with veneer tape and isn't much to look at. I remove most of the tape with a hand scraper, working with the grain as much as possible. Then I finish the job with sandpaper. Sometimes it's safer to forgo the scraper and sand the tape off, as pieces that are cross-grain to one another have a way of being torn out by the scraper. I use a hard cork block with 80-grit paper for the initial sanding. The flat block keeps the softer woods from abrading away faster than their harder neighbors, thus keeping the picture from becoming wavy. Because the felt bottom of an orbital sander is particularly prone to leaving a wavy surface, use one only for a final cleanup of cross-grain scratches, using 220-grit paper.

There are two repair problems that will probably occur at some time or other in your marquetry experience. The first is a "blister" in the veneer caused by improper adhesion. The blister is evidenced by a hollow sound when you rub your finger over the work. If an individual marquetry piece has not adhered, raise it with a knife, inject glue under the wood and reclamp, using cauls to localize the pressure over the repair. If the problem is in the middle of a larger expanse of background, slice the blister open along the grain with a knife, again inject glue beneath it and then reclamp the piece.

The second problem you may encounter is scraping or sanding through the veneer. The repair is made by inlaying a patch into the marquetry panel. Let's assume you have gone through at a particular spot. Select a piece of veneer, preferably from the same flitch, which has grain characteristics similar to the piece being replaced. The borders of the inlay patch should parallel the grain of the background and run from marquetry pieces inside the picture to the picture's outer edge, as above. This leaves you with a patch without end-grain butt joints, and it should be less visible. Make a tracing of the area to be recut and use the tracing as a pattern to mark and cut the patch. Bevel the cut so the piece will wedge into the panel when clamped. Set the patch on the panel and scribe around it with a knife. Use a router to cut the panel to the depth of veneer thickness, coming within about $\frac{1}{16}$ in. or $\frac{1}{8}$ in. of the knife line. Use a chisel to remove the rest of the waste material, occasionally checking the patch for a good fit. Glue and clamp, and hopefully your picture will be like new. This method can also be used to inlay veneer into a solid piece of wood, such as a tabletop. If you do inlay, try to avoid cross-grain constructions that will later loosen during seasonal movement. □

Silas Kopf does marquetry and makes furniture in Northampton, Mass. For more on this subject, see FWW #1, p. 33; #5, p. 38; #9, p. 70; #16, p. 67; and #25, p. 90. The Marquetry Society of America, PO Box 224, Lindenhurst, N.Y. 11757, publishes a monthly newsletter with technical information on the craft.

Making a Pencil-Post Bed
How to shape tapered octagonal posts

by Herbert W. Akers

I knew I was in trouble as soon as we walked out of the furniture store. We had just looked at several king-size pencil-post beds in solid cherry, all priced at about a thousand bucks. Then my wife asked me if I could make one. I took another look at the price tag and naively replied, "Sure." As I walked back to the car, I heard a little voice asking: How in the devil can you shape a 7-ft. long, 3-in. square post into an octagonal section with equal sides and a graceful taper? How do you even hold a post that size securely enough to plane it?

Before I was through making the bed shown here, I had answered those questions myself. Shaping the posts turned out to be easier than I'd thought—I planed them by hand, using a method similar to what boatbuilders employ to make masts and spars. Holding the posts was no problem either, once I had devised a vise made of pipe clamps and 2x4s.

Finding plans for the bed I wanted, however, wasn't so simple. Many country beds of the mid 18th century are called pencil-post because their posts are hexagonal in section, just like a wooden pencil. Others, however, are square posts ta-

Fig. 1: Pencil-post bed

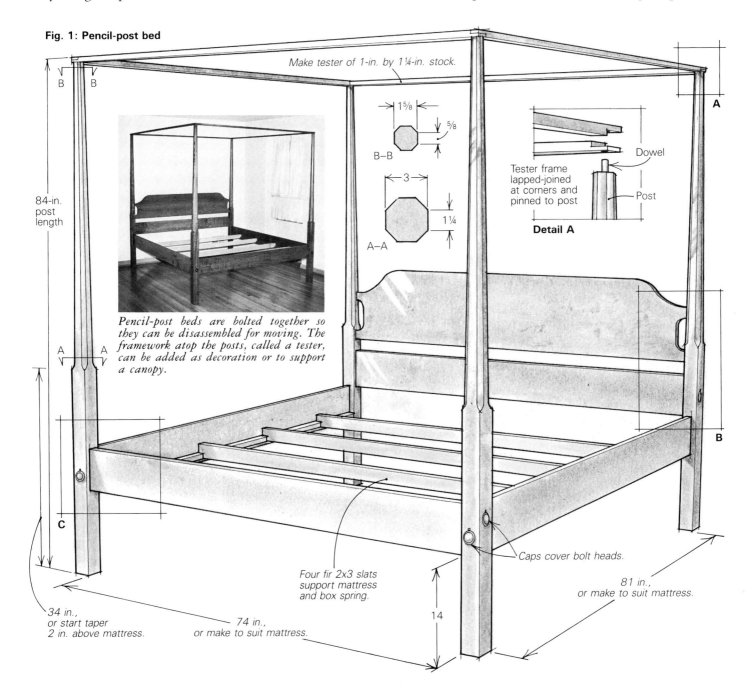

Make tester of 1-in. by 1¼-in. stock.

1⁵⁄₈   ⁵⁄₈

B–B

3

1¼

A–A

Tester frame lapped-joined at corners and pinned to post

Dowel

Post

Detail A

84-in. post length

Pencil-post beds are bolted together so they can be disassembled for moving. The framework atop the posts, called a tester, can be added as decoration or to support a canopy.

Caps cover bolt heads.

Four fir 2x3 slats support mattress and box spring.

34 in., or start taper 2 in. above mattress.

74 in., or make to suit mattress.

14

81 in., or make to suit mattress.

Drawings: David Dann

pering into eight sides. An exhaustive search at the local library turned up no plans, so in desperation I turned to a stack of old antiques magazines, and I got lucky: I found photos of several beds with octagonal posts.

By contemporary standards, pencil-post beds are quite lofty. Typically, the top of the mattress was 32 in. high, elevating the occupants well above the cold floor and leaving room for a trundle bed beneath. You can design the bed with a lower mattress, but if you do, consider also lowering the point where the taper begins on the posts, which is usually 2 in. above the mattress. Don't forget to measure the mattress and box spring you will actually use, and leave about a 1-in. clearance at the sides and ends for bedclothes. I found it essential to make a full-size drawing of the posts on taped-up sheets of graph paper.

Shaping the posts—Sixteen-quarter lumber is hard to find, and prone to checking anyway, so I laminated two pieces of 1½-in. thick cherry to make my 3x3s, taking care to match the color and grain. I made a quick-action vise consisting of

two Sears pipe clamps threaded into flanges screwed to the benchtop, as shown in figure 2. With this setup, I could securely grip about 27 in. of the post either on its corners or on its flat sides. The rest of the post extended out over the end of the workbench, so I could plane in either direction, depending on the grain of the wood.

Lay out the posts as shown in figure 3. Try to arrange your layout so that you'll be planing with the grain toward the smaller end of the post. You may want to test-plane it first, as grain-reading can be tricky with some woods. You'll be using this method over and over again to determine how much wood to cut away. The idea is to draw the guidelines, cut away material from the adjacent surfaces and then draw more guidelines on the newly cut surfaces. You alternate your shaping work, cutting the post's four corners first, then the four flats, then the corners again and so on. As you progress, the octagon will slowly take shape until each surface measures ⅝ in. at the top and 1¼ in. where the tapers begin. It may be tempting to simply scribe the octagon's final shape on the end of the post and taper down to it, but this would require re-

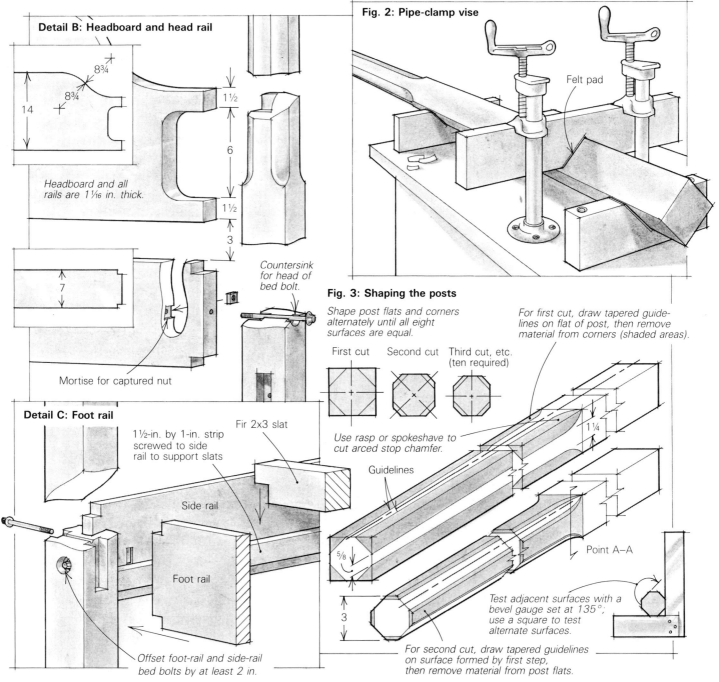

Detail B: Headboard and head rail

8¾ 8¾ 14 1½ 6 1½ 3 7

Headboard and all rails are 1¹⁄₁₆ in. thick.

Countersink for head of bed bolt.

Mortise for captured nut

Detail C: Foot rail

1½-in. by 1-in. strip screwed to side rail to support slats

Fir 2x3 slat

Side rail

Foot rail

Offset foot-rail and side-rail bed bolts by at least 2 in.

Fig. 2: Pipe-clamp vise

Felt pad

Fig. 3: Shaping the posts

Shape post flats and corners alternately until all eight surfaces are equal.

For first cut, draw tapered guidelines on flat of post, then remove material from corners (shaded areas).

First cut   Second cut   Third cut, etc. (ten required)

Use rasp or spokeshave to cut arced stop chamfer.

Guidelines

1¼

⅝

3

Point A–A

Test adjacent surfaces with a bevel gauge set at 135°; use a square to test alternate surfaces.

For second cut, draw tapered guidelines on surface formed by first step, then remove material from post flats.

moving too much material from one face at once, making it difficult to keep the taper uniform and the post straight.

I began shaping by cutting chamfers on the square post. Starting at the bottom of the tapers, I cut toward the top of the post with a sharp chisel until I could switch to a power plane which I'd used this project as an excuse to buy. A hand plane would be fine for this work, but a lot slower. Where the chamfers stop and arc into the square lower portion of the post, I used a ¾-in. rotary rasp chucked in an electric drill, although a spokeshave is the authentic solution. As you plane, keep a long metal straightedge handy to check for scooped-out spots in your tapered surface. Check the accuracy of your work with a square and a bevel gauge, as in figure 3.

As you near the final shape, check the dimensions of your post against the full-size drawing and sight down the post for straightness. On my post drawing, I struck perpendicular lines at 5-in. intervals, and then used dividers to make sure that all the faces were equal and that the width of my taper matched the drawing at these points.

If you end up planing against the grain and you tear out a chunk or two during the first few cuts, reverse your plane. You'll be cutting away enough wood to remove any blemishes as you approach the final shape. Just be sure to keep your plane extra sharp and to set the blade so that it takes a fine shaving.

Assembling the bed—I made a full-size drawing of the curved ends of the headboard and transferred this shape with carbon paper to the two glued-up boards that form the headboard. I mortised the posts first and then cut the headboard to fit. Since I wanted to be able to dismantle the bed for moving, I didn't glue the head-rail and foot-rail mortises and tenons. They are fastened with ⅜-in. by 7-in. bed bolts threaded into captured nuts, as in detail C (p. 85). A pivoting brass cap hides each bolt head. I got the bolts from Horton Brasses, Box 95, Cromwell, Conn. 06416. Get the wrench that goes with the bolts, or use a 12mm socket wrench. With no glue holding it together, I didn't want to risk an ill-fitting tenon shoulder where the headboard joins the posts, so I simply didn't cut shoulders, letting the full 1¹⁄₁₆-in. thickness of the headboard fit snugly into the mortises (detail B).

The side rails are stub mortise-and-tenoned into the posts and bolted. For strength, the two bolts that pass through each foot post should be a minimum of 2 in. apart. Most four-poster beds have the bolt for the side rail lower than the bolt for the foot rail, but it could be done either way.

Whether you plan to use a canopy or not, the bed looks better with the traditional bars that commonly join the tops of the posts. These are called the tester (pronounced "tee-ster") and they form the supports for a canopy. The laps that join the tester bars are not glued but are held together by dowels driven into the top of the posts.

I finished the bed with clear Watco oil, which darkened the wood just enough to enhance the grain of the cherry. A month later I followed up with a liberal application of Watco satin oil, and I think the final finish is exquisite.

This is not a small project, but because I drew my own plans and used techniques new to me, it's one of the most satisfying I've ever tackled. Trouble is, my daughter asked me if I could make one for her and I said "sure," again. I'll never learn. I wonder if she'll settle for pine. □

Herb Akers lives in Rockville, Md., and makes reproduction furniture as a hobby. Photo by the author.

Layout tips from the boatyard

by Michael Podmaniczky

A long straightedge or a chalk line does well for laying out guidelines on square-sectioned stock to be worked into an octagon. But this old sparmakers' marking gauge speeds the job, and you can also use it to mark out a swelled taper, as for a round mast or a boom.

It's made of a scrap that's a few inches longer than the greatest thickness of the taper to be worked. The two dowels that guide the gauge and the nails that do the scribing are inserted according to this geometry: In a square slightly larger than the section of the work, lay out the octagon as shown in the drawing. Then locate the dowels so that the distance between their inside edges equals the length of a side of the square. Position the scribing nails as shown.

To use the gauge, saw or plane the taper "in the square" on four sides of your stock. Then, with the dowels held

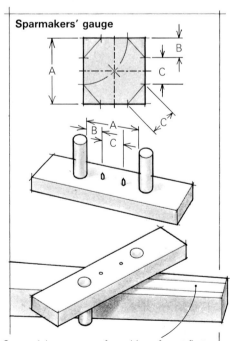

Cut straight tapers on four sides of post first, then use gauge to mark octagonal tapers.

tightly against the edges of the stock, scribe the corners of the octagon by drawing the gauge down the length of the piece. Drawknife down close to the line and finish with a smooth plane. A boatbuilder making a mast or a spar would continue shaping by first eyeballing the octagonal post to 16 sides, eventually planing off all the corners to form a uniform, round section.

For strength and weight, spars have noticeably swelled tapers. I suggest adding a subtler swell to octagonal posts, whether tapered or not. This slight bulging, called entasis, is commonly found in classic Greek columns. Entasis imparts an appealing visual correctness. Adding it will also help you avoid inadvertently hollowing the tapers. □

Michael Podmaniczky is a boatbuilder and patternmaker who works in Camden, Maine.

Methods of Work

Miter-gauge setting jig

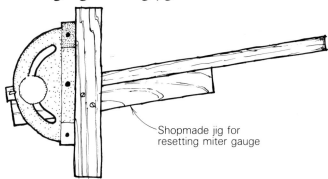

Shopmade jig for resetting miter gauge

Some tablesaw miter-gauge settings are the result of tedious trial-and-error, cut-and-fit procedures. Here's how to preserve that hard-won setting for future use. Cut two 1x2 strips about 1 ft. long. Clamp one to the bar and one to the gauge face. Glue and clamp the strips where they overlap. Reinforce this joint with a couple of screws or dowel pins. When the glue has cured, you can reproduce the setting anytime you like simply by pushing the jig against the gauge.

—*Tim Rodeghier, Highland, Ind.*

Drilling compound angles

Here's a simple method for drilling accurately through irregular workpieces, or for drilling tricky compound angles and having the hole exit where you want it. First clamp a board to the drill-press table and drill the board to match a dowel on hand. Point a short length of dowel and insert it in the hole.

Now mark the workpiece for the entry and exit holes, and center-punch the marks. Make the exit punch fairly deep. Place the workpiece's exit punch on the dowel point and drill on the opposite punch mark.

—*George Kasdorf, Ft. Wayne, Ind.*

Integral drawer pull

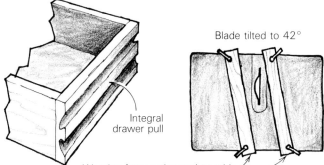

Integral drawer pull

Blade tilted to 42°

Wooden fences clamped to table

This flush, integral drawer pull can be made on the tablesaw. The profile seems to mirror gripping fingers, making it well suited to its task. To make the grip, tilt the blade to 42° and undercut the stock, running it 10° off line with the blade. Make several passes, raising the blade ⅛ in. or so each time, until you reach the final depth. As with all undercutting operations, the stock must remain flat on the table. To keep the board in place, I use two fences (straight pieces of wood clamped to the tabletop on either side of the workpiece) and a hold-down.

—*Ronald Neurath, Louisville, Ky.*

Segmented hinge column

This segmented joint works like a hinge for pivoting panels or doors, but also is a structural member capable of supporting loads like any other column. The hinge is composed of three basic elements: a pin, bushings and wooden joint segments. For the pin I use an ordinary threaded rod. The bushings are washers cut from brass shim stock. Wooden joint segments are made from a large dowel.

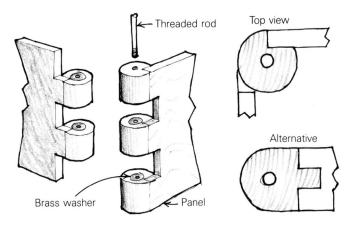

Threaded rod

Top view

Brass washer

Panel

Alternative

To make the hinge, first notch the dowel by passing it over a router mounted in a table. To keep the dowel from turning, tack a thin board to it. Cut the shaped dowel into segment lengths, keeping in mind that their length shouldn't exceed that of your drill bit. Next, drill the bushing hole in each segment. Proper alignment is important, so clamp a locating block to the drill-press table so that the bushing hole will be straight and centered. Assemble the segments on the threaded rod with brass bushings between, then glue the segments in place, one panel at a time.

—*Peter Kaphammel, Jr., Abbotsford, B.C.*

Vacuum attachment for the router

Routing produces a lot of dust and chips. It is much more efficient to collect this messy waste as it is produced rather than to sweep it up later. The sketch shows how I adapted my Sears router to hold my shop-vacuum nozzle: I positioned the nozzle so it filled the gap near the router's work light. It's supported in place with a wooden block (screwed to the base) and a steel band. To reduce air leakage through the holes in the router base, I added a solid base plate made from ¼-in. clear plexiglass. —*Harry M. McCully, Allegany, N.Y.*

Wooden block and shopmade plexiglass base reduce air leaks.

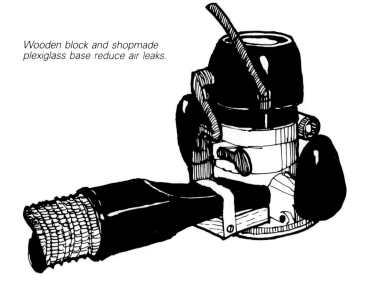

Designing Trestle Tables
Knockdown joinery challenges ingenuity and skill

by Kenneth Rower

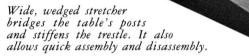

Trestle tables are bridges made of two or more standing frames and a top. If the frames are not individually stable they must be connected to one another or to the top. There are different ways to do this, most commonly by fitting a stretcher somewhere between floor level and the top. Most end-frames are T-form, but some are H-form or X-form, and these are sometimes braced on the diagonal to the top instead of being connected to one another. Many trestle tables are designed to knock down quickly. The simplest—indeed, the archetype—consists of a board on two horses, but most have a loose top and a detachable stretcher, which draw-wedged tenons join to the trestle posts.

A trestle table does not always require a knockdown frame; doorways, hallways and stairways are normally wide enough for maneuvering. The top alone can come off quickly, to reduce weight and bulk, and fixed joints can be made at the posts. But if flat storage is a requirement, or if the exercise is to build a rigid table that can be knocked down to elements with only a hammer, then the extra work is justified. Also, sizable draw-wedged tenons showing outside the posts are unsurpassed for strength, and an opportunity for expressive construction. But if flowing lines are planned for the frame, then it will be better to make fixed joints, without projections, at the posts.

Practical dimensions—A trestle table at standard dining height (29 in.) looks and works best when 6 ft. long or longer. At any length, the amount of top between the end-frames compared with the amount outside them is important. Putting about five-ninths between the supports and two-ninths out at each end balances the top against sagging, whatever its thickness (figure 1). But for tables much shorter than 6 ft., the resulting leg room at the ends becomes a problem—much less than 16 in. is uncomfortable. For elbow room, allow 24 in. per person along the sides. As to minimum dining width, around 30 in. is possible, 32 in. is better, and 36 in. provides space for serving dishes in the middle. The ratio between width and length is not critical, but as the

Wide, wedged stretcher bridges the table's posts and stiffens the trestle. It also allows quick assembly and disassembly.

plan approaches square, a leg-and-apron construction is more practical, for stability as well as comfort. A very long table may work better with another support in the middle, in which case the five-ninths/two-ninths rule is of course irrelevant.

The thickness of the top should be judged against the thickness of the posts. Probably the top should be thinner, but how much so will depend on the effect wanted. The width of the posts should be gauged against the width of the top. Two posts might be better than one under a very wide top, but twin stretchers could appear cumbersome. Flat stretchers placed at the floor and just under the top will give an airy effect (figure 2), but cannot do the stiffening work of a deep stretcher placed about halfway up a central post.

The trestle arms should stop about 3 in. short of the edges of the top, for knee room. The feet should be shorter yet, for toe space, but not so short as to allow the table to tip if someone were to sit on its edge. To clear minor irregularities in a floor, the lower edges of the feet can be relieved very slightly—$\frac{3}{32}$ in. is enough—starting 3 in. or 4 in. from each end. Careful beveling of the bearing parts will continue the thin dark line at the floor.

Stretcher depth and height off the floor determine the frame's lengthwise stiffness, as well as the apparent mass of the whole. In the standard knockdown design, the stretcher must

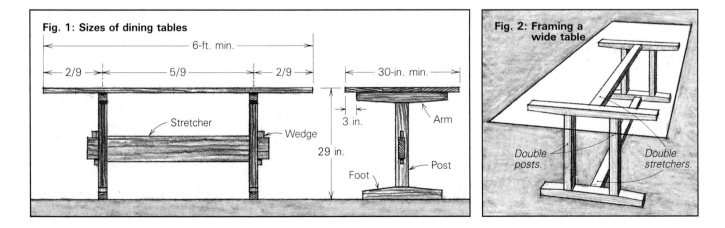

Fig. 1: Sizes of dining tables

6-ft. min. — 2/9 — 5/9 — 2/9

Stretcher

Wedge

30-in. min.

3 in.

29 in.

Arm

Post

Foot

Fig. 2: Framing a wide table

Double posts.

Double stretchers.

be thick enough to accept wedges that look right, and it is no bad thing to have plenty of weight down low in the frame.

Choices remain in the shaping of the frame parts and the treatment of edges, and different effects can be obtained for essentially the same table. For example, a frame trimmed with stopped chamfers on the posts and stretcher will look quite different from the same frame finished with through chamfers. The posts and the feet can be shaped to flow together at the joint, or they can be of different thicknesses to emphasize the change in direction. For wood of large section or uncertain seasoning, the latter arrangement has advantages.

Joinery—It is more complicated to plan and build a trestle frame than an apron frame. Instead of two sets of similar parts (legs and rails) and eight similar joints, there are four pairs of parts (posts, arms, feet and wedges) plus the stretcher, and three different sets of joints. The posts can be joined to the feet and arms by conventional mortise-and-tenon joints, or they can be bridle-joined by cutting open mortises at each end, with corresponding housings midway along each crosspiece. The latter is perhaps easier to do, and if cut with four shoulders is conceivably a stiffer joint in one direction, but it is particularly sensitive to shrinkage of the post. Certainly the bri-

dle joint is appropriate when the post is thicker than the foot.

Figure 3 shows several ways of joining a trestle to its top. For a fully fixed design, effective joints can be made with stout wood screws through the trestle arms into the top, the top acting somewhat as a stretcher. This, of course, requires careful truing of the mating surfaces (**A**). For a removable top, or if a purely wooden construction is preferred, the simplest approach, if the top is heavy enough, is to cut shallow stopped housings in the underside to fit snugly over the breadth of the arms. Gravity will keep things together well enough, although the housings should be cut hollow in their length to allow for some cup in the top, and long as well to allow for shrinkage (**B**). Alternatively, each arm can be shaped to offer a slightly tapered dovetail cleat along its upper edge, and the top housed to receive it. This device can be found on Italian Renaissance tables (**C**). The joint can be stopped so as not to show and to allow setback of the arm, but the cleat must then be considerably tapered and shortened so the top can drop over it and engage by sliding across the frame (**D**). Another method, which exploits the force of the draw-wedges in the stretcher, requires cutting barefaced dovetail cleats in the upper post tenons where they emerge from the trestle arms. Matching housings in the top are then locat-

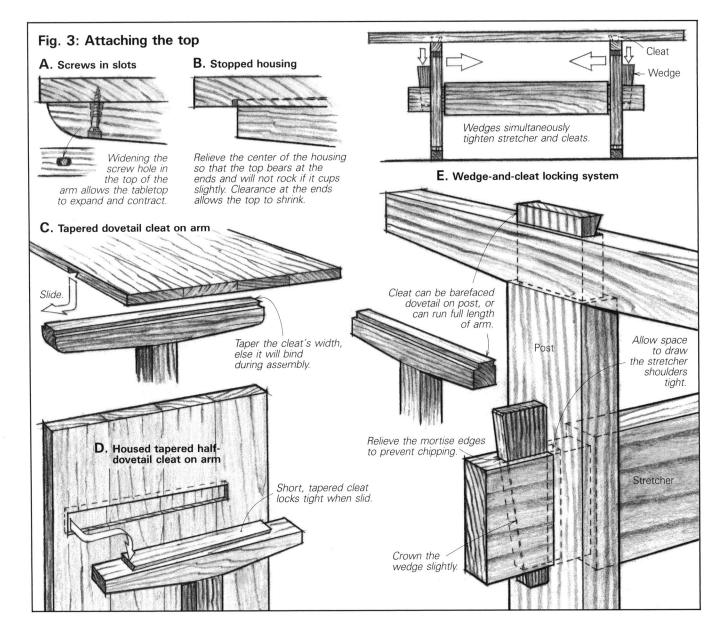

Fig. 3: Attaching the top

A. Screws in slots

Widening the screw hole in the top of the arm allows the tabletop to expand and contract.

B. Stopped housing

Relieve the center of the housing so that the top bears at the ends and will not rock if it cups slightly. Clearance at the ends allows the top to shrink.

Wedges simultaneously tighten stretcher and cleats.

Cleat

Wedge

E. Wedge-and-cleat locking system

C. Tapered dovetail cleat on arm

Slide.

Taper the cleat's width, else it will bind during assembly.

Cleat can be barefaced dovetail on post, or can run full length of arm.

Post

Allow space to draw the stretcher shoulders tight.

D. Housed tapered half-dovetail cleat on arm

Short, tapered cleat locks tight when slid.

Relieve the mortise edges to prevent chipping.

Crown the wedge slightly.

Stretcher

ed slightly farther apart than the cleats as measured when the frame is locked up. This method can instead use the full length of the trestle arm as the cleat. In either case, knocking home the stretcher wedges completes the joint by driving the end-frames toward one another (**E**).

When building end-frames, the post mortises can be chopped right through, ⅛ in. oversize in length, their ends squared, and the tenons later shimmed tightly with 5/32-in. slips, taken from the tenons themselves when the narrow shoulders are cut. Dowel pins secure the joints in the other direction.

Mortises through the posts for knockdown stretcher tenons are usually broad and exposed on one side, thus boring and paring is safer than chopping. The stretcher tenons should be a sliding fit in thickness and an easy fit in height, to prevent seizure if the wood swells.

Wedge mortises through the stretcher must be cut over-long to draw the stretcher shoulders tight against the posts. The slopes of the wedges should be slightly relieved toward the ends, and the extremities of the mortises chamfered, to prevent the wedges from catching when driven in or out. Wedge pitch is somewhat a matter of taste, but if it is too steep the wedge will bounce back when struck, and if too gentle the wedge may travel farther than anticipated. The wedges should be made first and used to lay out the mortises. A push fit is about right for the thickness. There is a temptation to make the wedges from harder wood than the rest of the frame, but such wedges may impress shallow grooves in the posts. It is better to use good pieces of the same stock, and to allow the slopes of the wedges to deform and lock against the harder end grain of their mortises.

Pins should also be the same stock as the frame, but selected for straightness in both planes (look at the rays as well as the rings). Square and octagonal pins hold best, but can visibly crush the surrounding wood on the driving side. Where the pins emerge they will be round, and so for consistency drive all pins from the same side. Center the pin holes about 1½ diameters from the shoulders of the joint.

Making the top—In the absence of a single wide piece (not impossible in, say, mahogany), certain strategies remain. A board one-quarter the width required but twice the length and thickness can be crosscut, then resawn. Random stock can be studied for possibilities of unobtrusive joints and some balance in color and grain.

If edge-joining, allow ¼ in. of width for each joint and another ¼ in. for truing the edges of the completed top. Mark the face side at the joints and glue them up one at a time, each time truing the face side of the boards already joined as well as that of the one to be added, to keep the plane of the whole flat. If this work is done well, and all glue cleaned away each time, little final effort will be required to ready the top for finishing.

Any variations in the surface of the underside need to be dealt with only where they count. When the top is fitted to the frame, parallel flats can be planed across the grain where the top bears on the trestle arms. Differences in thickness showing at the edges and ends can be trimmed away on a short bevel, working to a line gauged from the show side. Sometimes this is done anyway, to make the top appear thinner. □

Kenneth Rower is a joiner living in Newbury, Vt. Photo by the author.

Q & A

Walnut-husk stain—*I would like to make my own stain from walnut husks and currently have about 20 gallons of black muck. If I can get my furniture to look like my hands, I'll be satisfied. Would straining the muck through burlap and mixing it with denatured alcohol be enough? And is there a way to extract the color from the shells?*
—*Wesley Kobylak, Tuscarora, N.Y.*

GEORGE FRANK REPLIES: What you are trying to concoct is the famous *brou de noix* (literally, brew of walnut), the pet dye of all old-time French ébenistes. Since our professor taught us how to make it, *brou de noix* has been replaced by far better and easier-to-use aniline dyes. Still, maybe *brou de noix* has a nostalgic value and charm that some of us can still detect. I envy you your 20 gallons of black muck. Here's how we made the stuff into a wonderful stain.

The boss lady soaked the walnuts' green husks (not the hard brown shells or the edible fruit) in rainwater for a few days and then she put this muck over a slow fire, being careful not to let it boil. All the while, her hands became as pleasantly brown as yours. She added some soda ash (dry sodium carbonate) while brewing, approximately a heaping teaspoon per gallon, and let the brew simmer for two or three days. And that was it. She let it cool, strained it through an old linen cloth (the burlap which you ask about would work just as well) and then filled green bottles with the filtered liquid. She kept the bottles firmly sealed and in a dark area until we were ready to use our *brou de noix.*

If you insist on using alcohol, don't put it into the brew, but into the brewmaster. Rye would do, but go easy.
[GEORGE FRANK is a retired European master wood finisher.]

Form-laminating chair legs—*I am planning to make a chair with legs shaped roughly like a squared-off question mark. I want to laminate the legs, but I'm not sure how to make the forms or in what order I should make and glue the bends. How should I proceed?*
—*Ettore Zuccarino, Deerfield, Ill.*

TAGE FRID REPLIES: First, make up a two-piece jig to fit the shape you want to laminate, as in the drawing, and screw it

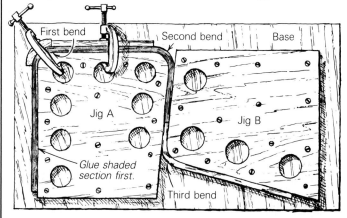

First bend · Second bend · Base · Jig A · Jig B · Glue shaded section first. · Third bend

to a plywood or particleboard base. Make the space between the two jig parts exactly the thickness of the lamination and cut holes in the jigs for clamps. A few coats of wax on the jigs and the base will keep the laminae from sticking to them. I would use wood as thin as possible so you won't have to steam it; 1/10-in. thick veneer would be fine. You can get it from Chester Stem, 2710 Grant Line Rd., PO Box 69, New Albany, Ind. 47150.

To make the leg, remove jig **B** and apply glue to all the laminae shown in the shaded area of the drawing. For the time being, the rest of the lamination will be straight. Clamp the leg on the top of jig **A** first, make the first and sec-

ond bends, and put clamps down each side of the jig. At the bends, make up a curved caul whose inside radius matches the outside radius of the bend. Make the caul flat on the outside so the clamp will have a solid bearing surface. Use as many clamps as you can and make sure you have good, tight gluelines. After the first glue-up has cured, remove the leg from jig **A** and apply glue to the rest of the laminae, using compressed air or a vacuum cleaner, if necessary, to force it between the pieces. Then put the leg back around jig **A**, screw down jig **B** and make the third bend. Remove jig **A** and clamp the leg, starting at the point where you applied fresh glue. A clamp somewhere along the straight section of jig **B** will hold the leg in place temporarily while you remove jig **A** and set the rest of the clamps. I suggest you use a slow-curing glue such as urea-formaldehyde.
[TAGE FRID is a retired cabinetmaker and professor emeritus at the Rhode Island School of Design.]

Vibrating bandsaw—*I built a 12-in. bandsaw from a Gilliom kit and the wheels are oak plywood. There is a slight vibration which I think comes from the tires being of uneven thickness. How can I grind the tires flat and even?*
—*T.T. Ormiston, Outlook, Sask.*
RICH PREISS REPLIES: Bumps or bulges in the tire could be caused by the wrong size tire, crud that got under the tire during installation, or a joint that isn't smooth. To find the high spots, rotate the wheel by hand and read the runout with a dial indicator, or clamp a block in a fixed position on the saw frame and see if the rotating wheel contacts it evenly.

Try spot-sanding with coarse sandpaper to knock down the high spots. If this doesn't work, use the belt-sander jig shown in the drawing below to bring the tire into round. Recrown

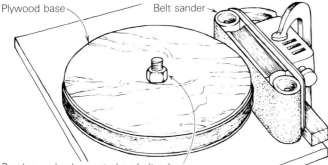

Plywood base
Belt sander
Bandsaw wheel mounted on bolt axles

the tire by hand-sanding or by mounting the belt sander on a beveled block—otherwise the blade won't track correctly.

If the vibration persists, the wheels themselves may be out of round or twisted. Remove the tires and true the wheels on a lathe large enough to accommodate the wheel diameter. Since the wheels are of wood, you can plane or sand out any twist, using winding sticks to check the results. Finally, check that the wheels are aligned and in the same plane when you mount them back on the saw. Hold a long straightedge across the face of the wheels—the straightedge should contact the rim and hub of both wheels evenly.
[RICH PREISS supervises the woodworking shop at the University of North Carolina at Charlotte.]

Gooseneck molding—*I'm building some reproductions of old Norwegian cabinets, and they have some pretty fancy crown molding at the top, which for the life of me I can't figure out how to make. I'd appreciate any help you can give me.* —*Dean E. Madden, Decatur, Ill.*
NORM VANDAL REPLIES: The type of cornice you describe is found on scrolled pediments, an important motif in period

architecture and cabinetwork. The molding itself is sometimes called a gooseneck.

The traditional way to make this cornice is to hand-carve the curved section, a process that seems more difficult than it actually is. The first step is to make the straight returns that are nailed to the top of the cabinet sides. You can make these by hand with a molding plane (*FWW* #37, pp. 72-77), with a shaper or with a molding head mounted in your tablesaw. Make sure to mill them long enough to allow for cutting the miters later.

Next make a full-size cardboard template of your gooseneck section that's exactly as wide as the return molding, as shown in the drawing. Transfer the shape to your stock and bandsaw the gooseneck. With the gooseneck blank held against the cabinet pediment, mark the point at which the miter will meet the cabinet corner.

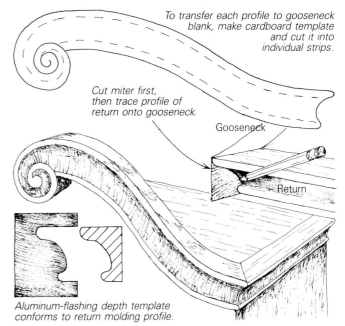

To transfer each profile to gooseneck blank, make cardboard template and cut it into individual strips.

Cut miter first, then trace profile of return onto gooseneck.

Gooseneck

Return

Aluminum-flashing depth template conforms to return molding profile.

Remove the blank and cut the miter. It may seem improbable to cut the miter before carving the molding, but it will prove to be helpful later.

Next cut a matching miter on the return, leaving it long at the unmitered end to allow for fitting later. Temporarily fasten the return to the cabinet and then place the gooseneck section on the pediment, butting the miters together. With a sharp pencil, trace the contour of the return onto the mitered face of the gooseneck. This represents the exact profile that the gooseneck must be where it joins the return. The layout lines for each separate profile of the molding should now be traced onto the gooseneck shape. Do this by first drawing lines representing the profiles on your template, then cut up the cardboard to make individual templates for each contour.

Before you begin carving, make another template out of aluminum flashing, using the contour of the return as a guide. As you carve the gooseneck, check the shape and depth of the profile with your aluminum template. Final shaping and truing should be done with a gooseneck scraper. Two important things to remember are that gooseneck moldings don't need to be as perfect or as consistent in profile as do straight sections, as long as they look correct, and that the only critical points are where the miter joins the two sections. See *FWW* #36, p. 80, for an article on cutting curved moldings with the radial-arm saw.
[NORM VANDAL makes period furniture and architectural millwork in Roxbury, Vt.]

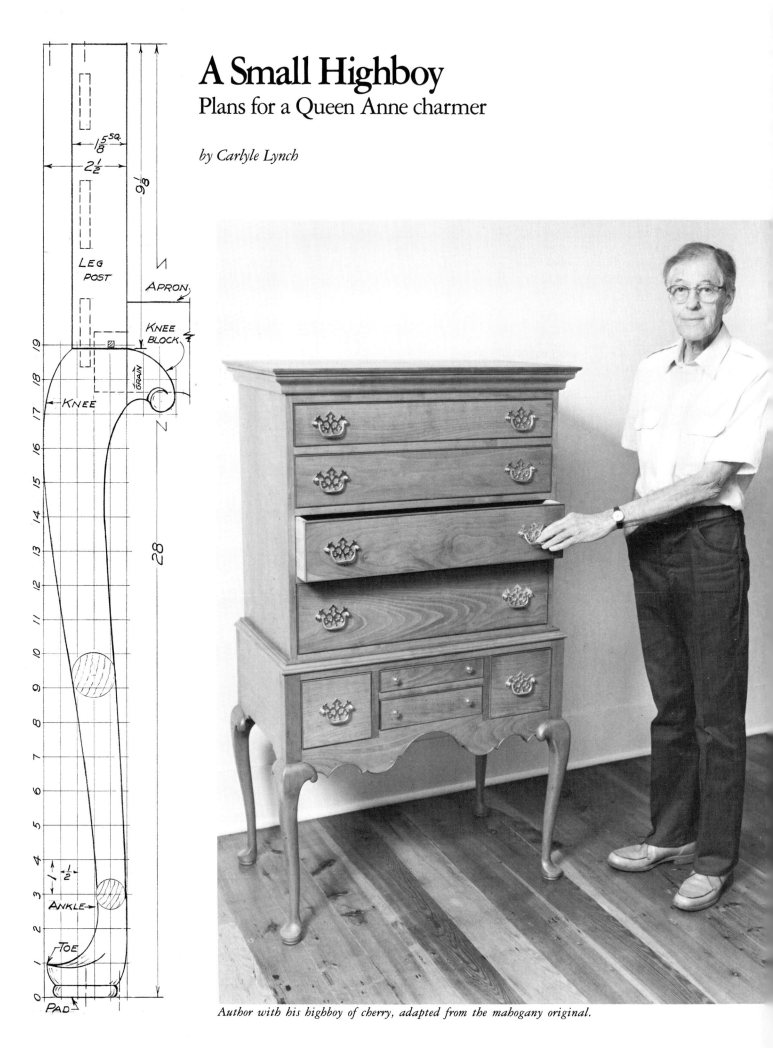

A Small Highboy
Plans for a Queen Anne charmer

by Carlyle Lynch

Author with his highboy of cherry, adapted from the mahogany original.

Photo: Hubert Gentry

The highboy is an imposing furniture form, too large for the spaces in which most of us live. But 18th-century cabinetmakers didn't always build grandly scaled furniture for stately halls. Shown here is a small, modestly proportioned highboy I found in the home of Mr. and Mrs. Richard P. Lewis in Augusta County, Va. Included in the drawings are a few adaptations—simpler moldings and a less arched front apron that accommodates one more drawer than the original. I built the piece to test these alterations. Here are the basic procedures; a bill of materials is given on p. 94.

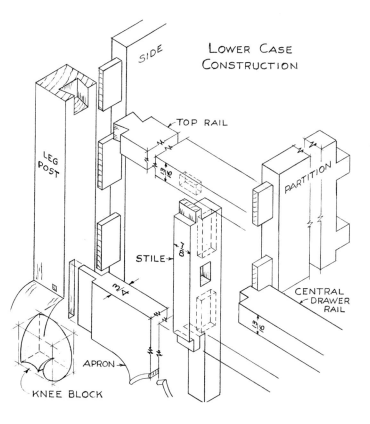

The legs—Begin by squaring the pieces for the legs. The article that follows on p. 96 gives a method for shaping cabriole legs with a bandsaw and hand tools. Here's how the lathe can be used, in addition to the tablesaw, bandsaw and hand tools, to shape the foot and ankle of these cabriole legs: Make a pattern from the drawing on the facing page, and lay out the leg on the two inside faces, so that the apron, sides and back will all fit flush with the post block. Cut the mortises in the post blocks while the leg blanks are still square.

To shape the legs, first draw diagonals on the leg ends to mark their centers, and punch a mark on each end $1\frac{1}{16}$ in.

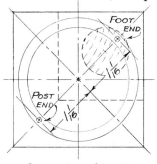

off-center, as shown in the drawing below. Mount each blank in the lathe on its true centers, with the foot end at the tailstock, and turn the foot. Shape it to the top of the pad, but don't finish turning the pad yet, or you will lose the offset center you need to turn the ankles. Remount the blank on the two opposing offset centers and turn the ankles. To someone not used to making cabriole legs, the setup looks forbidding. Use slow speed, and take light cuts with a sharp gouge or round-nose chisel held tight and fed slow. You can turn and sand 2 in. to 3 in. of the ankle, and sand to the top of the foot, before remounting the blank on its true centers to turn and sand the pads.

Take the blanks to the tablesaw, and with a smooth-cutting blade set for maximum height, cut the waste to form the post blocks. Set up a stop block to prevent going too far. In order to keep the post block flat on the table, cut two of the legs with the rip fence to the right of the blade, two with the fence to the left of it. Finish the cuts on the bandsaw and then rough out the rest of the leg. Bandsaw to the pattern line on one face, tape the scraps back in place, turn the leg 90° and saw again to the lines on the scraps. Final shaping is done with spokeshave, rasp and scraper.

The lower case—Mill out the apron, sides and back, then cut the tenons to fit the mortises in the leg. Cut the bottom edge of the sides to shape, but wait to scroll-cut the apron until a gentle fit of its tenons poses no danger of breaking it. Dove-

tail the top rail into the top of the front legs, and test-assemble the frame (drawing, above). Disassemble, and cut the mortises in the apron and the top rail for the drawer stiles, and in the stiles for the central drawer rail. Tenons are $\frac{5}{16}$ in. thick by 1 in. long, except the stile tenons, which are $\frac{1}{2}$ in. long. Use poplar, pine or other secondary wood for the partitions that mortise into the back edge of the stiles and into the case back. Nail three drawer runners and a kicker strip to each of these partitions.

Now add the cock beading to the apron edge. Cut strips of mahogany $\frac{1}{8}$ in. thick, $\frac{15}{16}$ in. wide, and long enough to bend around the curves with enough to spare for cutting the miter joints. Round one edge with a small plane. Use a small gouge to make a groove in a sanding block for smoothing the round. You can use this same block later, to sand the cock beading for the drawers.

Bend the apron beading strips between pairs of plywood forms, shaped to accommodate clamps. Make the curves of the forms a little tighter than the apron radii shown, to allow for springback. Also, make sure the curves on the forms are smooth, as rough or flat places can show up in the bent strips. Boil the strips in a shallow pan of water for ten minutes or so and clamp them in the forms while hot. When they're dry, finish-sand the beading and the apron face, miter the strips, and attach them with glue and small brads. Then fit and attach the short, straight pieces of beading.

Before gluing up the lower case, dry-assemble it to check

1. Mount blank on true centers and turn foot. **2.** Mount blank ¾ in. off-center and turn ankle. **3.** Remount blank on true centers and turn pad.

for fit and squareness. Disassemble, scrape and finish-sand all parts. Then glue the legs to the sides, clamping the two sub-assemblies together, if necessary, to make them lie flat. You can pin the tenons now, while these subassemblies are in clamps, or after the whole case is glued up. Drill $\frac{3}{16}$-in. holes (four in each side) into the post blocks and through the tenons, coat the inside of the holes with glue, and hammer in $\frac{3}{16}$-in. square pins. A small handsaw with set removed will trim off the pins that protrude, without marring the surrounding surface. Pare flush with a sharp chisel.

While the sides are drying, glue up the front frame, then glue the partitions between this and the back. When these are dry, finish gluing up the lower case, clamping and checking for squareness, and pin the two apron tenons and the four tenons at the corners of the back.

To shape the knee blocks, bandsaw the six blanks and glue each one to scrap wood with paper in the joint. Use the scrap to clamp in the vise while rough-carving the blocks. Match the shape of the blocks to the contour of the leg's knee. When they're shaped, pry the blocks from the scrap, scrape off the paper and glue, and glue the blocks in place. Now finish carving the blocks to fair smoothly into the leg.

The upper case—Begin the upper case by milling the stock and cutting it to length. Along the back edge of each side, cut the $\frac{1}{2}$-in. rabbet for the backboards, and cut the grooves to receive the buttons that will hold down the case top (detail A, facing page). Mortise the sides to receive the drawer rails—three front and three back. Cut the $\frac{1}{2}$-in. long tenons on the rails—twin tenons for the front, single tenons for the back. For the top and bottom rails, cut the half-sliding-dovetail slots in the top edge of the sides (detail B) and the dovetail mortises in the bottom edge. Fit the corresponding dovetail tenons in the top and bottom rails. Test-assemble the case, then take it apart and plow the slots in the inside edges of the drawer rails to receive the tenons of the drawer runners (detail C). The runners have $\frac{1}{2}$-in. long tenons that fit these grooves, and they will be left unglued; the distance between shoulders is $\frac{1}{8}$ in. short to allow the sides of the case to shrink. The inside edge of the top front rail is also mortised to receive the loose tenon of the top-drawer kicker strip. This does not connect to the back rail, but like the drawer runners will be attached to the side with a single screw. Test-assemble all parts, then take the case apart and glue it up.

The case sides are plain. The top that overlaps them is now molded on three edges and fastened with wood or metal tabletop buttons. Nail the molding strip under the top.

The drawers—All the drawers are constructed alike—dovetailed front and back, with the bottom slid into a groove in the sides and the front, and secured with nails to the bottom edge of the drawer back, as shown in detail D. (For a

BILL OF MATERIALS							
Amt.	Description	Wood	Dimensions T x W x L	Amt.	Description	Wood	Dimensions T x W x L
Lower case				*Drawers***			
4	Legs	mahogany	$2\frac{1}{2}$ x $2\frac{1}{2}$ x 28	2	Fronts	mahogany	$\frac{3}{4}$ x $6\frac{5}{8}$ x $7\frac{7}{16}$
1	Knee block (makes 3 pairs)	mahogany	$\frac{3}{4}$ x $1\frac{1}{2}$ x 15	2	Backs	pine	$\frac{1}{2}$ x $6\frac{5}{16}$ x $7\frac{7}{16}$
2	Sides	mahogany	$\frac{3}{4}$ x $10\frac{1}{2}$ x $15\frac{1}{2}$ s/s	4	Sides	pine	$\frac{1}{2}$ x $6\frac{7}{8}$ x $17\frac{1}{2}$
1	Apron	mahogany	$\frac{3}{4}$ x $4\frac{1}{2}$ x $28\frac{3}{4}$ s/s	2	Bottoms	plywood	$\frac{1}{4}$ x $6\frac{15}{16}$ x $17\frac{1}{4}$
1	Top rail	mahogany	$\frac{13}{16}$ x $1\frac{5}{8}$ x $28\frac{3}{4}$ s/s	2	Fronts	mahogany	$\frac{3}{4}$ x $2\frac{3}{8}$ x $11\frac{15}{16}$
1	Back	pine	$\frac{3}{4}$ x $10\frac{1}{2}$ x $28\frac{3}{4}$ s/s	2	Backs	pine	$\frac{1}{2}$ x $2\frac{1}{16}$ x $11\frac{15}{16}$
2	Drawer runners	pine	$\frac{3}{4}$ x $1\frac{1}{2}$ x $17\frac{1}{4}$	4	Sides	pine	$\frac{1}{2}$ x $2\frac{5}{8}$ x $17\frac{1}{2}$
2	Drawer guides	pine	$\frac{3}{4}$ x $\frac{7}{8}$ x $15\frac{1}{2}$	2	Bottoms	plywood	$\frac{1}{4}$ x $11\frac{7}{16}$ x $17\frac{1}{4}$
2	Kicker strips	pine	$\frac{3}{4}$ x $1\frac{3}{8}$ x $16\frac{3}{8}$	1	Front	mahogany	$\frac{3}{4}$ x $3\frac{5}{8}$ x $28\frac{7}{16}$
2	Drawer stiles	mahogany	$\frac{7}{8}$ x $1\frac{5}{8}$ x 7 s/s	1	Back	pine	$\frac{1}{2}$ x $3\frac{5}{16}$ x $28\frac{7}{16}$
1	Central drawer rail	mahogany	$\frac{13}{16}$ x $1\frac{5}{8}$ x 12 s/s	2	Sides	pine	$\frac{1}{2}$ x $3\frac{7}{8}$ x $16\frac{3}{4}$
2	Partitions	pine	$\frac{7}{8}$ x $8\frac{1}{2}$ x $16\frac{3}{8}$ s/s	1	Front	mahogany	$\frac{3}{4}$ x $4\frac{5}{8}$ x $28\frac{7}{16}$
6	Drawer runners	pine	$\frac{5}{8}$ x $\frac{3}{4}$ x $17\frac{1}{4}$	1	Back	pine	$\frac{1}{2}$ x $4\frac{5}{16}$ x $28\frac{7}{16}$
2	Kicker strips	pine	$\frac{3}{4}$ x 2 x $16\frac{3}{8}$	2	Sides	pine	$\frac{1}{2}$ x $4\frac{7}{8}$ x $16\frac{3}{4}$
1	Apron cock bead	mahogany	$\frac{1}{8}$ x $\frac{15}{16}$ x 40	1	Front	mahogany	$\frac{3}{4}$ x $5\frac{5}{8}$ x $28\frac{7}{16}$
14	Joint pins	mahogany	$\frac{3}{16}$ x $\frac{3}{16}$ x 2	1	Back	pine	$\frac{1}{2}$ x $5\frac{1}{16}$ x $28\frac{7}{16}$
1	Molding	mahogany	$\frac{3}{4}$ x 2 x $32\frac{1}{2}$*	2	Sides	pine	$\frac{1}{2}$ x $5\frac{5}{8}$ x $16\frac{3}{4}$
2	Moldings	mahogany	$\frac{3}{4}$ x 2 x 19*	1	Front	mahogany	$\frac{3}{4}$ x $6\frac{5}{8}$ x $28\frac{7}{16}$
1	Filler strip	pine	$\frac{1}{2}$ x $1\frac{5}{8}$ x $28\frac{1}{2}$	1	Back	pine	$\frac{1}{2}$ x $6\frac{5}{16}$ x $28\frac{7}{16}$
				2	Sides	pine	$\frac{1}{2}$ x $6\frac{7}{8}$ x $16\frac{3}{4}$
Upper case				4	Bottoms	plywood	$\frac{1}{4}$ x $16\frac{1}{2}$ x $27\frac{15}{16}$
2	Sides	mahogany	$\frac{13}{16}$ x $17\frac{7}{8}$ x $26\frac{3}{4}$	11	Cock bead	mahogany	$\frac{1}{8}$ x $\frac{7}{8}$ x 30
1	Top	mahogany	$\frac{3}{4}$ x $19\frac{9}{16}$ x $33\frac{1}{2}$	4	Cock bead	mahogany	$\frac{1}{8}$ x $\frac{3}{8}$ x 30
4	Drawer rails	mahogany	$\frac{13}{16}$ x $2\frac{1}{4}$ x $28\frac{1}{2}$ s/s		Stops	pine	from 1 x 2 stock
1	Top rail	mahogany	$\frac{3}{4}$ x $1\frac{3}{4}$ x $28\frac{1}{2}$ s/s				
4	Back rails	pine	$\frac{13}{16}$ x $1\frac{1}{2}$ x $28\frac{1}{2}$ s/s				
1	Back top rail	pine	$\frac{3}{4}$ x $1\frac{3}{4}$ x $28\frac{1}{2}$ s/s				
8	Drawer runners	pine	$\frac{13}{16}$ x $\frac{3}{4}$ x $13\frac{1}{4}$ s/s				
2	Drawer kickers	pine	$\frac{3}{4}$ x $\frac{3}{4}$ x $15\frac{1}{4}$ plus $\frac{1}{2}$-in. long tenon, one end				
	Backboards	pine	$\frac{1}{2}$ x $26\frac{3}{4}$ x $29\frac{1}{2}$				
1	Top molding	mahogany	$\frac{1}{2}$ x $1\frac{1}{2}$ x $31\frac{3}{4}$*				
2	Top moldings	mahogany	$\frac{1}{2}$ x $1\frac{1}{2}$ x $18\frac{3}{4}$*				
1	Molding backing strip	pine	$\frac{1}{2}$ x $\frac{1}{2}$ x 76				

Hardware: Ten brass pulls, four $\frac{5}{8}$-in. dia. brass knobs; available from Mason & Sullivan, 586 Higgins Crowell Rd., W. Yarmouth, Mass. 02673.

s/s = shoulder-to-shoulder. Allow $\frac{1}{2}$ in. to 1 in. extra length for each tenon or dovetail.

* Allow extra for final trimming.

** Dimensions include $\frac{1}{8}$-in. vertical allowance for humidity changes.

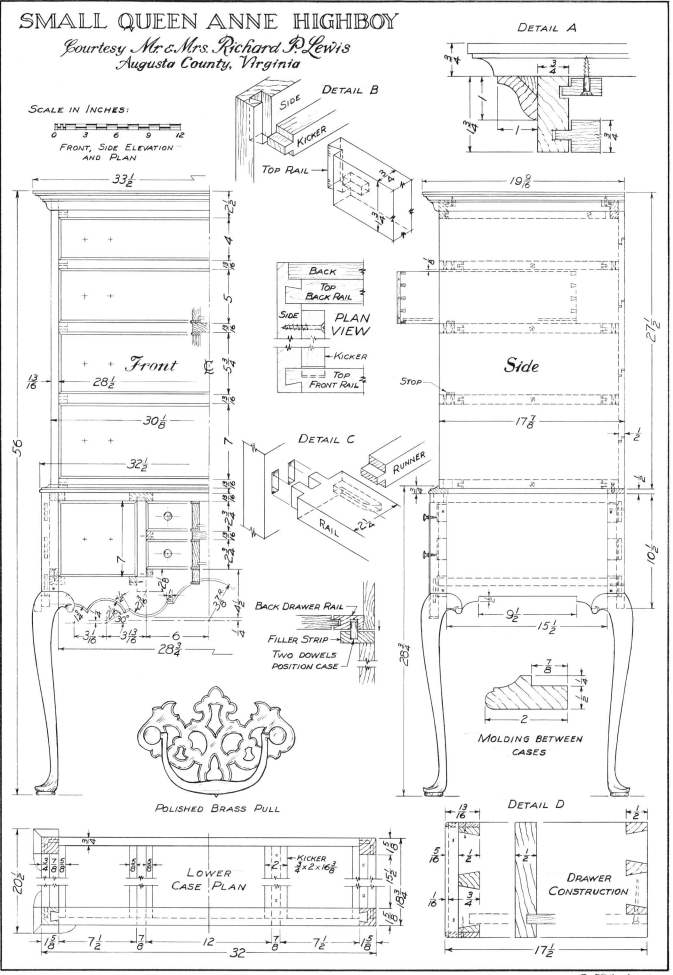

SMALL QUEEN ANNE HIGHBOY

Courtesy Mr. & Mrs. Richard P. Lewis
Augusta County, Virginia

SCALE IN INCHES:

0 3 6 9 12

FRONT, SIDE ELEVATION AND PLAN

DETAIL A

DETAIL B

SIDE
KICKER
TOP RAIL

PLAN VIEW

BACK
TOP BACK RAIL
SIDE
KICKER
TOP FRONT RAIL

DETAIL C

RUNNER
RAIL

Front

Side

STOP

BACK DRAWER RAIL

FILLER STRIP

TWO DOWELS POSITION CASE

POLISHED BRASS PULL

MOLDING BETWEEN CASES

LOWER CASE PLAN

KICKER 3/4 x 2 x 16 3/4

DETAIL D

DRAWER CONSTRUCTION

© E.C. Lynch 1983

95

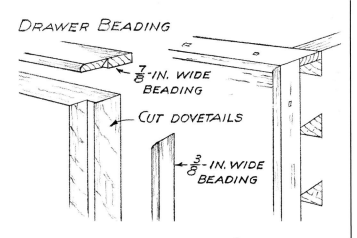

DRAWER BEADING

$\frac{7}{8}$-IN. WIDE BEADING

CUT DOVETAILS

$\frac{3}{8}$-IN. WIDE BEADING

detailed discussion of standard drawer construction, see *FWW* #11, pp. 50-53.) The cock bead is ⅛ in. thick and either ⅞ in. or ⅜ in. wide, depending on whether it goes on the top and bottom edges of the drawers or on the sides (drawing, above). Either way, it should stand about ³⁄₆₄ in. proud of the drawer face. Note that the drawer fronts should be at least ¼ in. shorter than their openings, to accommodate the beading, top and bottom, and to allow for possible swelling. When the drawers are glued up, but before the bottoms are slid in, rabbet the drawer sides for the ⅜-in. wide cock beading with a fine-tooth circular saw, guiding the drawer against both the miter fence and the rip fence. Do all final sanding of the fronts, and prepare the top and bottom beading. Cut these full-length and then miter the ends, actually only the front half of their width, to meet the narrower cock beading on the drawer sides. To miter, clamp the cock beading between a 45° angled block of wood and a backing board. Using the wood block as a guide, cut down with a sharp chisel. Apply the top and bottom beading with glue and nails, then miter and apply the beading in the rabbets along the drawer sides.

Finishing touches—Attach the drawer stops to the drawer rails in the upper case and to the drawer runners in the lower case. To ensure a close fit for the rabbeted moldings that provide transition between the upper and lower cases, position the moldings on the bottom of the upper case and miter them to length. Then, using a strap clamp, glue up the three molding pieces using the filler strip to complete the back of the rectangle. Attach this assembly to the top of the lower case. To key the two cases, drill two ⅜-in. holes in the top of the filler strip about 4 in. from each side of the case. Use dowel centers in the holes to mark the position of corresponding holes in the back rail of the upper case when the upper case is set in position on the lower case. Separate the cases, drill the holes, and then insert 1-in. long, ⅜-in. dowels for keys (see drawing, p. 95).

Rabbet the white pine planks for shiplapping and lay them horizontally in the rabbets you've cut in the back edge of the upper case sides. Space the planks ¹⁄₁₆ in. apart, to allow for expansion, and secure them with small nails. □

Carlyle Lynch, a designer, cabinetmaker and retired teacher, lives in Broadway, Va. His plans for a Southern huntboard appear on p. 75, and others of his drawings are available from Garrett Wade, Lee Valley Tools Ltd., or Woodcraft Supply.

Cabriole Legs
Hand-shaped, without a lathe

by Philip C. Lowe

Cabriole legs, all characterized by the cyma or S-curve, have taken various styles. The cabriole seems to have evolved from the ancient practice of shaping the legs of furniture after those of beasts, and so in Egyptian furniture you see cabriole legs ending in rather literal animal feet. The Chinese favored more abstract renditions. Chippendale, who borrowed many of his ideas from the Chinese, popularized the ball-and-claw foot, along with carved acanthus leaves decorating the knee. To my eye, the sparest, most pleasing form of the cabriole is the Queen Anne, which terminates in a spoon foot, also called a club or dutch foot.

The leg involves methodical shaping with hand tools. Traditionally, slipper and trifid feet were also hand-shaped. The spoon foot, however, was usually lathe-turned. But there are those who don't have a lathe, and even for those who do, the lathe has a disadvantage: it necessitates carrying the circular perimeter of the foot all the way around, which interrupts the flow of the line down the back of the ankle. Here is how to design, lay out, cut and shape a Queen Anne cabriole, with bandsaw (or bowsaw), spokeshave, rasp and file.

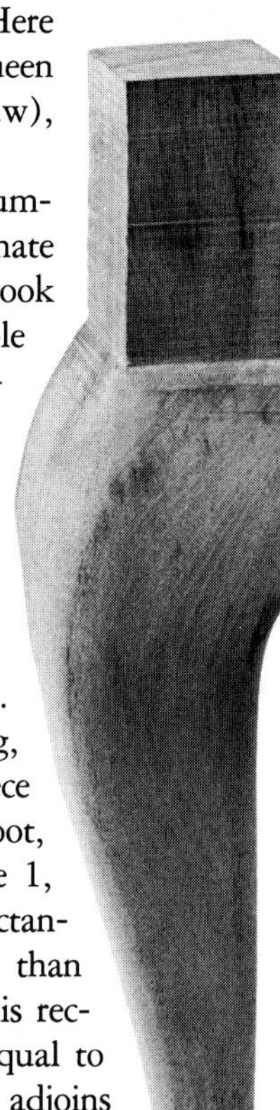

Consider first the rough thickness of the lumber you will use. Solid lumber is best, as laminate lines will interrupt the wood's figure and look offensive when the leg is cut. The most suitable thicknesses for cabriole legs are 10/4, 12/4 and 16/4, depending on the length of the leg and the size of the piece of furniture it will support. I always figure the working thickness of rough stock, after it is planed, to be ¼ in. less than it is nominally. For a typical chair or low table, 12/4 stock, which will yield 2¾ in. of working thickness, is suitable.

You'll need a full-size drawing of the leg, including the post block, knee, transition piece (also called the knee block), ankle, and foot, which is made up of the toe and pad (figure 1, facing page). On a piece of paper, draw a rectangle the length of the leg and ¼ in. smaller than the rough thickness of your stock. Within this rectangle draw the post block first, its length equal to the width of the rail it will join, or, if the leg adjoins a case, the width of the front, back or end. The width of the post block depends on the thickness of the tenons it will receive, as well as on the desired curvature of the knee. For 12/4 stock, a 1¾-in. square post block is common, readily accommodating ¼-in. thick tenons in ¾-in. thick stock.

After laying out the post block, draw the pad and foot. The pad diameter should be about half the width of the blank. Its thickness, from ¼ in. to ⅜ in., depends partly on the thickness of the carpet you expect your piece to stand on. The pad's function is to separate the lines of the leg from the floor. The height of the toe depends on the size of the leg, but on a chair or table leg it's usually ¾ in. to 1 in. from the floor. Sketch in the curves up to the ankle, whose diameter should be about two-fifths the thickness of the leg blank. This narrowest part of the leg should fall at about three times the height of the toe. Next develop the knee, sketching a curve that meets the bottom corner of the post block at about a 45° angle; if it is more horizontal than that, it creates an awkward shelf at the top of the knee. Aim for a tangency point with the outside of the blank a distance from the post block about three times the height of the toe.

Connect the knee to the ankle with a relatively straight line. It is important that you understate any curve here because your drawing is in only one plane, and when the blank is cut in two planes, the curve will be exaggerated. Draw the line of the back of the leg, leading all the way up into the transition piece. Keep this line relatively straight also, and see that the leg thickens gradually and proportionally to the toe, ankle and knee already drawn. The final curve into the transition piece should be relatively tight. If you regard the points of tangency at the knee, ankle and toe, you may be surprised at how much control you have in creating a pleasing shape. Keep in mind, however, that this is only a two-dimensional shape, and its final test will be in a solid piece of wood seen from eye level as part of a whole piece of furniture. Restraint at this stage promises a more pleasing leg in the end.

Next, make a permanent wooden pattern from your drawing. Tape the drawing onto a piece of ⅛-in. plywood, and with a large pin epoxied into a ¼-in. dowel, stipple the outline of the leg onto the plywood, poking through the drawing at ⅛-in. to ¼-in. intervals. Connect the markings on the plywood with a pencil. Repeat this procedure for the transition piece, then cut out both patterns and file their curves smooth.

Prepare the stock next, starting with pieces 2 in. longer than the sum of the two transition pieces (laid out above the post block) plus the leg. Usually the grain of the transition piece runs vertically, like that of the leg. Rip the stock to width at least the dimension of your rough thickness. Joint one face of the blank, either on the jointer or with a hand plane, and then joint an edge square to it. Thickness-plane the blank ⅛ in. larger than the finished dimension, and put the blank aside for a day or so, to give it time to warp in response to any stresses milling may have introduced.

When you have all the leg blanks milled, consider their grain orientation relative to one another. For visual compatibility, either the quarter grain or the flatsawn grain of each blank should face front. Mark the inside corner of each blank, and hand-plane the inside surfaces, removing mill marks and making sure that the surfaces are square to one another. Finish thickness-planing the blanks: plane the outside surfaces parallel to the inside. Crosscut the blanks to their finished length, saving the offcuts for the transition pieces.

To begin layout, set a marking gauge to the width of the post block, and scribe this width on the two inside surfaces (figure 2). Trace the outline of the leg below the post block. To keep the stock from rocking through the second bandsaw cuts, I include in the layout of the leg a pair of bridges—one at the top of the post, the other between the knee and toe. You could also tape the waste from the first cuts back on the stock before making the second cuts, but I find the bridges

easier and more stable. Scribe the position of the mortises on the post block, and cut the mortises while the blank is still square; it's easier to hold square stock.

Now, using a ¼-in. blade, bandsaw the leg: Cut relief kerfs for the bridges first, then saw the post block, staying 1/16 in. away from the scribe line. The post will be planed later, after it is attached to the rail. Saw the curve from knee to ankle, leaving the bridge between. Sawing right on the line will minimize spokeshaving later. Next, define the pad, cutting straight in from the bottom of the blank first, then sawing the curves at the bottom of the foot to meet these relief cuts. Finish sawing the back curve, and save both back-curve scraps. These have the pattern lines for the cut on the adjacent face and should be tacked or taped back in place to saw

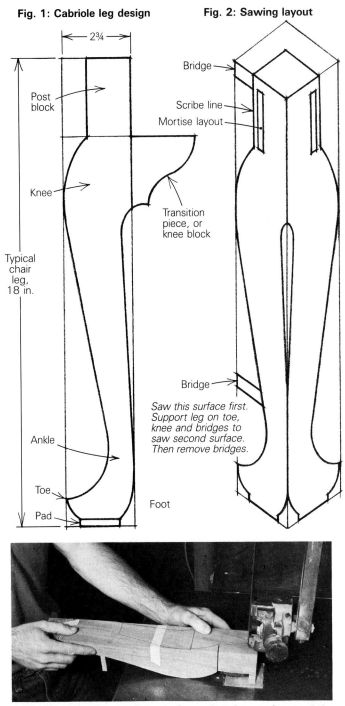

Fig. 1: Cabriole leg design   **Fig. 2: Sawing layout**

2¾

Post block

Knee

Typical chair leg, 18 in.

Transition piece, or knee block

Ankle

Toe

Pad

Bridge

Scribe line

Mortise layout

Bridge

Foot

Saw this surface first. Support leg on toe, knee and bridges to saw second surface. Then remove bridges.

Bridges—one between the knee and toe, the other at the top of the post block—keep the stock from rocking through the second bandsaw cuts. Waste from the first cuts has been taped back in place, to provide layout lines for sawing on.

A pipe clamp mounted in the bench vise, above, makes an ideal holding arrangement for working the length of the leg. Here a spokeshave fairs the bandsawn curves, in preparation for the modeling layout.

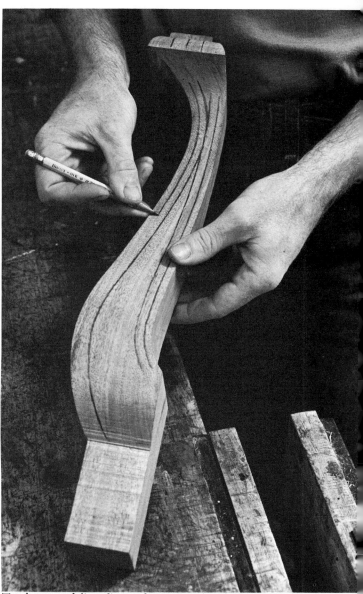

To draw modeling lines, the square for the pad is compassed round, and the other four surfaces are divided into quarters, left. Then each leg surface is penciled with lines parallel to the leg edges, above: two inside lines begin at half the ankle thickness and two outside lines begin at one-quarter the ankle thickness.

it. After sawing this second surface, turn the blank back to the first sawing position and saw off the bridges.

The next job is to fair the leg with a spokeshave, removing all the bandsaw marks, bumps and hollows. It is important here that the leg be kept square in section; irregularities are more difficult to see and smooth once you begin rounding the leg. Where the curves are tight and the spokeshave will not reach, you can use a rasp or a file. The leg is now ready to be laid out for final shaping.

Begin laying out the bottom, locating the center of the pad by drawing two diagonal lines from the corners of the square that will contain the pad, and scribing with a compass the largest possible circle the square will contain. Divide each surface of the underside of the foot into four equal sections: first draw a line from the center of each side of the pad to the top edge of the foot, then halve the distance between these lines and the corners of the foot.

To lay out the guidelines for modeling the rest of the leg, position a pencil point at the center of the ankle, and using your middle finger as a depth gauge running on the stock edge, draw lines from ankle to post block parallel to each edge of the leg. There will be a total of eight lines, two on each face. Reposition the pencil point halfway between these lines and the edges, and draw eight more longitudinal lines. Now the leg is ready to model.

Mount the leg bottom up in a vise, and saw the waste away from the pad square to leave a regular octagonal shape (figure 3A, facing page). Similarly, cut the corners off the toe square, but leave the corner at the back of the leg, thus forming only three-quarters of an octagon (figure 3B). Now use a rasp to round the outline of the pad and the foot (figure 3C). Check the shape of the foot periodically by looking down from the knee to see that it is situated symmetrically in relation to the rest of the leg. When the outline is round, use the rasp to fair the underside of the foot, from its perimeter to the perimeter of the pad.

Modeling the rest of the leg requires attention to holding it. As the surfaces become more curved, a bench vise becomes

98

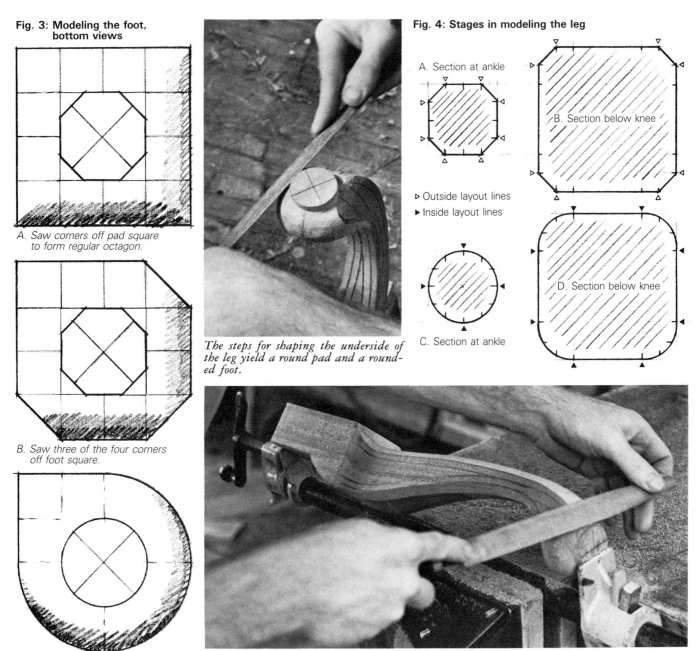

Fig. 3: Modeling the foot, bottom views

A. Saw corners off pad square to form regular octagon.

B. Saw three of the four corners off foot square.

C. Round outline of pad and foot with a rasp.

The steps for shaping the underside of the leg yield a round pad and a rounded foot.

Fig. 4: Stages in modeling the leg

A. Section at ankle

B. Section below knee

▷ Outside layout lines

▶ Inside layout lines

C. Section at ankle

D. Section below knee

A rasp chamfers the corners of the leg to the outside layout lines, then rounds the leg to the inside layout lines, as detailed in figure 4.

more frustrating. I clamp the blank lengthwise in a pipe or bar clamp and mount the clamp in my bench vise. This affords access to most of the leg's surfaces, and the blank is easy to reposition. Use a rasp to chamfer all four corners to the outside layout lines, from the ankle to the knee. This yields an irregularly octagonal section of varying proportion, depending on where it is along the length of the leg (figures 4A and 4B). The flat should taper to nothing at the foot and at the curve toward the transition piece. Next rasp the ankle round (figure 4C). Continue rounding the rest of the leg to the inside layout lines. The shape will become a square with rounded corners as you approach the knee (figure 4D). Flare the foot's top and back, to form a smooth-spreading curve.

When the leg is fair, remove the rasp marks with a file, followed by a cabinet scraper. Then sand the leg, except for the surfaces that will be blended into adjoining members.

The leg can now be joined to its aprons or case sides, after which the outside faces of the post block are planed flush, and the transition blocks are shaped and applied. Assuming the rest of the furniture piece is assembled, crosscut the transition block into the two blanks and orient each so that its grain (quarter or face) corresponds to the grain of the leg surface it will become part of. Plane the edge and end of the transition block for a close fit against the leg and the adjoining member (apron or case side). Position the pattern on the block and draw on it the shape of the transition piece. Bandsaw the piece, and glue it to the leg and adjoining member. A sharp, wide bench chisel then shapes the transition piece to the contour of the knee, and the areas that have not been sanded are sanded. ☐

Phil Lowe operates a cabinet shop in Beverly, Mass., and teaches cabinetmaking at North Bennet Street Industrial School in Boston. For more on cabriole legs, their history and other techniques for making them, see FWW #10, pp. 55-59, and #18, pp. 76-83. If you're looking to buy already made cabriole legs, contact Fallsview Studios, 165 Fairview Ave., High Falls, N.Y. 12440.

MACHINES

This wooden, 10-in. tablesaw has a robust sliding table with fixed crosscut fence.
It can crosscut wide panels
as accurately as cast-iron machines costing ten times as much.

A Wooden Tablesaw
An attractive, shopmade alternative to cast iron

by Galen Winchip

Early in my woodworking career, I remember arranging to use a friend's big radial-arm saw to make critical cross-cuts on wide panels for cabinets I was building. We spent hours fussing with the saw's adjustments, only to have it cut each panel frustratingly out of square. I longed for a sliding crosscut table—standard equipment on the heavy, industrial tablesaws that were way beyond my price range.

I had looked at the sliding tables then appearing as options on medium-duty saws, but they seemed flimsy and certain to sag when crosscutting heavy boards. Worst of all, these

devices were fitted with as many adjustment knobs, screws and levers as a radial-arm saw has, making them far from the set-it-and-forget-it crosscut machine I wanted.

I decided that the only way I'd own a sliding table was if I designed and built one myself out of wood. I had already constructed a half-dozen wooden woodworking machines, in-cluding panel saws, jointers (*FWW* #28, pp. 44-50) and lathes. I've found them to be well up to the rigors of daily use and, like a vintage wooden hand plane, they have the friendly feel that's absent from their cast-iron counterparts.

Photos: Pete Krumhardt

The saw's sliding table mechanism is self-centering and self-adjusting, and it won't bind or loosen as the wooden rail swells and shrinks. The guide rail and rip fence are laminated from thinner stock for stability.

For horizontal boring and slot-mortising, a chuck can be threaded onto the saw's extended arbor. The auxiliary table can be set in two positions: flush with the main table, or 5 in. below it.

I built two tablesaws with complicated tilting-arbor mechanisms, but because I wanted my third saw, described in this article, to be easier to build, I opted for a fixed arbor. I didn't include an adjustable miter gauge either, relying instead on jigs fastened to the sliding table. Most of the adjustments on this machine are achieved by planing or jointing a small amount of wood from a critical surface, or by inserting paper shims. Because I didn't have mortising machinery at the time, I extended the saw's arbor and added a table for horizontal boring and mortising. Of course, you can modify the design to suit your own needs. After I'd built my saw, alternatives and modifications kept coming to mind, and because I've included these changes in the drawings, the photos and drawings don't correspond exactly. If you do modify, keep in mind some basic wooden-machine-building principles, which I've outlined below.

Wood vs. cast-iron—If you set out to build a wooden chair, you wouldn't look to one made of plastic as your structural model, so it follows that cast-iron woodworking machine mechanisms shouldn't serve as models for wooden ones. Cast-iron is an unyielding, predictable material which can be machined into parts that will maintain close tolerances. Wood expands and contracts with the seasons, so you must design mechanisms that won't swell and seize up in summer, then shrink out of precision in winter.

The rail I devised for my sliding table is an example of one such mechanism. As the photo above shows, it's an angled-section member which supports guides shaped so that the table's weight keeps them accurately centered, regardless of dimensional changes caused by moisture or wear. There's no play in this mechanism, but the compromise is friction. The table doesn't move as freely as do commercial models that roll on steel bearings.

For a given cross-section, cast iron is about ten times as rigid as wood, thus wooden members must have larger cross-sections for equivalent stiffness. Obviously, cast iron is harder and denser too, so it can bear concentrated loads that would crush wood. The best way to achieve rigidity in wooden machines while avoiding crushing is to distribute loads widely. In a cast-iron saw, the arbor bearings might be mounted 2 in. or 3 in. apart, but in my wooden saw, they are about 19 in. apart. Spreading out these mounting points also masks minor construction inaccuracies and distortions caused by uneven movement of wooden components.

My favorite wood for machines is well-seasoned, straight-grained hard maple, though I've had good luck with cherry, beech and oak. Whichever wood you pick, it's a good idea to let it live in the shop for a few months so it can reach equilibrium moisture content before you work it. I always cull out the highly figured pieces because they are more likely to twist, bow or cup. You can further counterbalance some of the wood's inherent instability by laminating several thin pieces into one larger one, as I did for the saw's sliding-table guide rail and rip fence.

For sheet stock, I prefer particleboard with a density of at least 45 lb./cu. ft. It's cheap and strong, and can be finished nicely with paint or covered with plastic laminate. Fiber-

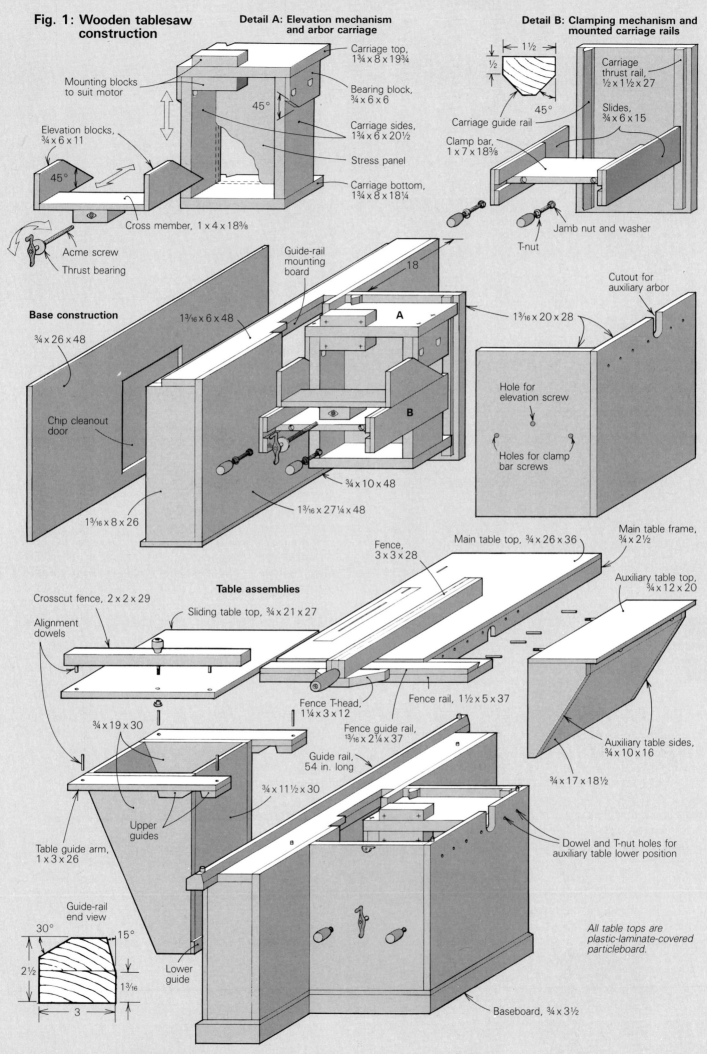

Fig. 1: Wooden tablesaw construction

Mounting blocks to suit motor

Elevation blocks, ¾ x 6 x 11

45°

Acme screw

Thrust bearing

Detail A: Elevation mechanism and arbor carriage

Carriage top, 1¾ x 8 x 19¾

Bearing block, ¾ x 6 x 6

45°

Carriage sides, 1¾ x 6 x 20½

Stress panel

Carriage bottom, 1¾ x 8 x 18¼

Cross member, 1 x 4 x 18⅜

Detail B: Clamping mechanism and mounted carriage rails

1½

½

45°

Carriage guide rail

Carriage thrust rail, ½ x 1½ x 27

Slides, ¾ x 6 x 15

Clamp bar, 1 x 7 x 18⅜

Jamb nut and washer

T-nut

Base construction

Guide-rail mounting board

18

¾ x 26 x 48

1³⁄₁₆ x 6 x 48

A

B

Chip cleanout door

1³⁄₁₆ x 8 x 26

1³⁄₁₆ x 27¼ x 48

¾ x 10 x 48

1³⁄₁₆ x 20 x 28

Cutout for auxiliary arbor

Hole for elevation screw

Holes for clamp bar screws

Table assemblies

Crosscut fence, 2 x 2 x 29

Alignment dowels

Sliding table top, ¾ x 21 x 27

Fence, 3 x 3 x 28

Main table top, ¾ x 26 x 36

Main table frame, ¾ x 2½

Auxiliary table top, ¾ x 12 x 20

¾ x 19 x 30

Fence T-head, 1¼ x 3 x 12

Fence guide rail, 1³⁄₁₆ x 2¼ x 37

Fence rail, 1½ x 5 x 37

Guide rail, 54 in. long

¾ x 11½ x 30

Auxiliary table sides, ¾ x 10 x 16

¾ x 17 x 18½

Upper guides

Table guide arm, 1 x 3 x 26

Dowel and T-nut holes for auxiliary table lower position

Guide-rail end view

30°

15°

2½

3

1³⁄₁₆

Lower guide

Baseboard, ¾ x 3½

All table tops are plastic-laminate-covered particleboard.

104

boards such as MD44 could also be used. Particleboard has one quality that cast iron can't match: it muffles the piercing, high-frequency whines that are rough on the ears. I don't recommend the lower-density particleboards sold for a song as shelving at the local discount lumberyard, because their larger particles are bound together with less adhesive, making them weaker and more difficult to join reliably.

Building the saw—As figure 1 shows, the saw consists of a particleboard cabinet that houses the motor, arbor and arbor-raising mechanism. A second particleboard cabinet—built in the form of a box-beam for strength and rigidity—supports the sliding table. The two are screwed and glued together to form a T-shaped pedestal that enhances the saw's stability by spreading its 400 lb. over a wider area than a cast-iron saw would occupy. I built my cabinets out of 1³⁄₁₆-in. and ³⁄₄-in. particleboard joined with glue and screws. Where possible, I reinforced the corner joints with glue blocks. If you want a lighter, more portable saw, build the cabinets out of plywood. Five-eighths to ³⁄₄-in. plywood should be rigid enough.

The blade is lowered and raised by the arbor carriage (figure 2), a box-like frame made of 1³⁄₄-in. thick hard maple glued and doweled together. Both the motor and the arbor bearings are bolted to the carriage, whose vertical travel is guided by two rails—one V-shaped guide rail and one flat thrust rail—screwed to the back of the saw cabinet. It's raised by two wedge-shaped elevation blocks that bear against similarly shaped blocks glued to the sides of the carriage. To operate the elevation mechanism, I chose a ⁵⁄₈-in. Acme-thread veneer-press screw. I discarded the swivel end and bought a flange-mounted ball thrust bearing at the hardware store. A small shoulder made by filing down the diameter of the veneer screw transfers the thrust to the screw's threaded collar, which is mounted on the raising mechanism.

I mounted the vertical carriage guide-rails first, then built the carriage frame, installing a ³⁄₄-in. plywood stress panel inside it to keep it square. I lapped the V-rail into the guide by moving the carriage back and forth over a sheet of sandpaper taped to the rail, a method that also works for the sliding-table guides, as shown in the photo on p. 107. Thickness the flat carriage rail so that the edges of the top and bottom members of the carriage are about parallel to the back of the saw cabinet. If the carriage rocks on the guides, plane a bit of wood off the flat rail to correct the problem.

I originally designed the arbor carriage to include the clamp bar shown in the drawings but not in the saw photographed for this article. The bar will lock the carriage firmly in place, but I never installed it. The machine works fine for sawing and drilling, but the carriage assembly vibrates when slot-mortising. The clamp would probably cure this. One other variation between the drawings and photos: I've drawn the V-shaped carriage rail on the sliding-table side of the saw rather than the other way around, as shown in the photos. Due to the motor location, the carriage's center of gravity is on the sliding-table side, and positioning the rails this way should give the carriage better balance and smoother action.

The arbor spins in two 1-in. ID, self-aligning, cast-iron pillow blocks bolted to the top of the arbor carriage, as shown in the photo at right. I turned my arbor shaft according to

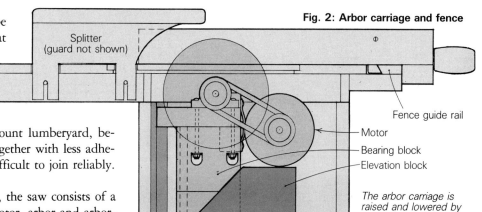

Splitter (guard not shown)

Fence guide rail

Motor

Bearing block

Elevation block

The arbor carriage is raised and lowered by the wedging action of the elevation blocks against the bearing blocks.

Thrust bearing

Elevating screw is ⁵⁄₈-in., Acme-thread veneer-press screw.

Arbor carriage

Stress panel

Arbor detail

0.625-in. dia., 12-TPI, left-hand Acme thread

3-in. dia. dished washer

Blade

0.875-in. ID, 3-in. OD cast-iron pulley keyed to shaft

Thread or Jacobs taper to suit chuck

Machine this face true as assembly.

To suit pillow block

1¼ in. to 1¾ in.

Fillets

1½   1½   19¾

Fence-dog detail

Bolt is kept from turning by steel pin passed through it.

Dog pivots on dowel.

T-nut

Knob

Washer

Fence guide rail

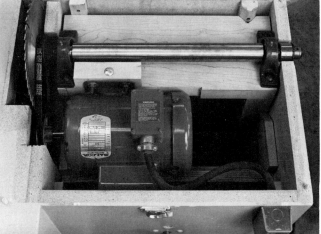

A V-shaped guide rail and a flat thrust rail steady vertical travel of the arbor carriage. For better balance, the V- and thrust rails should be reversed, as in figure 1.

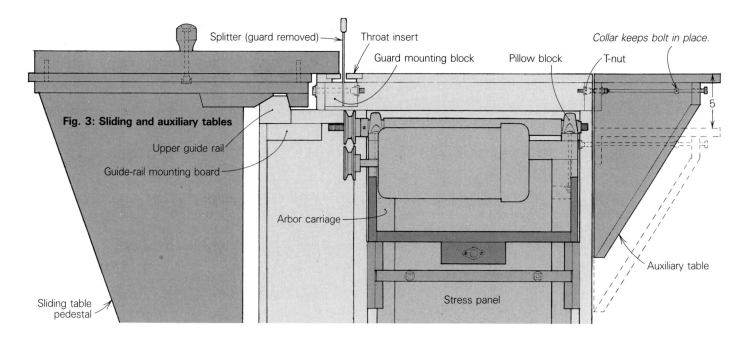

Splitter (guard removed) — | Throat insert | *Collar keeps bolt in place.*
Guard mounting block | Pillow block | T-nut

Fig. 3: Sliding and auxiliary tables

Upper guide rail

Guide-rail mounting board

Arbor carriage

Auxiliary table

Sliding table pedestal

Stress panel

the detail in figure 2. Machine the arbor out of stress-proof steel rather than mild steel. To keep stress risers from developing at the inside corners where the shaft diameter is turned down, have the machinist leave small fillets at these points. The auxiliary end of my arbor is machined to take a screw-on chuck, but if you do much slot-mortising, I suggest that you install a collet instead.

Once the arbor shaft has been machined so that the bearings and pulley are a light press fit, these parts can be installed, and the face of the pulley remachined to serve as the blade flange. The pulley must be either cast iron or solid machined steel, not stamped steel or die-cast white metal.

When it's time to calibrate the saw, you can shift the pillow blocks in their slotted holes to align the blade parallel to the sliding table's travel. Insert sheet-metal shims under one of the pillow blocks to square the blade to the table surface.

The motor is bolted to two blocks glued and doweled to the arbor carriage. I used a 1½-HP, fully-enclosed, fan-cooled motor. Since my saw is connected to a large dust-collection system, there's plenty of air swirling around to cool the motor. If dust collection isn't used, cut some cooling slots in the side of the saw cabinet.

The sliding table—The most critical assembly is the sliding table and its guide rails. The table consists of a triangular particleboard pedestal to which the two guide arms are attached. As the photo on p. 103 shows, the sliding table simply hangs on the upper guide rail, and it can be lifted off when it's not needed. The upper rail should be laminated, sawn to the cross-sectional shape shown in figure 1, and jointed true. The upper-rail mounting board, a 1½-in. thick maple plank glued beneath the top of the sliding-table cabinet, should also be machined true so that it won't bow the rail when it's attached. I glued the upper rail to the saw with a "paper joint" like that used in bowlturning, so it can be removed for remachining or for replacement. It's also bolted, since that was the most convenient way to clamp the glueline.

The sliding table's upper guides are glued and doweled to the arms, and positioned so that the guides rest on the inclined surfaces of the rail, leaving a small clearance gap between the underside of the arm and the top surface of the rail, as shown in the drawing above. This space is important—it

ensures that the guides will ride on the angled surfaces of the rail and it allows for wear. To make two identical arms and guides, I fabricated them as one assembly 6 in. wide, then ripped them in half to make two pieces 3 in. wide.

With the arms glued and screwed to the sliding-table pedestal, the assembly can be hung on the machine. The table's lower guide rides against the saw's baseboard (thrust rail), a member whose thickness must be adjusted so that the top of the sliding table will remain in the same plane as the main table throughout its travel. True up the table travel by trial and error, planing a taper on the baseboard if necessary. Lap the table guides to the rail, one at a time, using the sandpaper method described earlier and pictured on the facing page. Fit properly, the guides will push sawdust in front of them rather than packing it up into clods that will hinder smooth travel of the table.

Final assembly—The saw's main table is made of ¾-in. particleboard screwed to a frame that sits atop the saw cabinet, aligned by dowels and held fast by two draw latches. With the latches popped open, the saw table can be lifted off and the arbor carriage removed for maintenance and cleaning, an operation that requires no tools. To keep the sliding and main tables in vertical alignment, I equalized the effects of seasonal movement by orienting the annual rings in the guide rail horizontally and those in the main table frame vertically.

The auxiliary table, attached to the saw with dowels and bolts threaded into T-nuts (figure 3), has only two positions: flush with the main table (where it supports extra-long or wide stock), and 5 in. below the main table (for drilling or mortising). To create a smooth, durable surface, I covered all three tables with white plastic laminate. Make sure that the tables are in proper alignment before you cover them.

I strongly recommend that this and any tablesaw be equipped with a blade guard, a splitter or riving knife, and anti-kickback pawls. My guard assembly is from an old Rockwell Unisaw. It's bolted to a block glued to the inside of the main table frame. To adjust the knife in line with the blade, I inserted thin metal shims between the guard and the mounting block.

I prefer a fence whose length ends just before the splitter. This type of fence is less likely to cause a kickback, because

G. Winchip

With sandpaper taped to the guide rail, the table guides can be lapped to a perfect fit.

once the wood has been pushed past the blade's cutting edge, it won't bind against the back of the blade. For stability and ease of fabrication, I made the fence out of three pieces of oak laminated to the 3-in. finished thickness. The fence is glued and doweled to a T-head, and it's locked in place with the wooden dog mechanism shown in the detail in figure 2. I relieved the T-head so that it bears against the fence guide rail on just two points. By planing a small amount of material from one of these contact points, I can make coarse adjustments in the fence so that it's parallel to the blade. Finer adjustments can be made by planing a slight taper on the fence guide rail.

The crosscut fence is fastened to the sliding table by dowels and a bolt threaded into a T-nut. Make some test cuts with the fence clamped in place, and once you've got a perfect 90° cut, drill for the dowels and bolt the fence down. Adjust it later by planing a taper on its front side.

With the saw built and calibrated, you can paint the particleboard with an oil-based primer, followed by a coat or two of enamel paint. I finished the solid wood parts with Watco oil and then paste-waxed the sliding parts.

Aside from the lower cost (about $300 for this saw), I've found that the greatest advantage to building my own machines has been scaling their features to meet my needs. On this saw, for example, the tables could be made larger, or the crosscut capacity made greater, by lengthening the guide rails and supporting pedestal. My machine accommodates a 10-in. blade, but the design could be modified to accept a 12-in. blade and perhaps a 3-HP motor.

The machine described here has been in use now for 2½ years at the Iowa State University woodworking shop, a high-abuse place if there ever was one. So far, it has required only routine cleaning and lubrication, plus an occasional tightening of the arbor mounting bolts. In our shop we have two other saws, a 10-in. Rockwell Unisaw and a 14-in., 5-HP Oliver. Often these two machines sit idle while students wait in line to use the wooden saw. They tell me that its smoothness of operation, its adaptability to jig-work and its amiable disposition make it a more pleasant tool to use. □

Galen Winchip teaches woodworking and computer-aided manufacturing at Iowa State University at Ames.

Testing the wooden saw

When I flew out to Iowa this spring to try Winchip's wooden tablesaw, I had in mind comparing it to the sliding-table-equipped Rockwell Unisaw I've owned for three years. Having heard student raves about the wooden saw, I wasn't surprised to find it nicer on a couple of counts.

I did some ripping first, immediately discovering that the fence on Winchip's saw works better than the Unisaw's does. It's easier to position and clamp without the opposite end hopping out of alignment, as a lot of factory metal fences always seem to do, even on relatively expensive saws.

Apart from their size and construction material, I discovered the major difference between these two saws when I tried some crosscuts. With a couple of 8-ft. long, 15-in. wide panels on the sliding table, it took some muscle to make the cut—about the same effort you'd exert opening a heavy door. By contrast, the Unisaw table will slide one-handed. Although it's stiffer, the wooden table has no play and seemed more predictable than its steel counterpart, passing over the guide rail with an even swish instead of the clatter of steel on steel. A half-dozen crosscuts I checked were about 0.003 in. out of square across a 15-in. wide board. That's okay by my standards; slicing it finer calls for hunting down the renegade mils with a hand plane, a task that I suspect is no less frustrating than tickling the many adjusters on a steel table. I think Winchip is right about the guides' self-adjusting aspect, so the wooden saw should need less attention than a steel one.

The arbor carriage works as effortlessly as any I've used. Not having it tilt is a shortcoming I can live with, if only because it costs a thousand bucks less. The guard on this saw is a gem. It pivots handily out of the way for fence-setting, and it can be removed and, most importantly, reinstalled in seconds. I didn't much like the horizontal boring/mortising feature, though. For boring, 4500 RPM is too fast, and without a fence to guide it, impaling a chunk of wood on the bit is scary. Adding the clamp bar and a larger auxiliary table to accommodate fences and clamp jigs would help, especially for slot-mortising. I'd make two other changes: the sliding-table guide rail needs to be 2 in. longer, so that a full 24-in. wide panel can be crosscut, and a 3-HP motor would provide the extra power the saw needs to rip thick stock quickly, something it can't do with the smaller motor. —*Paul Bertorelli*

Winchip crosscuts two 15-in. wide panels on his wooden tablesaw.

P. Krumhardt

Repairing Bandsaw Blades
And how to make up your own from bulk rolls

You don't need welding equipment to braze narrow bandsaw blades. A propane torch can generate enough heat, and silver solder is strong enough for a good joint. Any small shop can deal with the nuisance of a broken blade by repairing it on the spot. And if bandsawing is a daily operation in your shop, you can save money by buying blades in bulk rolls. This also lets you choose from a variety of widths and teeth, some of which aren't generally available in made-up blades. One commercial supplier, DoAll (254 N. Laurel, Des Plaines, Ill. 60016), sells a skip-tooth, ¼-in. blade in 100-ft. rolls. Cut and soldered, each blade ends up costing about $3, and the entire process takes little longer than sharpening and honing a dull tool.

Bandsaw blades break for a variety of reasons. Sometimes a sharp, new blade will snap when you trap it by trying to saw too tight a curve, or when you skew the work. You can repair

Fig. 1: Scarf joint

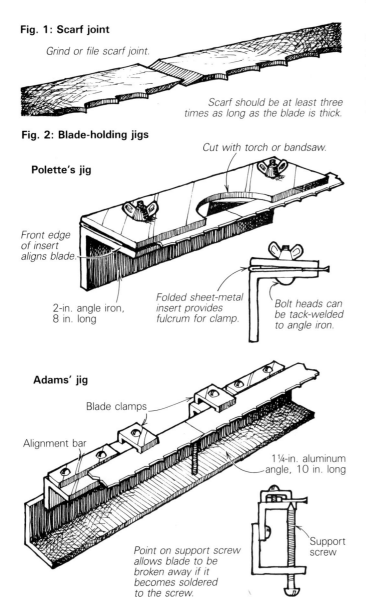

Grind or file scarf joint.

Scarf should be at least three times as long as the blade is thick.

Fig. 2: Blade-holding jigs

Cut with torch or bandsaw.

Polette's jig

Front edge of insert aligns blade.

2-in. angle iron, 8 in. long

Folded sheet-metal insert provides fulcrum for clamp.

Bolt heads can be tack-welded to angle iron.

Adams' jig

Blade clamps

Alignment bar

1¼-in. aluminum angle, 10 in. long

Point on support screw allows blade to be broken away if it becomes soldered to the screw.

Support screw

this type of break successfully, but fixing other kinds of breaks may be a waste of time. A dull blade, for instance, will break if it's pushed too hard, but repairing it won't be worthwhile unless you can sharpen it too (see facing page). Older blades, even ones that are still sharp, sometimes break because they've gotten brittle through work-hardening, having been flexed over the saw's wheels a few times too many. These blades aren't worth fixing either, because it's likely that they'll soon break in another spot.

You can probably buy silver solder and a compatible flux at the local hardware store, but be sure that it's about 45% silver with a melting point near 1100°F, or it will bead up on the blade without flowing. You'll need to make a holding jig (figure 2) from angle iron or scrap metal to position the ends of the blade while you solder it. The jig can be tucked away when you're not using it, then clamped in your bench vise when you need it.

Soldering metal is akin to gluing wood: success depends more on the fit of the parts than on the strength of the bonding material. Attempting to bridge an open joint with solder won't work. For this reason, the scarf joint (figure 1) should be a perfect fit and carefully aligned. First heat the blade ends red with the torch, then cool them slowly to soften the steel. The surfaces of the scarf should be at least three times as long as the blade is thick. The ends to be joined can be shaped on a bench grinder—either freehand or with a simple guide block—or they can be filed. One trick that ensures a matching joint is to lay one blade end over the other and bevel them both at the same time. The operation is easier than putting a bevel on a chisel, so use whatever method suits you.

Metal, like wood, must be clean for a good joint. Some low-temperature solders are hollow, and contain acid for cleaning the metal, making soldering a one-step operation. But high-temperature silver solders require a separate flux that is formulated to work with a particular solder's alloy and melting temperature. Flux performs several functions: when heated, it chemically cleans the metal, helps the solder flow and speeds heat conduction. Vapors from flux are very irritating, and some solders give off toxic fumes, so provide ventilation. Apply the flux to the scarf surfaces before you heat the joint. You can trap a flattened piece of cold solder in the scarf, or you can preheat the blade and drip solder onto it. If you drip the solder, it is not enough merely to melt it—you must get the blade itself hot enough to cause the solder to flow thinly over the metal and into the scarf.

As in gluing wood, the joint should be held tight while the solder sets. One jig, left, has a built-in adjustable screw support. Immediately after the initial soldering, you press down on the scarf with a screwdriver tip and reheat the joint until the solder flows. As an alternative that does without the screw, you can design the jig so you can grip the joint with a pair of pliers to clamp it and cool the molten solder. A traditional method requires brazing tongs (similar to blacksmiths' tongs). Set up the scarf with flux and cold solder, then grab

(continued on p. 110)

Bandsaw-blade sharpening jig

by Robert Meadow

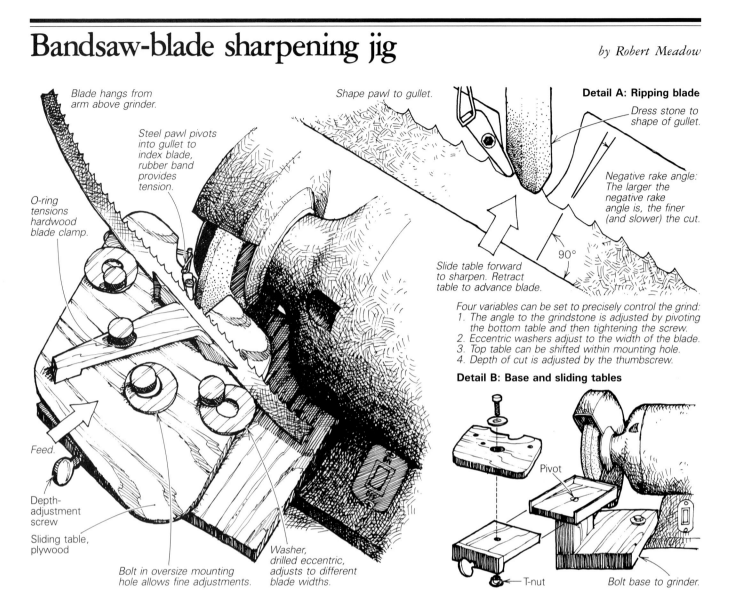

Blade hangs from arm above grinder.

Steel pawl pivots into gullet to index blade, rubber band provides tension.

O-ring tensions hardwood blade clamp.

Feed.

Depth-adjustment screw

Sliding table, plywood

Bolt in oversize mounting hole allows fine adjustments.

Washer, drilled eccentric, adjusts to different blade widths.

Shape pawl to gullet.

Detail A: Ripping blade

Dress stone to shape of gullet.

Negative rake angle: The larger the negative rake angle is, the finer (and slower) the cut.

90°

Slide table forward to sharpen. Retract table to advance blade.

Four variables can be set to precisely control the grind:
1. The angle to the grindstone is adjusted by pivoting the bottom table and then tightening the screw.
2. Eccentric washers adjust to the width of the blade.
3. Top table can be shifted within mounting hole.
4. Depth of cut is adjusted by the thumbscrew.

Detail B: Base and sliding tables

Pivot

T-nut

Bolt base to grinder.

Factory-fresh bandsaw blades leave a lot to be desired if you want to resaw slices thin enough for veneer or for instruments such as the lutes I build. The teeth are usually uneven, and they are sharpened to points like a crosscut or a combination blade, not square across like a ripping blade, which is the best shape for resawing. I built a sharpening rig that attaches to a standard bench grinder, adjusts to blades of various widths, and sharpens blades for ripping, with a slight negative rake and square-faced teeth. This not only improves a new blade, it greatly prolongs its life—the blade can be resharpened many times. I can adjust the mechanism and sharpen a 6-ft. blade in about 10 minutes. It will then cut slices that come off the flitch looking like they've already been sanded with 40-grit paper.

The setup is made from scrap and a few pieces of hardware. No doubt you can adapt a similar design for a dollar or two. The only real expense is the Nor-bide dressing stick used to shape the stone to match the gullets of the blade. That cost me $27.

The rig almost builds itself. First, attach the flat plywood base to your grinder. Next, choose your favorite blade, turn it inside out, and use the Norbide stick to true the grindstone to the shape of one of its gullets, or use the gullet shape shown in the drawing. Then, with the grinder turned off, line up the blade so that the stone fits the gullet—this will show you the height of the post, the angle at which the blade should be clamped and the angle at which the sliding table will have to move. The outside washers on the sliding table act as cams. They can be adjusted to different-width blades, and can also be used to change the sharpening angle slightly. Fine adjustments can be made by loosening the central bolt and shifting the upper layer of the sliding table. At the back of the sliding table, a thumbscrew controls the depth of cut.

The steel pawl, tensioned by a rubber band, indexes the blade. It pivots and clicks into each successive gullet as you slide the blade into position to sharpen the next tooth. When you reach the weld in the blade, you can just grind that tooth shorter freehand if the spacing is uneven. If you have a variety of blades with different-size teeth, you'll find it best to have interchangeable grindstones and pawls to fit.

I'm delighted with the results this gadget produces and I'm sorry I didn't make it years ago. It has had only one drawback so far: A friend of mine had been complaining that his 14-in. Rockwell bandsaw was too underpowered to resaw 12-in. stock. I made him an offer for the saw, then made the mistake of sharpening a blade for him. He promptly cancelled the sale. □

Robert Meadow runs The Luthierie, an instrument-making and woodworking school in Saugerties, N.Y.

Drawings: Jim Richey

the joint with the red-hot tongs. This activates the flux, melts the solder and clamps the joint all in one step. You can even get away with not clamping by taking advantage of the springiness of the blade. Align the scarf joint in the holder, then bend the ends of the blade until the joint is tight.

If you heat and cool the metal too quickly, it will be brittle. Manufacturers—who weld blades with an intense shot of electricity—reheat the joint at a lower voltage so it will cool slowly. But if the joint cools too slowly, the metal around the joint will be too soft. Conditions will vary depending on your torch, your solder, how you clamp and the speed at which you work. It's best to make a few practice repairs. Try to bend each joint. If the metal is too hard, it will snap. The remedy is to cool the joint more slowly. The blacksmiths'

tongs do this automatically, but cold pliers will probably leave the blade brittle. In this case, heating the joint with the torch until it turns the same blue color as the rest of the blade will temper it to the correct degree of spring. If the metal is too soft, it won't have any spring, and will bend easily. In this case, cool the joint more quickly.

After the solder has set, file away any excess from the sides and back of the blade—only the solder in the joint itself contributes to the strength of the bond. □

This article was compiled from information contributed by three woodworkers: Wash Adams, from Richardson, Tex.; Doug Polette, a professor at Montana State University in Bozeman; and John Leeke, of Sanford, Maine.

Japanese Resaws
Two small machines with big blades

by Rich Preiss

Resawing is a superb technique for getting the most out of your wood. You can slice thick planks to near their finished size and thereby lessen the amount of lumber that gets chewed up by the surface planer. After planing, resawn planks can be bookmatched to reveal attractive figure. Yet in many shops, resawing is difficult work. Large industrial bandsaws that do this task effortlessly are expensive and bulky; the smaller machines that shine at fine scrollwork bog down when you feed wide, thick stock into them. Two highly specialized bandsaws from Makita and Hitachi, two of Japan's best-known tool manufacturers, might resolve this dilemma.

These machines, which are scaled-down versions of the industrial bandmills that convert heavy logs to lumber, have been on the American market for three years now. Equipped with wide, coarse blades and geared motors, they are designed specifically for resawing. I borrowed one of each machine—a Makita 2116 and a Hitachi B600A—and tested them in my shop. I tried cutting all kinds of stock, from hard rosewood to softer oak and walnut. I used the machines for both resawing and ripping, and found that they did these tasks quickly and accurately.

The Makita costs about $1,936; the Hitachi, about $2,420 (figures vary, so shop around)—relatively high prices for bandsaws of this size, but a fraction of what you would pay for an industrial bandsaw that will resaw as well. I resawed boards up to 12 in. wide, dimensioned heavy timber and ripped boards to finished widths. I even resawed my own 1/16-in. thick veneer from wide boards, a job I wouldn't attempt with a standard bandsaw. This veneer was practically ready to use straight from the saw, requiring very little subsequent planing.

When I uncrated the saws, I was surprised at their small dimensions. Unlike other bandsaws that have base cabinets to elevate the table to a standard 40-in. working height, these resaws are designed for use at 29 in. to 30 in. This looked

odd to me at first, until I realized that it means you don't have to hoist large timbers or heavy boards to chest height, balancing them precariously during the cut. Of course, you still have the option of blocking the resaw to any height, but I found that I soon got more comfortable working over the material instead of behind it.

A second unusual feature of these machines is the seemingly small size of the motors. But these high-speed motors run the saws' drive wheels through a geared transmission and pulley arrangement that gives enough torque for this kind of work. The 2-HP Makita motor, with its greater RPM, makes for a smoother cut, but will lag sooner than the slower, 3-HP Hitachi. If you rely on these saws continuously, or for extensive resawing of maximum-width boards, larger motors can readily be adapted to the universal mounting plates on these saws. Both seem built heavily enough to take more power, especially the Hitachi.

The real eye-opener on both machines is the width of the blade—2⅜ in. on the Makita and 2⅞ in. on the Hitachi. The blades have swage-cut teeth tipped with Stellite, an alloy harder than steel but softer than carbide. The tips are fused to a thin blade body, resulting in a highly tensionable blade that cuts a narrow kerf. At $55 for the Makita and $75 for the Hitachi, these blades are expensive. But they run cool and should last a while. You can resharpen them once or twice by hand with a file, but when they get really dull, you'll have to take them to a sharpening shop equipped to grind Stellite.

The guides on both saws are conventional friction-type blocks made of Bakelite. They are as wide as the blade, and about ⅜ in. thick, with the middle section relieved so that the blade will run cooler. Both have thrust bearings behind the blade, but the Hitachi's bearings run in line with rather than at right angles to the blade axis—an unusual arrangement I'd never seen before, but one that seemed to work fine.

I preferred the Makita's blade-adjustment mechanism, es-

Photos: Cathy Preiss

Both resaws tested (Makita, left, and Hitachi, right, in the photo above) are surprisingly small. The saw tables are about 30 in. above the floor, a working height that makes it easier to balance the kind of heavy timber these machines are designed to cut. Blade guides are similar to those of conventional saws. The Makita 2116, top left, has two Bakelite guides adjusted with wing nuts. Those of the Hitachi B600A, bottom left, are similar, though slightly heftier. These saws will cut boards up to 12 in. wide; in the photo at right, Preiss uses the Hitachi to slice a 1/16-in. thick piece of veneer off a wide plank.

pecially the tracking control, which stays put without having to tighten an additional locknut, as on the Hitachi. The upper guides and thrust bearing on the Makita saw are fixed to a solid block, and are simpler to adjust than the Hitachi's, whose base tends to tilt when loosened.

I found quite a few other differences between these two machines. The wheel shafts and bearings on the Hitachi saw are about 50% larger than on the Makita. And like most industrial machines, the Hitachi has adjustable gibs on the upper blade-tensioning ways, enabling fine adjustment for future wear. The Makita lacks this feature, but I'm not sure it makes much difference to the average user anyway; nevertheless, it's a nice touch that's better to have than not. The Hitachi frame is made of fabricated steel, but is about 40 lb. heavier than the cast-iron Makita. The weight difference has little bearing on performance, though—either saw is stable enough to do what's expected of it.

Both saws are equipped with fences whose length ends at the front edge of the blade. The Makita's fence cleverly swings clear of the table, and it includes a vernier fine-adjustment control, two features that speed the work when you have to set up the saw several times a day. The stubbier Hitachi fence, however, locks more firmly and deflects less noticeably under feed pressure. In addition, it has a coarser rack-and-pinion adjustment that won't clog and bind when filled with sawdust, a problem that made the Makita fence annoying to work with. The Hitachi also has a spring-steel hold-down that I found handy for holding boards against the fence. The Hitachi has another feature I liked: a manual brake that quickly stops the blade for safety and for speeding adjustments.

After working with these saws for more than a month, I can only conclude that, for me, they aren't an essential basic machine. I don't do enough resawing or timber-sizing to justify a machine devoted to just that one purpose. Since I tested these saws, Hitachi has redesigned its blade guides to accommodate narrower blades, and one Makita dealer has devised a kit to do the same thing, but I haven't tested either. For my money, these saws are best kept to resawing, leaving scroll-work for the lighter—and usually less expensive—saws designed for that job. If I did have the need for one of these saws, I'd pick the Hitachi, despite its higher price. This machine's heavier, more sophisticated construction and greater power make it more akin to the kind of industrial-quality machinery we would all buy if we could afford it.   □

Rich Preiss supervises the architectural woodworking shop at the University of North Carolina at Charlotte. Since this article was first published, the Makita 2116 has been discontinued; some dealers, however, may carry used models.

Miniatures by Machine
Three router-powered setups for precision cuts

by Herbert Consor

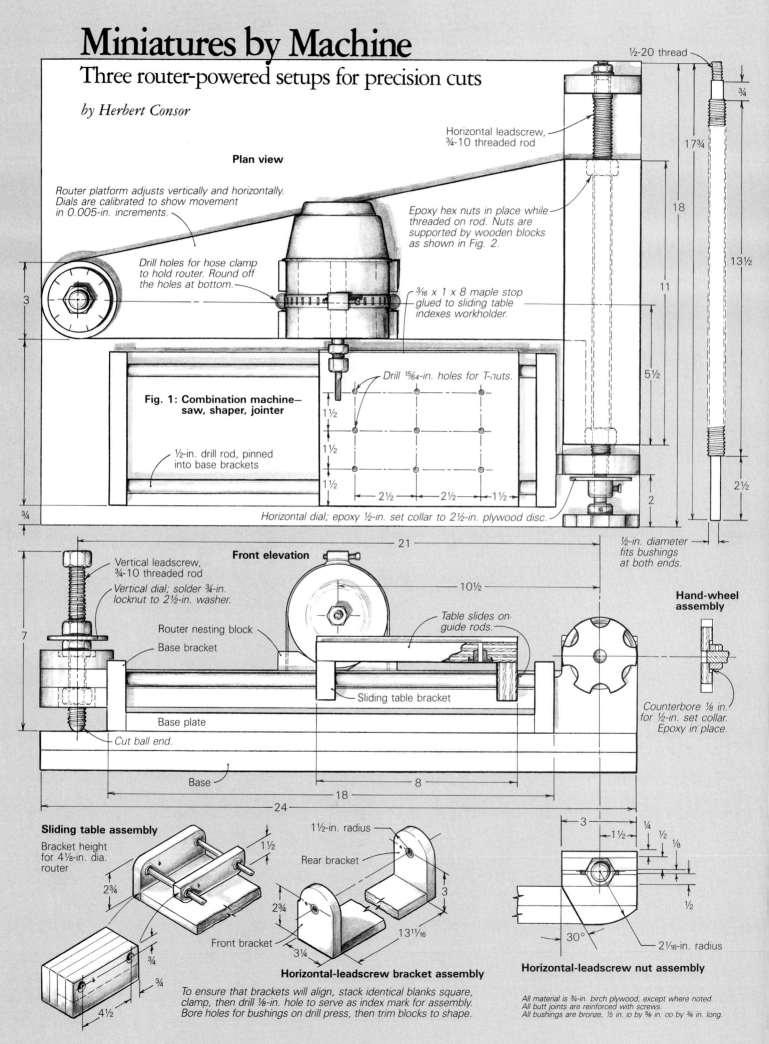

½-20 thread

Horizontal leadscrew, ¾-10 threaded rod

Plan view

Router platform adjusts vertically and horizontally. Dials are calibrated to show movement in 0.005-in. increments.

Drill holes for hose clamp to hold router. Round off the holes at bottom.

Epoxy hex nuts in place while threaded on rod. Nuts are supported by wooden blocks as shown in Fig. 2.

¾₆ x 1 x 8 maple stop glued to sliding table indexes workholder.

Drill ¹⁵⁄₆₄-in. holes for T-nuts.

Fig. 1: Combination machine— saw, shaper, jointer

½-in. drill rod, pinned into base brackets

Horizontal dial; epoxy ½-in. set collar to 2½-in. plywood disc.

½-in. diameter fits bushings at both ends.

Vertical leadscrew, ¾-10 threaded rod

Vertical dial; solder ¾-in. locknut to 2½-in. washer.

Front elevation

Router nesting block

Base bracket

Table slides on guide rods.

Hand-wheel assembly

Sliding table bracket

Counterbore ⅛ in. for ½-in. set collar. Epoxy in place.

Base plate

Cut ball end.

Base

Sliding table assembly

Bracket height for 4⅛-in. dia. router

1½-in. radius

Rear bracket

Front bracket

Horizontal-leadscrew bracket assembly

To ensure that brackets will align, stack identical blanks square, clamp, then drill ⅛-in. hole to serve as index mark for assembly. Bore holes for bushings on drill press, then trim blocks to shape.

30°

2¹⁄₁₆-in. radius

Horizontal-leadscrew nut assembly

All material is ¾-in. birch plywood, except where noted.
All butt joints are reinforced with screws.
All bushings are bronze, ½ in. ID by ⅝ in. OD by ¾ in. long.

Author's plans redrawn by Heather Brine

Despite having made a lot of full-scale and half-scale furniture, I found I was totally unprepared when I was first bitten by the $\frac{1}{12}$-size miniature bug. The techniques, equipment and measuring tools that had worked so well in the past just wouldn't cut the mustard. So I designed three router-powered machines for precision work: a combination machine (saw, shaper and jointer), a duplicating lathe, and a miniature pin router. Any one of them might prove just as useful for a woodworker making small, precise, full-scale parts.

Close cutting—A miniaturist has to work to precise dimensions or the piece just won't look right. So that I don't have to deal with unwieldy fractions, I convert measurements down to the nearest thousandth of an inch. In general, dimensions don't have to be machined *exactly,* but they should all be close. I usually work to the nearest 0.005 in., but sometimes closer. If each of the dimensions on the face of a typical cornice molding is enlarged by 0.005 in., for example, the equivalent full-scale error amounts to almost $\frac{1}{2}$ in. This is considerable, and just as such an error would ruin the looks of a full-scale piece, so will it ruin a miniature.

In designing the machines, I started out with some clear ideas about the problems they would have to cope with. Miniature parts, for instance, are too small to be safely held by hand. So as one of my first decisions, I borrowed the workholder idea from metalworking practices—the work would be rigidly clamped, and the cutter-to-workpiece relationship controlled by ways, leadscrews, cams, templates and stops.

I knew that normal cutting-tool forces could deflect, split or break the fragile parts. Supporting the work in the holder would partly prevent this, but I also wanted to minimize cutting forces. I accomplished this by allowing for very precise travel, and by using extremely high cutter speeds with controlled feed and depth-of-cut adjustments for taking light cuts. Despite my strong prejudice in favor of heavy cast-iron machinery, the tool forces are so low that the wooden construction of my machines hasn't led to problems.

In addition, I tried to design machines that required little precision metalworking to build. I don't have the equipment these days to do metal turning and milling, so I wanted to job out that work without spending a fortune. In the end, the total cost of outside work—machining the leadscrews and spindles—came to $40.

My three machines take care of all normal operations except drilling, rough-cutting and thicknessing. For the latter, a thickness sander is a must. Mine is an old belt sander rigged up with a sliding table. For the first two operations, I use conventional equipment.

Combination saw, shaper, jointer—The drawing on the facing page and the photo, below, will show you how this machine works. Its table, with various workholders attached, slides by hand on drill-rod support rods, and will carry a variety of workholders past the horizontally mounted router motor. Drill rod, instead of cold-rolled steel, offers greater stiffness, and its accurately ground surface makes a better fit and smoother movement in the bearings. The router's position can be accurately adjusted by means of the two leadscrews, one of which raises the platform the router is attached to, while the other moves the platform forward and back.

The two leadscrews are $\frac{3}{4}$-10 threaded rod with rolled thread instead of cut thread. You'll probably have to get them at an industrial supply house, but it's worth the trouble—the action is much smoother. Brass nuts make the action smoother still. One turn of the screws will move the embedded nuts $\frac{1}{10}$ in. (0.100 in.). Thus, on the horizontal leadscrew, an indicator dial with 20 divisions shows back-and-forth cutter movement in increments of 0.005 in. To allow vertical movement, the router platform pivots up and down on the horizontal leadscrew as the vertical leadscrew is

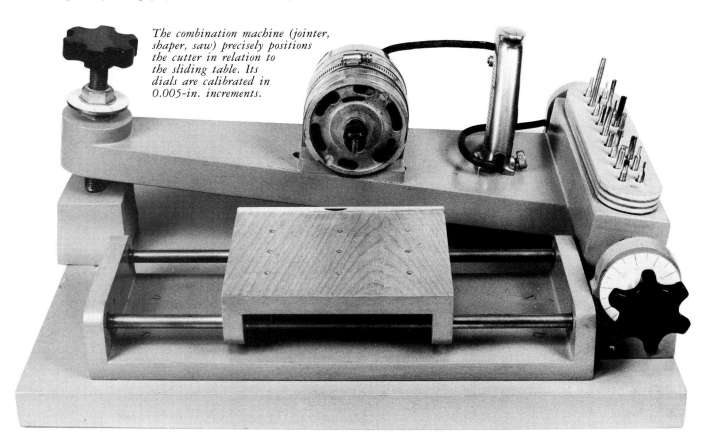

The combination machine (jointer, shaper, saw) precisely positions the cutter in relation to the sliding table. Its dials are calibrated in 0.005-in. increments.

The combination machine's router wears many hats, depending on which appliance is attached to its sliding table. Clockwise from above left, it performs as a shaper, making miniature moldings element by element in a series of passes; as a surface planer, tapering the sides of a pair of pedestal-table legs held in a workholder that maintains the correct taper angle; as a curved-molding shaper, with a pivoting workholder; and, below, as a tablesaw, with rip fence in place.

The tablesaw attachment, like the workholders, bolts to the sliding table's embedded T-nuts. Clamps, visible on the front guide rod, can either lock the table in place or restrict its movement for safety. In order not to extend the vertical leadscrew beyond the point of stability, Consor made various support blocks that raise the router platform higher than its normal operating range. When ripping, he pushes the work along the fence with the sliding table stationary. When crosscutting, he slides the table while the work is held against a stop block. For mitering, he sets up a stop block that holds the work at 45° to the blade.

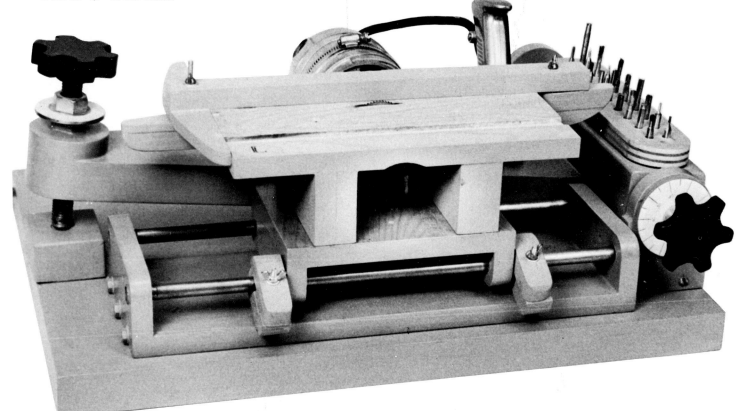

turned. Because the axis of the router is midway between the leadscrews, each full turn of the vertical leadscrew will move the router 0.050 in. up or down. Thus 10 divisions on the vertical leadscrew dial indicate increments of 0.005 in. Theoretically, the differing angles of the router platform introduce an error in the vertical dial reading, but the effect is inconsequential with the small angles involved.

As with most machine tools, different-size cutters preclude a fixed zero point. I bring the tool to a reference point on the workpiece, then shift to the exact cutting point by reading the dials. When I'm using the machine as a shaper (top left photo, facing page), this locating accuracy allows me to cut moldings one step at a time with straight and veining cutters. I round convex shapes by sanding them, or by grinding special cutters. You can freehand-grind one flute of a ¼-in. bit to shape, then grind clearance on the other (*FWW* #20, pp. 69-73). As in full-scale work, moldings are best cut on wide stock that is stiff and can be clamped. They are sawn off when finished. A tapered workholder allows me to duplicate tapered legs for one piece or for a production run. Circular moldings can be cut on a rotating jig, with the sliding table fixed so that the pivot point is at the centerline of the router.

To use the machine as a jointer, clamp the work to an attachment on the sliding table, and use the end of a ¼-in. bit to mill the edge of the work straight and smooth. It's similar to making a molding, but you make just one straight cut.

The tablesaw fixture, like most of the workholders, bolts to T-nuts in the sliding table, and it covers all but a few of the blade's teeth. After the ripping fence or cutoff gauges have been set for sawing, very exact final adjustments can be made within the width of the table slot by turning the dials.

Brackets ensure accuracy—Aside from the leadscrew adjustments, the accuracy of the machine depends on the table's traveling perpendicular to the router axis. In addition, the top face of the sliding table must be parallel to the router axis, and must not rise or fall as it moves from end to end. This alignment depends on the four brackets—two on the table itself and two on the base—that align the guide rods and the sliding table, as well as on the brackets that hold the horizontal leadscrew (figure 1). By carefully making and installing these brackets, you will achieve all the accuracy you can use.

To make the brackets, cut four identical plywood blocks, stack them flush and clamp them for drilling. Mark the stack (I drilled a small hole through it) so that you can align the blocks in the correct relationship when you set up the sliding-table assembly, then drill the holes on a drill press with a brad-point bit that will ensure a straight hole. I had planned to epoxy bronze bushings into the sliding brackets only where they are necessary to avoid wear, but I bought enough bushings from a local bearing-supply house for all the bracket holes. That way I could drill all the holes the same size and I didn't risk losing the centerline by changing bits. With this method, the spacing and relative heights of the holes will be the same in each set of blocks.

Trim the bottom of the two sliding-table brackets so they will clear the base, then mount them to the sliding table with the bushings, rods and base brackets assembled. Be sure that the table can slide freely. Epoxy the bushings to the brackets, then glue and screw the base brackets to the base, with the table and rods in place.

Use similar procedures for the horizontal leadscrew, but mount it so that its centerline is perpendicular to the guide rods. This alignment doesn't have to be absolutely accurate; you can rely on a carpenters' square to check it. Figure 2 shows details of some ways I mounted nuts on these machines.

After you have installed the router platform, mount the router nesting blocks so that the router axis is perpendicular to the front face of the sliding table. When this is done, use the machine itself to make a light cut on the edge of the sliding table; this will true it exactly to the line of travel of the table. I glued a thin maple strip to the trued face so that its edge projects slightly above the surface of the table. When I mount the workholders and fixtures shown in the photos, I just push them up against the strip to locate them in relation to the cutting line. This saves a lot of measuring time.

Duplicating lathe—Despite very fine cuts and a variety of tool shapes, I encountered problems in turning slender table legs and bedposts with a small metalworking lathe. Deflec-

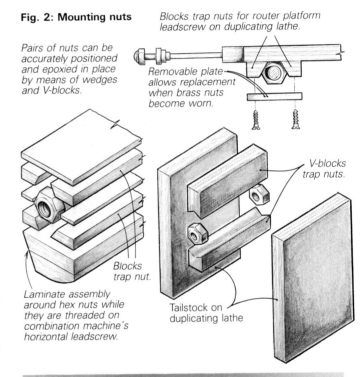

Fig. 2: Mounting nuts

Blocks trap nuts for router platform leadscrew on duplicating lathe.

Pairs of nuts can be accurately positioned and epoxied in place by means of wedges and V-blocks.

Removable plate allows replacement when brass nuts become worn.

V-blocks trap nuts.

Blocks trap nut.

Laminate assembly around hex nuts while they are threaded on combination machine's horizontal leadscrew.

Tailstock on duplicating lathe

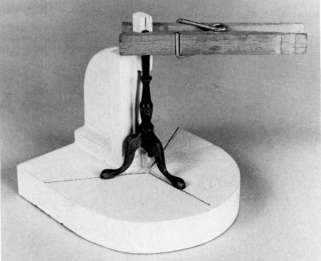

Miniatures not only need precision cutting, they call for special assembly fixtures for glue-up. The parts for this pedestal table are visible in mid-manufacture in some of the other photos.

tion of the workpiece caused out-of-round parts with non-uniform tapers and chewed-up surfaces. The template lathe, shown at right and below, cured these problems because it turns slowly, makes a light cut, and cuts mostly with the grain of the wood. In fact, the tool forces are so low that I don't usually need a steady rest or the tailstock support, and I routinely turn short parts down to as small as $\frac{1}{32}$ in. in diameter.

With this machine, the router platform is carried from end to end on a hand-cranked leadscrew. You can vary the speed of travel to suit the cut. The router pivots until the template follower meets the template.

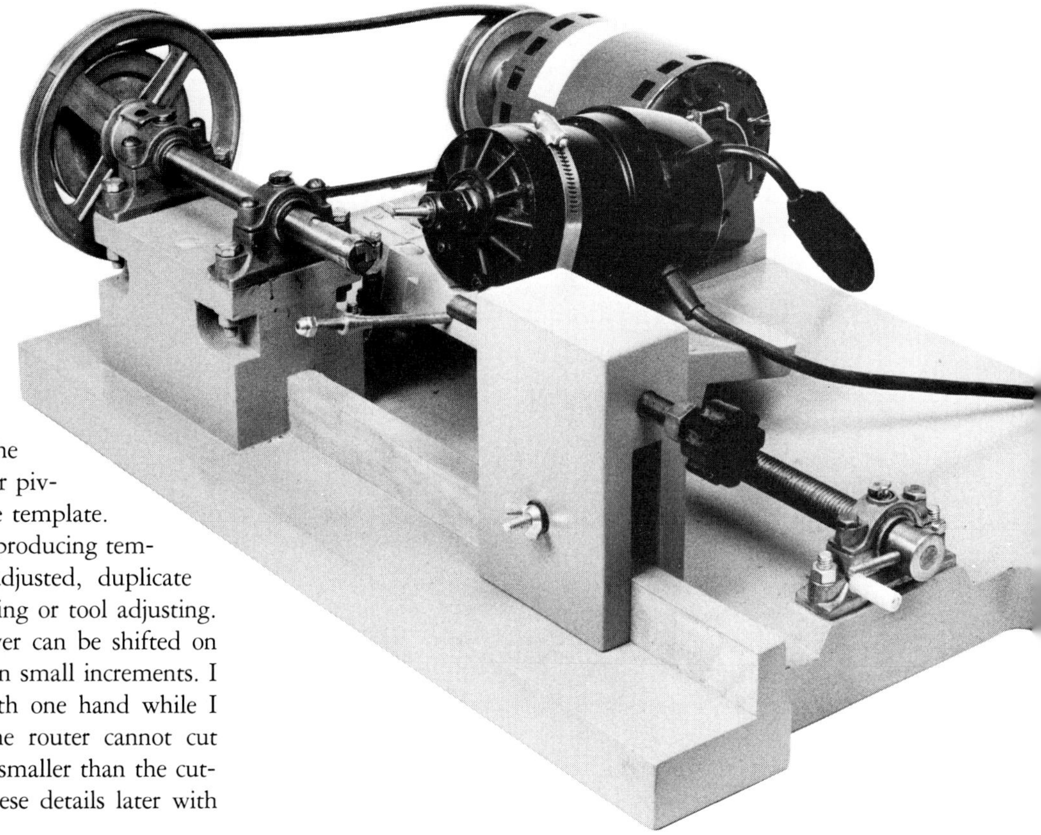

Figure 3 shows a method for quickly producing templates. Once the sliding wedges are adjusted, duplicate parts can be turned without any measuring or tool adjusting. A stepped spool on the template follower can be shifted on successive passes to cut the work down in small increments. I hold the spool against the template with one hand while I advance the router with the other. The router cannot cut sharp inside corners, or recesses that are smaller than the cutter diameter, but you can easily add these details later with needle files as the work rotates.

In construction of the lathe, no unusual precision is required. I mounted the pillow blocks for the headstock on a wood platform atop a block that I made from five vertical

Low cutting forces make this duplicating lathe ideal for turning fragile miniatures. The ¼-in. template follower, below, is fitted with a stepped spool that allows depth-of-cut to be gradually increased as the blank is cut down to final form.

Fig. 3: Lathe-template construction

The template is a series of ⅛-in. wide blocks glued to the top wedge. The height of each block can be figured from the table, below right.

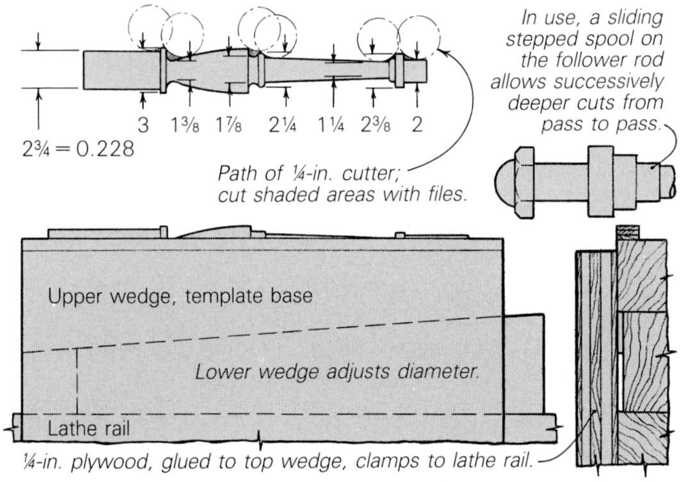

3 1⅜ 1⅞ 2¼ 1¼ 2⅜ 2
2¾ = 0.228
In use, a sliding stepped spool on the follower rod allows successively deeper cuts from pass to pass.
Path of ¼-in. cutter; cut shaded areas with files.
Upper wedge, template base
Lower wedge adjusts diameter.
Lathe rail
¼-in. plywood, glued to top wedge, clamps to lathe rail.

Fig. 4: Lathe spindles

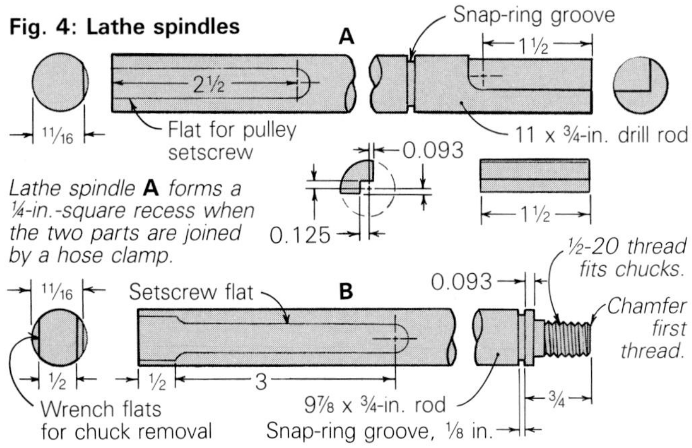

A
Snap-ring groove
1½
2½
11/16
Flat for pulley setscrew
11 x ¾-in. drill rod
0.093
Lathe spindle **A** forms a ¼-in.-square recess when the two parts are joined by a hose clamp.
0.125
1½
½-20 thread fits chucks.
0.093
11/16
Setscrew flat
B
Chamfer first thread.
½
½
3
¾
Wrench flats for chuck removal
9⅞ x ¾-in. rod
Snap-ring groove, ⅛ in.

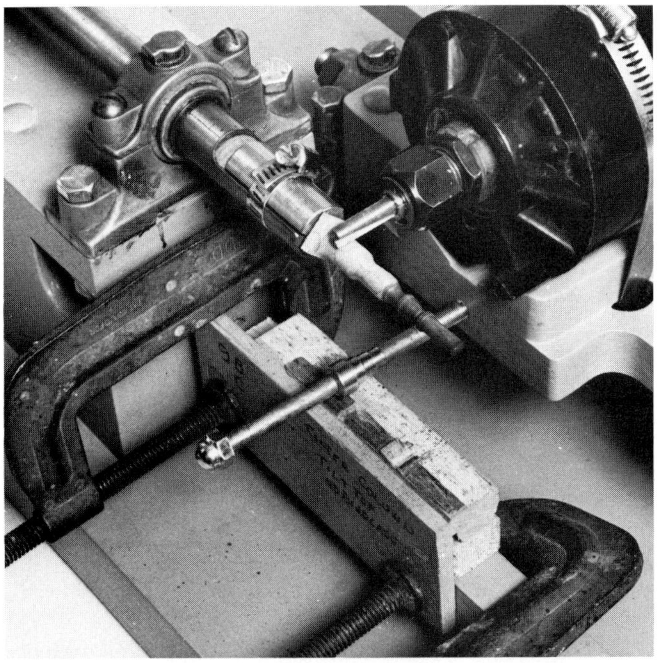

Template Heights

Diameter full-size	Radius full-size	Radius at 1/12 scale	Height above smallest radius
1¼	⅝	0.052	0
1⅜	11/16	0.057	0.005
1⅞	15/16	0.078	0.026
2	1	0.083	0.031
2¼	1⅛	0.093	0.041
2⅜	1 3/16	0.099	0.047
2¾	1⅜	0.114	0.062
3	1½	0.125	0.073

¾-in. thick pieces of wood laminated together. I left the center piece of the stack long to form the rail on which the tailstock rides, which is also the resting surface for the templates. To ensure that the template is parallel to the spindle, cut the top surface of the rail parallel to the top surface of the block.

First glue the headstock block and rail to the base. Then line up the pillow blocks: Take a 36-in. long, ¾-in. diameter drill rod (from which you will later make the spindles), insert it through the pillow blocks and sandwich it between two boards clamped to the sides of the rail. This ensures that the spindle is parallel to the rail. When everything lines up, epoxy the pillow blocks to the headstock block. Wait until the epoxy has set before you drill and bolt the pillow blocks.

The tailstock spindle is ½-20 threaded rod (which fits a standard ½-in. Jacobs chuck) running through two nuts epoxied into the tailstock (figure 2). The ¾-in. spindle in the headstock and the ½-in. threaded rod in the tailstock must line up exactly. Rather than attempting to line them up by measuring, I used the pillow blocks to register the height of the tailstock spindle. To do this, I supported a length of ½-in. threaded rod in the pillow blocks by means of two shopmade wood bushings. Centered by the pillow blocks, the threaded rod was thus in the correct position for the tailstock. I then threaded two nuts on the far end of the rod, and built up and epoxied the tailstock around the nuts.

The double-pulley drive provides speeds for low-speed turning as well as for high-speed sanding and filing. A simple, hinged motor mount provides quick belt-shifting.

The specific dimensions of the machine depend on the diameter of your router. In a horizontal position, the centerline of the router should be about ³⁄₁₆ in. above the spindle's centerline. The leadscrew should be at the router's center of gravity, so that the router's own weight will cause it to remain tilted up and out of the way when it isn't being controlled by hand.

The first spindle shown in figure 4 holds ¼-in. square stock. For smaller stock, use four shims for centering. For larger stock, cut down the surfaces to fit the chuck.

For offset turning, such as when making a cabriole leg, offset the end away from the chuck by inserting shims in the chuck. Brass shim stock or brass sheets obtained in auto supply stores will do nicely. Shim thickness may be determined by proportions or by trial.

A second headstock spindle is a ¾-in. rod threaded to receive a standard ½-in. drill chuck. This will handle dowels up to ½ in., which in full scale corresponds to 6-in. diameter work. This thread holds many small 3-jaw and 4-jaw chucks as well. For boring, use a chuck on the tailstock spindle.

Pin router—The photo, above right, shows my pin router, which cuts small-scale, complex shapes of the sort that you would bandsaw in full-scale work. The machine is an inverted form of the normal pin router, which has the pin in the table and the router suspended overhead on an arm. Inverting the design simplifies construction and improves visibility.

On any pin router, a pin and a bit, usually the same size, are aligned on the same axis. In use, the pin contacts the edge of a template (to which the work is clamped), and the bit cuts the work to the template's exact size and contour as you move it around the pin. In small-scale work, the template acts as a workholder as well, helping to support fragile stock. A typical template is shown in figure 5.

This inverted pin router allows better visibility for small-scale work. Bit and pin can be varied according to the work.

Fig. 5: Pin-router workholder

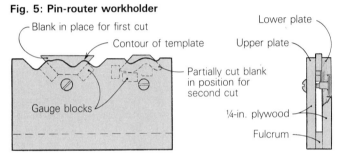

The upper plate is the template that bears against the pin; the bottom plate serves only to clamp the work to the upper plate. Gauge blocks, mounted to the bottom of the upper plate, locate the work in the sandwich. To concentrate clamping pressure at the cut and to minimize tear-out or splitting, put clamp screws and recessed T-nuts as close as practical to the cut, and make the fulcrum slightly thicker than the work.

Once you have carefully laid out and cut a template, you can make any number of duplicate shapes. This is a great timesaver for the preliminary cutting of Queen Anne legs, pedestal table legs (such as the ones in the photos on pp. 114 and 115) and other repeat patterns. Make the base and table, then install the router. The pin's height must be adjustable, to suit stock and template variations, and the pin must be removable, so that you can change router bits. I drilled a ¼-in. hole through a cap nut so that the pin would be a snug sliding fit, then installed a setscrew that would lock the pin's height. To support the pin above the router, I cut a sheet-metal holder and locked the cap nut to it with a jam nut beneath. With the pin through the cap nut and its end chucked in the router—to align it—I epoxied and screwed the sheet-metal holder to its base.

These three machines can help you overcome some of the wasted hours and frustrations I experienced in making the transition from full-scale to miniature work. Accept what you like, ignore what you will, find better ways, but do try your hand at miniatures. Even the most competent woodworker will find them a challenging and rewarding change of pace, and possibly a lifelong fascination. □

Herbert Consor, from Chagrin Falls, Ohio, is a retired engineer and manufacturing manager.

Super-Surfacers
Fixed-knife planers slice the wood paper-thin

by Paul Bertorelli

At all of the woodworking machinery shows in recent years, knots of incredulous people have gathered around small Japanese surfacing machines that can peel off a perfect shaving as long and as wide as the board they plane. Called super-surfacers, the machines are fixed-knife planers fitted with a powered belt that propels the wood under the knife, cutting like an enormous, inverted hand plane. They leave such a glass-smooth finish on the workpiece that it's hard to decide which is more interesting, that shimmering planed surface or the shaving. Evidently the onlookers haven't solved this dilemma either, because relatively few of these machines have been sold in this country.

This marketing flop seems curious. The Japanese have always had a knack for making products that Americans will buy by the shipload, but they couldn't seem to give away super-surfacers, despite the trade show demonstrations, which left little doubt that the machines work. So why haven't more been sold? Are they too expensive? Do they not perform as advertised? Or have these companies simply reached the outer boundaries of what sometimes seems like an insatiable American appetite for the latest gadget?

Hoping to answer these questions, we borrowed two super-surfacers and tested them in our shop for four months last summer. Later, I queried Hitachi and Makita executives to learn about the origin of these fascinating tools.

It turns out that the super-surfacers were developed for Japanese house carpenters, who must cut and fit heavy beams and plane them to a mirror finish before hanging them. Powered fixed-knife planers were first made 20 years ago, though the operating principle goes back at least a century to a traditional tool that made thin shavings for use as wrapping paper. This device, similar to the Western cooper's plane, consisted of a 1-ft. wide plane iron with the edge projecting up through a heavy table. Wood was pushed over the blade by means of a pivoting arm that gave the operator the considerable leverage needed to shove the chunk over the knife to make a shaving.

In a tradition-bound industry like Japanese carpentry, super-surfacers were slow to catch on. But demand has become brisk enough to support at least four manufacturers—Hitachi alone makes 5,000 super-surfacers a year—and sophisticated surfacers now find use in production shops and factories, where they do what sanding machines do in the West. The Japanese firm that holds the early patents on powered fixed-knife planers, Marunaka International, even makes auxiliary knife sets which cut simple chamfers, rounds and rabbets. And Marunaka is reportedly experimenting with fixed-knife shapers and molders.

Super-surfacers do not replace conventional rotary-head planers. In fact, a good rotary planer is needed in conjunction with a fixed-knife machine, since the latter works only when it starts with flat stock of uniform thickness.

In the United States, these machines remain a curiosity—dealers estimate that fewer than 250 of them are in use. I contacted a few woodworkers who have them and found that the machines seem to do the job they're designed for.

Eric Anderson, of Cape Neddick, Maine, who makes furniture and kitchen cabinets, bought a Hitachi super-surfacer last summer. "Before I got it," Anderson told me, "I basically did what everyone else does—I used a belt sander." Now, said Anderson, he routinely feeds rotary-planed stock and cut-to-size cabinet parts through the super-surfacer. He gets a far better finish in a fraction of the time.

One California woodworker I was told about couldn't care less about the shiny surface—it's the shavings he wants. He lined up four super-surfacers end to end in his shop, feeds incense cedar through, and then bags up the shavings to sell as closet odorizers.

Not all buyers like their super-surfacers. Clarence Gross, of Lima, Ohio, bought a rotary planer and a super-surfacer last spring, planning to use both for planing rough lumber. The super-surfacer disappointed him: "Oh, it would do it all right, but after a while I just kept using the other planer . . . took too many passes to plane rough stock," Gross said. Intrigued by such experiences, I was anxious to try these machines for myself.

Using the surfacers—I have to admit I was skeptical when we first decided to borrow and test two super-surfacers. I had seen the ads and read the sales hype, but I had no idea what I would actually want to do with these two machines parked in the middle of the shop. They seemed like expensive gimmicks to me, albeit well-engineered ones.

I didn't doubt that they could plane softwood nicely, but what about hardwood? Once they were set up (Makita's LP 2501 and Hitachi's FA-700), I scoured the shop for the nastiest wood I could find: bird's-eye maple, crotch walnut and a piece of rowed-grain padauk.

The first thing that struck me was how forcefully the surfacer's heavy rubber belt grabs the stock out of your hand and shoots it past the knife. The board clatters right off the outfeed roller table, the shaving whooshes off the knife. I was amazed to find that the surfacers planed the walnut and maple nearly perfectly and did a respectable job on the padauk. After four months of testing and casual use of the machines for three woodworking projects, I can see lots of uses for these things, though at $2,625 for the Hitachi and $2,800 for the Makita—plus $600 to $1,500 for the essential sharpener—I can't, as an amateur, afford one.

As I worked with these tools, I realized that in principle a super-surfacer works exactly like a hand plane. For an iron, it has a massive $5/16$-in. thick knife, 10 in. long, $2\frac{1}{2}$ in. wide and tipped with high-speed steel. A similar secondary knife mounts atop the cutting knife to serve as a chipbreaker. In

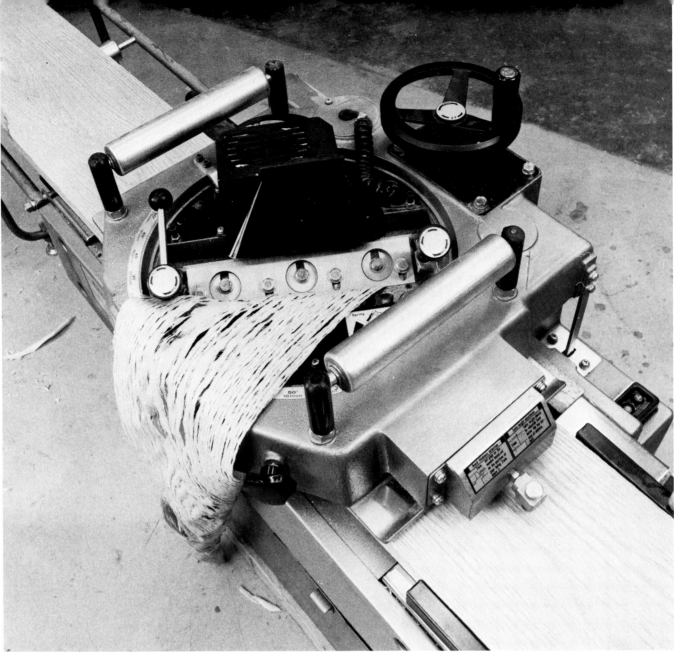

Like a well-tuned hand plane, a super-surfacer will peel off a perfect shaving of uniform thickness—but in a fraction of the time. This photo shows the Hitachi's knife set to about a 20° skew angle; the curled shaving is about 0.002 in. thick.

both machines, the knife assembly is bolted to a heavy cast-iron fixture which rides above the feed belt on adjustable columns. As with hand planes, super-surfacers require sharp knives and proper adjustment of both cutting depth and mouth opening. You adjust the mouths of these machines by moving a plate in the cutterhead and locking it down with bolts. In both softwoods and hardwoods, taking shavings about 0.002 in. thick leaves the best surface. Thicker shavings are possible, particularly in softwoods, but thicknesses over 0.008 in. or so draw protesting clanks from the feed mechanism, or else the board jams against the knife. The knives are bedded at a 35° angle—close to that of Japanese planes but shallower than the 40° to 45° of Western planes. You can vary the cut's angle of attack, from 0° (that is, the knife's edge at 90° to the length of the work) for soft, straight-grained woods, to 60° for harder, refractory woods. The effect is the same as skewing a hand plane in these woods.

I found one thing puzzling about both machines, however. Instruction sheets, though virtually incomprehensible, recommend higher angles of attack for softer woods than for hard. This made no sense—I skew a plane to ease the cut only in hard, tough woods. I later learned from Toshio Odate, a Japanese sculptor and sliding-door maker (*FWW* #34), that

to get the best surface on softwoods, the iron in a hand plane should bed at about 30°. Hardwoods, Odate said, plane best with an iron bedded close to 40°.

Odate went on to contend that when you rotate the turntable on a super-surfacer from 0° to, say, 45°, you lengthen the cutting bevel where it strikes the wood, effectively lowering the bed angle. To illustrate his point, Odate whittled a mock plane iron out of a scrap of wood. When he sliced one corner off at 45°, the compound angle formed where this cut intersected the cutting bevel was indeed less than the original bevel angle. A little trigonometry showed that skewing the knife's turntable to a 60° angle of attack produces an effective bed angle of 19°, about half the bed angle when the knife meets the stock head-on, at 0°. This effect applies to hand planes as well: when you skew the angle of attack, you are effectively working with a lower-angle plane, although the effect isn't significant at skew angles less than 40°. In addition, the bevel of a skewed plane slices somewhat sideways into the wood fibers, instead of encountering them head-on, thus reducing the likelihood of tearout. This allows the machine to plane hardwoods, although Odate says it would work better if it had a higher or an adjustable bed angle. As presently designed, the machines are best suited for soft-

The Hitachi (above left) and Makita (right) super-surfacers are both overhead, fixed-knife planers designed for finish-planing large, dimensioned timber. Both will plane wood up to 10 in. wide and 7¼ in. thick in a single pass. Width capacity drops to a 5-in. maximum when knives are skewed to 60°. Fixed-knife planing exerts enormous forces on the machine, and its knife, as the photo at right shows, is far heavier than any found in a hand plane. Knife and chip-breaker are made of ⁵⁄₁₆-in. thick steel. As with a hand plane, the high-speed steel-tipped knife must be sharpened frequently to get the best surface quality.

woods, even though American woodworkers are more likely to want to plane hardwoods.

Though they are identical in basic design, the Hitachi is generally sturdier and more sophisticated, and the one I'd pick if I were to buy. Its two spring-loaded, depth-adjustment knobs are easier to set than the Makita's pair of fine-thread bolts. The Hitachi has a pair of gauges for installing the knife correctly; the Makita has no such aids. Decoding the manuals takes real creative thinking—they're both awful.

We had no special sharpening equipment for our tests, but I wish we did. Ernie Conover, of Conover Woodcraft Specialties in Parkman, Ohio, who sells the Hitachi machine, recommends buying one of the two motorized grinders made especially for sharpening surfacer knives. The cheaper of the two grinders costs $600, but I think this extra expense should be considered part of the machine's price. You need razor-sharp edges and precise bevel angles to get the most out of a super-surfacer. Conover's method is to hollow-grind a 30° bevel on the grinder's 60-grit, 7-in. diameter wheel. Then he hones a 32° microbevel with a 600-grit, waterstone wheel. Between the coarse and fine wheels, Conover knocks off the wire edge with a hand slip-stone. Sharpening by hand is possible but difficult. I couldn't get good results.

I found it difficult, too, to measure knife durability. When planing poplar with a fresh knife, I got flawless surfaces through maybe 200 linear ft. Then surface quality dropped noticeably for about that much more work, before it was time to resharpen. A dull knife is most troublesome when you try to plane against the grain, which you must do somewhere along most boards. If you want to surface boards wider than the machine's 10-in. maximum, you can feed half of the width

one way, turn the board end-for-end and feed the other half. Increasing the angle of attack reduces fuzziness and tearout, but it also reduces the effective cutting width of the machine.

Dirt, Conover told me, is the knife's worst enemy. Wood must be clean and butt ends should be sawn off, or at least cleaned, and their leading edges should be chamfered before they are fed into the machine. Boards that have been sanded shouldn't be surfaced; abrasive particles could be embedded in the wood.

Having these machines around was fun, and I found that compared with sanding equipment of equivalent capacity they're cheaper and capable of a far better surface. So why haven't more woodworkers bought them? It's tempting to argue that the technology is just too alien to the American way of doing things; we sand, whereas the Japanese plane. I think the real reason, though, is simpler: the makers of fixed-knife planers haven't explained well enough what they'll do. These planers do have a place in shops where lots of flat stock has to be smoothly finished. If they are ever marketed sensibly for just that purpose, I'll bet you'll see a lot more of them. □

Paul Bertorelli is editor of Fine Woodworking *magazine. Fixed-knife planers are available in the United States from these Japanese companies: Hitachi Power Tools U.S.A. Ltd., 4487-F Park Dr., Norcross, Ga. 30093; Makita U.S.A. Inc., 16 World's Fair Dr., Somerset, N.J. 08873; Southwest Machinery Co., 9507 Santa Fe Springs Rd., Santa Fe Springs, Calif. 98670 (Marunaka International); and also from Shinko Machinery Works, Inc., No. 740 Matsutomi-Kamigumi, Shizuoka City, Japan (Grand Super Surfacer).*

Repouring Babbitt Bearings
A low-tech way to rescue old machines

by Bob Johnson

What woodworker hasn't dreamt of having a 36-in. or 42-in. bandsaw in the shop, a machine that can saw the thinnest stock one minute and then slab a 12-in. log the next? Most of us recoil from the price tags on such new machines. For the craftsman who would like industrial-quality machinery without paying new-machine prices, one answer is to seek the machinery of the 1880-1930 era.

Machines of that era are generally massive and well-made, and since most of them were built with babbitt bearings, industrial buyers are scared off, making such used machines available for surprisingly low prices. Aside from cleaning and painting, very often the only work required to put such machinery back into practical service is the rebabbitting of its bearings.

Modern ball and roller bearings have ended the age of babbitt in woodworking machines, but its heyday is still recent enough for there to be thousands of babbitt-bearing woodworking machines still in use

Old babbitt bearings are easily renewed by pouring molten babbitt, above, into the mold formed by the bearing shell and shaft. A torch warms the shell, keeping the metal from hardening prematurely. Babbitt, replaced by ball and roller bearings in new machines, still does its job in restorable, older machinery.

and many more that are out of service and in used-machinery emporiums which can be restored. Babbitt bearings last a long time and will continue to function even when worn. But best of all, when they do need replacement, the job can be done cheaply with a minimum of tools.

The principles of rebabbitting bearings are the same whether for a toy engine or a submarine propeller shaft. The metal is melted and poured, using the machine's bearing shells and shaft as a mold. When the assembly cools, the shaft is removed, if required, and the bearing surface is dressed with hand tools for a good running fit. Holes and grooves to supply and hold oil are cut in the finished babbitt.

Why babbitt?—Throughout the 19th century and well into the 20th, machine bearings were cast in a variety of alloys that have all come to be called babbitt. The name itself comes from Isaac Babbitt, who invented the recessed bearing box and lined it with metal alloy. Today, babbitt refers generally to a low-melting-point alloy made from some mixture of lead, copper, tin, zinc, antimony and/or nickel—a blend soft enough not to wear shafts and easy to renew when worn.

Most of the babbitt bearings in woodworking machinery are made with two-piece cast-iron housings that have a con-

siderably larger inside diameter than the shaft they will support. The molten babbitt is poured into the space between the shaft and housing to form the bearing. The hot metal runs into holes, slots or lips drilled partway into the housing, and this locks the bearing in place.

Some bearings, particularly those for vertical shafts, are one-piece and so are a bit more troublesome to pour. Machinery designers often did not allow much space for the babbitt, or for pouring it in between shaft and bearing shell.

One-piece bearings are not adjustable for taking up play, but a two-piece bearing can be adjusted by adding or removing shims until the cap is tight against the base (figure 1, p. 122), while still allowing the shaft to rotate freely. Many people try to adjust by tightening or loosening the bearing cap nuts until the shaft rotates freely, instead of by removing or adding shims. This is a poor practice, as it allows the cap to move, and usually causes the bearing to heat and wear rapidly.

How do you know when to rebabbitt? A quick inspection should tell. With two-piece bearings, tighten the cap bolts until the shaft won't turn, then back them off until it can be spun freely. Grab the shaft and give it a shake. There shouldn't be play in any direction. If the machine can be run, examine the end of the shaft while it's turning. If it wobbles instead of just rotating in place, new bearings are probably needed. Before you decide to rebabbitt, try eliminating the play by removing any shims left in the bearing.

Materials—In addition to standard shop tools such as wrenches, screwdrivers and hammers, you'll need some other tools and supplies for rebabbitting. First, you'll need a way to melt the babbitt and to heat the bearing castings, both for removing old babbitt and for pouring new. An oxyacetylene rig is best for both jobs, although a propane or MAAP gas torch can do small jobs. An ordinary household gas or electric stove gets hot enough to melt babbitt. Be sure to use an old heavy iron or steel pot—a 2-qt. saucepan is ideal. If you have a big bearing to pour, a plumbers' pot—a stove and crucible for melting lead—will save time and is more convenient. Hardware stores sell cast-iron plumbers' ladles in several sizes. These ladles have long handles and pouring lips. Each bearing

Fig. 1: Typical two-piece babbitt bearing

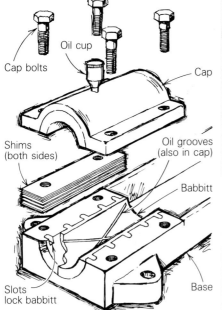

Cap bolts

Oil cup

Cap

Shims (both sides)

Oil grooves (also in cap)

Babbitt

Slots lock babbitt

Base

Lug for mounting bearing to machine, or bearings can be cast in machine

Restoring the bearings in an old machine takes but a few tools. You'll need a torch (propane will work, but oxyacetylene is better), a container to melt the babbitt in and a ladle to pour it. Babbitrite or other damming material contains the metal while it hardens in the bearing shell, light machine oil keeps the babbitt from sticking to the shaft, and the popsicle sticks are used to test the temperature of the babbitt before the pour.

After disassembling the bearings, Johnson's assistant melts out the old babbitt with a torch, above left, making sure he gets it out of all of the recesses, slots and holes in the bearing shells. The old babbitt is saved. With the addition of some fresh metal, it can be reused. Setting up a bearing for the pour calls for some artful placement of supports and damming materials. Above right, Johnson has placed wood blocks that will level and support this sawmill arbor exactly in the center of its bearing shells;

Babbitrite, a damming material, has been placed at both ends of the bearing to contain the molten metal until it has cooled. With the bearing shell braced on a level surface and the shaft firmly supported and centered in it, below, the molten babbitt is poured until it slightly overfills the shell. The shell is kept warm during the pour with an acetylene torch. Johnson pours two-piece bearings, such as the one shown here, in two separate operations—one for the bearing base and one for its cap.

must be made in a single pour, so make sure the ladle is large enough to do the job.

In 24 years of pouring bearings, I've never found that I couldn't reuse the old babbitt melted out of a machine simply by adding a little bit of new babbitt to make up the quantity required. If you're a perfectionist, you may decide not to take chances with an unknown old babbitt mix and to use all new. Babbitt is locally available from hardware stores or industrial supply houses and most sell two types, a high-lead alloy for slow-speed bearings and a high-nickel mix for high-speed ones. For most woodworking machinery, the high-nickel babbitt, or high-speed babbitt, is worth the cost—about $9 a pound from my supplier. We always use it on machine shafts that run at several thousand RPM, such as jointer and planer heads and tablesaw arbor bearings. We save money by using the old melted-out babbitt of unknown alloy only for slow-speed bearings, such as the drive gear and feed roll bearings on planers or bandsaw wheel shafts.

Babbitt is sold by weight in bar form, and some dealers will break a bar for you. Be sure you have enough. Nothing is more frustrating than to almost finish a perfect pour and run out of babbitt—you have to do the whole job again.

You'll need to seal the bottom, ends and oil holes of the bearing shell to stop the molten babbitt from running out. The handiest material is fireproof clay made for babbitting, which can be worked like modeling clay. There are various proprietary names—Babbitrite and Dambabbitt are two. The stuff is reusable and a can seems to last forever. Wood, cardboard, sheet metal, cloth, rope, string and other materials can supplement the damming material.

Preparation—Some machines have non-removable bearing shells cast right into their frames, others are made with a removable cap which bolts to a base that's cast into the machine, and others have both removable bases and caps. Whichever the case, before rebabbitting, all the old babbitt must be removed, and the bearing shell and the shaft must be clean and dry, free of all traces of loose rust, grease and oil.

If the bearings are removable, tip the bearing up and support it so that the old babbitt can run into your ladle or melting pot. Play the torch on the babbitt, starting at the bottom, allowing the babbitt to flow out. When the shell cools, inspect the surface to be sure that you've melted out all the corners, slots, and keyways provided to lock the babbitt in.

Machines with cast-in bearing shells are harder to clean. These will often have the babbitt-locking holes at the bottom of the bearing; if so, the holes can be used as drains for emptying the old babbitt as you melt it out. If there are no holes, you can sometimes drill one. Failing this, you'll have to chip the old babbitt out with a chisel, a task made easier by playing the torch on the metal so it flows and accumulates in a lump at the bottom, where it can be removed.

Machinery that has been out in the weather often has rust under the original babbitt. This should be removed by sandblasting, wirebrushing, or scraping and sanding after the old babbitt is out.

The shaft that will ride in the bearing must be clean, straight and polished to a bright, smooth finish. Flaws in the shaft will be reproduced in the bearing. Check the roundness of the shaft with a micrometer; it may require remachining if it is worn out-of-round or deeply pitted. We put old, worn shafts in a lathe and take a very light skim cut, and then polish them with fine sandpaper followed by crocus cloth. This is especially important in finely-fitted high-speed bearings. If you are dealing with a very long shaft or one that you can't prop into position for the pour, you'll need to make a babbitting mandrel—a piece of shafting the same size and finish as the original and long enough to extend beyond the bearing to some means of support at both ends.

Setting up—If there's an art in rebabbitting bearings, it's in the setup, wherein the shaft is secured in the exact position it will occupy in the finished bearing. You need room to pour the hot metal around the shaft, and it must not move during the pour and while the babbitt is hardening. Each machine requires its own special setup, so you have to be resourceful. Pour two-piece bearings in two steps, one for the cap and one for the base. Single-piece bearings are done in one pour. Here are some general guidelines for setting up:

With two-piece bearings, start by making up the shims that go between the bearing halves. I make brass shims of assorted thicknesses for each bearing, so play can be adjusted in variable increments. The shims can range in thickness from 0.1 in. to 0.001 in. Hard-finish paper will work for the thinnest shims. Use as many shims as you can, in equal numbers and thicknesses on each side, so your bearing will be thick and will last a long time before rebabbitting is required.

If the bearing shells are removable, place the bearing bases on a level surface; if they can't be removed, wedge and brace the machine so the bearing base is level in both horizontal planes. This will keep the babbitt from running to one side or one end when poured. When you're satisfied that the bearing is level, locate the shaft precisely in the center of the bearing, and in the final position it will be in the machine. Use dividers, sheet-metal guides, wooden wedges or whatever to measure and mark the location of the shaft. There are various methods for securing it there. You can sometimes support the shaft with small wooden blocks beyond each end of the bearing, or you might have to build a jig or cradle. Each situation is different. Use common sense, and remember that the shaft and shell must be in the relationship you ultimately want them, which usually means that the shaft is centered inside and parallel to the bearing base. Small, light shafts and mandrels can sometimes be supported by Babbitrite alone, but it is better to use a solid support.

There will be space between the shaft and the ends of the bearing shells, and this is where Babbitrite comes into play. Wrap it around the shaft and press it against the bearing shells to prevent the escape of molten metal. Holes in the bearing castings can be filled with Babbitrite, or with small dowels. Plugging oil holes with dowels saves drilling them out after the bearing is poured. Make certain that there is no unwanted egress for the molten babbitt.

Sometimes bearings are made in pairs or sets, such as on some jointer head assemblies. You must set up all the bearings at once, though the actual pour can be done a bearing at a time, without moving anything between pours.

One-piece or sleeve bearings are likely to be more successfully poured vertically. Brace your shaft or mandrel and make sure it is plumb—check on two sides 90° apart with your level, and secure it in position. If you have a large pulley that fits the shaft, it can be used as a base with small wedges under the rim to plumb the shaft. Slide the bearing housing over the shaft and support it at the point where the bearing will actually be. I find that the easiest way to support such a bearing is to bore a shaft-sized hole in a block of wood, split the block and then snug it to the shaft with a C-clamp. Put a layer of Babbitrite between the block and the bearing, and nail small pieces of wood to the block to center the bearing.

As it cools, the babbitt will pinch the shaft if you don't provide running clearance. Hard-finish letter paper is just thick enough to create enough clearance. Apply a light coat of oil to the shaft so the paper will stick to it, or use tape beyond the ends of the bearing. Instead of using paper, you can scrape the running clearance by hand after the pour. But be sure to oil the shaft in either case so the babbitt doesn't stick to it.

Check over your setup. Make sure the shaft is accurately positioned and braced, and that you've dammed every place where the babbitt could run out. You are now ready to melt the babbitt.

Bearings that are not adjustable, or that have a limited range of adjustment on the machine, should be set up together with their shaft in place, and then poured. Pouring the bearings individually off the machine allows less margin for error, so that when they are replaced they may pinch the shaft. If misalignment is not severe, scraping can often cure it.

The pour—Babbitt alloys contain metals that rapidly oxidize when heated, so it's unwise to leave the babbitt on the burner for long periods while you adjust the setup. We shorten the melt time even more by playing an acetylene torch flame directly on the lumps of babbitt in the melting pot. Impurities rise to the top of the molten babbitt and must be removed. Old-timers and old books sometimes suggest that you skim off the dross with a wooden stick, and this will work. However, the clean surface is an unstable composition that will quickly skin over again. It's better to leave the impurities floating on the top until you are ready to pour, then push them to one side and dip your pouring ladle in. Some old texts suggest putting powdered charcoal on the surface of the molten babbitt to help retard oxidation. Such things as pumice powder, fine sand, plaster or even shop dust can also be used. Each will retard oxidation and will float, making it easier to sweep aside with a stick before pouring.

Before you pour, you must heat the bearing shells. If you omit this step the babbitt coming in contact with cold metal is liable to chill and start to harden, giving rise to all manner of problems, from bearings of uneven, spongy texture to bearings with cavities, or those not filled by the pour. More babbitting problems arise from failure to perform this step than from all others combined, and those words—*heat the bearing shells*—should be branded on the brow of anyone pouring babbitt.

While your babbitt is melting, play your torch gently and evenly over all the bearing's exterior. You want it much too hot to touch, but nowhere near red-hot. The less space you have between shell and shaft, the hotter the shell should be, to ensure that babbitt will flow into all corners. This is especially true when you are pouring one-piece bearings. If the shaft is large, warming it with the torch will help. If you are pouring a bearing without the paper wrap, then you definitely should heat the shaft as well as the bearing shell, though take care—overheating can cause warping.

The time-tested way to check temperature is to insert a stick of soft wood (we use a popsicle stick) into the melted babbitt. If you can feel the stick wiggling, the babbitt is too hot. After three or four seconds in the molten babbitt, the stick should char on the end, but not burst into flame.

Put on heavy gloves and eye protection (molten babbitt splashing about causes nasty burns) and quickly dip up a ladleful, pushing the dross and impurities out of your way with your testing stick. Pour the babbitt into the bearing. Move quickly. Ideally, your pouring ladle should hold enough babbitt to fill the bearing shell in one go, but if you must pour another ladle, do so as rapidly as possible. With a helper and two ladles, you can pour from diagonally opposite corners of a horizontal bearing. Watch for overflows and especially for babbitt running out of openings you failed to plug. If babbitt is running out where it shouldn't, stop pouring, fix the leak and start over. Pour until there is a slight excess on the top. When you see the poured babbitt begin to harden, however, do not pour any more.

The pour is done. Now leave the assembly alone until it cools—when you can hold your hand on it, you can disassemble the setup and learn the degree of your success.

Finishing the bearing—If all's well, when you remove the shaft you will be greeted by a uniform, smooth, shiny, silvery babbitt surface. It will have no specks, streaks, blowholes or other irregularities. Some of these, if present, can be removed in finishing up, or ignored, depending on the size of the bearing and the degree of precision required. In most woodworking machinery bearings, you can ignore slight irregularities, especially those at the ends of the bearings, or those where oil grooves will be cut. Glaring irregularities will require a repour. How to decide? Check for the following problems.

Frosty patches: Usually in the center of a bearing, frosty patches can be caused by babbitt trapping air that didn't escape fast enough, or by impurities that got into the metal. If these don't cover more than a third of the bearing, you can still use it. Some small pockets in the center will act as oil reservoirs. If you feel grit on the babbitt surface, the babbitt must be removed, skimmed more carefully and repoured. If the babbitt is frosty all over, the metal was too cool when poured or the casting was not hot enough. Sometimes, uniform frostiness can result from impurities that did not rise to the top. The bearing will be spongy and weak, and should be repoured, with careful skimming after the melt.

Streaks or layers: This means the babbitt was not hot enough when poured, or more likely the casting was too cool and the babbitt began to chill. Light streaks may be removed by scraping and the bearing used; if they are deep, repour.

Looseness: If the babbitt is loose in the bearing shell when it cools, you probably left some oil in the bearing shell or housing, or some got in the babbitt itself, or some other contamination was present. You can repour, but you might be able to tighten the babbitt in the bearing shell by peening it gently with a ball-peen hammer, expanding the babbitt slightly. Peen from the center outward to the edges. This will leave dents in the bearing that you will have to scrape out.

Incomplete babbitt: Voids usually occur at the ends, and in most cases impair only the bearing's appearance. You can use the bearing anyway, or repour it. Sometimes there is a cavity in the bearing center—not a hole but a gentle depression, often not visible until you test the bearing. The cause could be a shaft that was too hot, or trapped air. Leave a small cavity to act as an oil reservoir, but one large enough to reduce the shaft/bearing contact by a third or more should be repoured.

Clean up the bearing by paring away excess babbitt with a chisel. Pare away the surplus babbitt protruding above the top and beyond the ends, drill out any oil holes and cut oil grooves. Though old books carry a bewildering variety of designs for oil grooves in babbitted bearings, you can use the originals, if they were visible, or cut a V-groove from the oil holes along the length of the bearing, stopping $\frac{1}{4}$ in. short of the ends so that oil will not run out.

Special tools are made for cutting oil grooves, but as these are hard to find nowadays, you can make one from a piece of $\frac{3}{8}$-in. iron rod, as shown in figure 2. The corner of an old flat file will cut oil grooves; small chisels and even pocketknives can also be used. The edges of these grooves and the points where drill bits have emerged through the babbitt are usually a little ragged, so smooth them off or chamfer them.

Final fitting of the bearing is done by scraping, the aspect of babbitting that many beginners fear most. It does take time and some judgment, but there is nothing mysterious or difficult about it. The amount and method of scraping depend on the speed of the shaft, the load on the bearing, and the degree of precision desired. Ideally, all bearings should be hand-scraped (or machined) to a perfect running fit. In practice, many bearings will fit their shafts well enough right after the pour, needing little or no scraping. Our rule of thumb is that woodworking machine heads that turn at high speeds, and parts requiring a perfect fit, such as a lathe headstock or the cutterhead of a large planer, should be scraped. However, the wisdom of taking the time to scrape rough, large or slow-speed bearings is questionable.

If you decide scraping is required, you'll need bearing scrapers and a small bottle of Prussian blue (machinists' layout dye), available from industrial supply houses. Lacking Prussian blue, ink or shoe polish could be used. Bearing scrapers can be purchased or made—they look like a 3-cornered file with the teeth ground off. Homemade scrapers of other shapes are often more useful than the store-bought kind. A flat file with the teeth ground off one face and one edge makes a fine scraper for large bearings. Babbitt cannot be sanded or filed. Not only will it gum, but abrasive sandpaper particles will become embedded in it.

Begin by coating the shaft with layout blue. Lay it carefully in the bearing, rotate it a couple of turns without sliding it lengthwise, then remove it. If the shaft is a perfect fit, the bluing will evenly cover the surface of the babbitt. More likely, though, you'll see blue spots where the shaft is making contact and the rest of the bearing will be shiny babbitt. Scrape gently at the blue spots, and try the shaft again. Shave gently rather than digging at the babbitt. Each time you try the shaft you should see more blued babbitt, meaning that the bearing is making better contact with the shaft. Continue in this fashion to any desired degree of finish.

A perfect fit is not impossible but requires much patience, and is not, in most cases, worth expending much time over. If a bearing must be that perfect, better to machine it with a reamer, a hone or a rotary cutter in a lathe or drill press—a job best done by a machine shop. Since babbitt is soft, it is somewhat forgiving, and after a period of time shafts will run in and wear the babbitt to a running fit. With or without scraping, however, if your bearing makes at least 50% contact with the shaft, pat yourself on the back and say well done.

Most woodworking machinery will have bearings con-

When the bearing is cool, Johnson uses an old woodworking chisel to trim the babbitt flush with the mating surface of the shell. Next he'll check shaft/bearing contact with machinists' layout dye and scrape out the high spots for a good running fit. He'll finish by scraping an oil groove along the bearing's length.

Fig. 2: A homemade oil-groove cutter

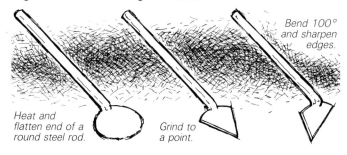

Bend 100° and sharpen edges.

Heat and flatten end of a round steel rod.

Grind to a point.

structed as I've decribed, but occasionally you may see an insert bearing—similar to car-engine connecting-rod bearings. These are often made of bronze or iron. Rather than making a new bearing of these metals, it's cheaper and easier to bore out the old shell to a diameter larger than the old insert, and pour a babbitt bearing in its place. For flat rubbing or sliding bearings, follow the steps—clean, set up, level up, heat and pour. Use an old plane to level off such a flat surface—grind a steep bevel on the iron as you would for very hard wood, and take light cuts. Or make a jig to hold a long scraper made from an old file.

Newly babbitted bearings require running-in. High-speed shafts will often heat new babbitt bearings until they have worn the bearing in. During this period, they should be oiled liberally with any kind of motor oil, and the caps kept snug against the shaft. But watch for overheating. In woodworking machinery, no babbitt bearing housing should get too hot to touch. If a bearing heats excessively, it will melt some of the babbitt at the running surface, and some of the components in the alloy may separate out and scratch or mark the shaft. If this happens, clean the shaft, lightly scrape the bearing, and check the fit of the cap.

If you take the time to restore, adjust and lubricate the babbitt bearings in machinery, you'll be amazed at how long the bearings will last. Being able to repair them easily and cheaply when they do wear out only adds to the enjoyment of owning and using these fine old machines. ☐

Bob Johnson restores vintage woodworking machinery and sells exotic hardwoods. He lives in Rossville, Ga. Photos by the author. For more on woodworking machinery, see FWW #30, p. 68.

Shop-Testing Five Jointer-Planers
Combination machines solve some problems, have drawbacks too

by James A. Rome

After the machine saws, a jointer and a thickness planer are likely to be the woodshop's most-needed stationary tools. It would be delightful to own a big, cast-iron jointer with an 18-in. planer to match, but, even ignoring the cost, most of us just don't have the room. Faced with this problem a year ago, I went on a mail-order shopping trip for a jointer-planer: a machine that would combine both functions into one compact unit.

I discovered that at least six companies build such machines, based on two design schemes. European and American manufacturers have preferred the over-under design in which a single cutterhead does both jointing and planing. The Japanese favor a side-by-side design—really just a medium-size jointer fastened to the side of a thickness planer—with two separate cutterheads running on a common shaft. The difference between the two basic designs is more than mere appearances. Although you can make a side-by-side go from planing to jointing by walking a step or two, its jointer head is only half as wide as its planer. The over-under machines can joint stock the same width as they can plane, but changing operations requires manipulation of tables and guards.

Lacking a useful way to compare one machine to another, I bought a Makita 2030 side-by-side, which I used happily for

a year, until an unfortunate accident (see box, p. 132) prompted me to replace it with the other Japanese combination, the Hitachi. When I offered to write about my experience with these two machines, *Fine Woodworking* arranged for me to test three more as well. In order of price, the test machines were the American-made Belsaw ($750), the Austrian Emco ($1,000), the Makita ($1,980), the Hitachi ($2,100) and the Swiss Inca ($1,568). I did not test another American-made machine, the $2,104 cast-iron Parks model #11, because it's available only on special order (Parks Woodworking Machinery, 1517 Knowleton St., Cincinnati, Ohio 45223).

Before getting down to specifics, let's review the basic functions of jointers and thickness planers. The jointer can start from a roughsawn surface and make it into a face side or edge: flat and smooth, free of twist, cup or warp. Once the cut has been started, the jointer is self-jigging in that it determines where it is going by referring to where it has just been. The thickness planer, on the other hand, power-feeds wood between its bed and cutterhead, and thus it requires one smooth, flat surface in order to create a true surface on the other side of the board. Many people, lacking a wide jointer, prepare both sides of a board by repeated passes through the planer. While this procedure will make both sides smooth

The Belsaw model 684, left, is one of two fabricated steel combination machines tested by the author. For conversion from a jointer to a planer, the hinged infeed and outfeed tables flip sideways, as shown in the photo above. The planer's maximum width of cut is 8⅜ in., the narrowest of all the machines tested. The guard leaves part of the cutterhead exposed during jointer operation, right, and because it's hinged on, rather than to one side of the table, it reduces the jointer's effective cutting width by nearly 2 in.

and parallel to one another, it won't remove all of the warp.

Setting up the machines was straightforward, no thanks to the instruction manuals, which were universally terrible. I went about my analysis with the needs of a serious but non-professional woodworker in mind, using these tools in the course of three months of small-project woodworking. I checked the jointer and planer tables for flatness, and measured the noise level generated by each machine. I paid particular attention to how each machine's knives could be removed and replaced, since precise knife adjustment is crucial to accurate planing and jointing (all five machines have two-knife cutterheads). To find out how the combinations would handle various woods, I planed oak, redwood, and goncalo alves, a hard tropical wood with interlocked grain.

The Belsaw 684 combination evolved from the company's popular 12-in. surface planer, the price of which has been kept low by the use of fabricated steel instead of cast iron. Unfortunately, in this case, cost-cutting has yielded a bulky, heavy tool (198 lb.) whose jointer is seriously flawed.

To convert the Belsaw from jointing to planing, you loosen a couple of catches and flip the tables sideways, so that the cutterhead shroud can pivot up from below, where it is stored when the machine is a jointer. A microswitch blocks motor operation unless the guard is installed, a safety feature the other two over-under machines lack.

As a planer, the Belsaw works reasonably well, given the 1-HP motor. Its feed rate of 28 ft./min. is brisk enough as long as you don't take too deep a cut in a single pass, in which case it stalls. The 8⅜-in. maximum width of the planer is inadequate for most cabinet work, and because the Belsaw lacks a depth feeler gauge, I found it hard to tell just when the knives start to bite. When I tried the dowel-cutting knife that Belsaw sent, the motor balked and blew my 20-amp circuit breaker. The other molding knives worked better.

Belsaw makes no attempt at sawdust control. Dust is dumped on the planer outfeed table, or under the jointer where it gets into everything, including the chain-and-sprocket depth-setting mechanism. To keep chips from jamming the works, you have to clean them out frequently by opening up the hinged side shrouds. There's also no anti-kickback device, but the machine's skinny rubber feed rollers probably grip the wood well enough to prevent it being shot out the back. None of the over-unders I tested has bed rollers, an omission that doesn't seem to hurt planing performance if you keep the tables waxed.

I found the Belsaw jointer almost unusable and somewhat unsafe. The fence, which tilts but doesn't slide, is inadequately supported and will deflect ½ in. horizontally, somewhat less vertically. The hinged tables are unsupported on the fence side. Press down, they give, ruining the flatness of the cut. Also, the jointer guard pivots on the infeed table rather than to one side of it, reducing the cutting width from 8⅜ in. to 6⅝ in. Worse yet, in use, the guard leaves a dangerously large triangle of cutterhead exposed.

Belsaw's knife-setting system seems elegant, but is difficult to use. Each knife fits into a dovetailed slot in the cutterhead where two bolts bear against the back edge of the knife, raising or lowering the knife to the desired height, which you measure with a plunger gauge that straddles the knife slot. I could adjust knife height easily enough, but when I tightened the locking wedge, the knives crept up. I had to loosen the

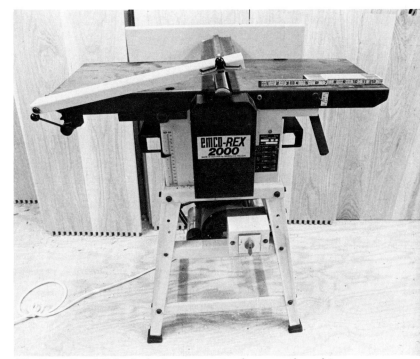

The Emco-Rex 2000, the basic power unit of a versatile multi-purpose machine, has the overarm jointer guard common to European stationary tools. It detaches for planer conversion.

wedge and start over with the knives low so that snugging the bolts pushed them to the correct height.

The Emco-Rex 2000 is made by the same folks who make Unimat lathes, the Emco-Maier Company. Strikingly painted in orange and black, the 2000 is the basic unit of a multi-purpose machine. You can add a tablesaw, a slot mortiser and a shaper. The Emco is made of fabricated steel, but is smaller than the Belsaw and, at 143 lb., is also lighter.

To convert the machine from a jointer to a planer, you remove the jointer outfeed table by turning a couple of bolted catch hooks a half turn. A plastic guard placed over the cutterhead is wedged in place by moving the jointer depth control, which is a lever instead of the usual knob or handwheel. The guard also acts as a duct which funnels shavings into an adapter that can be connected to your shop vacuum.

The Emco's steel feed rollers are deeply serrated and feed positively, but when I tried to plane off a light cut, they left noticeable marks in the surface, requiring another pass at a deeper setting to remove. Since the feed rollers aren't adjustable, this is a real drawback, because on hard woods such as birch or maple, you sometimes have to take a shallow cut to get a good surface. If the rollers lose their grip on the stock, anti-kickback pawls keep it from exiting violently.

To adjust the knives, you raise them with a screwdriver and push down with a block of wood. When the knives are correctly positioned, you tighten bolts to fix them in place. To measure knife projection, you place a plastic gauge across the jointer mouth and then hand-rotate the cutterhead. The knives are right when they just grab the gauge at the top of their arc, scooting it a marked distance. On my machine, the sheet-steel tables weren't flat, so the short gauge was useless. I had to make a longer one out of wood. Even then, knife-setting was a tedious trial-and-error affair.

The planing performance of the Emco was good, although leisurely, at a feed rate of 16.4 ft./min. With its 2½-HP induction motor, the Emco has plenty of power and never stalled, even when pushed hard. At the slow feed rate, thicknessing 100 bd. ft. of 4/4 lumber will likely take the better part of a day, and boards wider than the 10³/₁₆-in. maximum will have to be ripped down.

The Emco jointer guard consists of a sheet-metal stamping held above the cutterhead by an adjustable arm. For edge-jointing, it slides away from the fence; for face-jointing, you shove the board under the guard, an operation requiring you to lift your hands (or, better yet, push blocks) as you pass the guard. This little shuffle leaves an unjointed bump in the board, which the planer must skim off. I ignored the temptation to work without the guard: 10 in. of exposed cutterhead is too scary.

Because its tables are supported on both edges, the Emco jointer is more accurate than the Belsaw, but still too short for truing long stock. Anyone accustomed to an expensive jointer will find the movable, tiltable fence flimsy, yet it's solid enough, and would be quite good if you bolted a wide board to the fence to lengthen and stiffen it.

The Inca 343-190 jointer tables, bed and frame are made of pressure-cast aluminum, generously ribbed for strength and bending resistance, resulting in a tool that's very rigid, yet, at 114 lb., the lightest of the group. The tool I tested, which should be available this fall, is an improved version of the discontinued model 510. Its jointer tables are a usable 42½ in. long, and it will plane and joint boards 10¼ in. wide.

The Inca has an unusual feature for a planer in this price range: a two-speed feed (11.5 ft./min., 16.5 ft./min., and

Inca's combination is the only one of five tested that sports two feed rates, which are controlled by the lever above the motor. The flap screwed to the jointer fence covers the cutterhead when the fence is moved forward.

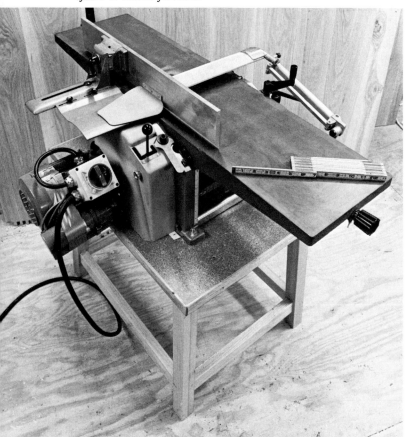

neutral) which can be changed by a shift lever while the wood is being planed. When I wanted to shift speeds, however, I always found myself standing on the side of the machine opposite the lever. Anyway, even at its high speed, the Inca is a slowpoke. I would have been glad to trade the speed changer for a decent depth feeler gauge, which the Inca lacks.

The Inca does a beautiful job of planing, especially if you take thin cuts, which you can do because the knurled feed rollers don't mar the wood the way the Emco's do. On the goncalo alves, the Inca tore out less than did the other planers, perhaps because its cutterhead knives are supported right out to their tips, thus limiting chatter. The Inca was outstanding at planing very thin pieces of wood (less than ⅛ in.). The standard 1½-HP motor is too small, however, and prone to stall. Garrett Wade, the Inca distributor, says a 2-HP (220V) motor is a no-cost option. I'd recommend it.

The Inca converts from planer to jointer similarly to the Emco. Also, like the Emco's, the Inca's jointer guard gets in the way. When face-jointing, wide boards chatter unless you press downward fairly near the cutterhead. I found this awkward to do. The jointer fence is one piece of solid, heavy aluminum supported on a ribbed pedestal a third of the way down the infeed table. This arrangement isn't rigid enough, and though it's stiffest where you apply pressure when edge-jointing, it deflects more than I like at the outfeed end. I was able to rig my shop vacuum to collect the planer's shavings, but couldn't do the same for the jointer—it dumps them on the planer table. A new plastic hood developed by Inca supposedly solves this problem.

Of all the machines tested, the Inca's knife-adjustment system is the most accurate. Each knife has two slots into which the head of an Allen bolt fits. Turning these bolts raises or lowers the knife. This system is handy if you have knives that are low at the center, as mine were. I raised both ends about 0.005 in. until the center was at the correct height, snugged the center locking bolts, then lowered each end to the correct height. To measure knife height, Inca supplies a very nice $80 dial indicator with an aluminum base, although I got just as close using the Emco method and a flat, straight piece of wood.

The Makita 2030 is one of a half-dozen stationary woodworking tools sold by Makita in the United States. Solidly constructed, it shows how the Japanese are using cast iron much the way Inca uses aluminum: relatively thin castings with plenty of stiffening ribs. You can also buy the machine with a 14-in. non-tilting circular ripsaw mounted alongside the planer (model LM3001). If you already own a radial-arm saw instead of a tablesaw, such a combination might be ideal. The Makita will plane boards up to 12 in. wide and joint to 6⅛ in. wide.

The Makita arrives ready to run (ditto the Hitachi), but the two columns upon which the machine is supported elevate it only 20 in. above the floor—uncomfortably low for my 6-ft. frame. I bolted the machine to a 2x4 stand on locking castors, raising the jointer table to about 35 in. above the floor. I included castors on the stand so that I could roll the 276-lb. machine around in my cramped shop.

Most Japanese stationary machines, including the Makita and Hitachi combinations, are powered by universal motors, not induction motors. Universal motors, which also drive routers, are small and light, but must whine up to high

(continued on p. 130)

Learning how to read the grain

by R. Bruce Hoadley

Before feeding a board into a surface planer or hand-planing it, it's important to read the board's grain, or you risk tearout. There are many routines for doing this. Most woodworkers simply examine the edge of a board to determine the inclination of the cell structure. But close scrutiny may sometimes be too time-consuming, as when feeding a large quantity into a jointer or a surface planer, or when you simply cannot see any useful detail because the lumber has roughsawn edges. Even-grained and fine-textured woods such as basswood pose similar problems.

One helpful gimmick when planing flatsawn boards is to use the board's U-shaped or V-shaped surface figure to determine grain inclination. As shown in figure 1, on the pith side of a board (the heart, or inside, of the tree), the tips of the Vs point with the grain, so you would hand-plane in that direction. On the bark side, the Vs point against the grain. My memory crutch goes like this:

Pith side, **Plane** with the **Points** (of Vs)
Bark side, **Backwards**

The rule works on boards with any visible V-shaped markings. After a while it becomes automatic. You instinctively glance at the end when you pick up a board; if you are working a pith side, you subconsciously hand-plane with the points, and so on.

Of course, with wood it's not always that simple. For example, you may have a board with Vs going in both directions. Let's assume you have a board that has a bark side surface with the appearance shown in figure 2. The "bark side, backwards" rule of thumb helps you recognize zones of the board, so you would hand-plane zones A and C from left to right, as shown, but zone B from right to left. If you keep in mind that the knives of jointers and planers actually cut in the opposite direction to the direction of feed, reading the Vs would also help you decide to send the board into a planer left-end-first. You can anticipate good results over most of the board (zones A and C), but with possible trouble where the cutterhead would be working against the grain (zone B). Knowing where the troubles will occur, you can take lighter cuts, slow the rate

of feed, or use alternatives (such as abrasive planers or sharp hand-tools) to minimize filling and sanding later.

Complete Vs are handy, but they're not always present. Consider the boards shown in figure 3, where the points of the Vs are gone and only their sloping sides are present. The drawing shows which way the Vs pointed in the wider board from which each strip was removed. Careful inspection reveals that within each growth ring the latewood edge indicates which way the Vs point. This is difficult to determine with even-

grained woods (such as birch or maple), but with uneven-grained woods (such as spruce, hemlock, fir, oak or butternut) it will be as easy as looking at the V-direction. Another way to state the rule is: On the pith side, within each growth ring, plane from early to late; on the bark side, backwards.

Every board came from a tree stem—the growth-ring figure can help you to interpret the inclination of the grain. If you learn to read it and work with it, you will have fewer surprises, and better surfaces in your finished work. □

Bruce Hoadley is professor of wood technology at the University of Massachusetts at Amherst, and the author of Understanding Wood, A Craftsman's Guide to Wood Technology *(The Taunton Press).*

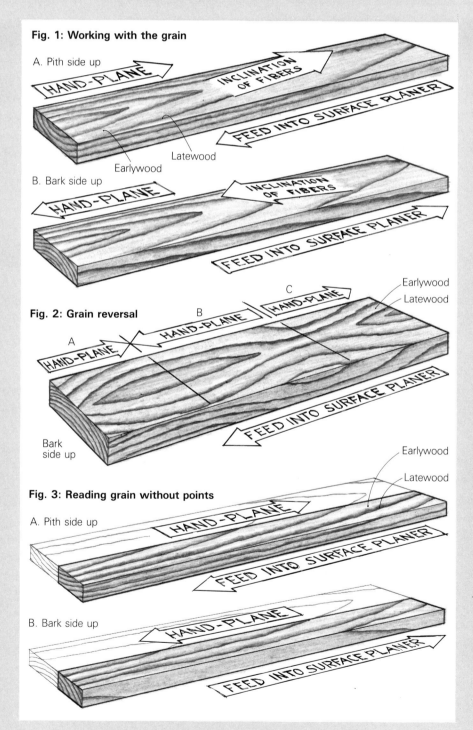

Fig. 1: Working with the grain
A. Pith side up
HAND-PLANE INCLINATION OF FIBERS FEED INTO SURFACE PLANER
Latewood
Earlywood
B. Bark side up
HAND-PLANE INCLINATION OF FIBERS FEED INTO SURFACE PLANER

Fig. 2: Grain reversal
A B C
HAND-PLANE HAND-PLANE HAND-PLANE
Earlywood
Latewood
Bark side up
FEED INTO SURFACE PLANER

Fig. 3: Reading grain without points
A. Pith side up
Earlywood
Latewood
HAND-PLANE FEED INTO SURFACE PLANER
B. Bark side up
HAND-PLANE FEED INTO SURFACE PLANER

Four unpowered bed rollers support boards fed through the Makita 2030. While you walk around the machine, stock can be temporarily shelved on two return rollers on top of the planer.

When the Makita fence is advanced over the cutterhead, the knives are left dangerously exposed as stock is fed.

speeds to develop their rated power. As a result, they are dangerously noisy (ear protection is a must) and, lacking torque, they bog down under load. The Makita's 2-HP motor is fine for most jointing and for planing narrow stock. It chokes when you try to plane more than $\frac{1}{32}$ in. off a wide board in a single pass. Set aside some time if you're going to mill a stack of lumber. And figure on cleaning up a mess—the planer tosses the chips onto the emerging board, the jointer leaves them on the floor. I liked the Makita's four adjustable bed rollers, especially the two outboard rollers which prop up long boards, preventing them from being sniped—gouged too deeply—as they emerge from the machine. Two return rollers atop the machine offer a handy perch on which to rest the board while you walk to the infeed end for another pass.

As a thicknesser, the Makita has great gauges. A plunger-type feeler gauge above the planer infeed table will tell you how much you're planing off a board before you feed it, and a nearby placard tells how much of a cut you can take for a given width without bogging the motor. The thickness indicator, also a plunger, is calibrated in eighths, reads easily, and can be set as a stop for repeated cuts to the same thickness. The jointer gauge (like all the others) is rudimentary at best.

After struggling with the short jointer tables on the over-under machines, I found it surprisingly easy to accurately edge-joint a long board on the Makita's 59-in. tables. The tradeoff, of course, is a $6\frac{1}{8}$-in. cutterhead that's not very useful for facing wide, warped stock prior to planing. Supported at two points, the fence is rigid (although mine was warped), it's movable and it tilts. It has one glaring problem, though. If it's moved forward, the cutterhead is exposed on the back side. None of the other machines tested has this hazard.

Setting knives in the Makita is touchy. Instead of fitting

into slots, the knives are sprung against a squarish cutterhead by steel clips and held fast by bolted-on, half-round covers. To adjust the knives, you stick a screwdriver through slots in the blade covers and pry up on the bottom edge of the knife. Two small wooden blocks, which span the jointer mouth or rest on machined surfaces above the planer cutterhead, push the knives to the correct level. Compared to the Inca, this is a crude arrangement, and it takes lots of trial and error to get right. The Makita does have one saving grace: the cutterhead has an external wheel, so you can rotate it by hand, with a pin to lock it at top dead center.

The Hitachi F-1000A, at 320 lb., is the heaviest machine I tested, and its four steel support columns make it sturdier than the Makita. Its planer and jointer capacity and running gear are similar to the Makita's, but the Hitachi lacks the outboard bed rollers, an annoying shortcoming which I remedied by mounting my own outfeed roller on a plywood outrigger. Rollers and castors can be bought from S.H.D., PO Box 13P, Sycamore Ave., Medford, Mass. 02155.

Though Hitachi claims 3 HP for the howling little motor that powers this machine, I couldn't detect any advantage over the Makita's claimed 2 HP. As planers, they perform equally, though the Hitachi is better at chip-handling. Planer chips are ducted through an oblong chute that exhausts out the side of the machine. Chips from the jointer are similarly ducted downward. I fashioned wooden plugs to fit into these ports, then drilled the plugs to accept the hose from my shop vacuum. I can run the machine all day without making a mess, though I have to empty the vacuum frequently.

Hitachi's knife-setting method is quite elegant and nearly as accurate as Inca's. Like the Makita, the knives are fastened to a squarish cutterhead by bolted-on plates. A detent pin on the handwheel locks the cutterhead at top dead center. The knives are spring-loaded, so you just pop them in place and push them down to height with a couple of magnetic clamps. They stay put while you tighten the locking bolts.

The Hitachi's cast-iron jointer fence is the best of all the machines I tested. It's heavy and easy to adjust, and it stays where you put it. I felt safer using the F-1000A, as well. It's festooned with bright yellow warning stickers, and has little niceties such as a metal cover over the cutterhead handwheel and a little metal flap that guards the exposed knives when the jointer fence is pulled forward. For storage in a tiny shop, the jointer has one other clever feature: its 63-in. jointer tables unlock and pivot downward about a foot from each end.

The Hitachi I bought has terrible gauges. The thickness gauge is calibrated in twelfths of an inch, and there's ¼ in. of parallax-producing space between the pointer and the scale. I cobbled up my own replacement out of a broken corner clamp and a metal rule. Originally, my machine had no feeler gauge at all, so I fashioned a crude version of the Makita gauge using the rest of the corner clamp and a stove bolt. Hitachi has since designed a gauge, and it's a beauty. It not only tells you where the blades will begin to cut, but how deep the cut will be. If you own an F-1000A without this, Hitachi's service manager, Hal Flora (10530 Lawson River Ave., Fountain Valley, Calif. 92708), will supply one for free.

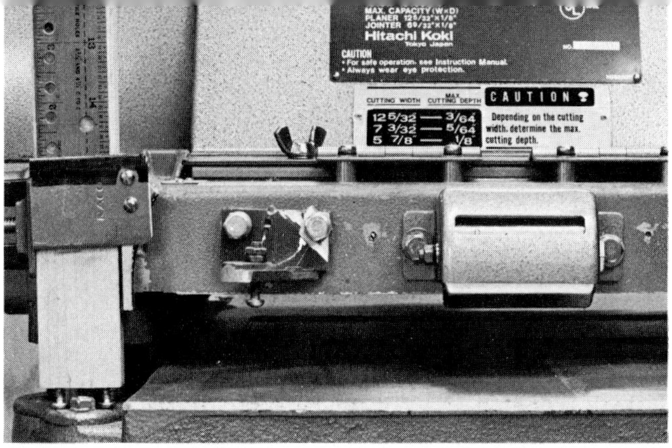

The Hitachi F-1000A has two bed rollers but no outboard rollers. Rome mounted his own outfeed roller on a plywood outrigger. With standard table extensions, the Hitachi has 63-in. tables, the longest of the tools tested. Before Hitachi supplied him with a new, well-designed feeler gauge, Rome made his own from a stove-bolt plunger mounted in a broken corner clamp, above.

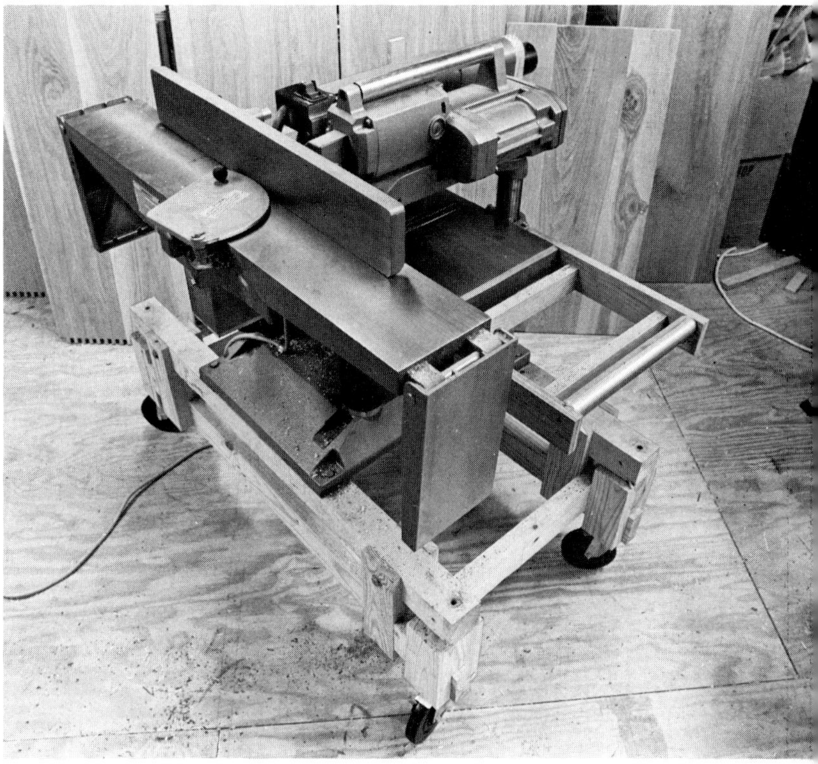

Which to choose? In picking a jointer-planer, I'd take several things into consideration. First, how wide a jointer do you need and how long must its tables be? The over-unders have wider jointers which are perfect for flattening one side of a wide, cupped board in order to give the planer a true surface to work from. Because the tables are so short, though, you'll have a hard time truing the face or edges of a long board. The side-by-sides have longer tables but narrower cutterheads, thus wide boards must be ripped before face-jointing and then glued back up to width. If you have to follow this routine, the wider side-by-side planers will be preferable for cleaning up your glued stock. Weight and size should be considered too. A small, light machine can be more easily pushed aside when it's not needed, but tends to move about when you're shoving big pieces through the planer.

I had a couple of friends try these machines, and all of us agreed that as planers they stack up about equally. But we found the over-unders compromised as jointers, especially the Belsaw, because of their shape: they're so wide that you have to lean over them, feeding the stock at arm's length. A wide

Comparison of Specifications

	Belsaw 684 (USA)	Emco-Rex 2000 (Austria)	Inca 343-190 (Switzerland)	Makita 2030 (Japan)	Hitachi F-1000A (Japan)
Price	$750	$1,000	$1,568	$1,980	$2,100
Watts input	1800	1920	1580	1400	1640
Advertised horsepower	1	2½	1½	2	3
Revolutions/minute	6,000	6,000	6,000	7,000	10,400
Feed rate (feet/minute)	28	16.4	11.5, 16.5	27.8	31.2
Cuts/inch	36.0	61.0	86.0, 61.0	41.9	55.6
Planer					
Blade width (inches)	8⅜	10 3/16	10¼	12	12 5/32
Maximum thickness (inches)	4½	5⅞	6 5/16	6¼	6⅝
Minimum thickness (inches)	¼	⅛	⅛	¼	3/16
Table dimensions (inches)	8 1/16 x 28½	9¾ x 17¾	10¼ x 15¾	11¾ x 23½	11⅞ x 24⅛
Jointer					
Blade width (inches)	8⅜ (6⅝ usable)	10 3/16	10¼	6⅛	6 9/32
Table size (inches)	9⅜ x 35⅝	12⅜ x 33¾	11 x 42½	6⅛ x 59	6⅜ x 39½* *63 with extensions
Weight (pounds)	198	143	114	276	320
Return rollers	0	0	0	2	1
Bed rollers	0	0	0	4	2
Sound level (dB)†	91	85	85	97	98

† Measured at ear level with a Radio Shack sound level meter, "A" weighting, no wood being cut. A difference of 3 dB *doubles* the apparent noise level.

jointer is nice, but what good is it if it's too short to true a long board? Then there's the matter of switching from one function to the other. Aside from the nuisance, you can't use both jointer and planer simultaneously. This can force you to use more inefficient sequencing while truing your wood.

I was disappointed with the Belsaw. Its low price isn't much of a value if half of the combination doesn't work. The people at Belsaw were helpful and happy to talk to me on their toll-free number, but goodwill can't offset a badly designed machine. Unless you are severely constrained by money, I can't recommend the Belsaw 684. On a tight budget, I'd consider Belsaw's model 804 planer-molder, about $550, and a separate jointer.

The Emco-Rex 2000 is probably the better budget choice. It gets the job done, but it requires more care and skill to get good results than do the more expensive machines. Its sheet-steel construction gives me doubts about its durability.

The Makita is a worthy machine which I liked better than the Belsaw or Emco. Yet it suffers in comparison with the Hitachi. The $120 lower price tag hardly offsets its drawbacks. Makita's lack of customer service (see box, below) persuades me to take my future business elsewhere.

My difficulty is in choosing between the Hitachi and the Inca, machines that have obviously been designed according to different philosophies. Both are well designed and well made, though one is light and elegant, the other heavy and sturdy. I favor the Hitachi's side-by-side design, but I admire the Inca for its compactness and engineering finesse. I think the Inca would be best for the craftsman who does careful, low-volume work and who doesn't often need to straighten long boards. I'm glad I bought the Hitachi, however. Apart from face-jointing wide boards, it can do all that the others can, with considerably more ease. It was the only machine on which the fence and tables were perfectly flat and straight. It's built like a tank, and the people who sell it are knowledgeable and helpful. For me, that's a winning combination. □

James Rome is a part-time woodworker and full-time plasma physicist. He works for the U.S. fusion energy program in Oak Ridge, Tenn. Photos by the author.

Don't answer the phone while adjusting jointer knives

I was installing the knives in my Makita 2030 jointer-planer when the phone rang. When I finished the call, I went back and turned on the machine, forgetting that I hadn't tightened the bolts. As the knives whirred up to speed, a horrible screeching noise ensued, followed by a shower of shrapnel. The jointer guard deflected most of the metal shards and I wasn't hurt.

After I regained my composure, I realized what I had done wrong. It was a cheap lesson in how *not* to set jointer knives. Valuable as the experience was, I learned even more when I tried to fix the thing.

Just taking it apart was a chore. The jointer tables are attached to the planer by hardened-steel drift pins. Driven into blind holes, these pins seem designed more for fast factory assembly than for easy removal. Hours of tugging finally opened up a gap large enough to insert a hacksaw blade into. Several blades later, I cut through the pins and separated the tables.

There followed another struggle to remove the jointer head from its press-fit into a bearing cup in the outfeed table. While doing this, I realized that if the drive belt connecting the motor to the shafts ever breaks, the jointer head will probably have to be removed to replace it. In principle, it might be possible to slide apart the coupled pulleys that connect the planer and jointer shafts, but in practice, forget it.

I had to decide whether to fix the

tables or to buy new ones. This decision was surprisingly difficult. Although Makita stocks parts at various locations throughout the country, each distribution center has different prices and tells a different story. Makita in Atlanta was willing to sell me a new outfeed table for about $400. Makita in New Jersey claimed that they had a sale on an old-style outfeed table and the price was

Rome's knife-setting accident tore chunks from both infeed and outfeed tables. Here they are reinstalled, after being built up by nickel welding and flat grinding.

$30. Makita in Atlanta said there was only one style of outfeed table. Makita in New Jersey said the sale was over.

I decided to repair the machine. It cost me $50 to get the cast-iron tables welded back together with nickel. It cost another $50 to have the tops of the tables ground flat. The nickel was hard enough to ruin several carbide tools. I had to belt-sand down the bottoms of the welds facing the jointer head.

Reassembling the 2030 was relatively straightforward. My struggles, however, were not over. Without the jointer blades, the machine ran smoothly up to speed. But when I installed the knives, it vibrated severely enough to walk across the floor of my shop. I weighed the blades and their cover plates, and found them to be perfectly balanced. I bought a new planer head (another $70) and readjusted the drive pulleys. The machine was still unbalanced.

In disgust, I sold it, as a planer only, to a friend. He found the problem. When I ordered a new spring-steel blade holder, Makita had sent me two of them stuck together. This raised the blade and its heavy cover about $\frac{1}{16}$ in., causing the out-of-balance condition.

My misadventures with the Makita explain why I am now the owner of a Hitachi F-1000A.   —*J.A.R.*

EDITOR'S NOTE: To sort out customers' technical problems, Makita has added a national service manager to its staff. Write to 12950 E. Alondra, Cerritos, Calif. 90701, or call (213)-926-8775.

Threading Wood

1. A router-table threadbox

by Andrew Henwood

I have always found setting up a hand threadbox (*FWW #6*) to be a fussy business. It has often taken me an hour or more of shimming the cutter in and out, up and down, and back and forth to get it right. Moreover, I was completely stymied recently when I tried to put 12 threads per inch on a ⅜-in. dowel. I spent half a day reducing a quantity of good dowel to round rubbish. Try as I might, I was getting all root and no crest.

I was unwilling to admit defeat. I wanted to make some little wooden clamps for delicate work, and I had put considerable time and effort into making a metal tap that did a dandy job of threading the hole. The tap wasn't going to be much use by itself.

I figured that to succeed I would have to use a high-speed cutter, so I decided to build a threadbox with a router to do the cutting. I managed to produce an acceptable thread on my first attempt, within an hour of the time I'd gotten the idea. I'll show you how to do it, then you can adjust dimensions to suit your own taps.

Take two squared scraps of close-grained hardwood, as shown in figure 1. Screw the pieces together face to face. Don't use glue—you will need to take the pieces apart again as you make the threadbox, and also when you set the router bit. Drill through both pieces with a 9/32-in. bit (the pilot size of my tap). Now take the two halves apart and enlarge the hole in the front half to ⅜ in. Thread the hole in the back block, carefully cleaning away the wood frayed by the entry of the tap. Refasten the halves together and cut out the keyhole slot across the bottom, giving it a good flare in order to provide clearance for chips and room for the router bit.

Next chuck a 60° V-groove bit in your router, and mount it under a router table. Make a cutout in the fence so the dowel can pass through, then set the fence loosely a couple of inches behind the bit. To adjust the fence, first disassemble the threadbox. Take the back (tapped) section and center it so that the bit is exactly in line with the first crest of thread. You can judge this most accurately if you adjust the height of the bit until it matches the contour of the thread. The threadbox will work best if the crest just enters from the surface at the left-hand side of the keyhole, so you should plane the block down a little to achieve this. Now place the block so that its front face is just a hair behind the point of the router bit. The back half of the threadbox is now correctly aligned, and you can use its position to set the fence on the table. Hold the back part of the threadbox down firmly while you snug up and secure the fence. Mark the position of the block on the fence so you can reorient the threadbox after it's been assembled.

Screw the two halves of the threadbox together again and clamp the whole unit to the fence, centered over the bit. Raise the router bit until the point is fractionally above the minor diameter of the threaded portion. Switch on the router, insert a dowel into the pilot hole, and rotate it clockwise as you apply pressure to push the dowel in. As soon as a turn or two of dowel is engaged in the tapped section, it will self-feed as you turn it.

A few pointers that may help: Make darn sure you provide a positive way to remove the waste, otherwise it will jam up in the thread behind the bit and wreck the work (my router vacuums the waste down through the keyhole slot). Also, I find that I get a better thread that is less likely to crumble if I

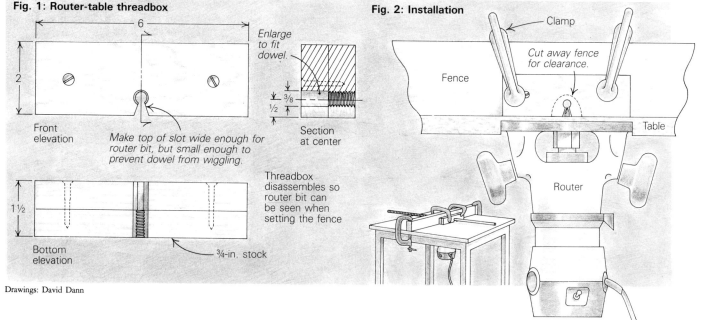

Fig. 1: Router-table threadbox

6

2

Front elevation

Make top of slot wide enough for router bit, but small enough to prevent dowel from wiggling.

Enlarge to fit dowel.

⅜

½

Section at center

Threadbox disassembles so router bit can be seen when setting the fence

1½

Bottom elevation

¾-in. stock

Fig. 2: Installation

Clamp

Cut away fence for clearance.

Fence

Table

Router

Drawings: David Dann

first dip the dowel in Watco oil or mineral spirits. Don't be in too much of a rush when feeding the dowel—in my enthusiasm I tried mounting the dowel in a brace for fast and easy turning, but I found that too much speed rips the crest off the thread. Feeding with the fingers lets you feel what's going on. I've found that it's a good practice to chamfer the end of the dowel for easy starting. The results will readily reveal whether the bit should be raised or lowered for the desired depth of cut. If the dowel won't feed, you have only to nudge the fence a trifle forward or back.

I can just barely stand the noise of routers, even with earplugs. I much prefer the quiet, crisp sound and feel of a hand threadbox as it slices its way around a dowel. But all in all, I don't suppose I ever would have gotten twelve threads on a three-eighths stick that way.

Andrew Henwood is an airline pilot and furnituremaker living in Georgetown, Ont.

---

2. A commercial threader

To speed production on their line of threaded novelty items, J&J Beall, of 541 Swans Rd. N.E., Newark, Ohio 43055, devised a threadbox that clamps to the base of a router. Shown here as a wooden prototype, it will be manufactured in reinforced plastic, with interchangeable leadscrew inserts (three sizes to fit the taps included). You attach the threadbox to a router, center and adjust Beall's three-flute V-groove bit, then simply screw a dowel into the wider end of the leadscrew. As the thread is cut, it automatically follows the leadscrew's pattern. The device will sell for about $130, and it is likely that more leadscrew sizes will become available, and eventually left-hand threads too. *—Jim Cummins*

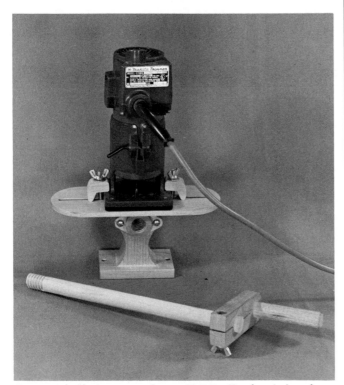

Any standard router attaches to J&J Beall's dowel threader.

3. Versatile threadbox cuts inside *and* outside threads

by Robert J. Harrigan

I needed some wood threads, and had in mind a jig for one size. After a while at the drawing board, however, I came up with a tool with interchangeable guides and thread sizes to fulfill all of my threading needs. All you really need to start making one is a tap and a matching threaded rod. The tool shown cuts outside threads up to $3\frac{5}{8}$ in. and inside threads up to $2\frac{7}{8}$ in. Some chipping occurs with ring-porous hardwoods such as oak, but it doesn't affect the action of the threads.

The key to the threadbox is the threaded feeder rod inside the box (figure 1, facing page). When you turn the handle at the back of the box, the workpiece rotates and advances past the cutter. The feeder rod affects only the coarseness or fineness of the thread, and has nothing to do with the diameter of the work you are threading. Change the feeder rod to suit the job. As a general rule, use fine threads on containers, and coarse threads when you are making clamps, so they will tighten up faster. A different guide disc is needed each time you change the diameter of the work, but you can make as many sizes as you need. Use plywood for the guide discs—you end up with a rounder hole than if you had used solid wood.

The large photo on the facing page shows the threadbox cutting an outside thread. I'm using a Weller model 601 motor tool. It rides in a track on the front plate that allows coarse adjustment of the cutter; fine adjustment is done with a machine screw that runs through an aluminum block. It's important that the work fit the guide disc precisely. If the holes and the work are slightly oval, the errors will double and the thread will show it.

To cut inside threads, you reposition the tool on an auxiliary plate that holds the tool in a horizontal position. Here also the work moves past the cutter as you turn the handle. The depth of the threaded section is limited by the length of the fly-cutter's shank, but a lot of thread would just be a nuisance on a container anyway.

When you want to make a long threaded dowel, such as for a clamp, tap a threaded disc to support the dowel as it comes out the front of the box. The bottom left photo on the facing page shows an extension plate I made to hold the extra disc. There is a rear extension plate also, which can be used to make dowels longer than the box. Use a scrap when you set the thread depth, and increase it little by little until a nut fits right. The dowel will chip when you take a series of light cuts like this, but when the depth is set correctly, you'll get a clean cut with one steady pass. Use the tap to thread the holes in the clamps. If you are working oversize threaded dowels, such as for a press, and you don't have a tap big enough to match

Fig. 1: Threadbox

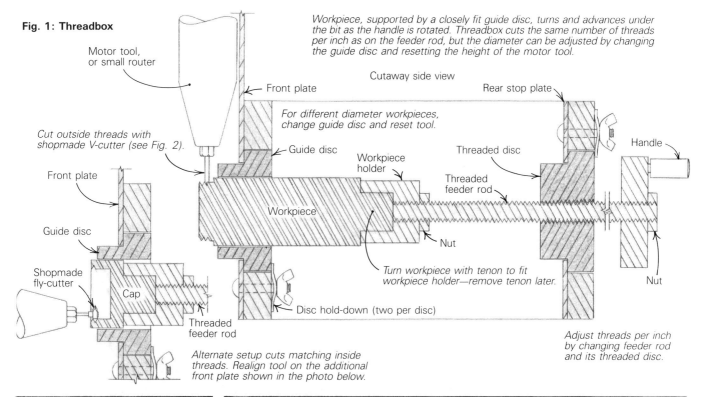

Motor tool, or small router

Workpiece, supported by a closely fit guide disc, turns and advances under the bit as the handle is rotated. Threadbox cuts the same number of threads per inch as on the feeder rod, but the diameter can be adjusted by changing the guide disc and resetting the height of the motor tool.

Cutaway side view

Front plate

Rear stop plate

For different diameter workpieces, change guide disc and reset tool.

Handle

Cut outside threads with shopmade V-cutter (see Fig. 2).

Guide disc

Workpiece holder

Threaded disc

Front plate

Threaded feeder rod

Guide disc

Workpiece

Threaded feeder rod

Shopmade fly-cutter

Cap

Nut

Turn workpiece with tenon to fit workpiece holder—remove tenon later.

Nut

Threaded feeder rod

Disc hold-down (two per disc)

Adjust threads per inch by changing feeder rod and its threaded disc.

Alternate setup cuts matching inside threads. Realign tool on the additional front plate shown in the photo below.

To cut inside threads, the motor tool is mounted on an auxiliary aluminum plate. Instead of the V-groove cutter that makes outside threads, a fly-cutter is used. The length of the threaded section is limited by the length of the bit's shank, but a container doesn't need many threads. Below, a front extension supports and indexes longer work.

In cutting outside threads, as the rear handle is turned, the work advances according to the pitch of the threads on the feeder rod inside the box. For adjusting to different diameters, the motor tool slides in a track; depth-of-cut is set with a fine-adjustment screw.

Harrigan's threadbox makes threads in various sizes.

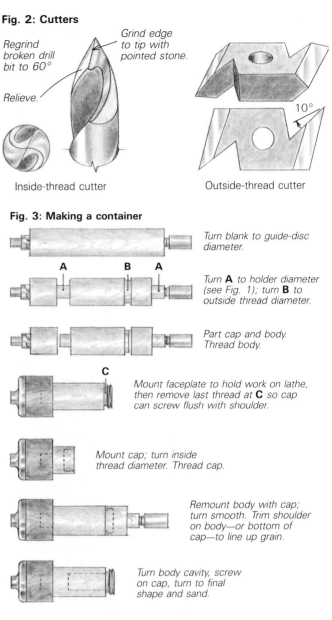

Fig. 2: Cutters

Regrind broken drill bit to 60°

Grind edge to tip with pointed stone.

Relieve.

Inside-thread cutter

10°

Outside-thread cutter

Fig. 3: Making a container

Turn blank to guide-disc diameter.

Turn **A** to holder diameter (see Fig. 1); turn **B** to outside thread diameter.

Part cap and body. Thread body.

Mount faceplate to hold work on lathe, then remove last thread at **C** so cap can screw flush with shoulder.

Mount cap; turn inside thread diameter. Thread cap.

Remount body with cap; turn smooth. Trim shoulder on body—or bottom of cap—to line up grain.

Turn body cavity, screw on cap, turn to final shape and sand.

the threads, simply make an inside-threaded plug that fits the dowel. Glue it, just as you would an embedded nut, where you need it.

I make my own V-groove cutters from broken drill bits $\frac{1}{32}$ in. wider than the thread pitch. I grind the end to 60°, then sharpen inside the cutting flutes with a pointed stone held in the Weller, using angles as shown in figure 2. Relieve the back of the cutting edge as you would a normal drill bit. I make fly-cutters from pieces of lawnmower blade—any high-carbon steel will do—screwed or bolted onto an arbor that fits the tool. You can buy high-speed bits instead, but they are bulky and won't cut as close to a shoulder.

To make a container, it helps to visualize the steps involved. Figure 3 shows how I do it. The most tedious step is turning the outside diameter so that it fits the guide disc. I use the disc itself as a gauge—I hang it over the tailstock center, and size the work from that end, turning off the lathe and sliding the disc along to check the fit.

When you turn the tenons that will fit into the holder inside the threadbox, it's better to turn them small rather than too large. You can always build them up with a turn or two of masking tape for a tight fit.

To avoid chipping, cut the body threads in one pass. When they are done, turn off an unthreaded neck below the threads on the body—if you don't, the cap won't screw on all the way. When making the cap threads, take a series of light cuts. You will find that you can remove the cap from the threadbox to check the fit without changing the cutter setting. Put a little more thread in the cap than you think you will need. This extra length will allow you to trim the bottom of the cap down later, so that the grain on cap and body will match when the cap is screwed tight.

When you turn out the end grain from the cavity, secure the blank to the faceplate with a couple of nails through the tenon for more support. □

Robert J. Harrigan has a stained glass and woodworking shop in Cincinnati. Photos by the author.

Truing dowels

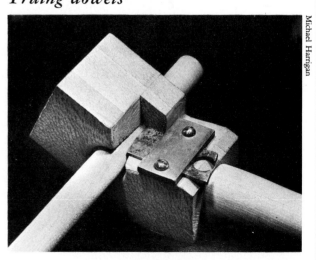

This lathe tool trues a dowel to exact size. Taper the entrance hole to the finished dowel size at the end of the blade, and relieve the blade's cutting edge at the corners to prevent the work from binding. —R.J.H.

Low-tech horizontal boring machine

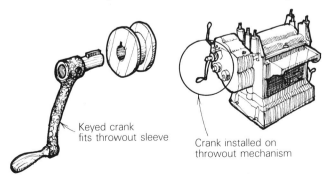

Sliding table

Thread motor shaft
for drill chuck.

Fixed table

Base

*To drill cross-grain,
slide table toward bit.*

*For end grain, turn table 90°,
clamp in position, slide work.*

My homebuilt horizontal boring machine features a sliding table that moves the stock into the bit rather than vice versa.

To begin, you'll need a ¼-HP to ½-HP, 1750-RPM motor, with its shaft threaded to accept a ½-in. drill chuck. I made the base, the fixed table and the sliding table out of ¾-in. Baltic birch plywood. Cut two square pieces the same size for the fixed table and the sliding table, then make all dado cuts at the same rip-fence setting to ensure that the dadoes align. Glue and screw hardwood runners into the dadoes in the sliding table. These runners should then fit either pair of tracks in the fixed table. Next bolt down the motor assembly and the fixed table to the base. Shim the fixed table so that the sliding table will be at the proper height relative to the bit. Glue and screw a fence to the top of the sliding table.

The height of the sliding table is not adjustable in this design. This presents no hardship for me because most of my boring is in 4/4 and 5/4 stock. I shimmed the fixed height so that my machine would normally bore 5/4 stock. To switch over to 4/4 stock, I place a sheet of ¹⁄₁₀-in. plexiglass on top of the sliding table.   —*Ed Devlin, Rothsay, Minn.*

Hand feed for the Parks planer

Here's a simple way to get an infinitely variable feed rate on a Parks Model 97 thickness planer, without altering any part of the machine. Simply install a hand crank on the throwout sleeve. Although no planer is 100% tear-proof, it sure makes a big difference once you get used to the feel of cranking wood through by hand. To make the crank, I started with an old farm machinery crank and fitted it to a short keyed shaft

Keyed crank
fits throwout sleeve

Crank installed on
throwout mechanism

that slides into the center hole of the throwout sleeve. To use it, I simply disengage the power feed and start cranking. Make sure you remove the crank before you use the power feed. This idea could probably be adapted to other planers that have a similar feed disengagement mechanism.
—*John Colombini, Pittsburgh, Penn.*

Pin-router adaptation for radial-arm saw

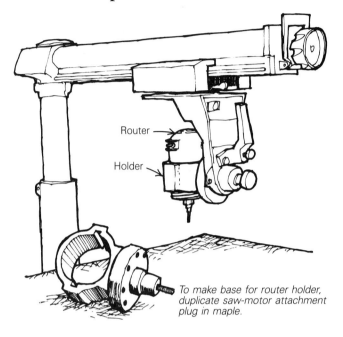

Router

Holder

*To make base for router holder,
duplicate saw-motor attachment
plug in maple.*

You can easily convert a radial-arm saw to a pin router. This tool will open up a whole new world of operations, and make many familiar tasks—such as rabbeting for bookshelves or cutting mortises and slots—much easier.

To convert my Sears 10-in. saw, I merely duplicated on the lathe, in rock maple, the saw-motor attachment plug where it fits the motor support arm. I laminated the ring assembly that holds the router from plywood. Then I glued and bolted together the laminated rings and the maple plug to form a single unit. Details of this fixture would vary to suit the saw/router combination. For specifics about setting up the pin and using templates, see *FWW #29*, pp. 63-65. Also, if the setup is combined with a machinists' dual-feed rotary table, to hold and move the work, very precise work is possible.

The router is normally used in the vertical position, but it can be rotated to any orientation (just like the saw) for special routing cuts.   —*Donald Wigfield, Moneta, Va.*

Installing jointer knives

Here's how to set knives in a jointer quickly and accurately. First crank the infeed table down so it's out of the way. Place a knife and a gib in the cutterhead slot, with the screws tight enough to hold the knife in place but loose enough so that it can be moved. The knife should project about ⅛ in. above the outfeed table. Now place a piece of plate glass on the outfeed table so that it projects over the cutterhead. Manually roll the cutterhead backward until the projecting knife lifts the glass at the top of its turning circle. Hold the cutterhead in place and gently press the glass down on the outfeed table, pushing the knife down into the cutterhead slot. If the knife was not exactly at the highest point of its arc, it will still be slightly too high. Rocking the cutterhead back and forth under the glass will level the knife with the outfeed table. Now tighten the gib, then repeat with the other knives.
—*Joe Robson, Trumansburg, N.Y.*

Making a Router Table
Poor man's shaper is a handy beginners' tool

by Donald Bjorkman

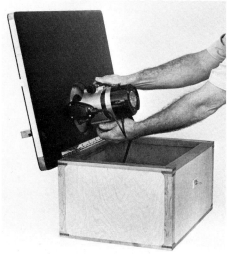

For both novice and experienced woodwork-ers, Bjorkman's router table is a versatile, easy-to-make tool that will perform many operations, including grooving, molding, and mortise-and-tenoning. It's constructed from the plywood and solid wood components pic-tured below, and the tabletop pivots on a continuous hinge, allowing access to the router for quick bit changes.

A router table is indispensable for shaping, molding and cutting joints, but the utility of many of the tables I've seen suffers for want of simple improvements, such as accu-rate, easy-to-adjust fences and a groove for a miter gauge. And the routers always seem tucked so far beneath the table surface that you have to be a contortionist to change bits or to make depth adjustments.

Using scraps left over from other projects, I designed and built this table to remedy those shortcomings. For rigidity and so it can be clamped to a convenient work surface, the table cabinet is of stress-panel construction—simple mortise-and-tenon frames with plywood solidly glued into a rabbet routed in the frames. I hinged the tabletop so that the router can be mounted with little fuss and the bits changed quickly. The router is positioned near the hinge so that its weight counter-balances the tabletop when the top is open, keeping undue stress from damaging the hinge.

As the drawing shows, the table consists of upper and low-er frames, joined at the corners by doweled vertical posts. I made the frame parts out of maple, then used a ⅜-in. rabbet-ing bit in a router to mill the rabbets for the stress panels after the frames were glued up. To make the panels, I scribed the rabbet outline directly onto pieces of ⅜-in. Baltic birch, cut them to size and rounded the corners on my disc sander. If you prefer, you could sidestep the stress-panel construction and make the table base out of plywood panels joined at the corners by a rabbet-and-groove joint or by screws.

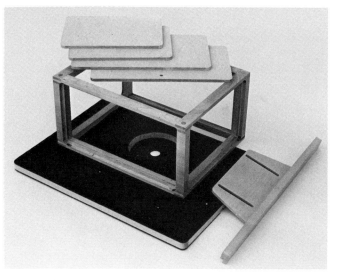

The top is a piece of ¾-in. particleboard edge-banded with hard maple. For a longer-wearing miter gauge groove, I let a strip of maple into the particleboard where the groove is da-doed. I sized the groove to fit my tablesaw miter gauge, but you could just as easily make your own wooden gauge. For a smoother, more attractive working surface than particleboard, I glued ⅛-in. tempered Masonite to the top. It's important to cover the back side of the top, too; otherwise, differential moisture absorption will warp the particleboard.

The Sears router I used is constructed in such a way that

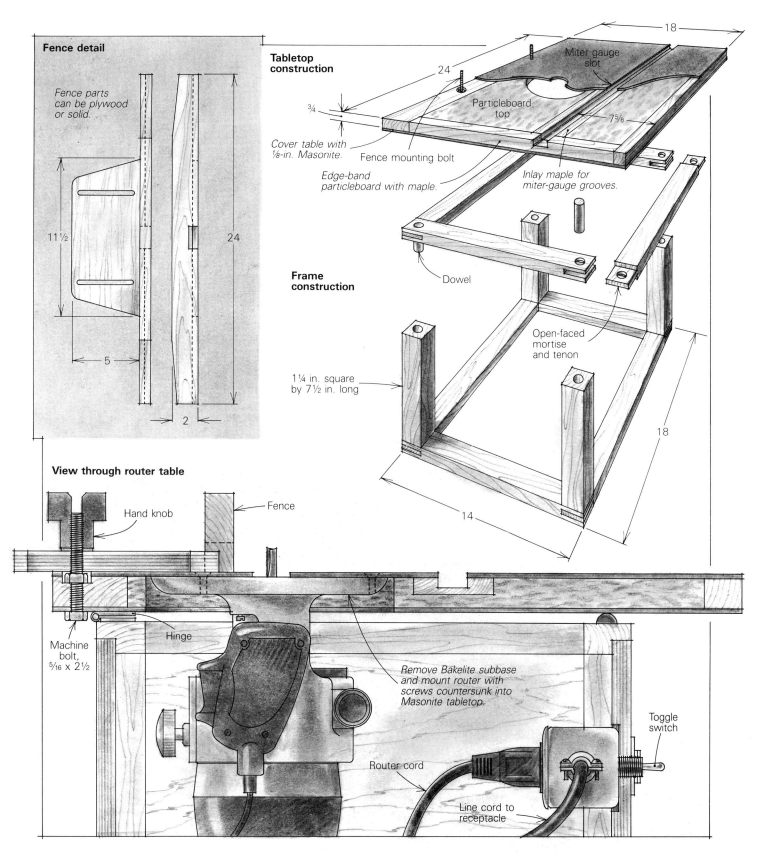

Fence detail

Fence parts can be plywood or solid.

11½

24

5

2

Tabletop construction

18

Miter gauge slot

24

¾

Particleboard top

7⅝

Cover table with ⅛-in. Masonite.

Fence mounting bolt

Edge-band particleboard with maple.

Inlay maple for miter-gauge grooves.

Frame construction

Dowel

Open-faced mortise and tenon

1¼ in. square by 7½ in. long

18

14

View through router table

Hand knob

Fence

Machine bolt, 5/16 x 2½

Hinge

Remove Bakelite subbase and mount router with screws countersunk into Masonite tabletop.

Toggle switch

Router cord

Line cord to receptacle

the motor can't be easily removed from the base. If you have only one router and it's of this type, you'll have to remove the tool's Bakelite base and fish the three mounting screws through the hardboard top each time you use the table. A router with a removable base (such as a Milwaukee or a Porter Cable) is more convenient: you can just buy an extra base and leave it permanently mounted in the table.

The router's power cord can be snaked out through the bottom of the table to be plugged in for each use, but I think it's safer to connect it to a switched receptacle mounted inside the cabinet. I wired mine to a toggle switch passed through one of the knockout plugs in the electric box and out the front of the cabinet.

To use the router table, I clamp the ledge formed by the lower frame to a pair of sawhorses. I've found that with a good selection of sharp bits, this little machine can do nearly as much as a shaper can, and for a lot less money. □

Donald Bjorkman teaches interior design at Northern Arizona State University in Flagstaff. Photos by the author.

Improving the Fretsaw
Pivot guides handsawing of marquetry veneers

by Ed Kampe

In marquetry, it's difficult to use a fretsaw freehand with only a bird's-mouth jig for support. With a few years of practice, you might become accomplished with this contraption, but I've already used up my three score and ten, and the designer in me insisted that there must be a better method. I wanted a jig that could be clamped to a corner of the kitchen table, something for the shut-ins or for the person in a wheelchair. Marquetry is a wonderful hobby that combines art and craft. An easy-to-use fretsaw might help more people enjoy it.

With that idea in mind, I rigged up this jig which is suitable for the double-bevel marquetry cutting method explained by Silas Kopf on pp. 79-83. Instead of the entire tool moving up and down, though, my modified fretsaw is clamped to a wooden arm which pivots on a carriage-bolt axle attached to the saw table. This setup has three advan-

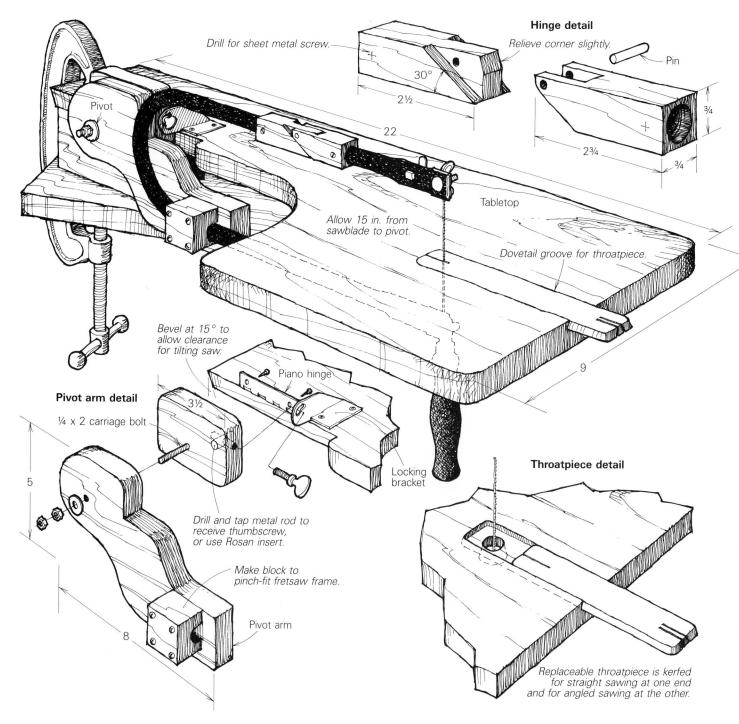

Drill for sheet metal screw.

Hinge detail

Relieve corner slightly.

Pin

30°

2½

2¾

¾

¾

Pivot

22

Tabletop

Allow 15 in. from sawblade to pivot.

Dovetail groove for throatpiece.

Bevel at 15° to allow clearance for tilting saw.

Piano hinge

3½

Pivot arm detail

¼ x 2 carriage bolt

5

Drill and tap metal rod to receive thumbscrew, or use Rosan insert.

Make block to pinch-fit fretsaw frame.

8

Pivot arm

Locking bracket

9

Throatpiece detail

Replaceable throatpiece is kerfed for straight sawing at one end and for angled sawing at the other.

Drawings: Jim Richey

tages. First, the saw is always held at the correct angle, freeing me from the task of sliding work and saw around in search of the narrow notch in the bird's-mouth. Second, the saw's hinged upper arm pivots out of the way when a blade must be threaded through the workpiece. And third, the veneer can be held stationary as the saw is stroked. This last feature is handy because when the blade reaches the bottom of its maximum stroke, it will have advanced about $\frac{5}{64}$ in., offering good control when cutting fragile or pointed parts.

As the drawing shows, I made my jig to about the dimensions of a small, power scroll saw. The table, saw bracket and tilting mechanism are of pine, but a good grade of $\frac{3}{4}$-in. plywood could be substituted. If unsupported, veneer will chip on the back side as it is cut. I solved this problem by inserting a throatpiece that slides in a 1-in. wide dovetailed groove milled in the tabletop. One end of the throatpiece is kerfed to accommodate the blade set at 90°; the other end has two kerfs at 12°, the angle I like for double-beveling.

The saw is clamped to a bracket, which is in turn attached to the table by a section of brass piano hinge. This allows the saw angle to be varied. A thumbscrew through a shopmade aluminum bracket locks the saw at the desired angle. I made my own barrel nut for the thumbscrew by drilling and tapping a $\frac{3}{8}$-in. steel rod. A wood screw, or better yet a thumbscrew threaded into a Rosan insert, would serve the same purpose. The best pivot point turned out to be 15 in. from the blade and just below the surface of the table.

If I had had access to a machine shop, I would have made the upper arm hinge from aluminum so that it could be smaller. As it was, I had to use wood, and maple seemed a good choice. So that you won't have to contend with clamping the odd-shaped pieces on the drill press, bore the blind holes for the saw frame before you shape the hinge parts. I didn't have the 0.515-in. ($\frac{33}{64}$-in.) bit to match the diameter of my saw frame, but an oversize $\frac{1}{2}$-in. masonry bit I found in my collection worked fine after I ground off a few thousandths of an inch. For accuracy, I drilled a $\frac{1}{2}$-in. hole first, and then, without changing the setup, enlarged it with my modified bit. Not all fretsaws have tubular frames (I got mine from Constantine's). If yours is of steel bar stock, you'll have to modify the mounting bracket and mortise the frame into the hinges.

I cut and shaped the hinge sections on my 4-in. Dremel saw. Doing it by hand is nearly as easy. With a backsaw, saw the angled cheeks and shoulders of the male section, then chisel the slot in the female part until you get a slip fit. For the hinge pin, I sacrificed a $\frac{5}{32}$-in. drill bit. Measuring the overall length of the hinge and subtracting the combined depth of the two holes tells you how long a section of the saw has to be cut out. Make sure that the blade clamps line up when you put the saw together. I fastened the hinge with sheet-metal screws driven through the wood and into the saw frame.

Installing a blade is easy. First, I clamp the jig to a comfortable work surface, which happens to be the desk in my den. I thread the blade through from the top and clamp it at the bottom. Resting the saw handle on my knee leaves both hands free to pivot the upper arm down and clamp the other end of the blade. □

Ed Kampe was a design engineer and general foreman in precision metalworking. He makes marquetry pictures in Zellwood, Fla.

Motor makes fretsawing fly

by Scott Littleton

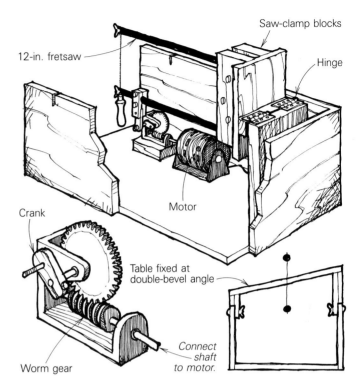

12-in. fretsaw

Saw-clamp blocks

Hinge

Crank

Motor

Worm gear

Table fixed at double-bevel angle

Connect shaft to motor.

As a marquetry beginner, I found that knife-cutting left my hands stiff and sore, so I set out to design and build a low-cost power scroll saw that would make a beveled cut. Ideally, a marquetry saw's blade should operate straight up and down. But a mechanism with a large throat to achieve this ideal seemed beyond my abilities. Some sketching showed me that a simple oscillating saw might work, since the force needed to cut veneer is small and the speed need not be great. One disadvantage of a rocking saw frame is that the cutting edge of the blade moves forward and back during the stroke. I found that with a short stroke ($\frac{3}{4}$ in.), the front-to-back motion is negligible.

I built my saw the simplest way I could and just slapped it together quickly, thinking it was an experiment to be improved on later. It works so well that the only improvement I may ever make is to increase the throat depth.

To make the saw, I clamped a 12-in. fretsaw between two bolted blocks. The blocks are attached to a hinged post mounted on a $\frac{3}{4}$-in. plywood base. To remove any side play from the saw, put the hinges in a bind, or use a piano hinge. Up-and-down motion is achieved through a small electric motor, a small worm gearbox (or gearmotor) and a simple crank mechanism. After having tried several speeds, I find that about 300 strokes per minute is my preference. The motor to power the unit need not be large. I've found that even a $\frac{1}{120}$-HP gearmotor (Dayton 200-RPM shaded pole gearmotor, stock #2Z812, about $18.50) will cut two thicknesses of oak veneer without noticeably slowing down. □

Scott Littleton lives in Salt Lake City, Utah.

TURNING, CARVING

Turning a Matched Set of Bowls
Patternmakers' tricks for consistent shapes

by Arthur F. Sherry

Getting the most from an outstanding piece of wood by making a one-of-a-kind bowl is part of the wood-turner's art. But turning a good matched set of bowls can be an equal challenge, calling for careful planning and execution. A matched set, to me, means consistent shape more than anything else. Bowls can be made of different woods, or be inlaid with elaborate designs. Yet if their shapes are the same, we instinctively know they belong together. Here are some patternmakers' tricks and templates that will help you turn a series of bowls, or almost anything else, exactly alike.

Wood never stops moving as its moisture content changes, of course. Plan to use dry wood, or your bowls will become oval after they have been turned. I frequently rough-turn bowls, then let them dry for a few days to stabilize before I finish turning. I've found species such as mahogany and walnut to be particularly stable, but you can apply these techniques to more highly figured species, too.

Start by designing the shape on paper. Then transfer the layout to a squared piece of ⅛-in. plywood (figure 1). Lay out the centerline of the bowl, marked C/L. Then, with a knife, scribe lines for the top and for the bottom of the bowl, perpendicular to the centerline. Draw the cross section of one half of the bowl on the template, and scribe rim lines (parallel to the centerline) to mark the outside diameter of the bowl. Notice that the side of the rim should be left at least ⅛ in. thick, so that after the inside has been turned you can mount the

bowl as shown in figure 4, for turning the outside.

Cut out, file and sand the template to shape. If I am making more than a few bowls, I copy this template onto another piece of plywood and use the master only for the final fit. I never touch the master to the spinning bowl.

To turn the inside of the bowl, screw the blank (bandsawn round) to a faceplate and mount it on the lathe. Turn the block to the final height of the bowl, plus $\frac{1}{64}$ in. for final sanding. Next turn the diameter, and stop to check it with both a square (so that the side is perpendicular to the face) and a ruler. I measure with a ruler, as shown in figure 2, instead of using calipers, because calipers have a tendency to give a little—a ruler is more accurate. First, mark the center of the blank while the bowl is turning, then stop the lathe and hold the ruler so it crosses the center point. If you stop the end of the ruler against a small wooden block held against the side of the bowl, the ruler will line up exactly with the edge of the rim.

You can hollow the inside of the bowl quickly at first, checking your progress with a template copy held against the spinning work. But stop the work often to check the fit as you approach the final form, as shown in figure 3. Keep in mind that the centerline of the template must end up at the center of the bowl, and that both rim lines on the template must line up with the rim of the bowl.

Stop turning when the inside of the bowl is about $\frac{1}{16}$ in.

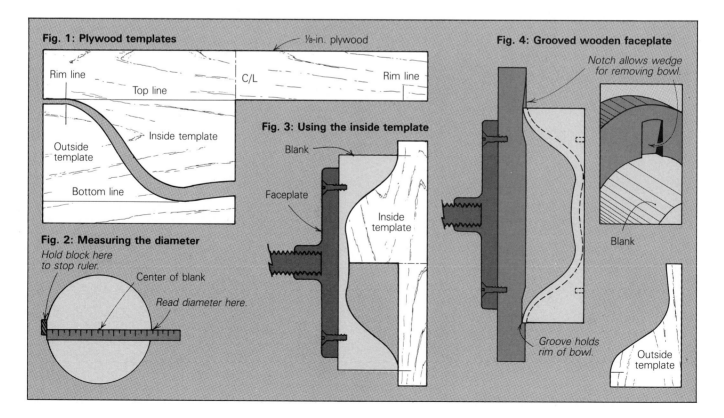

Fig. 1: Plywood templates

⅛-in. plywood

Rim line
Top line
C/L
Rim line
Inside template
Outside template
Bottom line

Fig. 2: Measuring the diameter

Hold block here to stop ruler.
Center of blank
Read diameter here.

Fig. 3: Using the inside template

Blank
Faceplate
Inside template

Fig. 4: Grooved wooden faceplate

Notch allows wedge for removing bowl.
Blank
Groove holds rim of bowl.
Outside template

full of these final marks, then switch to the master template. Rub the edge of the template with a little chalk or a crayon. Stop the lathe and rock the master back and forth in the bowl, gently transferring chalk to the high spots. Carefully turn away the marks, stopping and checking after every cut, until the master deposits an even spread of chalk along the profile of the bowl, but still about $\frac{1}{64}$ in. full of the reference points. Sand down to the line, using from 180-grit to 360-grit sandpaper, but leave the outside rim square so it can be mounted in the next step. Take every bowl in the set to this stage before proceeding.

To turn the outsides, begin by scribing a line that shows the location of the bottom of the rim. This will be the reference line for the outside template. Then check the diameters of all the bowls. There's always some slight difference, sometimes due to wood movement, sometimes to that last pass with the sandpaper. Select the smallest and turn a shallow groove in a wooden faceplate so that the rim of this bowl fits tightly (figure 4). There is no room for error here. Cut the opening with a skew chisel until its outside is slightly smaller than the rim of the bowl. Then turn the chisel over and rub, rather than cut, the last few thousandths away, until the bowl fits tightly and is difficult to remove.

We will hold the bowl in with a few tiny spots of glue, then use little softwood wedges or give it a light rap with a hammer to pop it out of the groove after the turning is done. Make some shallow notches in the faceplate before you glue the bowl in, so you will be able to get the wedges beneath the bowl's rim.

Mark a circle on the blank, approximately the size of the bottom of the bowl. Then turn the underside of the bowl using the center and rim line as guides, testing as before, until the chalk shows no more high spots. Switch to the master template and finish the bowl. Remove it with the wedges.

Enlarge the groove in the faceplate if necessary, to fit the next larger bowl, then repeat the process. When all the bowls have been turned, I use files and a piece of sandpaper glued firmly to a block to shape the rims, and I check the curve of

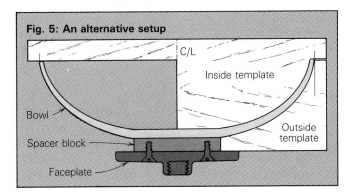

Fig. 5: An alternative setup

the outside edge with radius gauges (standard sheet-metal templates). Because matched bowls are usually used for food, I finish them with a non-toxic finish such as Constantine's Wood Bowl Seal, or a vegetable oil.

Once you understand how templates work, you can vary their use. A single-mounting setup that lets you work on the rim more easily is shown in figure 5. Its drawback is that the bottom cannot be as easily shaped. You have to glue uniform spacer blocks to the blanks and allow for their thickness in laying out the design on the template.

You can also take the guesswork out of long turnings. Just use several smaller templates along the length of the turning, each with its own set of reference points on the straight sections. If your lathe allows you to remove and replace your turnings accurately, do each step on all the turnings before proceeding to the next; if it doesn't, make a list of the steps so you can repeat them exactly in order.

As in all woodworking, accuracy on the lathe is as much a state of mind as it is a procedure. Templates will show you when you have gone far enough, but only your skill as a turner will prevent you from going too far. □

Arthur F. Sherry, of New York City, has completed four years as an apprentice patternmaker, and is now a partner in South Family Furniture, making custom furnishings.

Walnut-oil finish is safe for food   _by Antoine Capet_

A few hundred years ago, rubbed oil made do as a finish for everything from the cogs in wooden clocks to the gear on old sailing ships. When we think of rubbed oil, most of us probably think first of linseed oil, which is the most prevalent of the traditional oils, at least for outdoor items such as gateways and for seafaring. Yet many of us shy away from using it on bowls or other receptacles for holding food because modern, fast-drying linseed oils usually have poisonous chemical additives. The odor of linseed oil, also, while pleasant on a tool handle or in an artist's studio, quickly takes away one's appetite.

There are several other oils that can be used instead. A classic book on finishing, _Lexique du Peintre en Batiment,_ by Le Moniteur de la Peinture (Paris-Liège, 1935-36), lists other natural oils and their drying capabilities:

Oils, high drying capability—linseed, poppy, tung, walnut, hemp, sunflower.

Oils, moderate drying capability—colza, soya.

Oils, no drying capability—olive, peanut, almond, castor, grape pips.

Some of these rule themselves out. Tung oil is not edible, poppy oil (from artists' supply stores) is exorbitantly priced, and hemp oil is unobtainable these days. I've left the moderate-drying oils alone, because they seem to have no advantages. Olive oil, often mentioned as a salad bowl finish, has the drawback of never drying.

Walnut oil, though, the traditional French furniture polishing oil, deserves a closer look. It is not only edible, it is de-

licious. And it can be bought in health food stores and specialty food shops at a price that compares favorably with modern finishing oils.

Walnut oil's pleasant odor and non-toxic qualities are in sharp contrast to some other finishes I've tried. One commercial salad-bowl finish, though certified safe for bowls, has a strong smell of petroleum distillate that persists for a long time. Another "certified safe" finish requires that you wait 30 days before actually using the object.

There are additional advantages to using walnut oil on functional objects. Quick and soft finishes, waxes for instance, poorly resist spilled coffee, wet hands and damp fruit. Walnut oil takes these things in stride. Many hard-film finishes can chip, crack or peel away, but walnut oil penetrates deeply, and will conform to a dent without losing its ability to protect against moisture.

What then is wrong with it? Walnut oil requires time to build into a decent finish, ruling it out in a cabinetmaking shop that seeks a quick, high gloss. But for many of us, making things for our own pleasure, this is not so important.

I use walnut oil without a sealer, because it accentuates the figure best when allowed to penetrate deeply into the wood. I made some tests on fenceposts and found little difference in its drying time (about the same as raw linseed) whether I added small quantities of drier or not. But I found a pronounced acceleration when the oil was applied hot. It can be heated for a few minutes in a saucepan, about one-quarter full, until fumes begin to thicken. There's always a danger of fire, of course, but people safely fry with hot oil every day.

The smoother the surface texture, the less oil the object will absorb, and the faster it will shine. You can use a paintbrush to apply the oil, but it's better if you dip the wood, because the end grain will gulp up vast quantities, ensuring protection against future checking. Work the oil into the wood, rubbing surplus from the sides around into the end grain. After a day or so, polish it at high speed on the lathe.

I usually wait two weeks before giving the wood a second application, then two or three months, then a year or more between further treatments. □

Antoine Capet teaches contemporary British social history at the University of Rouen, in France.

Turning goblets

by J.H. Habermann

Turning a goblet presents a few problems, but once you see your way around them, the job becomes easy. **Design:** Some turners have enough confidence to let the shape evolve as they work, but I generally pick a shape I like—a favorite wineglass, for instance—and trace it with a device similar to those in *FWW* #18 (p. 83), a pencil mounted on a base that follows the profile of the glass to make an outside pattern.

Once you have traced the outline and allowed ¼ in. for the walls, you can plan to drill out most of the inside with Forstner or multi-spur bits chucked in the tailstock. This will save wear and tear on your turning tools as you remove the difficult end grain. Determine from your own pattern which size bits to use and how deep to drill, as shown in figure 1. Use calipers to measure the diameter of the glass at several points, then mark these dimensions on a template made from hardboard.

Wood: You can make almost anything into a goblet. Even native "weed trees" such as sumac work well. Goblets don't require scarce, chunky turning blocks; offcuts from furniture wood can be used. You can laminate thin stock either vertically or horizontally to get enough mass—just don't try to glue end grain. And leave some extra length. This allows you to turn a stub tenon for mounting the work in a wooden faceplate. You wouldn't want to waste this precious depth on a bowlturning blank, but here it doesn't matter.

Turning: Glue the stub tenon into the faceplate, aligning and clamping it with your tailstock, as in figure 2. When it is dry, rough-turn the outside of the top of the goblet, referring to the caliper sizes on the template, but do not turn the narrow stem yet. Chuck the appropriate

Fig. 1: Hardboard template, drilling guide

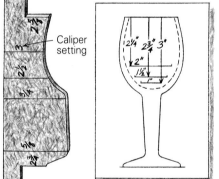

Caliper setting

Fig. 2: Stub-tenon mounting

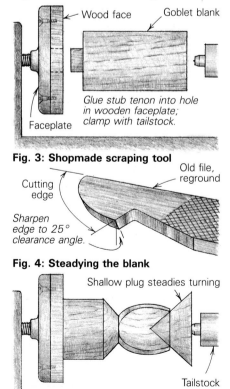

Wood face — Goblet blank

Glue stub tenon into hole in wooden faceplate; clamp with tailstock.

Faceplate

Fig. 3: Shopmade scraping tool

Cutting edge

Old file, reground

Sharpen edge to 25° clearance angle.

Fig. 4: Steadying the blank

Shallow plug steadies turning

Tailstock

drill bits in the tailstock, and drill out as much of the inside as you can.

True the inside by hand. Turners generally look down on scraping tools, but there's a lot of end grain in a goblet, and this is where scrapers excel. Commercial side-cutting scrapers such as Sorby's work well, but you can make your own by grinding old files, as shown in figure 3. I use my thumb and fingers as a thickness gauge.

When the inside of the goblet is true, insert a shallow plug (figure 4) and draw up the tailstock for stability. This will save you a lot of blown-up goblets as you turn the stem.

Using a combination of calipers and the template, turn the stem and clean up the shape. When I am duplicating a series, I make a full template that slips over the entire goblet while the lathe is stopped. This solves the problem of registering a half-template.

Before final-sanding, partially part off the base. Point the parting tool slightly toward the tailstock. This will give you a concave bottom that will be more stable.

Sanding and finishing: You will get far fewer circular scratches if you use an orbital sander to sand the work while it is turning. Work down to 280-grit, reversing the lathe once in a while if you can, and finish up with steel wool and a final polish with a handful of chips.

You will need to seal the goblet if you plan to use it. I have had great success with John Harra's DPS (deep penetrating sealer), which plasticizes in about a week. If you want a higher gloss, you can finish over this with a natural drying oil, or you can use commercial salad-bowl finishes. □

J.H. Habermann lives in Joplin, Mo.

Cutting flutes on curved turnings

For cutting reeds and flutes on curved and tapered turnings, I use a cutter mounted in a drill press, and a special indexing jig to hold the workpiece. Although making the cutter requires some time and moderate metalworking skills (or machine-shop expense), once it is done you can cut reeds and flutes on any shape with minimal set-up and excellent results.

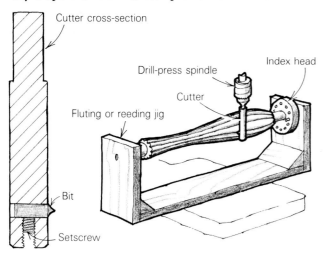

Make the cutter from a short length of ⅝-in. cold-rolled steel. Turn the top 1 in. of the cutter down to ½ in. so it can be chucked in the drill press. Drill a ¼-in. hole through the cutter ½ in. from its bottom, and file the hole square to accept a short length of ¼-in. tool steel for the bit. In the bottom of the cutter, drill and tap a hole for a setscrew, which holds the bit in place. Grind the bit to the shape of the profile desired for the reed or flute.

When the cutter is complete, you will also need a jig to hold the turning and to index the work as the flutes are cut. The jig can be either a simple one-time affair, or of a more elaborate, permanent design incorporating an adjustable tailstock. In either case, lay out the round indexing head carefully by dividing the circle into a number of equal angles according to the number of flutes required. For example, if 24 flutes are desired, then the pin holes on the index head will be 15° apart. On a permanent jig, you can use one indexing head for many combinations by laying out several concentric circles of pin holes, each with a different number of holes.

To cut the flutes, first turn and sand the workpiece, then fasten it in place between centers in the jig. With the jig in place on the drill-press table, lower the drill-press quill until the cutter bit is on the centerline of the turning. Lock the quill at this setting. With the drill press running at its highest speed, move the turning into the bit and across the table. The bit cuts the profile of the flute while the cutter body rubs along the turning, regulating the depth of cut. After the first cut, index the turning to the next hole and repeat the process until all the flutes have been cut.

—Kenneth Weidinger, Erlanger, Ky.

Three-jaw "overshoes" for bowlturning

Like many avid woodturners, I use a three-jaw chuck for bowlturning and other faceplate work. With it you can avoid screw holes in the bottom of the bowl, or skip the step of gluing on a waste bottom with paper between. But the three-jaw chuck is limited in the size range it can hold, and it contacts the workpiece at only three points, limiting the strength of its grip—if you overtighten it you will mar the work. I overcome these problems by adding wooden "overshoes" to the chuck. The overshoes, shown above right, are

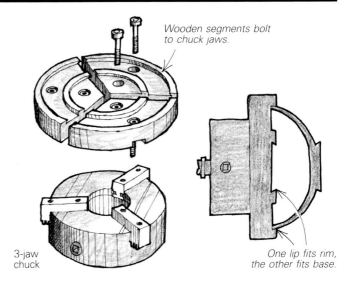

simply three 2-in. thick, wooden circle segments. I cut a groove in the back of each segment and bolt the piece to the jaw with two countersunk Allen bolts. Annealed chuck jaws, which can be drilled and tapped for the bolts, are available for most chucks; it's handy to have more than one set.

In the face of the wooden overshoes, I turn two recesses, slightly dovetailed, to fit the rim and the base of a bowl. I mark both the overshoe segments and their matching jaws—if removed, each overshoe must go back on the same steel jaw it came off of.

To use the overshoe chuck, I first mount the bowl blank on a large screw center and turn the outside to rough dimensions, taking care to size the base within a range that will fit the overshoe chuck. Then I reverse the blank, remount with the overshoe chuck gripping the base, and turn the inside of the bowl. When the inside is complete, I reverse the bowl in the chuck, gripping it by the rim to complete the outside. This technique is particularly useful when working green wood, which must be turned rough, then dried, and then remounted for turning to final shape and finishing.

—A.R. Hundt, Blackmans Bay, Tasmania

Reversing lathe rotation for sanding

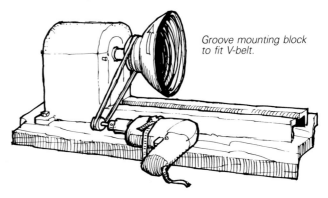

Here's how I reverse the rotation on my lathe for sanding turned bowls. This approach reduces the problem of the faceplate unscrewing from the spindle, as often happens if you reverse the motor or the drive belt. After the bowl is turned, I cut a pulley groove in the glue block. Then I chuck a plywood pulley mounted on a ¼-in. bolt into my electric drill. I mount the drill to the lathe bed and use a small V-belt to turn the bowl in reverse rotation. Be sure to remove the lathe's drive belt before starting up the drill—otherwise the drill motor would be fighting the inertia of the heavier lathe motor.

—Lawrence A. Fortier, Pleasant Ridge, Mich.

Disc Sander Sculpts Turnings

A way to cut spirals without an ornamental lathe

by William Hunter

I am a woodturner, and turning a bowl allows me to search a piece of wood inside and out for the fullest realization of the wood's potential. Sometimes the turned wood is so inherently beautiful that I cannot improve on it. But sometimes the form and figure warrant enrichment. One of my favorite ways to treat such a turning is to put it in motion, that is, to send the eye along a journey over its surface. I groove the bowl in regular or irregular spirals. Then I mount it on an asymmetric stand, a ribbon of wood sculpted to present the sculpted turning.

My method has evolved from 15 years as a sculptor and briar pipe maker. The effect is reminiscent of those formal patterns produced on a Holtzapffel ornamental lathe. But instead of employing mechanized cutters controlled by pulleys, cogs and ratchets, I sit in front of a stationary disc sander and move the piece freehand over the disc's spinning edge.

The method may seem dangerous. But in the several years I ran a five-man shop, and in the several teaching experiences I've had at the high school level, I've never witnessed a run-in with the disc sander that required more than a band-aid to cover a minor strawberry. This is the result of conscientious attention to safe practices: always wear safety glasses with side screens; work in adequate light; use a stable, comfortable stool; wear a dust mask; maintain a concerted mental attitude. The mechanics of this technique are not inherently dangerous. The edge of the disc is not sharp, and disc speed is relatively slow. If you do accidentally touch the disc, centrifugal force throws your hand free. Because there is no table on my setup, there is no chance of pinch or kickback.

I begin such a turning by selecting a piece of wood that, while beautiful in color, is not exceptionally figured. I bandsaw a circular blank, glue it onto a piece of hardwood of the same diameter as the faceplate, using 5-minute epoxy, and screw the glue block to a faceplate. Then I turn the outside of the form between centers and sand completely, from 80-grit down through 400-grit. I find that simple, closed forms work better than open, flared forms. Spheres are easier than spheroids with flat surfaces. In small work, I don't hollow the bowl until the very end.

To lay out a bowl, I first mark the limits of the spiral: With the lathe turning, I press a pencil to the wood ½ in. from the bottom of the bowl and ½ in. from what will be the

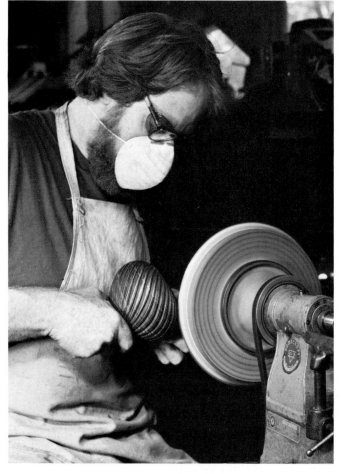

After the outside of a bowl is turned, regular spirals are laid out, above, by pivoting a compass from a block of wood, positioned first on one side, then on the other side of the lathe. A plywood disc mounted outboard indexes the blank. Freehand disc-sculpting, right, requires careful, measured, graceful movements. The sanding disc (which is the same piece of plywood that serves as the indexing wheel for layout) turns only 300 RPM to 500 RPM and is beveled on its back face to yield a definite edge against which the stock is drawn.

Photos: Leroy Radanovich and Bob Barrett

This 8-in. dia. marnut bowl on East Indian rosewood stand looks as if it were made on an ornamental lathe, but the spiral decorations were freehand-carved on the edge of a stationary disc sander.

lip of the bowl. I also make a mark around the bowl's largest diameter. This line will be the point where the spiral changes direction. It is also the circumference around which the spacing of the spirals is marked.

So that the spirals will be spaced evenly, I have mounted on the outboard side of the lathe a 12-in. plywood indexing plate. This plate (marked off in 28, 32, 40 and 48 increments, or however many you want) is a substitute for the lathe's smaller indexing plate. It is screwed to an outboard faceplate, offering a wider choice of indexing patterns and more control over tolerances. A pointer clamped to the lathe stand allows me to hold the bowl in position for each layout line. The spiral offers endless possibilities, but a good place to start is with 12 increments. As many as 24 increments work well on bowls up to 6 in. in diameter. I lay out each spiral with a compass pivoting from a block of wood clamped to the tool rest. Experiment with the compass and various tool-rest positions, looking for a pleasing sweep. Once decided, pencil an arc from the bowl top to the bowl center, crossing through each index mark. Reposition the tool rest on the other side of the lathe to complete the bottom of the arc, from the high point to the foot. Remove the turning, still attached to its faceplate, and examine the scribed lines to make sure that the layout is both accurate and aesthetically pleasing.

Now I move to the disc sander. This is the same plywood disc I have mounted outboard for an indexing plate: I cement 24-grit aluminum oxide (cloth-backed, resin bond) to the outside face and run the lathe at 300 RPM to 500 RPM. The slow speed affords better control for initial cutting, and the large diameter keeps the disc operating cool and also pre-

vents the paper from excessive loading. The edge of the disc is beveled at 30° toward its back side, so that there is a definite edge for cutting precise V-grooves. I cut with the outermost ¼ in. (or less) of the wheel, arcing the stock down along the edge, rather than pushing it straight in. I aim my cuts between the lines, trying to leave the pencil lines intact as reference until I approach finish-sanding. Disc-sculpting requires careful, measured, graceful movements, so it is important that you are seated comfortably, that your posture is relaxed and that your workspace is well lighted. Grip and wrist motion must be consistent so that all passes are equal. Therefore, you must maintain total concentration, without interruptions.

The first cut is very shallow and defines the basic form of the groove. Go once around the whole bowl, cutting about ¹⁄₁₆ in. deep in each groove. The second pass cuts deeper and wider into the established groove. You are now committed. Sometimes it takes only two passes to cut the desired arcs, sometimes as many as five. In this phase it is essential that each cut be equal and in sequence—never backtrack. Irregularities are better worked out with finer grits. It is also important to keep clear of the top and bottom guidelines; taper out the grooves later, with a finer-grit disc.

In the next phase I use an 8-in. Power Pad (available through Power Pad Mfg., 1223 W. 256th St., Harbor City, Calif. 90710) to refine form and to remove scratches. This is an industrial-quality foam disc that's flexible enough to sand contours easily. It's available in soft, medium and hard consistencies; I use mostly soft and medium. I cut my own sanding discs for the Power Pad from aluminum oxide and silicon carbide paper. It's less expensive than using pre-cut discs, but,

After the grooves are cut on the plywood sanding disc, Hunter uses a foam-backed disc to refine the shapes.

more important, you can control the amount of overhang. I use somewhere between $\frac{1}{32}$-in. and $\frac{1}{4}$-in. overhang, depending on whether I'm going for a hard line or a soft, rolled effect. Usually, $\frac{1}{8}$ in. is preferable. Also, after I cut an 8-in. disc out of $8\frac{1}{2}$-in. by 11-in. paper, I am left with enough scraps to use for lathe sanding and drum sanders. I recycle discs worn at the perimeter by cutting them down for 5-in. Power Pads and orbital sander discs.

I sand each groove in sequence, going two or three times around the bowl with the Power Pad in each grit. I begin with 80-grit aluminum oxide paper, then repeat the process with 150-grit aluminum oxide, 220-grit aluminum oxide and 400-grit silicon carbide. Then I move to the Sand-O-Flex flap sander (which can also be run on the lathe), using a combination of 240-grit and 320-grit, $\frac{1}{8}$-in. shred, for removal of sharp edges and concave finish work. Final-sanding is done on the Power Pad, with 400-grit and 600-grit, then I hand-sand. The piece is now ready for buffing.

The buffing process I use was originally designed for briar smoking pipes and works well on closed-grain hardwoods. The beauty of it is that, unlike metal buffing compounds, it does not clog the pores of the wood and it tones but does not discolor hardwoods. It is quick, and it burnishes the wood, adds luster and depth, and produces a hard, gem-like finish.

I use buffing wheels, compounds and waxes available from Pimo Pipe Supplies, Box 59211, Chicago, Ill. 60659. The wheels, designed for pipemakers, have a beveled edge that allows more detail in buffing. I generally use a 1-in. wide beveled buffing wheel, 9 in. in diameter. Wider wheels work best on broad surfaces because they provide a consistent polish with less danger of removing soft areas in the wood's surface. All of these wheels are designed to run at 1725 RPM, either with a $\frac{1}{2}$-HP motor or on the lathe. The compounds are colored waxes—green, red and white—impregnated with abrasive grits equal to 700-, 800- and 900-grit. I use four wheels. The first is a firm sewn muslin, which I use with green compound. The second is a softer sewn flannel, used with red compound. The third, a soft unsewn flannel, is used with white compound. The fourth, a very soft flannel, is for the hard carnauba wax. It is important not to overload the wheels with abrasives.

If all has gone well, you now have a spiraled bowl, the exterior of which is complete. Time now to return to the lathe to hollow the bowl. I prefer a closed form for my spiral-grooved turnings because it allows me greater surface area to explore sculptural techniques.

I find it helpful to begin with a $\frac{3}{4}$-in. drill bit in the tailstock, to clear the center and define the bottom of the piece. I hollow-turn with a combination of handmade chisels, using a spear point for clearing waste and a roundnose for finishing. (For a detailed discussion of hollow-turning, see *FWW* #16, pp. 62-66.) After I'm satisfied with wall thickness, usually $\frac{1}{8}$ in. to $\frac{1}{4}$ in., and that the last chisel cut is smooth, I cut the bowl from the faceplate, beginning with a parting tool and finishing with a backsaw. I finish the bottom on the disc and belt sanders.

Freehand disc-sculpting is workmanship of risk. It takes hundreds of passes with the disc's edge before you capture the spiral and you hold the finished form in your hands. Then you feel its weight for the first time, to know the thickness of its walls, and the piece comes to life. □

Freehand disc-sanding also lends itself to less regular, asymmetric decoration, as in this 6-in. dia. Indian rosewood bowl.

Bill Hunter is a professional turner in El Portal, Calif.

An answer to breathing dust

Turning tropical woods, fossilized walrus tusks, soapstone and amber was a health hazard in my shop. Solving the problem has been quite a challenge.

My first step was to set up an exhaust system built out of parts from an old line-finisher (a shoe repair bar). These machines are outdated in the shoe industry and can be picked up relatively cheap: $100 to $200. They have a great 6-in. exhaust system built in. I cannibalized the one from our machine, and hooked it up to a 1½-HP motor and 6-in. stovepipe. This handled most of the dust from my lathe, but some left the force field, especially during power-sanding. So I experimented with a box, as shown in the drawing, that totally enclosed the headstock, the tool rest and the piece, yet still allowed work on the piece. For most turning, the box, in conjunction with the line-shaft exhaust system, worked. There are some drawbacks, however. You need several sizes for different scale work, power-sanding is possible only awkwardly through the top, vision is limited, and the setup slows you down. Also, for turning soapstone (with its high asbestos content) and fossilized walrus tusk (which I'm highly allergic to), I needed more protection—I could still see small amounts of dust escaping. The lathe box is close to what I need, and I regard it as a must, so I'm still trying to improve it.

Meanwhile, I sought advice through the occupational safety program at San Francisco General Hospital. For only $15, a team of experts, both medical and industrial, spent an evening discussing my problem with me. Two weeks later I received a package of safety information, including specs on the 3M Airhat, mentioned in the article "Respiratory Hazards" in *FWW* #41.

To be absolutely assured with this system, you have to get a licensed industrial safety engineer to come and test the particulate content of your shop. The cost of such a test was almost the cost of the $400 Airhat, so I took the chance, figuring that if I had no allergic reaction when working walrus ivory, I would be adequately protected against other substances as well.

The Airhat includes a protective Lexan face shield, a beard collar, an air hose, and a battery and filter pump you wear on your belt. In conjunction with my lathe box and exhaust system it works great. I had *no* allergic reaction to walrus tusk at all. I have found the system as comfortable as a face shield, and I prefer it to a dual-filter respirator and

goggles. The helmet has several adjustments for proper fit. The battery pack and pump are light and behind you, out of the way. The hum of the pump isn't a problem; after a couple of minutes it seems to go away. I also wear a lab coat now, so *all* dust is left in the shop.

In my opinion, here are the positive aspects of the Airhat:
—It provides total face protection, even if you wear a beard, and partial head protection from "fly-off."
—There's no facial pressure or sweat as with a respirator-and-goggle combination; it's actually cool and pleasantly breezy inside.
—I've had no fogging problem.
—It provides dust protection in shop areas that don't have exhaust.
—Talking is easier than in a dust mask.
—It doesn't interfere with large ear protectors or eyeglasses.
—It's been easy to maintain and clean.
—You feel secure and healthy inside it.

Working materials like the ivory of this 4½-in. dia. bowl requires special attention to dust collection.

Here are the negative aspects:
—It costs $400.
—Its batteries need to be charged for 12 to 16 hours after every 8 hours of operation. You'll damage them if you "top off" the charge frequently. An extra battery can be ordered, but this still requires orderly attention.
—It takes longer to put on and take off than other respirators, and it's tough to train yourself to use it *all the time.*
—You sound weird on the phone.
—Shop partners have a tough time taking you seriously.

I highly recommend the Airhat in conjunction with some form of shop exhaust system. I've had no experience in a totally dust-filled room using only an Airhat. —*W.H.*

Dust-free and breezy inside his 3M Airhat, Hunter turns a bowl in the dust-collection box drawn below.

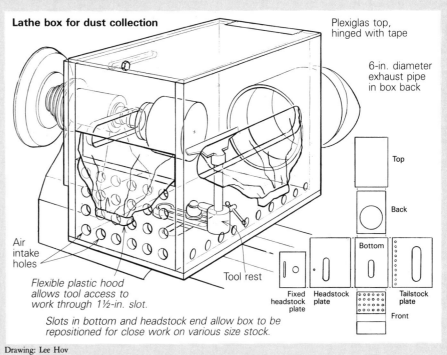

Lathe box for dust collection

Plexiglas top, hinged with tape

6-in. diameter exhaust pipe in box back

Top

Back

Bottom

Air intake holes

Tool rest

Fixed headstock plate

Headstock plate

Tailstock plate

Front

Flexible plastic hood allows tool access to work through 1½-in. slot.

Slots in bottom and headstock end allow box to be repositioned for close work on various size stock.

Drawing: Lee Hov

Knife Work
Make the knife and carve a spoon

by Rick Mastelli

Winter nights are long in Sweden. When farmers go into the forest to cut the year's firewood, they make a point of also collecting bent limbs and crotches, blanks from which to whittle spoons in the evening months. In rural Sweden many men still wear knives, not as weapons but as ready tools, and it is part of the ritual of conversation to punctuate a sentence with a shaving from a stick. In some parts of the world whittlers carve figures or ornaments, and there are always some who just make chips. In Sweden spoons are traditional, and still popular. The centuries have yielded a deep understanding of hand-tool techniques, as well as of the form of the wooden spoon—together they evidence a refined simplicity.

A week-long workshop I attended last summer focused on these hand-tool techniques. The place was Country Workshops in Marshall, N.C., and the teacher was Wille Sundqvist, a wiry, 57-year-old Swede whose relationship to craft is long and thorough. As a boy he learned to carve by watching his father and grandfather, both of them farmers and winter woodworkers. When he was six years old, he discovered the first principle of knife work while squabbling with his brother. His brother grabbed the knife's handle and he gripped the blade, and when they pulled, he learned indelibly how knives slice. At 20 Sundqvist hurt his back in a forest accident, and so had to find a career other than farming. He went to wood-

Sundqvist uses innumerable knife grips and strokes. These two are among his most powerful, because they slice away from the body and require no 'safety stop' to protect the carver from the blade. At right, the hand that holds the blank rigid is lodged above the kneecap. The knife is held at an angle in the hand such that the stroke leads with the handle, the tip of the blade trails. The slice is powered from the shoulder and back, with elbow and wrist locked. Above, the slice is also from the handle toward the tip, but here leverage against the chest helps power it.

Photos: Rick Mastelli and Drew Langsner

Sundqvist demonstrates the grip and stance for grinding an ax. The backing board helps to maintain even pressure on the ax head as it is run diagonally over the grindstone.

working school, where he apprenticed with the illustrious furniture designer Carl Malmsten. Later he taught woodworking at Malmsten's school, and in various elementary and preschool programs, then for ten years he taught others to be woodworking teachers. Since 1969 Sundqvist has been consultant to the Handcraft Society in the province of Västerbotten, researching traditional handcrafts and helping the disabled and the elderly become productive craft workers.

In Sundqvist's hands, ax and knife are powerful, precise tools. Throughout the week at Country Workshops we ten students were awed. Sundqvist could waste thick, measured slabs from an ornery dogwood branch, or with the same surety scribe vigorous detail into a spoon handle. Every inch of the knife blade or ax edge, every contour of their handles, had its purpose and right use. He showed us a profuse variety of traditional grips and strokes—useful not only because they direct the cut but also because they provide built-in safety stops, in that the cuts end when part of the hand or arm comes in contact with the work (or part of the carver's body), thus keeping the knife from slicing flesh. When you are sure of your stop, you can work with confidence and direct more energy into the cut. Not only his hands, but the whole of his body worked. Barefoot, shirtless, in shorts, he showed the interaction between thrust and safety stop, brace and swing, grip and lever. He did not say much; English does not come easy for him. We learned by watching him work.

It's shocking how much we modern craftsmen underestimate the basic tools. Knives sold for carving come with spindly handles and stubby blades, their bevels dubbed round by the buffing wheel. Axes are sold with their bevels made bulbous by a sanding belt, and with handles so skinny that your fingers bottom out on your palm. No wonder we figure these tools are good only for hacking at firewood. The quality of an

artisan's work increases directly with his understanding of and respect for his tools. Thus Sundqvist began by having us make knives. We spent a full day fitting a 3½-in. long, laminated Swedish steel blade into a chunk of applewood, then shaping the wood to fit our own hands. We took another day fitting the knife into a wooden sheath with a leather collar we sewed wet around the knife's handle. After the leather dried and shrank, the knife could be eased out and snapped securely back into place, and afterward it hung from our belts to remind us how handy a knife can be.

We sharpened our tools so there was no rounding at the edge, and no secondary microbevel, for the surfaces that produce the edge have to be flat. Dubbing is right for edges that are meant to split wood; dubbing keeps the tool from sticking in the wood. And a microbevel is okay for a chisel, whose flat back registers the cutting edge. But for a knife, the bevel itself is that registration plane. When it is flat on the wood surface, the edge must be there too, ready to cut. These blades were manufactured by Erik Frost in Sweden and are called Sloyd knives by most woodworking supply outlets. You can see the lamination line halfway up the bevel. The softer steel sandwiching the harder makes the knife less brittle and easier to sharpen. We sharpened to a greater angle than is usually recommended: 25° for knives and gouges, 28° for axes. For knives, the bevels on either side of the blade are equal. For axes, if you are right-handed, you sharpen the left-hand bevel longer than the right, for more surface with which to guide the cut. Axes can be honed by moving the ax head over a stationary stone, but I found it easier to clamp the ax upright in a vise and move the stone over the bevels in small circles. Sundqvist showed us how to keep our eye on the bevel opposite the stone, looking for a thin line of honing oil to be scraped off the stone's surface and to run down the edge. Maintain the finest flow of oil, and your bevel will be flat. This technique also works for honing the carving gouges used to hollow the bowls of spoons. You hold the tool upright in one hand, bevel away from you, and rub the face of a stone

Fig. 1: Plans for a Sloyd knife handle

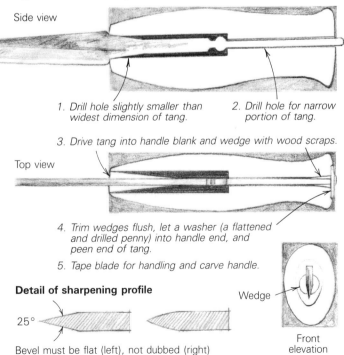

Side view

1. Drill hole slightly smaller than widest dimension of tang.

2. Drill hole for narrow portion of tang.

3. Drive tang into handle blank and wedge with wood scraps.

Top view

4. Trim wedges flush, let a washer (a flattened and drilled penny) into handle end, and peen end of tang.

5. Tape blade for handling and carve handle.

Detail of sharpening profile

25°

Bevel must be flat (left), not dubbed (right)

Wedge

Front elevation

Making a spoon begins with a green crook that you split at the pith using the ax, driven by a maul, as a wedge (above). The top and bottom of the spoon are shaped first (above right), then the sides (right). Careful, measured strokes, always aimed below the hand that holds the blank, define the basic shape.

up and down, flat against the bevel. Rotate the tool slowly back and forth to present the whole of the bevel to the slip stone, all the while looking for the dribble of oil to leak over the edge. To remove the burr, slip the round edge of the stone up and down, flat against the inside of the gouge.

Any close-grained, dense wood will make a good spoon. The natural curves of branches make for a stronger utensil, because the grain can follow the shape. We had a pile of green crooks and crotches to work: rhododendron, dogwood, black birch, apple. At times it seemed that the spoons we were making were only vehicles for practice with knife and gouge. Eventually the tool and hand would work effortlessly for a while, and the infinite possibilities of the spoon would replace the challenge of simply using the tools. How make a lump of wood hold food, be comfortable to the hand and mouth, please the eye, enjoy use? The bowl of the spoon needs to be thin, to fit the lips, and so for strength it ought be oriented to minimize end grain. The stem of the spoon should position the bowl below the plane of the handle, and to satisfy the eye it should be narrow, so for strength it ought be thick and continue down like a spine, supporting the bowl. The top of the handle should be thin, to fit the hand, so for strength and visual balance it should be wide. A wide

surface calls for decoration, so at the top ("to keep the eye from flying off," as Sundqvist puts it) you need a finial. Making a spoon, you learn how deep is the challenge—design that is infinite with possibilities, all coordinated by tradition and function. Suddenly, the wooden spoons you buy at the supermarket are two-dimensional.

It's surprising how much like a spoon you can shape a branch with only an ax. First the ax splits the branch in half (you drive it with a maul, like a wedge), to ensure that the pith will not be part of the spoon. The trick for the rest of the ax work is to support the blank solidly on the chopping block and far enough forward so that an overswing will not end in your leg. Hold the blank so that the thrust of the stroke is below your fingers. You shape the side view of the spoon first, including most of the bottom of the bowl, then you define the outline of the bowl and handle. This order gives you more stock to hold on to longer. The strokes that shape the stem near the beginning of the bowl are the most critical, because an overswing here can easily crack the bowl. For a more mincing stroke, you hold the ax closer to its head.

Now you sit down with your knife and a couple of gouges. The green wood cuts like cheese. The diverse grips for safe, forceful knife and gouge work are recorded in the photos of

154

Fig. 2: Plans for a Swedish spoon

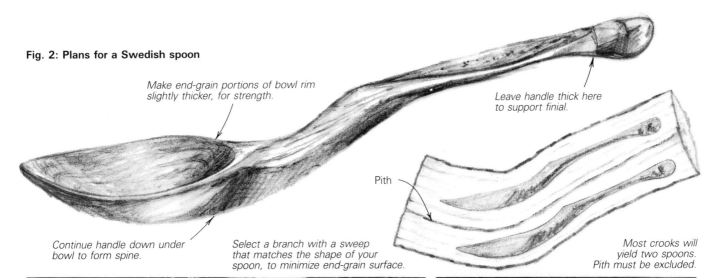

Make end-grain portions of bowl rim slightly thicker, for strength.

Leave handle thick here to support finial.

Pith

Continue handle down under bowl to form spine.

Select a branch with a sweep that matches the shape of your spoon, to minimize end-grain surface.

Most crooks will yield two spoons. Pith must be excluded.

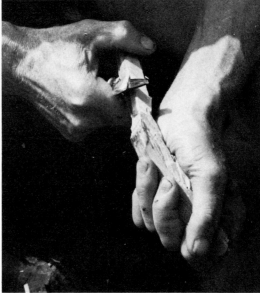

Most of us pare by slicing from the stout end of a knife toward the tip. Sundqvist gets greater power arcing the blade from tip to handle, often using his thumb for leverage. Each stroke has its safety. Above, the thumb is held out of the knife's direction on the spoon end. At right, Sundqvist modifies this stroke to slim the middle of the spoon's handle by repositioning the thumb 90° to the stroke and rotating the knife in the palm about 30° toward the blank. Short, arced strokes stop before the thumb is touched.

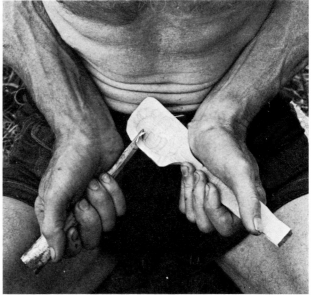

It doesn't take long to shape the blank with the knife before it's time to hollow the bowl. Gripping the gouge as shown at left keeps the stroke short and safe. Most of the strokes are cross-grain, and they stop when the hand contacts the spoon. The rim of the bowl calls for special grips. The knife grip above may look dangerous, but it has its safety and is surprisingly controlled. The trick here is to put your little finger on the flat of the blade, which positions the heel of the hand along the back. Then both arms are braced against the ribs, and the hands move together like a pair of scissors. With the wrist cocked, it is not possible for the knife to reach the body.

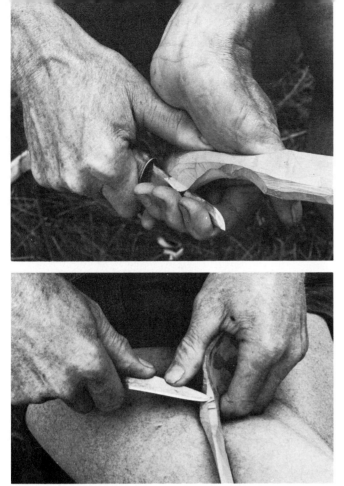

These two strokes are both powered by the hand not holding the knife. They show how Sundqvist uses the whole length of the blade: the stout portion for heavy cuts, the tip for fine work. At top is the still-green blank. Wet wood is easier to shape, but to smooth the surface, the spoon is first dried overnight. Dry wood, above, frays less.

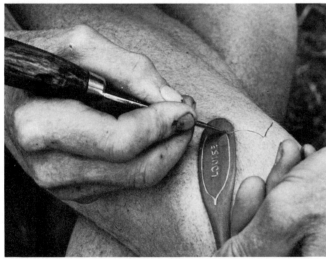

Gift spoons warrant decoration. Sundqvist first pencils in the shapes and letters, then uses the tip of the knife locked at about 60° to the surface, first in one direction, then the other, to remove a triangular chip of whatever length.

Sundqvist at work. Most of these positions feel strange at first, but by the time the calluses form, you have a physical memory. Your body reaches for the necessary posture to handle that excess of wood at the rim. For the underside of the handle, it reaches for another position. You don't think about it, you feel for it. But each time before you power the stroke, you think, *where is this edge going to stop?*, and you balance the tensions, or you adjust your hands so the edge doesn't end in your flesh. It's absorbing work. The conversations I enjoyed late into the night, unable to release my work for the day, were indeed punctuated with shavings.

When the shape of the spoon is there, you rub the blank with a boiled potato to fill the pores and forestall checking. The blank dries over the stove until morning. Green wood is easy to carve, but it is trouble to smooth. The next day you lightly go over your dry blank with the knife, and then you sand, until your spoon is fit for hand and lip.

Sundqvist was a remarkable teacher. He would devote himself entirely to one student at a time. He would listen to your question or watch you work for a moment. Then, unable to tell you what to do, he would show you. It was unnecessary to explain to him what shape you had in mind. He would see it in the blank. It may have taken you half a day to realize what you were doing, but he knew in half a minute—you would see what force could be exercised, how much wood could be made to disappear, if only you held the knife *this* way. It was unnerving at first to hand over that precious lump of wood, with all your feeble little nicks in it, and then watch great chunks of it fly. But it was your own vision Sundqvist handed you back. And then he would hold your hands in his and shape them to the task.

He cared about every piece of worked wood. The more effort that had gone into it, the more valuable it became. There were no mistakes we could make nor defects in the wood we could uncover that did not summon his healing energies. I watched him painstakingly patch a misbored hole in a knife handle, even an incipient check in a spoon bowl. The pieces hardly seemed worth the trouble—they still looked like ax offal. But he saw them as works, and his fixes made them all the more valuable. When finished, they were special pieces, marked by their making. Craftsmanship, Sundqvist demonstrated, is measured as much by the mistakes you correct as by the ones you avoid. □

Rick Mastelli is producer/director of Taunton Press' video department. He wrote about chairmaking in FWW #33.

A Sundqvist spoon, traditional craft.

Bent Bowl Gouges
Reforge your tools for finish-turning

by Douglas Owen

Owen turned this elm-burl bowl green, finishing it with one of his bent gouges. He says, 'It is difficult to season burr woods without all the little knots cracking badly. I couldn't sand the wet wood on the lathe, and I didn't want to sand after the wood had dried. I wanted to keep the wrinkled surface that comes from the wood's drying and warping, the more the better in this case. So I had to get a fine finish directly from the tool. I got what I wanted from one of the first bent gouges I made.'

The idea of tools bent along their length came to me at a woodturning seminar I attended two years ago, where I had a go on a bow lathe with the turning hooks as used by turners of old (see pp. 159-160). Also, David Ellsworth was there demonstrating the amazing cranked tools he uses to make his bowls, which are hollowed out through a small hole in the top (*FWW* #16, pp. 62-66). Woodcarvers have always used tools shaped like mine, and for the same reason—to get into places where a straight tool can't.

I have never liked scrapers. They blunt quickly and produce a rough surface. I use the conventional deep-fluted, U-section bowl gouge as a roughing-out tool. I finish with a shallow, long-and-strong gouge. It is ground straight across and used on its side, with the bevel rubbing for a slicing action. This means it can reach only so deep into the bowl before the bevel loses contact.

I forged the gouges shown below from straight long-and-strong ones. The forge was the woodstove in my living room; the fuel, barbecue charcoal; the draught, from a windy day. By blocking most of the grate with firebricks, I didn't have to use too much charcoal. For an anvil I set a blacksmiths' fuller in a lump of wood—a fuller is a rounded iron wedge that fits into the square hole in an anvil, for shaping iron. I heated the gouge red, placed its end over the fuller, and struck it with a heavy hammer. I had to repeat the process several times to get the full curve. To reharden the gouge, I heated the newly bent end bright red and plunged it into a bucket of cold water. It's important here to hold only the cutting end of the tool in the hottest part of the fire; otherwise thin tools tend to warp and thick ones may crack. Then I ground the tool smooth with small grindstones in an electric drill. I tempered it by heating it in my kitchen oven for one hour at 350°F, which brought the polished steel to a medium straw color, and then letting it cool slowly.

I always test new tools with a sharp masonry nail. If I can scratch the tool just behind the edge, I reharden and retemper. I have never found a chisel or a gouge that cannot be made excellent this way.

The tangs I either cut off short or bury deep in the han-

dle. If the handle is securely joined to the wide part of the tool shank, turning tools cut with less vibration. For handles I like a simple cylinder, though I'll rummage among the tools I'm not currently using for a handle before I'll make one. I frequently make a new handle when the first one does not seem quite comfortable. For ferrules I have used short pieces of plastic pipe, but I often don't bother. The handle can still split when driven on with a ferrule in position. Metal ferrules are cold on the hands. A handle should not be too long, too short, too fat, too thin, too light or too heavy. These are all matters of personal taste.

I grind the bevels hollow, stopping just short of the edge. I hone, using a fine oilstone, several times before having to regrind. I round over the heel of the bevel, to prevent its rubbing and marring the wood, and to make it slide smoothly.

Recently I tried one of my bent gouges inside a large elm goblet. I was delighted with how quickly I could get it smooth, even though cutting from rim to bottom was going against the grain. These gouges also work happily a long way over the tool rest. No doubt dig-ins are possible, but using the gouges only as finishing tools, I've had nothing nasty with them. □

Douglas Owen makes his living as a turner near Bainbridge, England. Photos by the author. For more on forging, see FWW #4, pp. 50-52, and #9, pp. 58-61.

Owen forged his bent gouges, excellent for finishing bowl insides, from straight long-and-strong gouges. The bent part is kept short to make the gouges easier to use.

Turning Tools That Cut
A book from Sweden favors some old tools

by James Rudstrom

My father's shop was equipped with all sorts of wood-working tools, and I was gradually introduced to their secrets. We had quite a number of machines, but no lathe. I guess one just didn't seem necessary for building houses and cabinets, and our economy permitted only necessities.

I was in ninth grade when I first tried turning. I don't recall being taught anything other than scraping, with the exception of attempting to make V-cuts with a rather dull skew. Several of my would-be masterpieces were ruined when the skew, instead of making its path toward the bottom of the V, skittered in the opposite direction, scarring everything in its path. That was my first experience with the cutting method of turning, although it took 20 years or so before I understood what I was up to.

I don't remember if it was because of my shop, his kids or his interest in English that I got to know my neighbor, crafts teacher Wille Sundqvist (see pp. 152-156). In any case, we hit it off well from the beginning. In 1978, while he was teaching an evening course in my shop, Sundqvist mentioned a book that he was writing on turning. We had touched on the subject before, but not at length or in depth, probably for the same reason that I hadn't gotten to turning before—I still didn't have a lathe in my shop.

Sundqvist and another turner, Bengt Gustafsson, have published their book, *Träsvarvning enligt skärmetoden* (LTs förlag, Stockholm, 1981). *Turning, The Cutting Method,* as its title translates, is not a large volume, but it covers many aspects of lathe work that have been more or less forgotten. The book touches on lathe construction, tool design, tool care, safety, the turning of cylinders and profiles, bowlturning, green-wood turning and more. It is well illustrated with photos and drawings. Unfortunately, it is not available in English yet; the authors are exploring the possibility of U.S. publication. Until then, here are some of the book's most interesting points, for English-speaking woodworkers.

The cutting method presented by Sundqvist and Gustafsson would definitely be suited for efficient use on treadle lathes and other low-tech machines. High RPM are unnecessary; in fact, undesirable. In most cases, the tools advocated are almost opposites to those in the "long-and-strong" school. "Short, sharp and sensitive" is the name of this game. If you're interested in trying the approach, you'll find that some of these traditional tools are hard to come by. You may find some treasures at auctions and flea markets. But most of us will have to modify standard tools, make our own or find someone who can. Even with the right tools, this kind of turning requires industrious practice, but in return there's little dust, surfaces that require little or no sanding, and the good feeling when fine shavings reel off the workpiece.

Tool rests—Many of the standard and auxiliary tool rests on the market maintain too much distance between their point of contact and the tool's cutting edge. When you use a short, light tool, it is essential that the tool be supported as close to the cutting edge as possible. The usual type of rest, which has a flat for the bearing surface (figure 1), will shift this contact point away from the stock when the tool is positioned at the steep angles often used when cutting, especially in faceplate turning. The cleanest cut is usually obtained at a steep angle, very close to the threshold of kickback. Resting short finishing tools at point B in figure 1 will obviously increase the risks of chatter and kickback. Sundqvist and Gustafsson suggest the solution in figure 2. Notice the removable pins that prevent tools from slipping into the chuck.

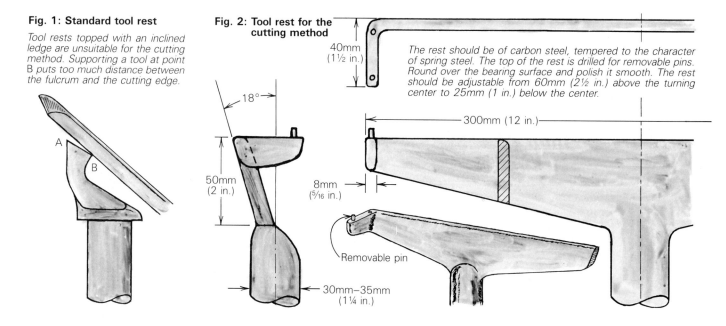

Fig. 1: Standard tool rest

Tool rests topped with an inclined ledge are unsuitable for the cutting method. Supporting a tool at point B puts too much distance between the fulcrum and the cutting edge.

Fig. 2: Tool rest for the cutting method

40mm (1½ in.)

18°

50mm (2 in.)

8mm (⁵⁄₁₆ in.)

The rest should be of carbon steel, tempered to the character of spring steel. The top of the rest is drilled for removable pins. Round over the bearing surface and polish it smooth. The rest should be adjustable from 60mm (2½ in.) above the turning center to 25mm (1 in.) below the center.

300mm (12 in.)

Removable pin

30mm–35mm (1¼ in.)

Photos and drawings adapted from *Trasvarvning enligt skärmetoden*

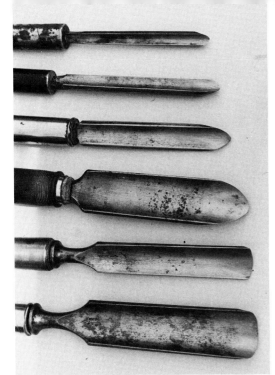

The tools at left were made by regrinding standard carvers' and turning gouges. Smoothing gouges (upper four) have an edge more curved than the edge of roughing gouges (lower two). Above, a gouge smooths the inside of a bowl.

Fig. 3: Gouges

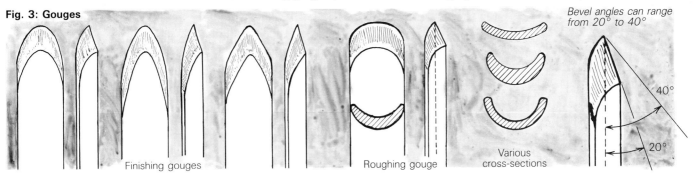

Bevel angles can range from 20° to 40°

Finishing gouges

Roughing gouge

Various cross-sections

40°

20°

Gouges—Two main types of gouges are mentioned: those used for roughing out and those used for forming and finishing. Examples of different edge shapes are shown in figure 3. Note that the angle of the bevel can vary between 20° and 40°, following the general rule of a greater angle for harder or more figured wood. Many of the gouges on the market are too long for finishing work. The authors prescribe using imagination in regrinding standard turning gouges and in experimenting with the great variety of carvers' gouges available. In some cases, you might want to forge your own.

Skew chisels—The skew is perhaps the most versatile of all the turning tools used to cut. In the hands of a skilled turner, the skew can make profiles appear as if by magic. The short and rather thin skews recommended here should have a taper, being thicker toward the handle, as shown in figure 4, to lessen vibration. The corners along the length of the tool are rounded and polished for a better feel in the hand and to facilitate a light, gliding movement over the tool rest. The normal angle of the skew should be 70°, although different angles and variations from straight edges are common. Hand-forged skews were often flared at the edge and had long bevels, making them thin and liable to overheat on modern lathes with high RPM, especially when turning harder wood. Bevels otherwise are between 20° and 40°, as with gouges.

Turning hooks—Among the more valuable subjects in the book is that of turning hooks or hollowing hooks. These low-speed tools are near-forgotten things of the past. In essence, the turning hook is a gouge with its cutting edge oriented 90° to the length of the tool. It can have a double edge or a

Fig. 4: Skew chisels

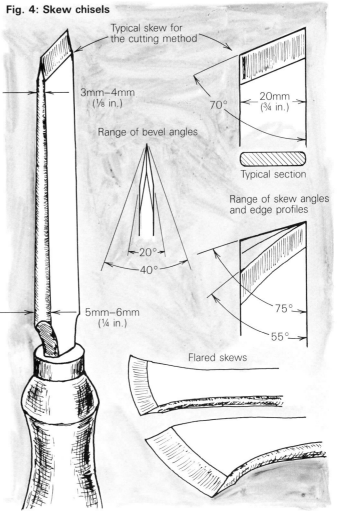

Typical skew for the cutting method

3mm–4mm (⅛ in.)

Range of bevel angles

70°

20mm (¾ in.)

Typical section

Range of skew angles and edge profiles

20°

40°

5mm–6mm (¼ in.)

75°

55°

Flared skews

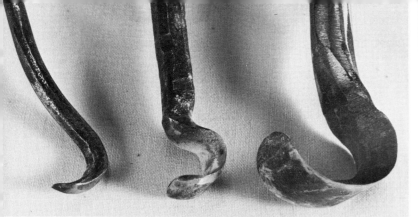

Turning hooks are actually gouges with the cutting edge turned 90°. The tool at left in the photo above was forged from a pitchfork tine. In the photo at right, a hook hollows a bowl.

Fig. 5: Turning hooks

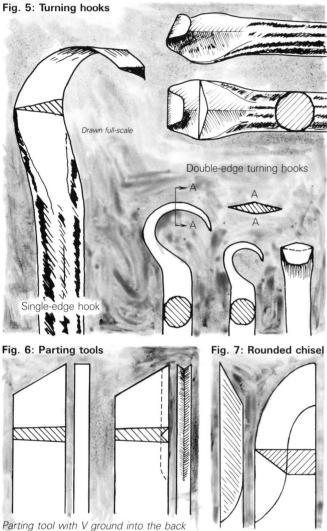

Drawn full-scale

Double-edge turning hooks

Single-edge hook

Fig. 6: Parting tools   **Fig. 7: Rounded chisel**

Parting tool with V ground into the back edge (right) cuts cleaner.   *(Shown in use, below.)*

A rounded chisel (figure 7) planes surfaces in faceplate turning. Its bevel rides the work.

single edge, as shown in figure 5 and the photos above.

The turning hook cuts with the grain when working cross-grain on a faceplate, starting from the outside and cutting toward the middle. Cuts in end grain are the opposite, starting from a bored hole in the middle and working outward. To work in tight places, some turning hooks have the bevel ground on the inside rather than the outside. Turning hooks more than ⅝ in. across are best for softer woods. Long handles are also recommended for larger hooks, to help prevent chatter and kickback. Sometimes a bent or an angled handle facilitates holding the tool at an efficient, safe edge angle.

Other tools—A parting tool with a flat back will do; one with a V ground into the back (figure 6), however, will produce a cleaner cut. The blade is thinner toward the bottom edge to provide clearance. The tool needs plenty of metal beneath the cutting edge, and a long, sturdy handle to help avoid chatter and kickback.

For faceplate turning, the book recommends a rounded chisel (figure 7), which can be fashioned from a scraping tool.

Tool length—It is difficult to give definite rules for turning-tool length. Generally, large skews, roughing gouges and parting tools are about 450mm (18 in.) in overall length. Tools used for making profiles and doing other finishing work should be very short, 300mm (12 in.) or less. It should be possible to move these tools in front of you without having to hold your breath and pull in your stomach. Experienced turners work with smooth movements, switching hands when necessary. ☐

James Rudstrom is a school psychologist in Vilhelmina, Sweden.

160

Lathe template fixture

A few months ago, while teaching lathe duplication methods to my cabinetmaking class, I discovered a novel and efficient method of rapidly producing identical turnings. Mount a template of 16-ga. metal on a swinging arm at the back of the lathe. After the stock has been turned round, swing the

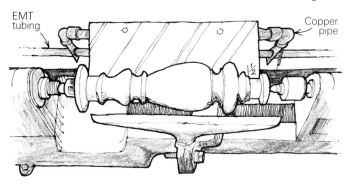

template against it with a light spring, maintaining enough tension to prevent excessive bounce. By cutting from the front in normal fashion and referring visually to the template at the rear, you will be able to quickly and accurately produce any number of identical turnings.

To keep each turning the same diameter, scratch a final diameter reference on a short, straight run at each end of the template. Work each end of the turning to these reference diameters first, then the gap between the reference diameters and the template will show the maximum cut depth to be taken from the workpiece's high spot.

My version of the duplicator is made from ¾-in. copper pipe, copper pipe elbows and a length of ½-in. EMT conduit. Solder up a U-shaped assembly from the copper pipe, flatten the pipe on each of the U's legs and drill to pivot on the conduit. Flatten the crosspiece of the U and drill to attach the template. Adjust the angle at which the template hits the work by heating the joints of the U and turning the template to the proper position. —*Doug Christie, Fort Grant, Ariz.*

Portable exhaust fan

The various home-workshop exhaust systems I'd seen either were too expensive or would simply suck all the precious heated air from the shop. The latter problem is important when you live in a northern climate and like to spend long winter nights over a lathe. The dust-exhaust system I built solves these problems. It is inexpensive, portable and of low velocity (so as not to empty all the heat from the shop). I mounted a 70-CFM bathroom fan on a 4-ft. long maple strip notched to hang on nails adjacent to my work areas.

The fan is vented through a standard dryer vent using 3-in. flexible bathroom vent hose. Since the vent hose is 3 in. in diameter and the dryer vent is 4 in. in diameter, I installed a PVC hose reducer to mate the two sizes. For convenience and neatness, you can run the electrical wire through the hose

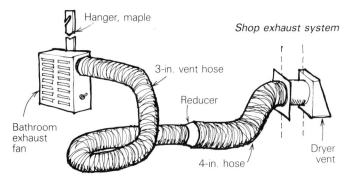

Shop exhaust system

or tape it to the outside. I installed a toggle switch on the fan box for turning the fan on and off.

The fan is handy for drawing paint fumes away, in addition to its main job of removing dust. But the darned idea works so well that even chips are drawn into the hose—I have to uncouple the hose and dump them out about once a month. —*Ronald R. Stolz, Guelph, Ont.*

Preserving green bowl blanks

To eliminate checking on green bowl blanks, simply store them in your freezer until you're ready to turn. I even use the freezer for storing work in progress if I'm interrupted before completing the rough-turning. This method is especially useful if you have a large number of green blanks and don't have time to rough them out so that they will dry properly. For long-term storage, wrap the blanks in plastic bags to avoid freezer burn and surface drying.

Another advantage of the method is that the frozen blanks turn without building up heat at the cutting edge—your gouge will need sharpening less frequently. Also, spalted wood, soaked and frozen, holds together much better.
—*Joel N. Kutz, Brockport, N.Y.*

Centerfinder for woodturners

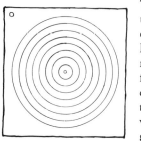

This plexiglass centerfinder will be useful to woodturners who split odd-shaped workpieces from the log. To make the gauge, first mount a piece of scrapwood to the faceplate and trim it to a round disc. Now attach a piece of ⅛-in. thick clear plexiglass to the scrapwood disc and scribe a series of target-like circles into the face of the plexiglass through its protective paper. Drill a center hole to fit your favorite scratch awl. To complete the gauge, spray the grooves with a colored enamel, drill a hang-up hole in one corner and remove the paper. To use the gauge, hold it on the end of irregular stock and adjust it until the largest possible circle falls completely over wood. Then mark the center.
—*Nels Thogerson, Ames, Iowa*

Improved hot-glue faceplate technique

To avoid screw holes and to speed assembly, I attach turning blanks using hot-melt glue chips and a torch-heated faceplate. Aluminum faceplates work better for this method because they conduct heat well and cool quickly. If your faceplate is iron, you can attach a thick aluminum face to the faceplate with flat screws.

First, be sure the bottom of the blank is flat. Then heat the faceplate with a torch and place it on the turning blank to warm the wood. Cut thin discs of hot-melt glue (no gun needed) and place them on the heated blank in amounts proportional to the bulk of the blank. Use enough to secure your doubts as well as your wood. Place the faceplate on the blank, and clamp in position until cool.

After turning is complete, aim a torch at the faceplate, heating it enough so the wood falls off with a gentle tap. While the glue is still hot, clean up the faceplate with a rag and scrape the glue from the bottom of the turning.
—*Randy Kalish, Belen, N.Mex.*

EDITOR'S NOTE: Several readers have expressed concern for the safety of previous faceplate attachment methods using hot glue or double-sided tape. Kalish's method seems more secure than these. Nonetheless, each reader should test this, or any other new technique, to be sure it is safe in his own application.

Carving Running Patterns

How to chop out picture-frame moldings by the yard

by Miles Karpilow

This complex Spanish design derives from a series of straightforward cuts.

The great picture frames, such as the richly carved portrait frames of the Louis XIV and Louis XV periods in France and those of 17th-century Spain, are carved with the whole frame in mind, so that the pattern is symmetrical, running from the center of each side to the corners. To make one of these, you have to know the size of the frame before you can begin to carve. But there is another way to make frames—you can carve a running pattern on a length of molding, and then cut it to whatever size is needed. By its nature, this is production work, and it goes quickly. Each cut may not look like much, but it sets the stage for the next, with no wasted motion and with far less fuss than one would imagine. There are fine examples of such continuous carved frames from virtually every historical period, from the Italian Renaissance through the end of the 18th century, when handcarving generally gave way to machine-made moldings with embossed patterns or cast ornamentation.

Like their more aristocratic cousins, running-pattern frames were usually finished with several layers of gesso followed by gold leaf. The patterns are similar to those found in furniture, but because the heavy gesso obscures the detail, the carving tends to be cruder. For a crisper look, some designs were reworked by carving the gesso. The scope of these carvings runs from simple beads, popular in the Renaissance and again in the Neoclassic period of Louis XVI, to the wide, flamboyant carvings of the Spanish and Italian Baroque. The origins of several patterns can be found in medieval manuscript decoration. One motif, peculiar to Spain, consists of spoon shapes and elephant ears. There are many versions of this, one of which I've described on pp. 164-165.

The word "bead" originally meant to pray—hence rosary beads, and eventually anything that looked like them, such as the beads on a necklace. Carved beads are actually a series of half-beads in high relief, as if a necklace were emerging from the wood. The molding is first planed into a sort of half-dowel shape running its length. The plane used is called a beading plane because it produces the shape that can be carved into beads. The shape on the molding is also called a bead, whether it is carved or not.

During my eight years as a carver and gilder, I developed a great respect for historical models. Robert Kulicke, the man I worked for and learned from, was very wary of what he called "inventing in the past tense." Chances are that our understanding of any period has been too much modified by our own, and that our attempts to work out new designs for a period will look inadequate and distorted to the next generation. But sometimes a carver has to take that risk. On one occasion I had to come up with something for an important 17th-century drawing, and nothing we had available would do. I decided to scale down and modify an existing model, and a short time later found an original frame virtually identical to my invention. Nearly every period frame we made, however, was copied from a specific model, and in most cases we owned the original, to which we continually referred in order to keep from straying. When possible, we'd scrub a section down to the bare wood to analyze the cuts. If you have a carved molding that you wish to duplicate, this is the route to take whenever possible. Examine the carving to figure out the minimum number of cuts and the most efficient order.

The carving technique is basically punch and shape. Each carving is a fixed number of strokes. When the chips fall away, you need to do very little secondary shaping. The interaction of the molding profile with the surface indentation creates an enormously rich texture, even though the execution is deceptively simple and satisfyingly quick. One traditional carver of my acquaintance, trained in Europe before World War II, was used to spending days on one delicate Louis XV panel and months on whole rooms of boiserie. He refused to believe me when I told him how quickly a particular frame could be carved, until I brought him into the shop to watch. He was convinced, but he walked away muttering "chip-chop," which, of course, is just what it is.

Any running pattern consists of a series of similar units strung together. The trick is to do the same cut of each unit all the way down the line, then turn around and do the next cut, and so on. I generally start out with pencil marks for the center of each unit and then do the rest by eye. If it's a carving I haven't done in a while, I'll carve one complete unit and use that as my guide. Sometimes it is necessary to do a few units before you get it just right, but one awkward unit—if it isn't *too* far off—will blend into the complete frame.

For this kind of carving, the molding profile is critical. If it isn't just right, the carving won't look right either. A bead on a molding has to be round, without a peak, and only slightly higher than its width. If hollows are too deep, they will interfere with your punch cuts. Steps have to be wide enough so that they don't break off, and rabbets have to have enough meat on top for the same reason. Once, when I was carving a Louis XVI molding, I found myself having to glue most of the beads back on, a tedious and costly process. I did a little research and discovered that the bead should not sit on top but go in at an angle, as shown in figure 1, so that you're carving toward the solid part of the frame instead of directly down on the rabbet. As a further precaution, you can place a strip of wood in the rabbet to support the lip.

Most professional framemakers have moldings made to their specifications by a mill, but the part-time framer cannot have a stock of hundreds of feet of moldings in all the profiles he may want. There are many ways to deal with this. Shapers, routers, and even a tablesaw (*FWW* #35, pp. 65-67) can make moldings. I use block planes, molding planes and gouges. Back-bent gouges are particularly helpful. One caution, however: If you are going to carve the molding, remember not to sand the milled stock. Fine abrasive particles lodge in the wood and will quickly dull your tools.

My favorite wood for frames has always been basswood. It is the blandest wood I know of. It hardly ever asserts itself—just sits there and lets itself be carved. Jelutong, a southeastern Asian wood, is very similar in character. Neither of these woods looks particularly good with a natural finish, so they are best used when the frame will be gessoed and gold-leafed. Wormy chestnut finishes nicely, and is pre-antiqued in the bargain, but it isn't much fun to shape and can also be stubborn to carve. Honduras mahogany is an excellent choice for a natural finish. French frames were generally carved in oak, but the European variety of oak is finer and softer than our white oak. The Spanish carvers used a species of pine that is a little harder than those generally available in this country.

Bench—A carvers' "bench" is a work surface that can be set on top of a sturdy table or supported by a framework of 2x4s. My favorite is a 2x12 with a 2x6 fastened along the top to form a step. The molding will be nailed to this, so you'll want lumber with few knots, but good kiln-dried construction lumber is adequate. An 8-ft. bench is portable, and can be clamped on top of a regular woodworking bench. But if you're planning a production operation, 12 ft. or 16 ft. is better. The height should fit the individual. I like about 40 in., so I can rest my forearm on the work. The bracing should be about 2 ft. deep for stability, which leaves room for a 1x12 along the back, on which you can lay your tools.

Nail the molding to the bench with 4d or 6d finish nails and set them, even if they don't go through an area to be carved. This not only holds the work more firmly, but protects the tool edge from an accidental brush with them. As an added precaution, when you know that a cut will be made

directly over a nail, interrupt yourself and give the nailset an extra punch. Better time spent setting nails than regrinding chisels. When the work is finished, pry the molding from the bench. Remove any nails left in the bench with a claw hammer and pull the ones left in the molding out from the back with a pair of nippers. Never pull nails out from the front.

Tools—Because most cuts are made with one punch, the shape of the tool determines the shape of the carving, and you will eventually need a fair number of tools. When I was carving full-time, I got up to about 30, which served me for 12 or 15 different designs ranging from delicate to heavy moldings. The tools range in width from $\frac{1}{16}$ in. to 1 in. Most frame carvers call all their tools chisels, including the gouges. This is less confusing than it might seem, because each tool is numbered according to its width and the shape of its curve. A $\frac{1}{2}$-in. #8 and a 1-in. #8, for instance, have different widths but the same curve proportionally. A #7 has a slightly broader curve, and a #1 is a straight chisel. With a couple of exceptions, tools are ground straight across, with the bevel on the outside of the tool, opposite the cannel. For the carvings I'll discuss in this article you'll need the following: $\frac{5}{8}$-in. #1, $\frac{1}{8}$-in. #1 (ground to a $\frac{1}{2}$-in. radius), $\frac{1}{4}$-in. #8, $\frac{5}{8}$-in. #8, $\frac{3}{4}$-in. #8, $\frac{1}{2}$-in. #7, $\frac{1}{4}$-in. skew, and a medium-weight mallet. In addition, you should also have a soft, long-bristle wire brush for clearing away chips, a hammer, a nailset, a flat bench chisel or a prybar for removing the molding from the work surface, and a compass/divider.

Carving beads—One of the most popular styles of the late-18th-century period of Neoclassicism was a simple row of beads, often used alone as trim on a number of moldings ranging from about $\frac{7}{8}$ in. to about 2 in. wide.

Choose a chisel slightly wider than the diameter of the bead on the molding. For a molding bead of just under $\frac{1}{4}$ in., as shown in figure 2, start at the left-hand end of the piece, holding the $\frac{1}{4}$-in. #8 chisel in your left hand at a 45° angle toward you, so that it lines up with the angle of the bead, and 45° to your right, with the cannel down. There are three cuts plus cleanup. The first cut just breaks the surface. Beads have a way of splitting out, so don't strike too hard with the mallet. There are various adjustments to avoid split-out. One,

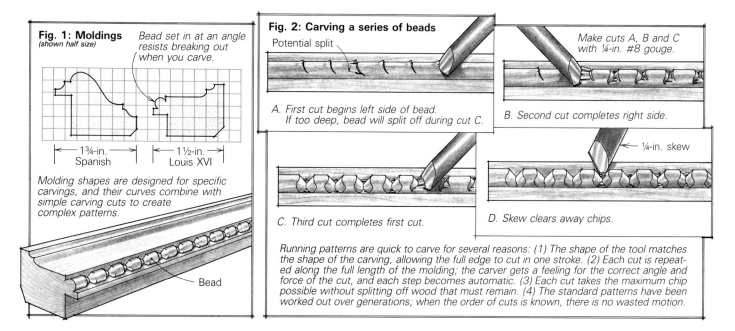

Fig. 1: Moldings
(shown half size)

Bead set in at an angle resists breaking out when you carve.

|← 1¾-in. →| Spanish

|← 1½-in. →| Louis XVI

Molding shapes are designed for specific carvings, and their curves combine with simple carving cuts to create complex patterns.

Bead

Fig. 2: Carving a series of beads

Potential split

A. First cut begins left side of bead. If too deep, bead will split off during cut C.

Make cuts A, B and C with ¼-in. #8 gouge.

B. Second cut completes right side.

C. Third cut completes first cut.

¼-in. skew

D. Skew clears away chips.

Running patterns are quick to carve for several reasons: (1) The shape of the tool matches the shape of the carving, allowing the full edge to cut in one stroke. (2) Each cut is repeated along the full length of the molding; the carver gets a feeling for the correct angle and force of the cut, and each step becomes automatic. (3) Each cut takes the maximum chip possible without splitting off wood that must remain. (4) The standard patterns have been worked out over generations; when the order of cuts is known, there is no wasted motion.

of course, is cutting lighter, but cutting down at a steeper angle can also help. The cuts should be $\frac{7}{16}$ in. apart. In the beginning you may want to use a ruler or a divider to mark the spaces, but you should learn to space evenly by placing the tool so that the previous cut is centered in the space between the one before it and the one you are about to make. You are looking one space behind as you cut. Remember, you are not a machine, and a little unevenness is desirable.

The next cut is the mirror image, only deeper. Starting at the right-hand end, hold the tool in your right hand and the mallet in your left, and go back the other way. This time go all the way down, until the corners of the gouge reach the bottom of the beading. If your first cut was deep enough, there should be no splitting out. As you place the chisel,

watch the bead you are forming. There should be a neat little ellipse, nearly round. There should also be no space between the beads. The third cut finishes the first, and the outside edge of this cut should touch cut number two. The final cut is with a skew, used as a knife to slice out the chips.

When you start out, it's a good idea to make eight or ten first cuts, then finish off a few of them. If they are all right, continue to the end. If not, practice a few more. A variation, generally used with other carvings such as ribbons, is the "pencil and pearl": three beads followed by a single long one that is about the length of three beads. The long bead is simply the half-round shape with rounded ends. □

Miles Karpilow makes furniture in Emeryville, Calif.

Carving a Spanish molding

This is a very popular carving that occurs in many different widths besides the 1¾-in. shown in figure 1 and in the photos. Start by marking off 3-in. divisions with the compass. If you want, you can also mark off the centers of these too. Photo **A** shows the carving after a series of cuts made by punching down with the mallet. These are numbered in the order they were made, but mirror-image cuts aren't numbered separately. You can vary the order of these cuts somewhat, but it's important to maintain the overall proportions. You will need most of the tools listed on p. 163. For a wider molding, select wider tools and wider divisions.

The first cut (*1*) is chopped straight down on each of the 3-in. divisions with the flat chisel (or the rounded one) at the very top of the molding. Now take the ¾-in. #8. With the top edge of the tool in the first cut, chop straight down (*2*), almost perpendicular to the face of the molding, fairly deeply, especially along the lower portion. Cut all these along the length of the molding, then turn the gouge around and cut the mirror images. The next cut (*3*), still with the ¾-in. #8, begins at the bottom end of the previous cut. Be sure to hold the gouge so that a line drawn through its corners would be at 90° to the molding length. Make the mirror-image cut in the opposite direction, keeping the shape symmetrical. The next cut (*4*) is similar. When you are more familiar with the carving, you can make cuts *3* and *4* as part of the same run. Then using the rounded #1 chisel, make a cut (*5*) halfway between the original 3-in. divisions. The cut should be right on the hollow of the molding and a little deeper at the top. Using the same tool or a straight-ground flat, continue the cut over the top of the molding (*6*), chopping fairly deeply.

Each unit (between arrows) results from the cuts described in the following series.

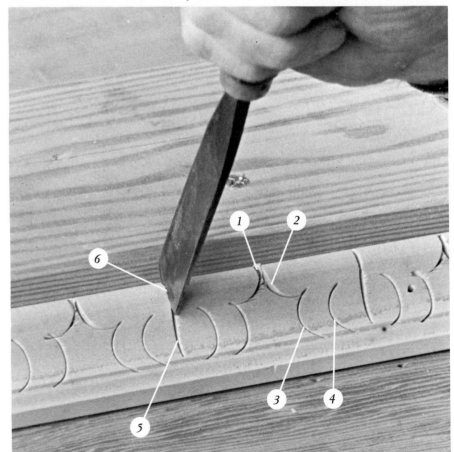

A. *The first six cuts, and their mirror images, chop out the basic proportions along the full length of the molding.*

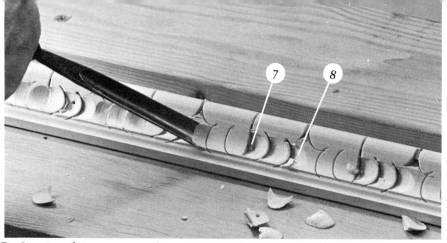

As shown in photo **B,** take the ⅝-in. #8, cannel up, and make a series of slicing cuts (*7*) starting from about ¹⁄₁₆ in. from the outside curve of the punch cuts *3* and *4,* aiming at about a 30° angle toward the base of punch cuts *4* and *5.* Cut *8* is similar, but at a shallower angle, starting from the original 3-in. divisions and aiming toward the base of cut *3.* The whole surface between the outside curves of cuts *3* will be lowered and left slightly crowned. When you get used to them, you can make cuts *7* and *8* in the same pass.

For *9* (photo **C**), turn the tool over, cannel down, and round into straight cut number *6* at the molding top. I find that two taps with the mallet, holding the tool a little higher for the second tap, gives just the right shape. Take the ½-in. #7, cannel up, and make cut number *10,* angling up toward cut *9.* This enlarges the hollow that you began with the innermost mirror-image cuts at *7.* When working soft wood, you may not need the mallet for these cuts.

To make cut number *11,* use the same tool, cannel down, and tighten the curve begun by cut *9,* as shown in photo **D.** The "saddle" is next and is begun by cutting up (*12*) toward the base of cuts number *2.* Cut *13* comes around and over at the top of each saddle with the ⅝-in. #8, cannel up. At the top it should come in no more than ⅛ in. from the edge of the molding.

In photo **E,** cut *14* broadens cut number *13* with the same tool, but cannel down. The last cuts (*15*) are the scallop cuts along the bottom. These are chopped straight down with the ½-in. #7 and cleaned out with the skew.

Mitering carved moldings—There is a technique that will ensure that at least three of the four corners of the frame will come out symmetrical. There is waste involved, but it must be weighed against the time saved by carving in the length. Start by cutting both miters on the first piece. Then trim the adjacent corner. Keep trimming until the carving on that side is a mirror image of the unit on the end of the first piece. When put together, there should be no protruding edges. Proceed this way with the next two pieces. You will then have three matching corners and you can only hope that the fourth will be close. It rarely will match, so after the frame is joined, take a small chisel and improvise. If done properly, it will take a very astute eye to see the difference. —*M.K.*

B. *Cuts 7 and 8 pare away the waste up to chop-cuts 3 and 4.*

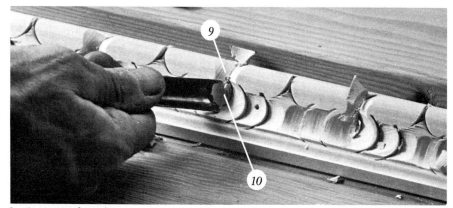

C. *Cuts 9 and 10 begin to bring out the mound for the saddle.*

D. *Cuts 11, 12 and 13 refine the saddle's edges and rough out its top.*

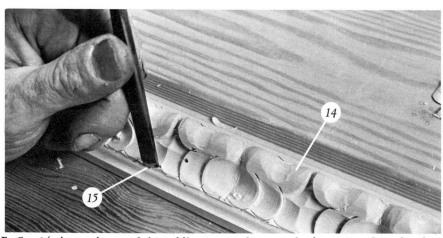

E. *Cut 14 shapes the top of the saddle. Cut 15 chops out the decoration along the edge.*

Photography Associates/Bill Tchakirides

These bowls came not from the lathe but from single, flat boards that were bandsawn into tapered concentric rings and glued together before being shaped with abrasive discs. The bowls can be of one kind of wood or of several contrasting woods.

Un-turned Bowls
They may be round, but you don't need a lathe

by Peter Petrochko

About eight years ago, I discovered a way to make wooden bowls of many sizes and shapes, even though I didn't own a lathe or know how to use one. Playing around with a bandsaw I'd just bought, I found I could saw a flat board into tapered, concentric rings that could then be glued into a stack and shaped, using sanding discs and carving tools, into a finished bowl. I've since made hundreds of bowls this way, some in sizes and shapes that would be impossible to achieve on the lathe.

Small, shallow bowls can be made with as few as one ring; deeper ones may consist of as many as a dozen rings, all cut from the same board. For design variation, I sometimes saw the rings from a blank laminated up from several different-colored woods. Typically, my bowl blanks are boards as wide and as long as the bowl's major diameter and from ¾ in. to 2½ in. thick. The bowl's height, shape and wall thickness are governed by the initial shape cut out of the board, its thickness, the number of rings and the angle of their taper—variables that can be precisely controlled at the bandsaw. Besides it being unconventional and fun, I've found that turning a flat board into a bowl is the essence of economy.

Peter Petrochko turns boards into bowls in his Oxford, Conn., shop. Photos by Andy Badinski, except where noted. Sanding discs described in this article are sold by Sculpture Associates, 40 E. 19th St., New York, N.Y. 10003.

Many bowl forms are possible—round, oval, free-form—but don't draw a shape with smaller radii than you can easily cut on your bandsaw. I use a ¼-in. wide, 6-TPI, skip-tooth blade. I mark off perpendicular reference lines, which I later use to align the sawn rings. Next I draw a guidemark completely around the top surface of the bowl blank about ¼ in. in from its outside edge. This line marks the cut for the bowl's top ring.

Before cutting the first ring (**A**), I set my bandsaw table at about 20°, an angle that I've found produces a workable taper. I start my cuts parallel to the grain because this yields a cleaner joint later on, when I glue the bandsaw kerf shut. Saw carefully and exit the blade where it entered—a tapered ring of wood is now cut loose from the blank.

To mark out the next ring, I trace the inside bottom edge of the first ring onto my blank (**B**). Before I saw, I decide on the vertical shape of my bowl, which is determined by the ring taper angle. For a shallower shape, I start with the table set at 30° or more and I increase the angle by about 5° or more per ring. Starting around 18° and increasing the taper of each ring by 3° or 4° makes a more vertical bowl. I start the second cut on the opposite side of the blank from the first so that when the bowl is glued up, the kerfs will be staggered. I saw rings in this manner until my original blank is much smaller, but not too small to be a stable bottom for the bowl. Once I've chosen the size of the base, I trace onto it the edge of the ring that will be just above it. With a gouge, I hollow out the base inside this line.

At this point, I take the pleasure of test-stacking all the rings over the base so I can see what the bowl will look like. Photo **C** shows a three-ring bowl. Before the rings can be assembled, the bandsaw kerfs must be glued. I use urea-formaldehyde glue (Weldwood's Plastic Resin) and spring clamps for each joint, with cauls to spread the pressure. Sometimes I sandwich a piece of veneer in the kerf to highlight it. I let the rings cure for a day, unclamp them, and file off any excess glue from each seam so that the rings will stack flat and tight.

I've developed a direct approach to gluing up my bowls: I pile a few hundred pounds of concrete blocks atop a bowl inverted on a firm, level surface. I sometimes use large screw clamps, similar to a veneer press, but the blocks are

Petrochko's band-saw method lends itself to tapered shapes such as this mahogany bowl.

A. *Sawing the first ring.*

B. *Tracing the second ring.*   **C.** *A bowl makes its debut.*

handier, even if cruder (**D**). Be mindful of the stack's center of gravity. If it's skewed, the rings will slide out of alignment or, worse yet, the entire thing may come crashing down.

Next I'm ready to give the bowl its final shape. If you are making a round bowl and you have a lathe, you could screw it to a faceplate and finish it just like a turned bowl. Instead, I disc-sand it. I prefer industrial-grade discs made by Merit.

A scrap of rug on the bench keeps the bowl from slipping while I rough-sand the outside. Smaller bowls have to be clamped to the bench. First I shape the outside of the bowl with a 36-grit, 7-in. disc, and then I refine it with finer, 5-in. discs mounted in the drill press. I sand the inside next (**E**), starting with a 36-grit, 3-in. disc on the drill press. I wear a face shield because the coarse disc sends glue beads flying. Medium and fine sanding, done with 80-grit to 150-grit discs, take much less time. After sanding, I finish the bowls with either mineral oil or 8 to 16 coats of Behlen's Salad Bowl Finish. When the finish has dried, I sand with fine wet-or-dry sandpaper, using vegetable oil as a lubricant, followed by fine steel wool. For the final sheen, I buff my bowls with a pad charged with polishing compound. □

D. *Clamping the bowl.*

E. *Sanding the inside.*

Bandsawn Baskets
Spiral your way to a collapsible container

by Max Kline

The idea for these collapsible baskets came from those fold-up drinking cups that were popular as novelties years ago. You simply bandsaw a continuous, spiraling kerf into a flat board at a slight angle, so the segments wedge against each other when the basket is opened. These baskets are useful for holding all sorts of things, from fruit to floral arrangements. When collapsed, they make nice tabletop trivets.

I make the oblong baskets from a ¾-in. thick board, 12½ in. by 6½ in. You could make larger baskets, but I don't recommend smaller ones because accurate sawing becomes difficult. I've made round baskets using the same technique, but I don't find them as attractive. Any wood species will do, although it should be knot-free, not too brittle, and resistant to checking. Very hard, light-colored woods such as maple and ash will sometimes burn when cut, particularly if the blade is dull. This burning is practically impossible to sand off.

To make a basket, scale up the pattern shown in the drawing and attach it to your board with rubber cement or double-faced tape. A new pattern is needed for each basket, so I photocopy them a few at a time to keep on hand.

As the drawing indicates, cut the handle with the bandsaw table set at 90°. I use a ¼-in., 6-TPI, skip-tooth blade. After the handle has been cut and removed, tilt the saw table to about 6°—an angle that seems to produce the best bevel to wedge the segments together when the basket is opened. Increasing the angle makes a shallower basket, but if you decrease it too much, the segments will drop through without wedging and you'll have a wooden "Slinky" toy. Thicker wood, say, 1-in., can be sawn at about 5°. As you saw around the pattern lines, the board will become harder to

Collapsible-basket pattern

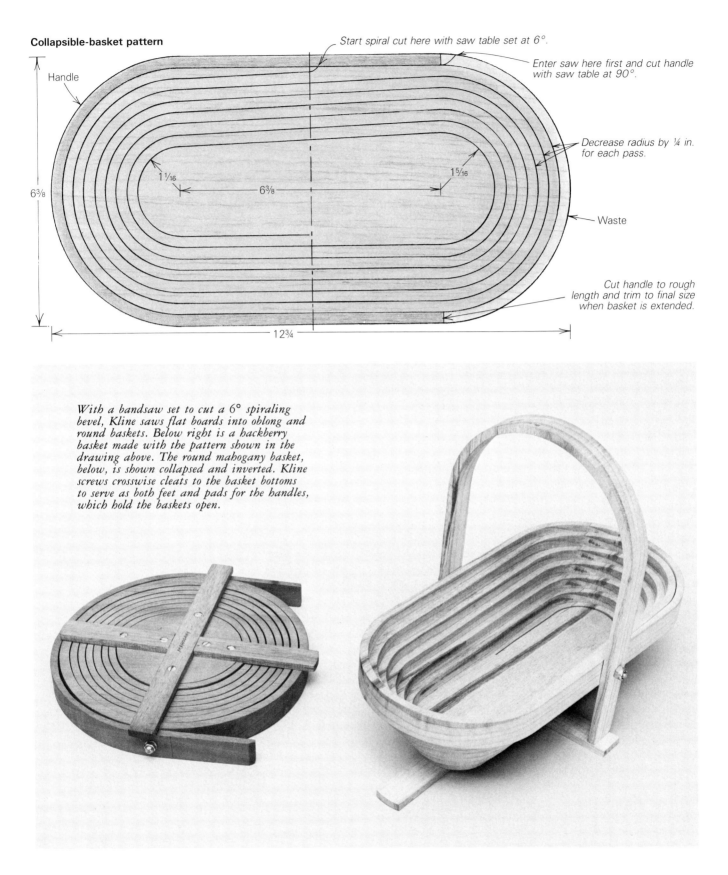

Handle

Start spiral cut here with saw table set at 6°.

Enter saw here first and cut handle with saw table at 90°.

Decrease radius by ¼ in. for each pass.

1 1/16

6 3/8

1 5/16

6 3/8

Waste

Cut handle to rough length and trim to final size when basket is extended.

12 3/4

With a bandsaw set to cut a 6° spiraling bevel, Kline saws flat boards into oblong and round baskets. Below right is a hackberry basket made with the pattern shown in the drawing above. The round mahogany basket, below, is shown collapsed and inverted. Kline screws crosswise cleats to the basket bottoms to serve as both feet and pads for the handles, which hold the baskets open.

control because the spiraling cut makes the blank springy. To maintain an accurate cut, grip the stock tightly at the sides and squeeze the segments together. When you reach the end of the pattern, back the blade out.

Next, glue back in place the free end where the saw entered. I sand the handle and the outside contours with a 1-in. belt sander. If you follow your pattern accurately, you shouldn't have to sand the inside of the basket. Attach the handle with flat-head stove bolts countersunk on the basket's inside and fastened with brass or chrome cap nuts. My pattern produces an extra-long handle which must be trimmed and positioned so that it holds the basket open at its full height but stores snugly when the basket is collapsed. Screw or glue the two lengthwise cleats and one cross-cleat to the basket bottom, and finish as you desire—I use Watco oil, followed by wax. □

Max Kline is a retired chemist. He lives in Saluda, N.C.

169

The Louisville Slugger
Custom-turned bats for baseball's heavy hitters

by Paul Bertorelli

A major league bat must be within an ounce of the weight specified by the player who will use it.

When I played sandlot baseball, I devised the cleverest batting strategy that my childhood grasp of physics would allow. I grabbed the biggest bat in the box, reasoning that no pitcher could possibly throw a ball past such a fat target held anywhere near the strike zone.

Until I visited the Louisville Slugger baseball bat factory, I hadn't connected my abysmal batting average with the trouble I had swinging those monsters off my shoulder before the ball whizzed by. At the famous Slugger plant, I learned that hitting is the end product of a refined equation in which four guys standing at lathes figure prominently. I'd read about how big-league bats are custom-turned for each player, so I went to see how it's done.

The Slugger factory—known properly as the Hillerich and Bradsby Co.—is actually not in Louisville at all but across the Ohio River in Jeffersonville, Ind. They've been making bats in the Louisville area since 1884, when the founder's son, Bud Hillerich, took to turning them for a local ball team in his father's job-shop turnery. Players found Hillerich's bats to be a great improvement over the crude, shapeless clubs they'd been accustomed to, and by the turn of the century, H&B was established as the premier maker of major league bats.

My tour of the plant began with a walk through the timber yard, where thousands of 3-in. by 40-in. white ash billets are left to air-dry. High tensile strength, resiliency and, most of all, lightness make ash the preferred bat wood, though hickory has also been used. Rex Bradley, H&B's timber and professional-bat expert, told me that the billets are shipped in from seven mills situated along the Pennsylvania-New York border, where soil and climate conditions encourage the moderately fast growth rates that result in ideal bat timber. Fast-growth timber is avoided because its greater ratio of dense

latewood makes the same size billet heavier, giving hand-turners less leeway in matching size and weight.

The billets are dried to about 10% moisture content, rough-turned, and sorted by weight and quality. The best will become major league bats; the rest softball and adult league models, the vast majority of the million or so wooden bats that H&B turns every year. As you would expect, the bat factory is a noisy place, with most of the floor given over to ranks of squat, semi-automatic lathes that spin out bats as fast as workers can load in blanks. Off in one corner, away from the din, was what I had come to see: the hand lathes and four turners who together make 20,000 major league bats a year.

Each bat is custom-turned to suit the swing, grip and whims of the player who will wield it. Bill Williams, an H&B vice president, told me that modern players prefer lighter, shorter bats over the heavy clubs I thought were the key to hot hitting. "Babe Ruth used a 42-ounce bat," Williams said. "You don't see any that heavy today. Most of the bats we make are around 32 to 35 ounces." That's because modern players face a more cunning variety of pitches than did their predecessors.

In Ruth's day, a batter might have faced the same pitcher three or four times in one game. By the end of the day, he would have seen enough of the pitcher's tricks to adjust his swing accordingly. Today's player has to contend with a starting pitcher and any number of relievers, each one with a different curve, fastball and slider. Because it can be snapped more quickly, a lighter bat allows the hitter to scope the approaching pitch an instant longer before he decides to swing, thus increasing his odds for a hit. The batmaker's challenge is to shave off as much wood as he can without weakening the bat's slender handle.

I watched Freeman Young turn a bat for Mike Jorgensen, a New York Mets utility fielder. Jorgensen likes a 32-oz. bat that's 35 in. long, requiring Young to skim the handle down to near its breaking point. Young picked a blank from racks sorted by weight, chucked it in his lathe and went to work. His toolkit is sparse: three gouges, a knob-sizing tool, and a yardstick with a knife in one end to mark the bat's length. With a 1¼-in. gouge, Young roughed the shape by eyeballing a bat he took from H&B's artifact room, where a sample of each of the hundreds of past and present models is kept. If no model exists, the turner looks up a card on each player that describes the diameter of his bat at 15 points along its length. He turns those diameters, checking with a caliper, then connects the points with a fair curve.

"I like to do the knob and the handle first," Young said, after he slid his gouge along the lathe's long, continuous tool

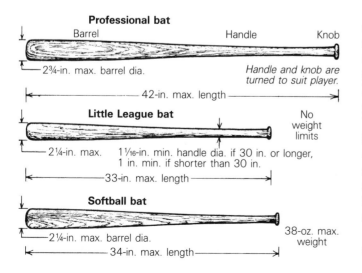

Professional bat
Barrel — Handle — Knob

2¾-in. max. barrel dia.

Handle and knob are turned to suit player.

42-in. max. length

Little League bat

No weight limits

2¼-in. max.   1¹⁄₁₆-in. min. handle dia. if 30 in. or longer, 1 in. min. if shorter than 30 in.

33-in. max. length

Softball bat

2¼-in. max. barrel dia.

38-oz. max. weight

34-in. max. length

rest. "That way if it breaks, I won't have wasted my time on the barrel." Other H&B turners do just the opposite, figuring that turning the barrel first reduces the blank's weight, minimizing whip and reducing the risk of breakage. Young set his sizing tool a bit larger than the model's knob diameter. The extra material is needed because the sizing tool's high angle of attack scrapes rather than cuts, leaving a rough, cratered surface. Young smoothed the knob to size with a ½-in. gouge. He switched back to a larger gouge to slim the handle and lower barrel, lubricating the tool's travel along the rest with an occasional swipe of an oily rag. As he neared the finished size, Young checked his bat against the model by lining up his caliper with a position marker consisting of a steel rod that slides along another rod mounted behind the lathe and parallel to its centers.

I could see the bat flex as the tool cut the narrowest part of the handle, but before it began to whip, Young hooked his callused left hand behind the spinning work to support it. Oddly, the turners here had never heard of bracing slender work with a steady rest. I doubt they would use one anyway. They have to hustle to make their daily quota of 32 bats, and a steady would just slow them down.

Once Young had duplicated the model, he turned down both ends with a parting tool, gave the new bat a once-over with rough sandpaper and tossed it onto a scale above his lathe. It weighed 32½ oz. "I like to get 'em right on . . . an ounce either way is okay for the major leagues," Young said. Final-sanding, finishing (lacquer) and the famous Slugger burned-in brand happen in another part of the plant. In the 10 minutes that had elapsed between centering the blank and weigh-in, Young hadn't stopped his lathe, neither to remove the completed bat nor to chuck a fresh blank.

Watching Young work, I realized that turning a bat is easy compared to the arcane task of selecting the right timber. "Ballplayers are notoriously superstitious about their bats," Bradley, a one-time minor leaguer himself, told me. "Ruth liked to have pin knots up around the barrel, Pete Rose won't use anything but wide-growth ash. To us, timber is timber, but we try to give a player what he wants so he won't have any doubt in his mind when he steps up to the plate." Some players even visit the plant to supervise the turning, having a little removed here and there until the balance is just so.

This infinite adjustability has, in part, kept wooden Sluggers from being driven to extinction by aluminum bats, the weapon of choice in Little League and college baseball. Aluminum bats can't be tailored to each player, but the metal is arguably a better bat material than wood. For its weight, it's stronger than ash, and it never has wind shakes or worm holes. Weak hitters do better with aluminum because the metal bats have a larger "sweet spot," that area of the barrel which imparts the most power when it strikes the ball squarely.

Tradition, however, is likely to have more to say about the survival of wooden bats in the majors than any volume of debate over how well they work or don't work. "It really comes down to pleasing the ballpark crowd," said Williams. "An aluminum bat just can't match the sound that a wooden bat makes when it hits the ball." □

Hillerich and Bradsby offers tours of its plant and base-ball museum. For more information, write the company at PO Box 35700, Louisville, Ky. 40232. Paul Bertorelli is editor of Fine Woodworking.

Four woodworkers at H&B hand-turn most of the bats swung by major league players. To make a bat for a particular player, the turner duplicates one of the hundreds of current models filed in the artifact room, above.

Above, turner Freeman Young sets his sizing tool to the model bat's knob diameter. He'll size the knob on the new bat and then shape it with a small gouge.

To keep the slender handle of a light bat from breaking, Young steadies the spinning work by hooking his left hand behind it. The thumb presses the gouge to the tool rest, ensuring a precise shearing cut that leaves a smooth surface.

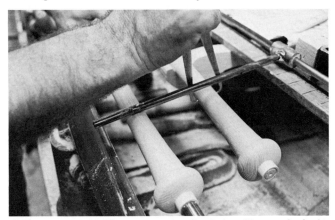

As he turns a new bat to near its final size, Young checks his work against the model with calipers. He aligns the measuring instrument via a position marker that slides along a steel rod mounted behind the lathe and parallel to its centers.

Turning Giant Bowls
Ed Moulthrop's tools and techniques

by Dale Nish

Says Moulthrop, 'Each bowl already exists in the tree trunk, and my job is simply to uncover it and take it out. I love the heft and the solidness of these huge blocks. I love to feel their weight as they resist the leverage of a big cant-hook, or to sense the tug of gravity as the hoist slowly separates a fifteen-hundred-pound block from the ground.'

When I first saw one of Ed Moulthrop's 36-in. diameter bowls, I was intimidated at the thought of turning it. It had evidently required a tree trunk for a blank, about a half-ton of green wood. I have since visited Moulthrop in his Atlanta shop, to learn about his monster lathes, harpoon-size tools and sophisticated techniques for controlling moisture-related wood movement in such hefty treen.

Moulthrop produces about 250 of these bowls each year, marketing them in craft galleries in New York, Atlanta, Scottsdale (Ariz.) and San Francisco. Although he's been turning since he was 14 years old, it was 10 years ago that he quit his thriving architecture practice of 30 years to do it full-time. His work has been exhibited in more than 40 art museums, including the Smithsonian's Renwick Gallery and the Vatican Museum, as well as being part of the permanent collections of New York's Museum of Modern Art and Metropolitan Museum of Art.

Moulthrop uses only southeastern woods, exceptional pieces of tulip magnolia (yellow-poplar, *Liriodendron tulipifera*), wild cherry, sweet gum, white pine, black walnut and orangewood, magnolia, and persimmon. He feels that native woods are amply exotic, if you find the right logs. His bowls are limited mainly to a few basic shapes: hollow globes, for which he is best known, lotus forms, and chunky donuts. The simplicity of his designs serves to enhance the elaborate, colorful figure of the wood.

Moulthrop builds his lathes (he's built five in an improving series) specifically for large faceplate turning. For rough turning, he uses the one drawn on the facing page (and pictured on p. 175); for finish turning he uses a similar design, but a lighter structure (p. 177). In the former, the base is ¾-in. plywood glued to 2x4 corner supports. The top is a 24-in. by 35-in. section of a 1¾-in. thick exterior solid-core door reinforced with angle irons along its top edges. Moulthrop metal-turned the headstock from a scavenged, 3½-in. diameter steel shaft mounted in giant pillow blocks 18 in. apart. The centerline of the shaft is 38 in. from the floor, a comfortable height for Moulthrop, who's about 6 ft. tall. The tool rest, positioned a little below shaft center, is attached to a 5x7 solid cherry beam. The beam slides in and out from under the table, and is held in position by two large clamps.

Inside the base, a 2½-HP gear motor, controlled

Dale Nish teaches industrial education at Brigham Young University in Provo, Utah. He is the author of Creative Woodturning *and* Artistic Woodturning, *both published by the Brigham Young University Press, and is working on a book tentatively titled* Masters of Woodturning.

Moulthrop's tools include hooks and lances up to 96 in. long.

by a foot switch, is mounted on a hinged table, with the weight of the motor providing tension on a heavy ¾-in. wide V-belt. The motor output is 80 RPM. With four 9-in. pulleys on the motor, and four pulleys on the headstock shaft approximately 15 in., 10 in., 8 in. and 6 in. in diameter, speeds range from 50 RPM to 120 RPM. This may seem slow, but on a 30-in. diameter bowl, 80 RPM means a rim speed of 628 ft. per minute, about the same as a 6-in. bowl turning 400 RPM.

Moulthrop's tool rest is made from a 16-in. long piece of ½-in. by 3-in. by 4-in. angle iron, bandsawn to shape. A steel connector bar (⅞ in. by 2 in. by 16 in.) pivots from the cherry beam, cantilevering the tool rest in various positions. The top edge of the rest is drilled with a series of holes that take an 8d tempered nail, which serves as an adjustable stop to lever tools against, similar to the way tools are used on a metal-spinning lathe. A pin projecting from the bottom of the rest locates a support, which braces the rest against the floor when it's extended far from the beam.

The three basic tools Moulthrop has designed and developed for his work are the lance, the loop and the cut-off tool. All are forged from either salvaged tapered-reamer stock or hex-bar tool steel,

Moulthrop's production includes bowls up to 40 in. in diameter.

Moulthrop's roughing-out lathe

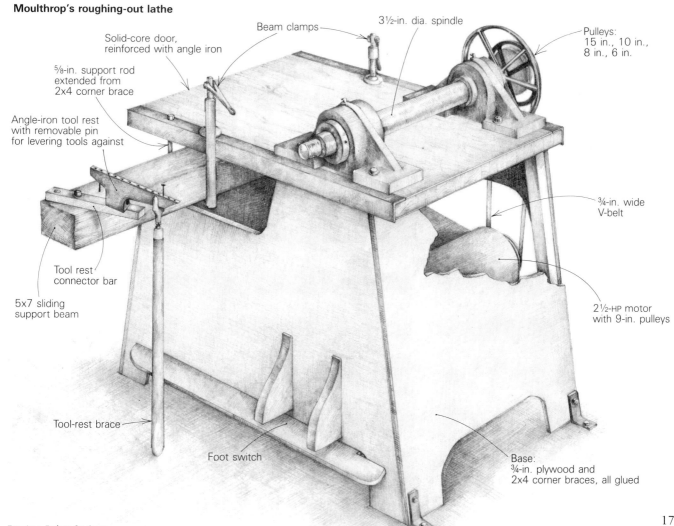

Solid-core door, reinforced with angle iron

Beam clamps

3½-in. dia. spindle

Pulleys: 15 in., 10 in., 8 in., 6 in.

⅝-in. support rod extended from 2x4 corner brace

Angle-iron tool rest with removable pin for levering tools against

¾-in. wide V-belt

Tool rest connector bar

5x7 sliding support beam

2½-HP motor with 9-in. pulleys

Tool-rest brace

Foot switch

Base: ¾-in. plywood and 2x4 corner braces, all glued

Drawings: Barbara Smolover

Moulthrop's tools

The lance

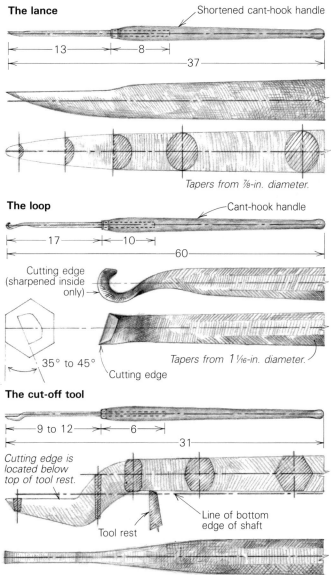

Shortened cant-hook handle

13

8

37

Tapers from ⅞-in. diameter.

The loop

Cant-hook handle

17

10

60

Cutting edge (sharpened inside only)

35° to 45°

Cutting edge

Tapers from 1¹⁄₁₆-in. diameter.

The cut-off tool

9 to 12

6

31

Cutting edge is located below top of tool rest.

Tool rest

Line of bottom edge of shaft

The wood yard, a grove filled with turning blanks.

Attaching the faceplate with lag bolts.

⅞ in. to 1¼ in. in diameter. The lance is Moulthrop's dream tool, replacing skews, gouges and round-nose chisels for all exterior work. The tool-steel shaft is epoxied deep into a shortened cant-hook handle, so the two become one continuous piece, free from vibration. The lance is a model of cutting efficiency, never used flat as for scraping, but always with the edge at 45° to nearly vertical, levered against the tool-rest stop.

For inside work, Moulthrop uses a loop not unlike the turning hooks used by turners of old (see pp. 159-160). After forging, the loop is tempered and then sharpened on the inside only, using a high-speed tool grinder and cone-shaped stone. Like the lance, it's used to cut, not scrape, always levered against the tool-rest stop.

Moulthrop's cut-off tool, a giant parting tool, is unique because its cutting edge is located below the level of the tool rest. The force of the turning workpiece thus keeps the tool aligned in the cut, safe from flipping over.

Moulthrop's wood storage yard is a grove of trees shading open areas covered by plastic sheets. Log sections waiting to be turned are left standing on end on the plastic, their weight forming depressions in which rainwater accumulates. Shavings

heaped on top of the bolts and generously scattered over the plastic retain moisture in the rainy Atlanta climate, helping to forestall checking. The aim is to keep the bolts as wet as possible for as long as possible.

The damp climate also fosters staining and spalting of the wood. Colors seem to mature, sapwood darkens, and stains penetrate the bolt from both ends. All this adds an extra dimension of color and character to the pieces. Bolts may be turned fresh-cut, or kept for 6 to 24 months before they're rough-turned, still wet. In the interim, the older bolts may breed fungus, mold and even mushrooms. Before too long, however, these pieces will rot beyond usefulness.

Such large blanks require careful mounting. Moulthrop squares the ends of the bolt with an electric chainsaw, removing ½ in. of wood from each end so that he can see the color and figure. He lays out a circle on the end of the bolt delineating the best color and figure, not necessarily centered on the heart of the bolt. After chainsawing the bolt's diameter to its rough size, he rolls it into his shop, purposely located downhill from his storage area—a valuable feature, considering that some of the large bolts weigh 1500 lb.

The faceplate shown above was made from an old sprocket gear found in the salvage yard, Moulthrop's favorite shopping

First cuts with the lance braced on the thigh.

Roughing the bowls in steps.

place. It is 9 in. in diameter and ¾ in. thick. It has been threaded to fit the headstock shaft: 2-in. diameter, 8 threads per inch. The faceplate is carefully positioned in the center of the blank, and is mounted with heavy screws or ⅜-in. lag bolts, depending on the weight to be held. Moulthrop often drives additional lags between the teeth of the gear, as security against a massive mishap. After the bowl is finish-turned, the screw holes will be filled. Moulthrop uses epoxy mixed with wood dust to match the color of the surrounding wood.

In the typical roughing-out position (pictured above), Moulthrop holds the butt of the lance handle against his thigh so that the tool cuts at about the center of the piece. His right hand and leg steady the handle and control the tool's movement, while his left hand holds the tool firmly on the rest and against the tool-rest stop. His two arms and the tool form a triangle, providing maximum control as the lathe turns at 50 to 120 RPM.

The lance shears. The shank is held against the tool-rest stop and the rounded portion rides the surface of the turning work as the point penetrates the wood. After roughing the blank round, Moulthrop shapes the contour in a series of steps which are then faired. He typically removes shavings up

Smoothing the outside shape.

A. *Boring the clearance hole.*

Hollowing a closed bowl

Plan view

Numbers indicate the order of cuts and the corresponding position of the tool on the rest.

8 11
11 7 9
6
3 4 5 10
2

1 (clearance hole bored with auger)

2,3,4,5,10

6.7.8.9.11

B. *The hook begins hollowing the bowl.*

C. *Undercutting the inside.*

D. *Several months in a solution of PEG stabilizes the wood.*

E. *After finish-turning (facing page), a flexible-shaft grinder smooths the outside. The dust pick-up cone, right, attaches to a 12-in. exhaust duct.*

F. *The flexible shaft also reaches the inside of the bowl.*

Using lance and loop, Moulthrop refines the shape of his bowls after PEG treatment, but on a lighter-duty lathe.

to 1½ in. wide and ½ in. thick. These peel off like long woolly caterpillars as water sprays from the moisture-laden log.

To hollow the bowl (facing page), Moulthrop first bores a 1¼-in. clearance hole with a brace and bit, held stationary while the lathe turns at slow speed. He marks the depth on the auger and drills to within 2 in. of the bottom.

The loop cuts from the center out, levering on the tool-rest stop, which must be repositioned periodically as the cut progresses. Wall thickness on small bowls is gauged by feel. On the larger bowls, where the reach is too long, Moulthrop drills ⅟₃₂-in. gauge holes and measures the thickness directly with fine wire. The rough bowls have a wall thickness of about ¾ in. at the opening to 1 in. or 1½ in. at the base. Later the base of the bowl will be thinned, from the inside, to ¾ in.

Polyethylene glycol 1000 (PEG) is the key to being able to turn such large bowls taken from anywhere in the log, even including the pith and knots, without the bowl splitting or warping. The PEG replaces the moisture in the wood and stabilizes it (*FWW* #19, pp. 68-71). After green turning, Moulthrop dates the rough bowl and immerses it in a 40% solution, vats of which line his tank yard outside his shop. The 4-ft. diameter, 36-in. high aluminum vats are also from his favorite salvage yard. Soaking time varies with the temperature of the season: about 60 days in the summer (average temperature 80°), about 90 days in the fall, and about 120 days in the winter. Small bowls don't require as long a

soak as large ones, but leaving them longer doesn't hurt. Because of the work invested in them, Moulthrop often allows more time for large bowls, just to be safe.

After soaking, the pieces are drained and set outside on a drying rack for a week in the sun. Final drying takes about two or three weeks, in a small room conditioned by a household dehumidifier.

The finishing lathe (above) is similar in design to the rough-turning lathe, except that it is lighter and has a smaller motor, since only light cuts are now made. The tools, however, are the same: the lance for outside work, the loop for inside.

Sanding begins with grits as coarse as 16 or 24. Both inside and outside are worked by hand or with discs on a flexible-shaft machine. Small holes and defects are usually patched with a mixture of sanding dust and hard-setting epoxy, just before final sanding with fine-grit paper.

The bowl's finish may be of several types; many are possible, but all finishes are sensitive to the moisture that PEG attracts. Moulthrop has been experimenting with his present finish for ten years now, but he feels it still needs further development. For those starting out with PEG, he recommends polyurethane as the easiest finish. It must be applied in conditions of low humidity. Moulthrop buffs with 0000 steel wool, followed by tripoli and rouge in oil applied with a cloth while the piece is rotating on the lathe. The last step is to remove the faceplate, patch the screw holes and hand-finish the bottom. □

FINISHING, GLUE

Which Glue Do You Use?

Chemical types, not brands, make the difference

by George Mustoe

Like the alchemists' attempts to transmute base metal into gold, much human effort has gone into the search for the perfect glue. This goal is probably as unrealistic as the dreams of alchemy, but the inventors' struggles have not been without reward: adhesives manufacturing is a big growth industry in the United States, and per-capita consumption is about 40 lb. per year.

Not surprisingly, "What kind of glue did you use?" is a frequent query heard whenever woodworkers gather. Unfortunately, these exchanges generate some old wives' tales, among them the colorful but incorrect assertion that cyanoacrylate "superglue" is derived from barnacles (*FWW* #37).

Because wood is a relatively weak construction material, most adhesives produce bonds that are stronger than the surrounding lumber, so claims of extremely high strength are seldom meaningful to the woodworker. Instead, the most important characteristics are setting rate, viscosity, resistance to water, flexibility, color, sandability, and gap-filling properties. As a woodworker who happens also to be a chemist, I've developed a keener than usual interest in the literally hundreds of glues sold today, discovering in the course of my research that only about a dozen kinds are useful for woodworking. Within each category, I've found that different brands will usually perform equally, so the choice for a particular project is best made by understanding the chemical makeup and characteristics of the glues we use.

In this article, I'll cover those glues that are best suited to general woodworking. In a second article, I'll talk about epoxies, hot-melt glues, cyanoacrylates and contact cements, all specialty glues that are usually more expensive, though not always better, than our old standbys.

Protein glues—The natural world abounds with examples of sophisticated adhesives which display impressive tenacity; barnacles and mussels, for example, cement themselves to beach rocks and ship bottoms with a substance that resists prolonged immersion in salt water. Though the chemistry of these natural adhesives is poorly understood, most sticky secretions are combinations of various complex proteins. Thus it is not surprising that early artisans discovered that the best raw materials for glue were protein-rich animal products such as skin, bone and blood.

Today, despite the advent of modern synthetic adhesives, animal-protein glues are still common. They can be divided into three types: hide and bone glue, fish glue, and blood glue. Of the three, hide and bone glues are of the greatest interest to the woodworker. The use of fish glue, which is derived from the water-soluble proteins in fish skins, is limited to industry, mainly for attaching labels to bottles and occasionally as a tack-improving additive to white glue. Blood glues, once developed as water-resistant adhesives for early military aircraft, are made by dispersing beef or pig blood in water, with wood dust, lime or sodium silicate added as thickening. They're most often encountered in vintage plywood, but are practically impossible to buy today and have no significant advantages over readily available synthetics.

Hide and bone glues, on the other hand, are far from obsolete. Besides being widely used in industry for products such as gummed paper tape, sandpaper and bookbindings, hide glue finds plenty of uses in the woodshop. The setting time and spreadability can be varied, and the adhesive cures into a colorless, nontoxic, sandable glueline which can be undone by the application of moist heat—a feature that is attractive to luthiers, for instance, who may need to remove the soundboard of an instrument to repair it. Water also softens hide glue, and some furniture conservators use a 50% vinegar solution to speed the disassembly and repair of antiques.

Hide glue consists of protein derived from collagen, the main ingredient of skin and connective tissue. The glue is prepared by cooking animal hides, hooves and tendons into a protein-rich broth which is then cooled to a gelatinous solid, sliced, dried and ground into a coarse powder. In retail stores, hide glue is commonly sold as a pre-mixed liquid, but it can be bought in powder form, in which case it must be mixed with hot water. For an explanation on how to mix hide glue, see *FWW* #42, pp. 74-75. Liquid hide glues have two advantages over mix-your-own: you don't need a heated glue pot, and the slow setting rate may be valuable for complicated assemblies. During the heyday of hide glue, it could be bought in 18 grades, each with a different viscosity and setting time. Today, woodcraft suppliers usually offer only a single, high-grade product. Setting time can be slowed by adding more water, but this leads to a slightly weaker bond.

Many other proteins have adhesive properties. Soybean-based glue is used in some interior plywood. Casein or milk glue, which has been detected in medieval picture frames, is made from skim milk, and is used today for laminating interior beams and trusses. This glue is a light-colored powder that must be mixed with cold water and allowed to stand about ten minutes before use. Unlike the other protein glues, casein sets both by evaporation and by chemical reaction, forming calcium caseinate. The resulting neutral-colored bond is highly moisture-resistant but not waterproof. Casein can be used in cool weather and on woods containing up to 15% moisture. It is particularly effective with oily woods such as teak, yew and lemonwood. Powdered casein glue is available from National Casein, 601 W. 80th St., Chicago, Ill. 60620.

Petrochemical resins—Casein glue is sometimes confused with polyvinyl acetate (PVA) white glues. Part of this confusion stems from the milky appearance of white glue and also because dairy-related companies such as Borden, who once marketed casein, now sell PVA glue. Developed during the 1940s, PVA glue is part of a family of synthetic resin glues

that have largely replaced animal glues in the woodshop.

Derived from petroleum compounds and acetylene gas, white glue consists of minute PVA globules suspended in water. When the glue is spread on wood surfaces, the water evaporates and/or diffuses through the surrounding porous material, and the globules coalesce to form a tough film. Because of its reputation as a cheap hobby cement, white glue is sometimes undervalued as a woodworking adhesive. Actually, its low viscosity, rapid setting time and fair gap-filling qualities make it an excellent choice for general woodworking. It dries into a clear, slightly flexible glueline, and it remains fresh on the shelf almost indefinitely. PVA is nontoxic, making it safe for use around children.

The major disadvantages of white glue are its low resistance to moisture and the gummy, thermoplastic nature of the dry film: it turns rubbery under the heat of sanding and clogs the sandpaper. You can minimize clogging by removing excess glue with a sponge or a damp cloth before the glue sets, or by trimming away hardened glue with a chisel or a scraper. The soft film also causes PVA-glued joints to "creep" out of their original alignment when subjected to continuous stress. While this may allow joints to adjust to seasonal variations in humidity without cracking, it's not a desirable quality if great structural strength is needed.

Be cautious when buying white glue. Competition among the 40 to 50 manufacturers of PVAs has kept the price low, but with the predictable advertising hype. Weldbond, for instance, calls its PVA a "concentrated...universal space-age adhesive...not similar to any other type of bonding agent being offered." In fact, the adhesive contains a lower percentage of solids than Elmer's and several other brands of white glue. Weldbond's most significant characteristic may well be its relatively high price. In testing white glues, I found only one that yielded inferior results, a generic white craft glue distributed by a local hobby shop. Its adhesive properties compared favorably with leading brands, but the glue reacted with most woods to produce gray or black stains. Chemical analysis revealed that the glue was contaminated with high levels of dissolved iron.

In recent years woodworkers have been attracted to another type of PVA adhesive, aliphatic resin or yellow glue. Actually, the label is a bit of a marketing ploy, since both yellow and white glues are technically aliphatics, which means that they consist of long chains of molecules. Yellow glues have qualities similar to those of white glues, but they contain polymers that speed tack time and improve moisture- and creep-resistance, at the expense of a slower final cure. Yellow glues are

also less thermoplastic, so they won't gum up sandpaper as badly. Borden's Elmer's Carpenter's Wood Glue and Franklin's Titebond are two of the best-selling brands.

Yellow glue may be more difficult to apply because of its thick consistency, but it is also less likely to squeeze out when clamped. The viscosity increases as the glue ages in the container. Manufacturers recommend that the glue be used within 6 to 12 months of purchase, but some workers successfully store it for up to two years by stirring in small amounts of water to reduce the viscosity. Up to about 5% water can be added without affecting bond strength. Freezing can ruin white and yellow glues, both in the bottle and as they cure. Manufacturers add compounds to improve freeze-resistance, but any PVA that seems curdled should be discarded.

Water-resistant glues—Modern industrial processes have been revolutionized by the development of highly water-resistant synthetic resins, beginning in 1872 when the German chemist Adolph von Baeyer (of aspirin fame) discovered that he could produce a solid resin if he reacted phenol with formaldehyde. This basic chemistry forms the foundation of the plastics industry and has given birth to a family of versatile, reliable adhesives. Phenolic resins, because of their cost and heat-curing requirements, are used mostly in industry and for exterior plywood and water-resistant particleboard. But a chemical cousin of the phenolic resins, urea-formaldehyde resin, is cheaper and easier to use, making it an adhesive of choice when water resistance is needed, or when long open time between spreading the glue and clamping up is desirable.

Phenolics and urea-formaldehydes cure not by evaporation, but by cross-linking or polymerizing their molecules into hard films that aren't softened by water. The small-shop woodworker will be most familiar with the type that consists of a light brown powder which must be mixed with water before use. Weldwood and Wilhold manufacture this adhesive, both under the label "plastic resin glue." Another type, Aerolite 306, is sold with a hardening catalyst that speeds curing.

Urea-formaldehydes are good general-purpose wood adhesives, especially for woods of relatively high moisture content. They cure into hard, brittle films which won't clog sandpaper, but, for the same reason, they are poor gap-fillers. The medium brown color when cured blends well with most cabinet woods, although bonding may be inhibited in some oily species such as rosewood and teak. Most urea-formaldehydes aren't recommended for marine use, but they are sufficiently water-resistant to withstand sheltered outdoor applications.

When high strength is not essential, urea-formaldehyde can

Adhesive	Application characteristics	Properties after curing	Recommended uses
Hide glue (hot)* (Behlen Ground Hide Glue, Behlen Pearl Hide Glue)	Fast tack, viscous, min. curing temp. 60°F, moderate gap-filling ability, nontoxic, requires glue pot	Transparent, not water-resistant, can be sanded	Musical instruments, furniture
Hide glue (liquid)* (Franklin Liquid Hide Glue)	Slow-setting, low viscosity, min. curing temp. 70°F, moderate gap-filling ability, nontoxic, may have strong odor	Similar to hot hide glue	Assembly procedures that require slow setting
Casein glue* (National Casein #30, slow cure; National Casein #8580, fast cure)	Glue must stand 10 to 20 minutes after mixing, min. curing temp. 35°F, moderate gap-filling ability, nontoxic	Neutral opaque color, high water-resistance, sands cleanly	Interior structural applications, especially good with oily woods and in cool working temperatures
White glue* (Elmer's White Glue, Franklin Evertite, Weldbond, Wilhold R/C-56)	Cures rapidly, low viscosity, min. curing temp. 60°F, moderate gap-filling ability, nontoxic, almost unlimited shelf life	Transparent, low water-resistance, creeps under load, clogs sandpaper	General woodworking, not recommended for structural or outdoor applications
Yellow glue* (Elmer's Carpenter's Wood Glue, Franklin Titebond)	Fast tack, moderate viscosity increasing with age, min. curing temp. 60°F, moderate gap-filling ability, nontoxic	Nearly transparent, moderate water-resistance, less likely to creep under load than white glue, can be sanded	General woodworking, indoor use only
Urea-formaldehyde glue* (Weldwood Plastic Resin Glue, Wilhold Plastic Resin Glue)	Glue powder must be mixed with water, min. curing temp. 70°F**, poor gap-filling ability, releases formaldehyde vapor, uncured glue is toxic	Medium brown color, high water-resistance, sands cleanly, thick gluelines are brittle and may crack under stress	General woodworking, structural uses indoors or in sheltered outdoor locations, bonding may be inhibited with oily woods
Resorcinol glue (Elmer's Waterproof Glue, U.S. Plywood Resorcinol, Wilhold Resorcinol)	Moderate viscosity, min. curing temp. 70°F**, good gap-filling ability, releases formaldehyde during curing, two-part system must be mixed, uncured glue is toxic	Opaque reddish color, waterproof, withstands most solvents and caustic chemicals, can be sanded	Marine use and outdoor construction

* Water-based adhesive may cause warping of veneer or thin panels.   ** May be rapidly heat-cured at 90°F to 150°F.

be extended by adding up to 60% wheat flour or fine wood dust. The thermosetting nature of urea-formaldehyde glues can be both boon and bane. In a shop cooler than 70°F they will cure poorly or not at all, but at 90°F the mixture's pot-life is only one to two hours. Once the glue is spread and the pieces clamped, curing can be hastened by heating the glue-line to between 90°F and 150°F. Urea-formaldehyde's thermosetting qualities make it the most popular adhesive for use with the radio-frequency curing apparatus described in *FWW* #38, p. 26.

One drawback of urea-formaldehyde glues is the emission of formaldehyde gas during and after curing. Besides being a suspected carcinogen, this vapor may irritate the skin and eyes and cause headaches. The problem is liable to be most pronounced in homes constructed with urea-formaldehyde-glued paneling, but it's a good idea to work with this adhesive only in a well-ventilated shop.

The development of urea-formaldehydes marked a milestone on the road to the perfect waterproof glue sought by boatbuilders for centuries. Ironically, completely waterproof adhesives didn't appear until the wooden ship was nearly extinct. Today, resorcinol-formaldehyde glue is the most popular waterproof wood adhesive, with epoxy resin trailing as an expensive second choice. Resorcinol glue was developed during World War II for gluing the plywood used in bombers,

helicopter blades and antimagnetic mine sweepers. Today, it is used to bond marine and exterior plywood, and for laminating outdoor timbers. For the home shop, resorcinol is sold retail as a two-part system consisting of a dark red liquid resin, and a solid powder containing paraformaldehyde and an inert filler (usually powdered nutshells). Two brands are Wilhold and U.S. Plywood, both marketed as waterproof glue.

Resorcinol is fairly costly, and once mixed it must be used within an hour or two. For these reasons, it should be the glue of choice only when a completely waterproof joint is needed. It requires a minimum setting temperature of 70°F, and solidifies within eight hours, though it doesn't reach full bond strength for several days. Acidic hardwoods such as oak may require 100°F to 110°F temperatures for maximum bonding. The final glue film is extremely durable, tolerating boiling water, caustic chemicals and drastic temperature variations. Resorcinol glue is easy to apply and can be cleaned up with a damp rag. Disadvantages include the dark reddish glueline and the release of formaldehyde during curing.   □

George Mustoe is a geochemistry research technician at Western Washington University in Bellingham, Wash. He wrote about making cross-country skis in FWW #31, and his article on respiratory hazards appears on pp. 186-189 of this volume.

Why glue joints fail

When wood joints fall apart, as they occasionally do, the glue is automatically suspect. Usually, though, bond failure occurs not because the glue isn't strong enough, but because the wrong adhesive was used, the wood's moisture content was too high or too low, the surface was improperly prepared, or the joint was clamped incorrectly.

The wide range of glues available will meet any woodworker's requirements, but for most indoor woodworking, white and yellow glues are the best choice, except for veneering, where water-free glues such as epoxy or hot-melt sheets will keep the veneer from curling. Powdered resin glues can give erratic results due to sloppy mixing or poor temperature control, but they are excellent when a hard, machinable glueline is required, and for moisture-resistant exterior work.

Too much or too little moisture in the wood is one of the most frustrating causes of glue failure. Consider this example: The center of a 2-in. thick board is liable to contain more moisture than the surface. If the lumber is planed and edge-glued before it reaches equilibrium moisture content, the porous end grain of the wood will dry and shrink faster than the middle, straining or breaking the glueline. To avoid this, stack and sticker your lumber after milling, postponing gluing until it has stabilized. An extra coat of finish on the end grain when your project is done will minimize subsequent stress on the glueline.

Climatic extremes can drive wood to equilibriums that will make gluing troublesome. In the desert Southwest, for instance, moisture content sometimes falls to 4%, which can draw the water out of PVAs before the joints can be assembled. Conversely, the glue won't harden at all in wood much wetter than 12%. In these environments, using adhesives that don't cure entirely by evaporation—urea-formaldehydes and casein glues—will help. Temperature can also be a factor in glue failure. Below 50°F, PVAs come out of solution and cure in chalky, weak gluelines. At high temperatures, say, above 100°F, they are liable to skin over before assembly, which makes a strong bond virtually impossible.

Typically, adhesives bond to only the top layers of wood, so the surface must be smoothly cut, with no torn or partially detached fibers. Providing that it is straight and true, the best surface for edge-gluing is one left by a sharp hand plane. Next best is to use a jointer or even a sharp circular saw, preferably one that leaves indetectable sawmarks. Dull jointers and planers, on the other hand, produce a glazed, burnished surface which swells in contact with glue, encouraging failure. A sanded surface is similarly undesirable because the loose fibers left behind by the abrasive soak up glue but will part readily when the joint is stressed. Wood surfaces oxidize quickly, so try to mill and glue on the same day; machining a fresh surface on lumber that has been stacked for acclimation is advisable.

Mating surfaces should fit snugly without massive clamping pressure, but joints should have enough space to permit a glue film to develop; hammer-tight tenons or dowels will squeeze out most of the adhesive as they are assembled. If a joint is sloppy, don't rely on your glue's gap-filling qualities to rescue it. Better to recut the joint, or to salvage it with a strategically placed veneer shim.

Deciding how much glue to apply is a dilemma often not solved until it's too late. The ideal glueline is as thin as possible, but without starved spots. Thicker lines are generally weaker because they contain air bubbles or trapped solid particles, as well as internal stresses that develop as the adhesive shrinks during curing. Most glues, particularly PVAs, perform best if they're spread on both surfaces, and the surfaces then placed together and allowed to stand for about 10 minutes before being clamped. This "closed time" gives the adhesive time to penetrate and coalesce before the clamps squeeze it out.

To bond successfully, glues require surprisingly little clamping pressure—10 PSI is plenty, more will just squeeze out the glue, starving the joint. The most common clamping problem is an uneven glueline caused by poorly distributed pressure. Obviously, each job calls for its own setup, but a joint is clamped correctly when the glue squeezes out a bit just as the two parts mate, gap-free. Exert more pressure after that and you risk starving the joint or racking the assembly. For edge-gluing, a good rule of thumb is to space clamps at intervals equal to twice the width of each board. So two 4-in. boards should be clamped every 8 in., with generously dimensioned clamping blocks to spread the pressure and to protect the wood. Before actually gluing, dry-clamp your parts. If a joint won't close, fix what's wrong so you won't be tempted to draw it up later with crushing clamp pressure, introducing stresses that make failure probable. —G.M.

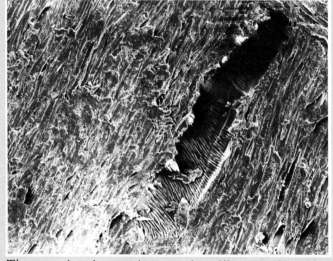 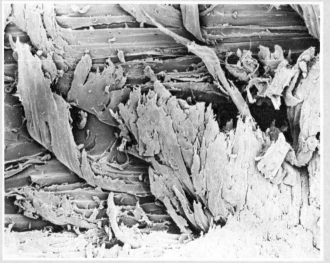

These scanning electron microscope photos illustrate why a crisply cut surface is better for gluing than a handsawn one. The photo of hand-planed maple at left shows cleanly sheared fibers which allow liquid glues to penetrate. The partially detached fibers of a sawn surface, right, limit glue absorption to top layers and break readily under stress.

Outdoor Wood Finishes
Varnish is pretty, but paint's tougher

by William C. Feist

If properly protected and sheltered from the elements, wood is a remarkable durable material. Even when buried or submerged in water, it can retain its strength for many years. Unfinished wood exposed to the harsh effects of wind, rain and sun, however, coupled with the decaying action of fungi, may become useless within a year or two.

Water is the worst enemy of wood left outdoors. Rain and heavy dew are readily absorbed by unprotected wood. At first this causes differential swelling between earlywood and latewood, raising the grain so the wood looks—and is—weathered. Eventually moisture cycling creates enough stress to warp boards, straining fastenings and often cracking the wood. Sunlight, too, takes a toll. Ultraviolet radiation rapidly breaks down the lignin that binds wood fiber together. Sunlight initially affects the top layers of wood, bleaching some species while darkening others. Continued exposure causes slow disintegration.

Sometimes people prefer the look of weathered wood. Usually, though, we want to protect wood that must be left outside, by applying some sort of finish. There are basically two kinds of finish: those that form a film on the wood surface—paints and varnishes—and those that penetrate the wood—water-repellent preservatives and pigmented or semi-transparent stains.

Of all the finishes, paint provides the most protection. A properly applied paint film limits checking and warping by keeping water out, and its pigments (depending on amount and type) filter ultraviolet rays. Paints are classified by their solvents as either solvent-borne or waterborne. Solvent-borne paints are suspensions of inorganic pigments in an appropriate vehicle that binds the pigment particles to each other and to the wood surface. For practical purposes, alkyd-resin paints are the same as oil paints, since alkyds are synthetic substitutes for natural linseed and tung oils. Waterborne, or latex, paints are suspensions of inorganic pigments and latex resins in water. These resins can be any of a number of plastic compounds, including polyvinyl acetate, polyvinyl chloride and acrylic, the same basic resins used to make white glue, garbage bags and Plexiglas, respectively.

Although the impervious film of an oil paint provides the best shield from liquid and vaporous water, it's not necessarily the most durable. No matter how well sealed, wood still moves with seasonal humidity, stressing and eventually cracking the paint. Latex paints, particularly the acrylics, remain more flexible, and even though they pass more water vapor, they hold up better by stretching and shrinking with the wood. Our test fences at the Forest Products Lab show that the all-acrylic latexes, applied in two coats over an oil-based or stain-blocking latex primer, last longest.

Most paint complaints involve cheaper products, leading me to believe that high-priced paints are probably worth the extra money. Better paints usually contain 50% solids by weight. Paints with less than 50% solids may be cheaper by the gallon, but they will cost more per pound of solids, and you'll have to apply more or heavier coats to get equal coverage. At FPL we evaluate paints by generic type. *Consumer's Report* (256 Washington St., Mount Vernon, N.Y. 10550), however, does extensive weather-testing by brand.

A coat of a water-repellent preservative before priming and painting greatly prolongs the life of the paint. Film finishes usually fail first at joints, so give these points, particularly any exposed end grain, an extra coat of water-repellent.

Whether oil or latex, two coats of paint should follow the primer. Our research shows that a single coat over a primer may last four or five years, but two coats can last up to ten. The optimum thickness of primer and paint is 0.004 in. to 0.006 in., about the same as newsprint. Thicker films are liable to fail prematurely, creating a rough, cracked surface

Photos: Forest Products Laboratory

Paint is wood's best defense against the elements, and a water-repellent is paint's strongest ally. Five years ago, the window above was treated with a water-repellent preservative before painting; the one below wasn't.

that can be made smooth again only by a laborious stripping back to bare wood.

Oil paints may adhere better to weathered paint surfaces than latex paints do. If you're in doubt, try this test: Clean and paint an inconspicuous spot with latex and let it dry overnight. Press a bandaid onto the paint, then briskly snap it off. If the bandage lifts a chip of paint, you'll have to clean the surface and try again, or switch to an oil-based paint. Never paint over mildew, for it will just grow through. Instead, clean off the mildew with a solution of ⅓ cup liquid detergent mixed with 1 quart household bleach and 3 quarts warm water. Never mix bleach with detergents containing ammonia; the combination releases a lethal gas.

If you want to show off the lavish joinery of your picnic table through clear varnish, be prepared to refinish often. Even the toughest varnishes have only a fraction of the durability of paints, often breaking down in a year or less. This is because ultraviolet light penetrates the film and attacks the wood, whose breakdown cracks the varnish, which then sloughs off. Hardwoods, with their lower lignin content, may be a better choice for varnish, but you'll still need to maintain the finish regularly. Some varnishes contain ultraviolet-inhibitors, which protect the film itself but not the wood underneath.

Marine spar varnishes, made from tung and linseed oils with driers added, have been the traditional clear outdoor finishes. Phenolic-based varnishes and polyurethanes, essentially liquids that cure into plastic films, are more resistant to moisture and abrasion than oil varnishes are, but all types weather about equally. Two-part polyurethanes are tougher and perhaps more ultraviolet-resistant, but they are expensive and difficult to use, and have a short pot-life.

Varnish built up in many thin coats instead of two or three thick ones will usually perform best. As many as six coats may be needed, with a sanding and a fresh coat once a year. To prolong a varnish finish, shade it from the sun. If you hide varnished outdoor furniture under trees, however, rinse it occasionally to remove bird and leaf excretions, which can also attack the film.

The best compromise between opaque, grain-obscuring paints and short-lived varnishes may be clear water-repellent preservatives or colored semi-transparent stains. These products protect by partially sealing out moisture and light, and by penetrating the wood, leaving it slightly exposed and working in concert with the elements to weather the surface without degradation. These materials are easy to apply and durable, and are particularly effective on roughsawn wood.

Water-repellent preservatives are mixtures of petroleum solvents, paraffin, resins or drying oils, and preservatives (mildewcides) such as pentachlorophenol and copper naphthenate. They don't form a film and therefore don't protect the wood against water vapor or ultraviolet light. They do, however, exclude liquid water, thus inhibiting the growth of mildew and other fungi, making them suitable for any outdoor woodwork that will benefit from some weathering. Semi-transparent stains are water-repellents plus pigments that impart some ultraviolet-shielding. These stains are made in many colors, and since no film is formed, they won't crack or blister. Don't confuse these stains with opaque stains—specially formulated thin paints best used when you want the wood's texture but not its grain to show. An important caution: Pentachlorophenol is toxic and a skin irritant. Stains and water-repellents containing it shouldn't be used on outdoor furniture, playground equipment, or decks around swimming pools. Also, penta can kill plants. Newer waterborne water-repellent preservatives may be less hazardous to use.

Stains and water-repellents are more versatile than paints or varnishes. They can be applied over hardwood or softwood, rough lumber, smooth boards or plywood. Water-repellent preservatives are best dipped, but a liberal brush coat to the point of refusal is fine. The treatment should last one or two years, and should be repeated when water soaks in instead of beading and running off, or when the wood looks dry and gray. To refinish, simply clean the surface with a bristle brush and then brush on more.

Depending on the color and the amount of grain you want to show through, one coat of stain might do. But as with paints, two coats are better. Brush on the second coat before the first has dried. An hour or so later, wipe off any excess to keep glossy spots from forming. Two coats of stain may last ten years, and a recoating then should last even longer because the stain will soak into surface checks that opened up as the wood weathered. □

Add oil, color, and stir

If I were shopping for an outdoor wood finish, I'd probably pick a semi-transparent stain. I would want it to be oil-based, for penetration and durability. It should contain a water-repellent. And I'd want it to have some sort of preservative, particularly if I lived in the South or along a humid coast, where mildew is likely to be a constant problem.

Paint stores usually have these stains in great variety, but if they're too expensive for you or the wrong color, you can mix your own from this formula we developed at FPL about 25 years ago. The amounts listed will make 5 gallons. You can scale down the recipe for a smaller amount.

Boiled linseed oil	3 gal.
40% pentachlorophenol solution	½ gal.
Paraffin (melted)	1 lb.
Burnt sienna (brown iron-oxide) tinting color	1 pt.
Raw umber tinting color	1 pt.
Mineral spirits	1 gal.

Melt the paraffin in a double boiler, taking care not to get it too hot. Add the linseed-oil/mineral-spirits solution, and when the mixture has cooled to about 70°, add the penta and blend it with the other ingredients. Don't breathe the fumes from any of these materials, particularly the penta. Work outside, and wear gloves, goggles and an organic-vapor respirator.

One nice thing about this finish is that you can modify it in many ways. The tints listed make cedar-brown, but you can try any combination of the universal tints sold by paint stores. If mildew is a problem, use half as much linseed oil, making up the volume with mineral spirits. —W.C.F.

William Feist is a wood-finishes research chemist at the USDA's Forest Products Laboratory. This article was adapted from research and consumer publications produced by FPL and by Purdue University. For more information, write to FPL at PO Box 5130, Madison, Wis. 53705.

Respiratory Hazards
Choosing the right protection

by George Mustoe

When the first woodworker whittled a stick with a sharp rock, millions of years of evolution had already provided safety devices to protect him against the occupational hazards of shaping wood. Living in a landscape sculpted by windstorms and volcanic ash eruptions favored the development of physiological defenses against airborne irritants. Nasal hair filters large particles, while the cilia-lined and mucus-coated respiratory tract keeps all but the smallest dust from reaching the lungs. Unfortunately, nature's defenses are meant to counter occasional dust storms and pollen outbreaks, not the dust and vapors encountered by present-day woodworkers. Though woodworking is relatively clean compared with other manufacturing, woodworkers face two hazards: wood dust produced by sawing and sanding, and toxic vapors emitted by adhesives and finishing agents.

How dangerous is wood dust?—The dust problem has usually been considered to be an unpleasant but unavoidable aspect of the craft. Vacuum filters are often connected to power saws and sanders, but most woodworkers still find themselves breathing more wood than they like, producing the familiar symptoms of sneezing, coughing, runny nose and phlegm. To some degree these are natural reactions, as the body traps and moves dust up and out of the respiratory tract. But the defenses can be overloaded. Just how hazardous is this dust? Inorganic dusts from coal, silica and asbestos have long been known to provoke serious lung damage. Recent research strongly suggests that the relatively larger-sized particles generated by sawing or sanding wood also pose a threat, not to the lungs but to the upper respiratory tract. While some abrasive dust is generated by abrasives themselves, the concentrations are not regarded as hazardous.

A 1968 report in the *British Medical Journal* described an unusually high rate of nasal cancer, *adenocarcinoma,* among furnituremakers in the Oxford area. This disease occurs in only 6 out of 10,000,000 people among the general population each year, compared to 7 out of 10,000 among the furnituremakers, who typically worked with beech, oak and mahogany, often in factories lacking dust-collection systems. The figures suggest that about 2.5% of all woodworkers will develop nasal cancer within 50 years of entering the industry. The disease wasn't found in wood finishers, who typically work in separate shops, suggesting that nasal cancer is linked to dust rather than to chemical exposure. Neither were high cancer rates found among carpenters, who worked mostly outdoors where dust doesn't persist. A 1982 survey of medical records from 12 countries found that 78.5% of nasal adenocarcinoma victims were woodworkers, further indicating the potential hazards associated with dust exposure.

Current data on the relationship between cancer and wood is confusing because woodworkers commonly work with other materials as well. For example, several 1980 reports indicate

If you have a beard, no mask will seal adequately against your face. Instead of shaving, you can wear an air helmet, which blows filtered air over your face. The helmet shown above is 3M's model #W316 ($400), available from Direct Safety Co., PO Box 8018, Phoenix, Ariz. 85040.

greater than expected rates of colon, rectal and salivary-gland cancers among woodworkers employed as patternmakers in the U.S. auto industry, but these workers are exposed to plywood, treated lumber, and plastics as well as to solid wood.

Though the relationship between cancer and wood products is just beginning to be explored, particular wood species are definitely known to cause allergenic reactions among many people (*FWW* #9 pp. 54-57). Rosewood, yew, boxwood, cashew, satinwood, teak, ebony and mahogany are among the well noted examples. Western red cedar is particularly notorious because not only is the dust irritating, but the wood contains irritating volatile oils that can evade dust-collection systems. The most detailed descriptions of its effects come from Japan, where occupational asthma was first reported among woodworkers in 1926 after large quantities of cedar were imported from the United States to repair damage done by the Tokyo earthquake. Since 1965, Japanese mill workers and carpenters have again evidenced allergic reactions, as furniture factories have greatly expanded their use of Western red cedar. A 1973 investigation of 1,300 furniture workers revealed that 24.5% suffered some kind of allergic response to red cedar, sometimes developing symptoms within 30 minutes of contact. These symptoms include dermatitis, conjunctivitis, rhinitis and asthma attacks. Sawmill workers are particularly likely to suffer from eye inflammation (conjunctivitis). In Japan, saws are by law equipped with dust collectors, suggesting that irritation comes from exposure to volatile oils. These oils eventually evaporate from the sawn lumber, and respiratory ailments experienced in later processing are more likely dust-induced. In the United States, respiratory irritation has also been linked to inhalation of redwood dust, leading to a form of *pneumonitis* known as "sequoisis." British furniture-makers use the term "mahogany cough" to describe the medical condition *coryza*, an acute inflammation of the nasal membranes accompanied by profuse discharge.

What to do about dust—There are three ways to reduce your exposure to dust. In some situations you can choose another tool that produces less dust; a plane, for example, can substitute for a belt sander. Second, you can trap the dust at its source, using vacuum collection (*FWW* #12, pp. 76-78, and #25, pp. 58-59). Adequate ventilation is the best defense against respiratory dangers, but for those who won't or can't spend the money for a dust-collection and ventilation system, there is a third alternative: you can wear a mask.

Dust masks have been used since Roman times, and simple respirators are described by Pliny the Elder in his *Natural History,* written during the first century AD. Early masks consisted of animal bladders or rags worn over the nose and mouth. During the 1800s, major advances in mask design were aimed primarily at protecting firefighters: masks were developed to filter toxic gases as well as particulates. Chemical warfare during World War I led to further developments. In the United States, this research was led by the Bureau of Mines, which later set performance standards for civilian-use respirators. At present, the National Institute of Occupational Safety and Health (NIOSH) evaluates respirator performance, and specifies acceptability for specific models.

Many woodworkers use "nuisance-dust" masks, which are designed to trap large-diameter, non-toxic particulates. These devices offer fairly good protection for general woodworking, but they are inadequate for dusts released from home insulation, chemically treated lumber or allergenic species. Nuisance-dust masks, though they are light, comfortable and inexpensive, are not manufactured to meet NIOSH standards. The 3M company's popular model #8500 disposable paper mask is available at hardware stores for about 30¢. Another common nuisance-dust mask design, the Norton Bantam model #7200 ($3.50) or the Willson "Dustite" ($3.00), for instance, uses a replaceable filter element.

Given the new-found dangers of wood dust, it is better to use what NIOSH approves as a "toxic-dust" mask, which provides about twice the filtration efficiency of nuisance-dust masks. Disposable types such as those shown below can be purchased locally or from mail-order safety-equipment suppliers. For a permanent facepiece with disposable filter ele-

NIOSH-approved disposable toxic-dust masks include 3M's model #8710 ($1.25), left, and Norton's model 7170 ($3.75), both available from Edcor, Box 768, Kansas City, Mo. 64141.

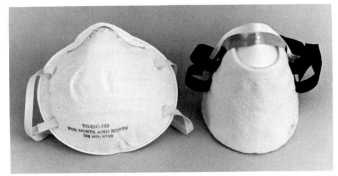

ments, a toxic-vapor mask (to be discussed shortly) can be fitted with NIOSH-approved toxic-dust filters.

While a mask can offer significant protection, its effectiveness may be reduced by 90% or more if you wear it over a beard. One alternative to shaving is a positive-pressure air-purifying respirator, which fits like a helmet and blows filtered air over your face. These are expensive; 3M's air helmet, model #W316 (facing page), runs about $400. It includes a face shield and a rechargeable battery, and weighs about 3½ lb.

Solvent vapors—While the body's respiratory defense mechanisms can filter moderate amounts of dust, toxic vapors present a more serious threat. Hydrocarbons seldom occur in nature, thus we have developed only a limited ability to trap and detoxify these compounds. Unlike inhaled particles, vapors from paints, glues and solvents are readily absorbed into the bloodstream, often causing toxic reactions in organs other than the lungs. The liver and kidneys are particularly vulnerable.

Volatile compounds are widely used in wood finishes and adhesives, and there is no easy way for a worker to judge their hazards. Odor alone is not reliable. For example, highly-odoriferous acetone ranks relatively low on the toxicity scale, while mild-smelling epoxy gives off very toxic vapors. People all too often assume that the mere presence of products on store shelves indicates their safety, a mistake that is compounded by the tendency to ignore warning labels.

The hazards in using synthetic organic compounds are best known from cases where large numbers of industrial workers developed similar symptoms. The home worker, unprotected by expensive ventilation systems, may be at even higher risk. In 1969, ninety-three Japanese workers were found to be suffering from polyneuropathy resulting from exposure to hexane-based glue, used in home manufacture of sandals. Symptoms included muscle weakness, impairment of sensation, and temporary paralysis in the arms and legs. Reactions continued long after contact with the glue ceased, and four years later eleven of the workers still showed some ill effects.

Understanding the toxic properties of solvents is difficult because of the complex biochemical processes that occur once the solvents enter the body. For example, methylene chloride (a major ingredient in paint remover) metabolizes to form carbon monoxide, and methyl alcohol is converted to formaldehyde. In both cases, the toxic effects are partly due to these intermediate metabolites rather than to the original solvent. Many new products reach the market before their health hazards are well understood. When epoxies were introduced to industry in the late 1940s, numerous incidents occurred. A 1947 study revealed that 47% to 100% of workers at various electrical assembly plants suffered skin ailments from epoxy exposure. Many people become sensitized after repeated contact, but the full range of risks remains unknown. Animal studies suggest that at least some epoxy resins are carcinogenic.

Organic vapors are tissue irritants and central nervous system depressants. Workers are most likely to notice irritation of the eyes, skin and respiratory tract, as well as headache, dizziness, confusion, loss of appetite, nausea, malaise and fatigue. Though these symptoms usually disappear within hours or days, the long-term effects may pose different risks. Kidney and liver damage may result from chronic exposure to many solvents, particularly the chlorinated hydrocarbons (methylene chloride, perchloroethylene, etc.) and the aromatic compounds (toluene, xylene, benzene). A 1981 study by Swedish investi-

Several companies make twin-cartridge organic-vapor respirators, usually available in small, medium and large sizes. American Optical Corp.'s 'Sureguard' model #R5051P (shown being worn at right) is priced at about $17, and has an optional hemispherical fiber pre-filter to trap mists and dust. The Norton 'Protex' model #7531 (held at right) is similar, but uses a flat pre-filter pad. It sells for about $26. The 3M model #8712, worn and held at left, does not have a replaceable filter, but costs only about $8. The mask's wide, soft plastic facepiece is unusually comfortable.

gators revealed that painters with more than 25 years' experience showed a 15% greater than expected death rate from cancer. These deaths included unusually high incidences of cancers of the esophagus, larynx and bile ducts. The study also showed abnormally high rates of fatal diseases of the respiratory tract and upper gastrointestinal tract.

What to do about toxic vapors—Though exposure to vapors can be minimized by providing good ventilation, this remedy is not always feasible for woodworkers. Open doors and windows that vent fumes also invite airborne debris and insects to land on wet surfaces, and in winter one may be loathe to allow heat to escape. Most frustrating is the prospect of stripping floors or painting walls in a room that has inadequate ventilation. The danger level is not known for many compounds, and harmful exposure may not produce immediately noticeable effects. Concentrations of methylene chloride vapor as low as 300 parts per million (PPM) can cause drowsiness and reduced coordination after 3 to 4 hours of exposure. This concentration can easily be reached when paint remover is used with poor ventilation. Other compounds are much more toxic; the wood preservative pentachlorophenol, suspected of causing cancer and chromosome damage, is considered hazardous at vapor levels of only a few PPM. Allowing 2 teaspoonfuls to evaporate in an 8x10 room would exceed the danger level.

Besides working with adequate ventilation, wearing an appropriate mask will provide additional protection against even small concentrations of many of these vapors. The modern organic vapor respirator is a direct descendant of the World War I gas mask, with several modifications. The glass-windowed, full-face mask is still used when eye-irritating vapors or gases are encountered, but the half-mask style is most common. This consists of a soft rubber facepiece containing one or two vapor-absorbing cartridges. These typically contain about half a cup of activated carbon or charcoal granules, though silica gel and synthetic molecular-sieve resins are sometimes used. The vapor-absorbing property of these compounds comes from the extremely large surface area of their porous particles. Cartridges are available to protect against a variety of toxic substances. They are made by impregnating the cartridge material with reactive compounds: a filter treated with iodine will absorb mercury vapor, while one impregnated with metal oxides will absorb acid fumes. The standard "organic vapor" cartridges have been found to provide protection against all but 18 of the 197 substances tested. These filters absorb the most common vapors emitted by wood finishes and adhesives. One exception is methyl alcohol. For this reason, when alcohol is needed as a solvent for shellac or other materials, it is safest to substitute denatured ethyl alcohol.

Respirator performance is evaluated by NIOSH. Testing is performed using carbon tetrachloride at vapor concentrations of 1,000 PPM. A cartridge is considered spent when the vapor concentration of air passing through it reaches 10 PPM. Under these conditions, cartridge life must be at least 50 minutes. As vapor levels during wood finishing are likely to be much under 1,000 PPM, the actual lifespan of a cartridge is usually 4 to 16 hours.

In addition to the vapor-absorbing cartridge, the organic-vapor respirator usually comes equipped with a fiber-filter disc designed to remove particulates such as paint-spray mist. In particle-free environments, these filters can be removed to make breathing easier. Or the mask can be used with a filter alone, simply as a dust mask. Masks generally contain a low-resistance port for exhaled air to leave the mask. This exhalation valve prevents exhaled air from leaving through the filter, keeping moisture from saturating the absorbing medium. If the exhalation valve leaks, or if the mask does not seal against the face, the mask is ineffective, allowing unfiltered air to enter. Make certain that your mask fits tightly and that the exhaust port functions.

Respirators have some drawbacks. They restrict your field of vision and make talking difficult. Breathing requires more effort than normal, and some people suffer claustrophobia. These problems tend to become less noticeable as you become accustomed to wearing a respirator. The benefits of both dust and organic-vapor masks are most apparent at the end of the day. Gone are the clogged nostrils, gummy throat and rasping cough. Solvents no longer produce headaches, respiratory irritation or that vague hung-over feeling, and you no longer have to rush through the application of a finish just to get away from the smell.

As a woodworker, I try to produce items that will last for many years, and it seems only an extension of that goal to expect my own components to hold up equally well. Though I sometimes feel like a giant anteater as I wander around the shop wearing my bulbous black proboscis, the health benefits seem well worth the minor inconvenience. □

George Mustoe, of Bellingham, Wash., has worked as an analytic chemist. He also makes harps.

What's in a label: common solvents in the woodshop

Aliphatic hydrocarbons: Also known as "paraffins," these petroleum derivatives consist of chains of carbon and hydrogen atoms. Gaseous forms include *methane, butane* and *propane;* molecules containing five or more carbon atoms are liquid at room temperature. *Pentane, hexane, heptane* and *octane* are major constituents of gasoline, kerosene, mineral spirits and VM&P (varnishmakers' and painters') naphtha. Hexane is widely used in rubber-based liquids such as contact cement and rubber cement. Isobutane and propane serve as propellants in some spray cans.

Aliphatic solvents are generally less toxic than other classes of organic liquids, though they are not risk-free. Common symptoms resulting from excessive exposure include skin and respiratory irritation and central nervous system (CNS) depression.

Aromatic hydrocarbons: These compounds are ring-shaped molecules distilled from coal tar. These liquids are powerful solvents, but their use is limited by low flash-points, high volatility and high toxicity. Three compounds are common: *Toluene* (*toluol*) and *xylene* (*xylol*) are often added to aliphatic solvents to increase their effectiveness. *Benzene* is not used in most areas, owing to its high toxicity and carcinogenic properties, but it is commonly present in small amounts as a contaminant in commercial-grade solvents. Benzene is commonly confused with benzine, an alternate name for VM&P naphtha, a variety of mineral spirits.

Alcohols: Denatured ethyl alcohol (*ethanol*) is widely used as a solvent for shellac, and consists of grain alcohol made poisonous to drink by the addition of methyl alcohol or some other toxic liquid. *Methyl alcohol (methanol,* "wood alcohol") is used in lacquer thinner, paint remover, shellac, and aniline-based wood stains. Methyl alcohol can be absorbed through the skin and its vapors are much more toxic than those of denatured alcohol, so the latter product should be employed for general shop use.

Ketones and esters: This group includes a number of compounds which contain oxygen as well as carbon and hydrogen. *Ethyl acetate, butyl acetate* and *amyl acetate* are esters used in nitrocellulose lacquer. Common ketones include *acetone, methyl ethyl ketone* and *methyl isobutyl ketone.* Esters and ketones typically have strong odors and high flammability. They are particularly likely to irritate the skin because of their ability to dissolve natural oils, and they may produce respiratory irritation and symptoms of CNS depression. A ketone derivative, *methyl ethyl ketone peroxide,* is used as a catalyst for polyester resins. This strong oxidizing agent will cause serious damage to the skin and eyes, and demands careful handling.

Glycol ethers: These are another type of oxygenated organic compound used in solvents, most commonly in slow-drying lacquer. Glycol ethers are highly toxic, and can cause liver, kidney and CNS damage. In addition, they may adversely affect reproductive organs, causing birth defects and miscarriages.

Halogenated hydrocarbons: This group of compounds contains fluorine, chlorine, and less commonly iodine and bromine. Gaseous forms such as *freon* have been widely used as spray-can propellants, but these are now restricted because of evidence that their use is destructive to the earth's protective ozone layer. Though some of the fluorocarbons have low toxicity, the chlorinated hydrocarbons rank high on the list of hazardous solvents. Degreasers and dry-cleaning agents such as *dichloroethane, trichloroethane* and *perchloroethylene* are generally weak solvents, being most effective for removing wax, grease and oil. (Mineral spirits is a safer solvent for removing oil and wax residues.) *Carbon tetrachloride* is no longer widely used because of its toxicity, but *methylene chloride* remains a common ingredient of paint remover and spray finishes. These volatile solvents produce hazardous vapors, and liquids can be absorbed through the skin. In addition, air-supplied respirators, not air-purifying organic-vapor (charcoal cartridge) respirators, should be used to protect against methylene chloride, as air-purifying cartridges will not adequately remove this essentially odorless material. Health risks include liver and kidney damage, CNS depression, narcosis and possibly cancer. Unlike most other solvents, halogenated hydrocarbons are not flammable, but when heated they break down to produce phosgene and other poison gases. The solvent vapors commonly have anaesthetic properties, and *chloroform* and *halothane* (*bromochlorotrifluoroethane*) have been widely used in medicine for this purpose.

Mineral spirits (VM&P naphtha, white spirits): These are distilled from petroleum, and consist mostly of the aliphatic hydrocarbons *hexane, heptane* and *octane.* Composition varies according to the source of the crude oil and manufacturing differences from batch to batch, and chemical analysis reveals the presence of as many as 100 separate compounds in some samples. Mineral spirits are grouped into three categories. Low-boiling-point (140° to 180°F), "odorless" spirits consist mostly of aliphatic compounds with fast evaporation rates and relatively weak solvency. Medium-boiling-point (200° to 300°F), "low odor" spirits are predominantly *heptane* and *octane* fortified with small amounts of *xylene* and *toluene.* High-boiling-point (300° to 400°F), "regular odor" mineral spirits comprise about 75% of all solvents used in the paint industry. They consist of 15% to 25% aromatic hydrocarbons. Mineral spirits are less toxic than most other solvents, but vapors can cause skin and respiratory irritation and CNS depression. Toxicity increases in proportion to the aromatic hydrocarbon content, so odorless spirits are best for general use.

Turpentine: This is produced by steam distillation of pine gum, and consists mostly of carbon-ring compounds called *turpenes.* Pine gum contains about 68% solid rosin, 20% turpentine and 12% water. Turpentine has a strong, characteristic odor, but its physical properties are very similar to mineral spirits, which has largely replaced it as a solvent. Turpentine is more chemically reactive, and will discolor upon long exposure to light or to air. Its vapors can cause respiratory irritation as well as dizziness, headache and other signs of CNS depression. It is a strong skin irritant, and can cause severe allergic reactions after repeated contact.

Lacquer thinner: Lacquers are usually made by dissolving a cellulose derivative in a suitable solvent, though modern formulations may include alkyd resin, natural rosin or other dissolved solids. Lacquer thinner usually consists of about 30% esters and ketones as the active solvent, diluted with aromatic and aliphatic hydrocarbons. The ester, ketone and aromatic content makes these solvents very volatile and relatively toxic, so they should be used only when needed and not as a general substitute for mineral spirits when thinning liquids or cleaning brushes. —*G.M.*

189

Sanding canoe paddles

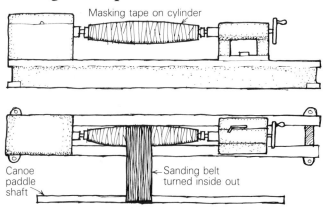

This setup speeds up the tedious job of rounding canoe-paddle shafts. I suspect it has other applications as well.

To start, turn a wooden cylinder 18 in. long and 3 in. in diameter. Wrap it with masking tape, building it up in the middle to form a crown. This will help center the sanding belt as you work. Then turn a sanding belt inside out and place it over the wrapped cylinder.

I prepare the handle by squaring off a blank, then chamfering the corners, except where the blades will be glued on. I then stick the handle into the sanding-belt loop, pull tight and sand round. It takes a little practice at first, but eventually you will be able to make a difficult task simple.

—Wright E. Bowman, Jr., Honolulu, Hawaii

Collapsible finish containers

Collapsible plastic bottles for photographic chemicals (available from photo-supply houses) make excellent working and storage containers for tung oil and other finishing materials that skin over or polymerize in half-empty cans. As the finish is used up, the bottles can be folded like an accordian before the top is screwed on, which eliminates just about all the air. *—T. Carpenter, Calgary, Alta.*

Graining tool

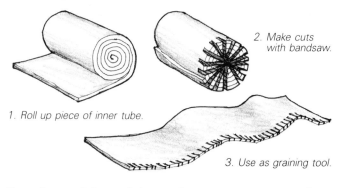

1. Roll up piece of inner tube.

2. Make cuts with bandsaw.

3. Use as graining tool.

To make a graining tool that works on any contour, including intricate molding, roll up a strip of inner tube and notch its end randomly on the bandsaw with cuts about ⅛ in. deep. Then using a glaze of artists' oil colors, linseed oil and varnish, you can produce a striking grain pattern—with practice.

—J.B. Small, Newville, Pa.

Inlaying with dental silver

You can inlay silver into wood using the silver amalgam that dentists use to fill teeth. Draw the design on the wood, scribe the outline, then deepen the cut to ³⁄₃₂ in. or so with a small chisel or a rotary bur. Undercut the edge of the design to hold the amalgam (a dentists' inverted cone bur is ideal).

Now pack silver amalgam into the groove. After the alloy has set, smooth the surface with a flat tool. After 24 hours, level and polish the inlay with wet-or-dry sandpaper, finishing with 600-grit.

The inlay won't polish to a mirror finish, but will take on a softer sheen, something like pewter. It will need a coat of finish (tung oil works) to keep it from tarnishing.

For small designs (three initials about 2 in. tall, for example) the cost is minimal, probably about $1.00.

—Lawrence Warner, Encino, Calif.

EDITOR'S NOTE: My own dentist's reaction was "Now, why didn't I think of that?" Intrigued, he showed me some premeasured plastic capsules (about the size of a cowboy's bullet), with powdered silver alloy in one end, mercury in the other, and a seal in between. A vibrating machine shakes the capsule end-to-end, and a little metal pellet inside the capsule breaks the seal and mixes the two ingredients, much like the agitator ball in a can of spray paint. He explained that different companies market different kinds of capsules with varying seal arrangements, amounts of silver, alloy mixtures and working consistencies, but none of the variables should affect the amalgam's use for inlay. The capsules he demonstrated contained silver the volume of a pea, and cost about 60¢ each.

He gave me a couple of capsules to try at home. There I found I could mix the amalgam by simply taping the capsule to the blade of a portable scroll saw and running it for 30 seconds at high speed. I also found that, in a pinch, you can mix the mercury and silver powder in a shot glass, using a rounded dowel as a pestle. Inlaying was no problem, but the silver would fill the pores of open-grained wood around the inlay, and had to be picked out later with a pin.

One cautionary note: Free mercury is poisonous, as is mercury vapor. After mixing, the amalgam is non-toxic. *—J.R.*

Disposable foam brush

I use this homemade foam brush with its disposable insert on those little oil-finish or paint jobs where it is more work to clean a brush than to do the job.

I fold ½-in. thick foam carpet padding around the end of a ¹⁄₃₂-in. aluminum stiffening strip, and clamp it with a rubber band in an aluminum holder. After the job is done, you can throw away the foam and wipe off the aluminum.

—Harry M. McCully, Allegany, N.Y.

Sanding drum

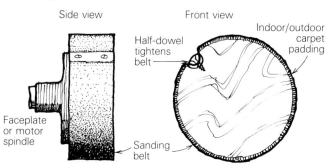

Side view

Front view

Indoor/outdoor carpet padding

Half-dowel tightens belt

Faceplate or motor spindle

Sanding belt

To make this sanding drum, glue up a slightly oversize round blank as wide as the sanding belt you plan to use. To determine the diameter, divide the belt length by *pi* (3.14). Turn down the blank so that the belt plus padding fits snugly, and tighten as shown. *—C. Thorne, San Luis Obispo, Calif.*

Smoke Finishing
Rubbed-in soot colors pine

by Robert B. Chambers

An acetylene torch, starved of oxygen, produces a large, yellow flame instead of a tight, blue cone. The yellow part of the flame is incandescent carbon, much of which is deposited on the wood.

When the surface is evenly wiped, some carbon particles remain as a coloring agent, and will be sealed in by top coats of polyurethane. Under the finish, the wood continues to age naturally.

Here's a smoked finish that can give provincial furniture a mellow patina. An acetylene torch, starved of oxygen, lays a coat of pure carbon on the wood. When you wipe the carbon away, the surface retains enough to give the piece a translucent glaze that allows the wood to age and develop natural color beneath it. Unlike the burning process popular for plywood in the early 1950s (*FWW* #18, p. 36), smoking does not raise the grain pattern or char the wood. I learned the technique from a graduate student in one of my woodworking classes when we were trying to create a driftwood effect for a stage design that had to bear close scrutiny.

I have used smoke finishing on pine, birch, basswood and little bits of Philippine mahogany. It works best on white and sugar pine, but does not work well if the wood has a high pitch content: the process brings the pitch to the surface, the carbon sticks to it, and you end up with black streaks. Small specks of pitch can look interesting, but for a uniform effect, the clearer and drier the wood the better.

Generally, smoking will give you the same highlights and dark, low areas as a stain, but it doesn't interfere with the wood's natural color the way stain does.

As with any finishing, begin preparing the surface by thoroughly sanding or scraping. All traces of glue must be scraped or sanded away, or you will have light spots. After sanding, blow off the dust. It can build up in corners and crevices and keep the carbon from reaching the wood. If you don't have compressed air, a damp rag will work, but do not use a rag dampened with anything flammable. Be sure the wood is completely dry and dust-free before you begin smoking, or the coat won't be even.

The smoking itself is done with a standard oxygen and acetylene welding rig equipped with a heating tip. Do not use a standard brazing tip—the flame spread is too small and will result in burn lines. If you don't have an acetylene rig, you can get similar results by barely browning the wood with propane—don't blacken it—and then rubbing lampblack into the wood. This will give you an idea of what the finish looks like, but the acetylene will give broad coverage and work much better on an actual piece of furniture.

Set the oxygen pressure at 8 lb. and the acetylene pressure at 8 lb. Light the acetylene first and turn it up to a "mild roar." At this point little bits of black soot will be descending all around you. Add oxygen gently until most of the smoke is gone, but don't add so much that you get a secondary blue cone in the middle of the flame. It takes very little oxygen.

Now use the torch with long, even, slightly overlapping strokes to "spray" the wood black. Keep the torch head about 8 in. to 10 in. from the wood, depending on your particular rig. Follow through on each pass so that you begin the spray before you get to the work and continue it off the work in one steady motion. If you stop or backtrack you will get buildups, just as you would in spray painting. Continue

until the piece is uniformly black. You will have a deposit of soot on the work—but no charring of the wood itself.

Wipe the piece down thoroughly with clean rags, changing them frequently, until it takes a lot of elbow grease to get more carbon off the wood. Wrap the cloth around slivers, wedges or pointed dowels to wipe corners and crevices.

Now you are ready to seal the finish. My old standby is Sears satin polyurethane. I have found that it will harden the soft pine I like to work with, and make the wood stand up to the destructive spills, stains and teenagers of a normal household. It's best to spray on the first coat. If you do use a brush, though, just flow on the first coat with the grain. Brushing it will pick up the carbon, causing streaks. Experiment on a scrap to get a feel for it. Fine steel wool and a tack rag between coats will give you a good finish after about three or four coats. After that I usually finish up with a coat of Goddard's paste wax applied with 0000 steel wool and buffed with a soft cloth.

The first time I used this technique I was delighted with the immediate results, but I'm even more pleased by the way the wood continues to age and warm under the finish. □

Robert B. Chambers teaches in the theater department of Southern Methodist University and runs Design Imagineering in Richardson, Tex. Photos by the author.

SPECIALTIES

Letting the Wood Bend Its Own Way

A flexible method for laminating compound curves

by Seth Stem

by Seth Stem

Wood sawn into thin strips and bent is almost animate in its flexibility. With the rudimentary formwork shown in the photo below, author Seth Stem laminates a stack of strips into a sweeping compound curve.

One of the most exciting ways to design with wood is to bend thin strips freely in space, letting form and line depend as much on the wood's natural flexibility as on any preconceived shape. When I first started bending wood, I discovered that the woodworking I had done before was really rigid, beginning and ending with fitting one flat plane of wood into another. I had learned little about the pliant nature of wood that makes dramatic sweeps and curves possible. Such curves may seem to be more in the domain of the sculptor than the furnituremaker, but I've found challenging, direct and practical application of these forms.

Traditionally, wood has been bent either by plasticizing it with steam or by cutting it into thin strips for wrapping around a form and layering up to thickness. This latter method suits the kind of furniture I design and build, although the technique described in this article is considerably different—instead of building the form and forcing the wood to fit it, you bend a single thin strip until you get a curve you like and then you build the form to suit. This method's real value is as a design tool. Compound curves—those which bend in more than one plane simultaneously—are difficult to envision, let alone to draw. I often find considerable disparity between the curve I imagine and the one the wood is actually able to assume. I start my lamination projects with a series of thumbnail sketches, followed by a scale model made of 12-ga. copper wire held together with hot-melt glue or tape. The model, though, takes me only part of the way through the design, because to bend thin strips of wood compoundly, you have to twist them. This process creates shapes difficult to predict with a model. I really don't know how a compound curve will come out until I actually begin bending the wood. My model, then, serves only as a guide for making a full-size, mock-up bend. Once I've bent a single strip to the curve I want, I build a simple but sturdy framework to both guide the shape of the curve and support the weight of clamps when I glue on more strips. When the bend has cured, I shape it to the desired cross-section with hand tools.

Cutting the strips—After I've made the sketches and models, I select the wood. Color and figure are a consideration, but the species' ability to bend is just as important, particularly if I'm planning tight curves. Oak, ash, hickory, beech and elm bend well. Maple, poplar, teak, mahogany, and softwoods such as pine and fir should be limited to gentler curves.

Ideally, lumber should be knot-free, straight-grained and, if possible, air-dried, since it will be less brittle than kiln-dried lumber and will bend better. If you plan severe bends, cut your laminate strips so the annual rings run across their width, and position the heartwood toward the inside of the curve, as in figure 1. If you have rift-sawn (quartersawn) lumber and you plan a severe bend, simply rip your laminae from the edges of the boards. This method is quick and you'll be able to maintain grain continuity. If you have only plain-sawn lumber, first rip the boards to the laminate width and then resaw to the proper thickness. This method is quite wasteful, and grain continuity is sacrificed if you have to build up a thick lamination.

Strips sawn from the center of a plain-sawn board will have short grain, which is more likely to break, particularly in a severe bend. Put the fragile short-grain pieces to the inside of the curve, with the more pliable long-grain pieces supporting the outside.

Expect about 50% waste in converting rough stock into strips. That means a board 6 in. wide in the rough will make a stack of ⅛-in. thick laminae 3 in. high. The strips should be cut a few inches longer than the length of the finished curve and about ¼ in. wider to compensate for slippage, splaying, glue removal and subsequent shaping of the bend. Before sawing, I witness-mark the face of the board with a large V, as a guide in maintaining grain continuity during assembly.

How thick should the strips be? That depends on the severity of the bends. You can get a good idea of the right thickness by cutting a test strip and bending it to the breaking point. Keep in mind, though, that the moisture in the glue will relax the wood's fibers, so a sharper curve is possible than with a dry strip. Curved laminations spring back slightly; if this will create problems in your design, you can minimize it by using thinner strips. If radical curves are wanted, dry-bend the laminae in your form after they've been soaked in hot water for an hour or steamed for 20 minutes. This will make the strips easier to bend and it will lessen springback by giving the wood fibers "memory." Let the strips dry for a day or two before gluing them.

I find that a bandsaw fitted with a 4-TPI, ½-in. or wider blade is the most efficient tool with which to cut laminate strips. It's fast and safe, and the saw's narrow kerf minimizes waste. I rig the saw with a fence or guide block set to cut a strip about 1⁄32 in. to 1⁄16 in. thicker than the final size I want. The extra material will be planed off later when the strips are smoothed for gluing. Rip a strip off each edge of the stock, joint both edges of the board to remove the sawmarks, and rip two more strips, continuing until the board is too narrow to be jointed safely.

The strips will be smooth on one side, but you'll have to remove the sawmarks on the other side. To do this, I use either a tablesaw set up with a 40-tooth carbide blade or a thickness planer. The carbide blade acts as a planer, producing a clean surface excellent for gluing. Install a wooden throat plate on your saw and run the blade up through it, so the slot is the exact thickness of the blade. This way, thin strips will be supported as they pass by the blade.

The advantage of the tablesaw method is that thin or ir-

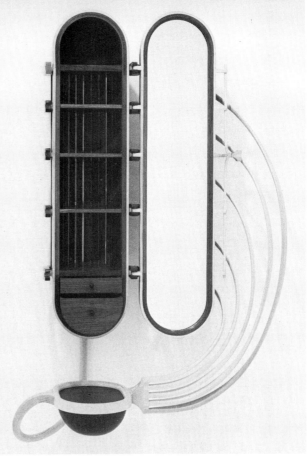

Laminated compound curves can be strong visual and structural elements of functional furniture. For this wall cabinet, Stem laminated maple strips into fluid arcs that connect the tray at the base of this cabinet to its sides.

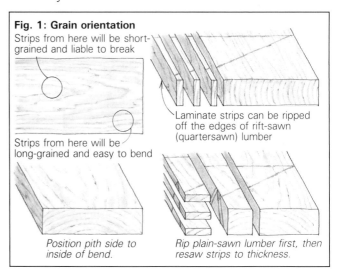

Fig. 1: Grain orientation

Strips from here will be short-grained and liable to break

Strips from here will be long-grained and easy to bend

Position pith side to inside of bend.

Laminate strips can be ripped off the edges of rift-sawn (quartersawn) lumber

Rip plain-sawn lumber first, then resaw strips to thickness.

For a good glue bond, laminate strips must be free of sawmarks. One way to remove them is to attach a wooden auxiliary fence to the tablesaw and, with the strips held against the fence by featherboards bolted into holes tapped in the saw's table, pass the strips by the blade. A 40-tooth carbide combination blade will leave an excellent gluing surface.

regularly grained strips can be smoothed without tearout or breakage. But make sure the blade is parallel to the fence (not just square to the table), because any thickness error will be multiplied in a stack of strips. Check for uniform thickness by trimming two strips and laying them side by side on a flat surface. Feel the adjacent edges for a ridge. Flip one strip over, and feel for a ridge again. Any thickness discrepancy will be apparent.

To check for uniform thickness, lay strips edge to edge.

Flip one strip and feel for a ridge.

The thickness planer does a good job of removing saw-marks from straight-grained material, but it's likely to chew up figured wood, in part because thin strips bear unevenly against the machine's bed rollers, which results in uneven, grabby planing. Bridging the planer's bed rollers with an auxiliary bed made of Formica-covered particleboard or a similarly smooth material should solve this problem. I've planed veneer as thin as $\frac{1}{28}$ in. with an auxiliary bed on a Makita 2040 planer. Sharp knives, of course, will limit tear-out and will leave a better surface for gluing.

Though it's more hazardous and wasteful, strips can be ripped directly on the tablesaw, without planing off the saw-marks. But I don't recommend setting the fence to the strip thickness and then ripping with little space between the blade and the fence—a repetitious operation that invites an accident. A safer way is to support the stock with a wooden form, as in figure 2. Push the form and stock forward with your right hand while applying pressure against the form, in front of the blade, with your left.

You can save yourself the waste and the relatively hazardous work of milling strips by buying $\frac{1}{10}$-in. thick veneer, a material especially well-suited for making wide bends. These sliced veneers are available in many species from Chester B. Stem, Inc., Grant Line Rd., New Albany, Ind. 47150. You may have to purchase a complete flitch, which is expensive, about $150 minimum plus shipping. But getting out your laminae from flitches saves time and makes grain-matching automatic. To cut the strips, I clamp part of the flitch to a bench, chalk lines to mark the strip width on the top piece of veneer and cut the whole stack with a portable circular saw.

Bending form—The key element of successful compound-curve lamination is the bending form. It must be versatile enough to conform to the curve, yet strong enough to hold the laminae rigidly in place during glue-up. A bend even 3 ft. long acts as a powerful lever, exerting tremendous force when a stack of laminae are bent. Nothing is worse than having parts of the form pop loose during glue-up. The fixture I describe here shows one way to support and clamp the laminae; see the boxes on pp. 198-199 for some other ideas. Any device—2x4s tacked to the ceiling and floor, steel pipes, even the shop's supporting posts—can be pressed into service, so long as it supports the laminae and remains firmly in place.

Begin the form by making a base plane, which can be particleboard or plywood if your design is small, or the shop floor if it's larger. I sometimes strike a grid pattern on the base as reference points to aid the layout of the curves, but I translate the model lines to the form mostly by eye—the spontaneous nature of this method makes it difficult to more exactly duplicate the model.

Once you've laid out the curve on the base, mark reference points where both ends of the curve will rest on it and temporarily screw down two 2x4 blocks to serve as anchors for clamping both ends of a laminate strip, as in the photo at the top of the facing page. You're now ready to try a mock-up bend—a single strip that will illustrate the actual form, and will tell you what kind of radius can be bent with a certain thickness strip and what sort of compound curve is possible.

With one end of the test strip clamped down, start bending it in the direction you want it to go. Remember, strips of wood will bend easily only in one direction; you'll have to twist them to get compound bends. Take your time. Experiment with strips of varied thickness and try different bends and twists. Once you've got a pleasing curve, stand back, look it over from various angles and compare it to your model. The mock-up strip should describe fair, consistent curves with no unintended kinks, flat spots or quick turns. Don't be afraid to play around with the strip and form until you get just the curve you want.

Using the mock-up strip as a guide, you can now make the bending fixture from construction lumber (2x2s, 2x4s, plywood, etc.), fastened together with hot-melt glue and drywall screws. But first rebuild the end blocks, anchoring them with stouter stock, or at least reinforce them with corner blocks and screws. Then make a series of 2x2 braces and locate them on about 2½-in. centers, as in the middle photos on the facing page. These braces will hold the curve's position in space and will also support the weight of the clamps. You should support the curve anywhere along its length where the weight of the clamps is liable to distort the bend. But if you use lightweight clamps, such as the rubber inner tubes and bolt-clamps I'll describe later, you won't need to brace the curve as stoutly. I like to keep 2x2s, screws and hot-melt glue handy during the glue-up to shore the curve if it sags unexpectedly. To keep from gluing the bend to the form, cover with masking tape those parts of the supports that may come in contact with glue. Mark the point at which your mock-up strip intersects the braces, so you'll have a way to line up the laminate stack when you make the actual bend. Then remove the mock-up strip from the form.

Clamping and gluing—Each compound curve calls for its own clamping scheme, depending on the severity of the curve and thickness and width of the laminae. Quick-action or C-clamps will work, but if you're attempting a large bend you may not have enough, or there may be insufficient space

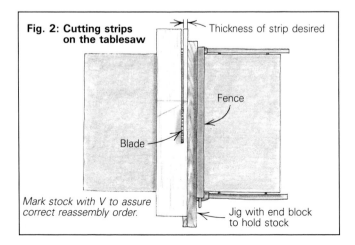

Fig. 2: Cutting strips on the tablesaw

Thickness of strip desired

Fence

Blade

Mark stock with V to assure correct reassembly order.

Jig with end block to hold stock

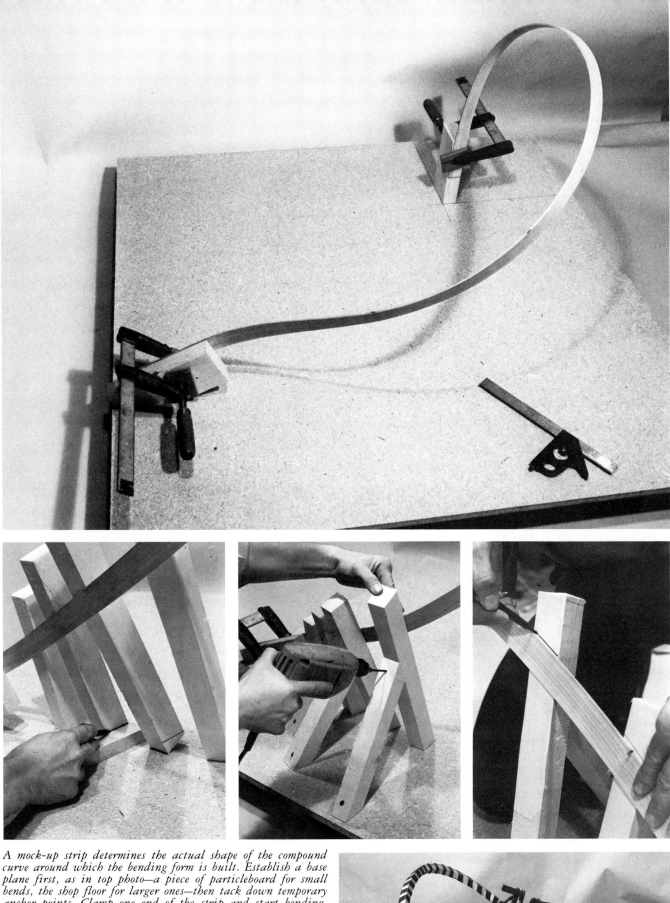

A mock-up strip determines the actual shape of the compound curve around which the bending form is built. Establish a base plane first, as in top photo—a piece of particleboard for small bends, the shop floor for larger ones—then tack down temporary anchor points. Clamp one end of the strip and start bending, twisting the strip to make it curve compoundly. When you've got the bend you want, build a form out of 2x2 lumber to support it. A scrap held against the bottom of the 2x2s, above left, provides reference for marking the base angles, which can then be cut on the bandsaw. Fasten the supports with hot-melt glue and screws, then add 2x2 braces for additional strength, above center. Before removing the mock-up strip, mark its position on the formwork, above right, so you'll be able to relocate the strips for the glue-up. Compound bending calls for clever use of clamps. For the bend shown at right, Stem used quick-action clamps, an old bicycle inner tube wrapped candy-cane fashion around the laminate stack, and shopmade bolt-clamps. Let glue cure overnight before you remove the bend from the form.

to fit them all in. Here are alternative clamping methods:

Cut the valve stems out of an old bicycle inner tube, tie off one end and wrap the tube around the laminae in a spiral, candy-cane fashion, stretching the tube as you pull it tight. Inner-tube clamps don't work well on laminations over 2¼ in. wide because the pressure bears mostly along the edges of the strips. Laminations wider than 2¼ in. can be clamped by this method if a ¼-in. thick strip is used as a batten between the inner tube and the laminae, as in the drawing at right. Rope or heavy

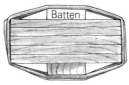

string can be used similarly, though it doesn't have the elasticity. It is good for adding pressure to trouble spots.

Lightweight, inexpensive clamps can be made of two 1-in. by 1-in. by 3½-in. wood bars connected by two ¼-in. or ⁵⁄₁₆-in. bolts or threaded rods, as in figure 3 on the facing page. A slot in the top bar allows the clamp to be put in place quickly, with both top nuts already started. Wax the wood parts to resist glue. The bolts can be spun on quickly using an electric drill fitted with the socket adapter shown in the drawing. As the laminae are bent, their edges will sometimes splay out of alignment, especially if clamps are tightened unequally. A handscrew, clamped across the edges of the

A platform fixture for a fancy table

by Baile Oakes

When I was commissioned to design and build the white ash dining table shown below, I worked out the forms and jigs as I went, starting with a sturdy, perfectly level platform fixture built of plywood and 2x4s, around which the bentwood table grew.

I first transferred to the fixture table a full-scale plan view of the bends that form the table's rails. Where the legs sweep up to join the rails, I fashioned a form and then anchored a single laminate strip which I bent and twisted until I got the leg shape I wanted. The legs were glued up by bending all the laminae at once, supported by a form of steel rods and angle iron. I put a strip of sheet metal between the clamps and the outermost laminae to spread clamping pressure and to protect the wood against marring.

So I would have less shaping to do, I tapered the leg laminae in a thickness sander, using a form similar to the one described in *FWW* #14 on p. 49. With complex compound bends like those on this table, I use epoxy glue from Chem-Tech, 4669 Cander Rd., Chagrin Falls, Ohio 44022— its 4-hr. working time is a necessary luxury because the bends take so long to complete. My shopmade clamps are similar to Seth Stem's, but instead of wood bars I use steel strap, angle or channel iron connected by ⁵⁄₁₆-in. machine bolts. To keep the laminae from splaying, I put the clamps in place finger-tight before I make the bend.

After the glue cures, I shape the laminae with a drawknife, Surform, spokeshave, file, cabinet scraper, and airbag sander, pretty much in that order. The table shown was dyed a rosewood color with powdered dyes and then finished with an oil/varnish mixture. □

Baile Oakes makes furniture in Westport, Calif. Photos by the author.

In compound-bend laminating, the bending form can sometimes be as involved as the object it's intended to produce. For this glass-topped white ash table, left, Oakes made a platform fixture from plywood and 2x4s. He made dozens of clamps out of steel strap, angle or channel iron connected by bolts or threaded rod.

strips, will push the stack back into alignment.

The ideal glue for bent lamination should have a long working time and a high resistance to gradual slippage or cold creep, as the laminae try to straighten themselves out after the bend. The glue should also be sandable after curing, without it gumming up sandpaper or abrasive discs. An adhesive called Urac 185 (made by American Cyanamide) meets these requirements. It is sold in quarts and gallons by Nelson Paint Co., PO Box 907, Iron Mountain, Mich. 49801. Urea-formaldehyde glues (such as Weldwood's Plastic Resin) work nearly as well and are sold by most hardware stores. Urea-formaldehyde glues are powdered resins which, when mixed

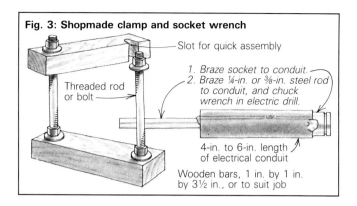

Fig. 3: Shopmade clamp and socket wrench

Slot for quick assembly

Threaded rod or bolt

1. Braze socket to conduit.
2. Braze ¼-in. or ⅜-in. steel rod to conduit, and chuck wrench in electric drill.

4-in. to 6-in. length of electrical conduit

Wooden bars, 1 in. by 1 in. by 3½ in., or to suit job

Bending with the help of steel hands

by Steve Foley

Playing around with a pliable strip of wood is an illuminating but sometimes frustrating way to arrive at compound curves. If you grab one end of a thin strip and start bending and twisting, any number of shapes will emerge—you'll sense, however, that even more would be possible if you could just grab the thing in the middle and give it a twist this way *and* that.

Having spent many hours yearning for more bodily appendages to do just that, I have developed this universally adjustable device which can lock onto various points of a wood strip twisted and curved in space. The idea is to bend a strip using the fixture as extra hands, and then build the necessary formwork around the strip to support clamps when you glue up more strips. This device is good for one-shot pieces, but I've also found it invaluable for building forms that can be reused.

All the materials were gotten from the local welding shop/junkyard—one of those places where they weld up leaky gas tanks with the gas still in them. You could substitute any kind of scrap parts you can get, so long as the device is adjustable yet rigid when all the parts are snugged down.

As the drawing shows, the fixture consists of a central column with adjustable telescoping arms that can be positioned anywhere to support a strip. Build as many collar-arm assemblies as you think you might need. Though my device is rather cumbersome, it works, especially with helical bends. And it was put together on a budget, always a preoccupation in the small shop. It can be modified for individual needs, and I'd like to hear about any improvements or refinements anyone can suggest.   □

Steve Foley works wood in Lake Oswego, Ore.

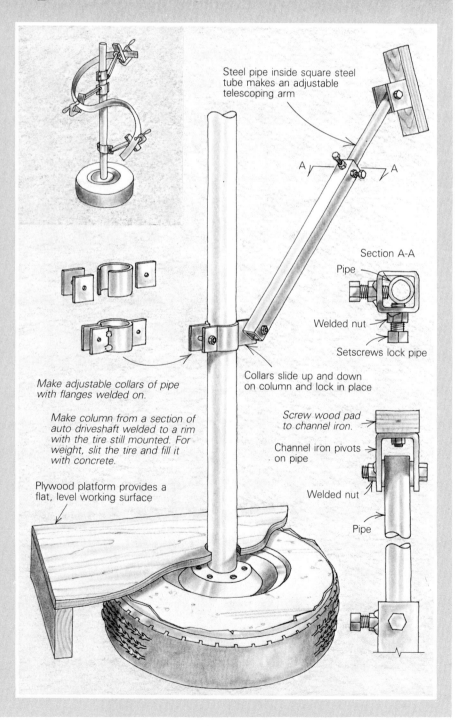

Steel pipe inside square steel tube makes an adjustable telescoping arm

Section A-A

Pipe

Welded nut

Setscrews lock pipe

Collars slide up and down on column and lock in place

Make adjustable collars of pipe with flanges welded on.

Make column from a section of auto driveshaft welded to a rim with the tire still mounted. For weight, slit the tire and fill it with concrete.

Plywood platform provides a flat, level working surface

Screw wood pad to channel iron.

Channel iron pivots on pipe

Welded nut

Pipe

with water, have a working time of about 20 minutes under normal conditions, less if you're working in a warm shop. Working time can be extended by chilling the glue in a refrigerator or by adding ice cubes to the mixture.

For a proper bond, the glue must be well mixed and lump-free. Also, make sure you store these glues in tightly sealed cans—premature contact with atmospheric moisture will crystallize the powder, ruining its bonding qualities. You could use yellow glue (aliphatic resin), but it is thermoplastic and thus quickly gums up and ruins sanding discs and belts. I never use white glue; it has little resistance to cold creep.

Glue-up is messy work. I suggest you do it on a bench covered with newspaper or plastic. With a brush or a 2-in. wide paint roller, apply glue to both sides of all but the outermost two laminate strips.

When all the strips are coated, align their edges and clamp one end of the stack in the form. As you make the bend, the glue-coated strips will resist, but you'll feel them sliding past each other as they seek mechanical equilibrium. Continue the bend, lining the strips up with the marks on the supports. Take your time—don't force the wood where it doesn't want to go, or you'll open up gaps between the strips.

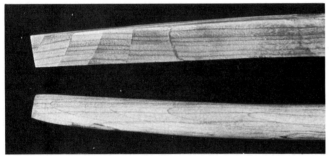

A graceful, dramatic compound bend can be ruined by insensitive shaping. Angular shaping of the top lamination in this photo has exposed gluelines and reveals a discordant grain pattern. The lower one was rounded and the resulting shape is more harmonious with the wood's figure.

Furniture often wants symmetrical or mirror-opposite bends, for looks and strength. To make such bends, draw a grid on the formwork base as in the photo above, and locate the supports for both curves on the same lateral lines, equidistant from the grid's centerline.

Start clamping at one end of the bend and proceed to the other, thus forcing out gaps between strips. With inner-tube clamps, wrap the strips before you actually make the bend. This will reduce splaying and will also make tighter radii possible (the inner-tube wrapping supports the outer strips against breaking, and since the inner tubes stretch during the bend, they apply more clamping pressure). But bend *slowly,* so the individual strips can slide by each other to conform to the curve.

When the curve is all clamped up, check for open gluelines and use your finger to scrape off the oozing glue. Close any gaps with additional clamps.

Clamping time depends on temperature and humidity. Urac 185 and urea-formaldehyde adhesives will usually cure overnight. Check the cure with a chisel. If the hardened squeeze-out chips like glass, it's set; if it dents or gives, don't remove the clamps, or delamination is likely.

Shaping and sanding—After the glue has set, remove the clamps and unwrap the inner tubes. Sand off excess glue with a 16-grit to 36-grit abrasive disc on a body grinder or on an electric drill. Be careful not to remove too much material at this point. Once the glue has been cleaned off, you can further shape and refine your bend with a #49 cabinetmakers' rasp or a half-round Surform plane, followed by a cabinet scraper. Be sensitive about your shaping, however. Cutting into the face of the laminae is likely to reveal unattractive, randomly spaced gluelines. Better to use soft-edged, rounded shaping that will produce forms more sympathetic to the wood's grain patterns and to the shapes you are likely to build using this method of lamination.

Drawknives, spokeshaves, planes, knives and other edge tools can be used for shaping, though I prefer abrasive tools, especially for initial cleanup. Holding a bend for shaping sometimes calls for resourcefulness, but a quick-action clamp or a patternmakers' vise will usually do.

One or more completed bends can be joined together with conventional joints such as a mortise and tenon or a spline. As you would expect, these joints are difficult to lay out, so I prefer to simply design my bends so that they merge smoothly and can be glued long-grain to long-grain. For a better glue joint, flats can be planed on the bends along the length of the joint.

Used singly or joined together, laminated shapes can be strong elements—visual and structural—of chairs, cabinets, tables and other functional furniture. Before I learned this technique, I felt my woodworking constrained by method—my designs were too often dictated by the processes I was familiar with and, in retrospect, I had a lesser understanding of what wood as a material is truly capable of. Now I have a larger technical vocabulary with which to express my ideas, and one flat plane fitted into another is only a small part. □

Seth Stem teaches furniture design and construction at the Rhode Island School of Design in Providence, R.I. Photos by the author; drawings by David Dann. For more on lamination, see FWW #6, p. 35; #7, p. 62; #14, p. 48; and #17, p. 57. Two books on the subject are Tage Frid Teaches Woodworking: Shaping, Veneering, Finishing, *by Tage Frid, published by The Taunton Press; and* The Wendell Castle Book of Wood Lamination, *by Wendell Castle, published by Van Nostrand Reinhold Co.*

Decorative door joint

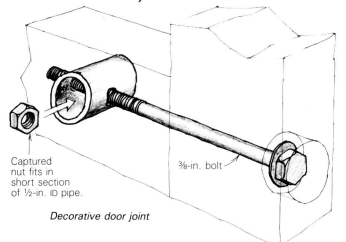

Captured nut fits in short section of ½-in. ID pipe.

⅜-in. bolt

Decorative door joint

This homemade barrel-nut adaptation uses short sections of ½-in. ID iron pipe and captured ⅜-in. hex nuts. I installed several of these fasteners in an old weathered door to pull together the loosened glue joints. The joint would work in other applications as well, such as machine stands and workbench carriages. You can plug the holes in the pipe after the bolt is tight, allowing the metal to show like an inlaid ring.
—*Jack Niday, Balboa Island, Calif.*

Fold-away ladder

Projecting handles, bolted to wall, form retainer bracket.

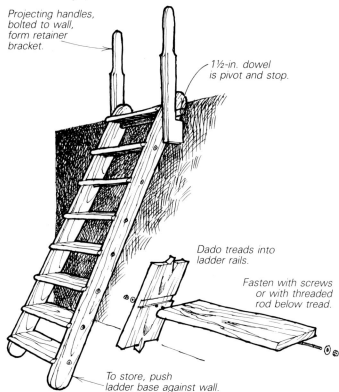

1½-in. dowel is pivot and stop.

Dado treads into ladder rails.

Fasten with screws or with threaded rod below tread.

To store, push ladder base against wall.

Needing some form of access to an overhead storage area, I rejected a stepladder (shaky and dangerous) and permanent stairs (loss of valuable shop space). The solution was a sturdy, shopbuilt, fold-away ladder. It's always there when it's needed and a simple pull locks it into place. Because the steps are wide and the slant is not so steep (20° from vertical), the ladder is safe and reassuring. The projecting handles at the top make the most unstable phase of descent—mounting the ladder at the top—hardly more precarious than descending your front porch steps. —*William Lego, Springfield, Va.*

Router-table fence for edging discs

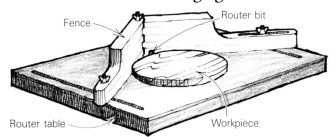

Fence

Router bit

Router table

Workpiece

I developed the fence shown above to shape the edges of round rings, such as clock bezels, on the router table. The fence can shape both outside and inside edges of circular blanks. For shaping the outside edge, some part of the profile must remain uncut to provide a bearing surface against the fence, otherwise the disc would just keep spiraling smaller. The fence is made by laminating 2-in. wide, ½-in. thick plywood strips into two arms that fit together in a finger joint that pivots on a ¼-in. bolt. The other ends of the fence arms fasten to the router table with wing nuts. Slots in both sides of the router-table top and in one arm of the fence allow adjustment for different-size circles and different-width rings.

The dimensions of the fence don't really matter, but I've found that the angle between arms cannot be less than 90° for safety and should not be more than 135°. At angles greater than 135°, the workpiece rolls away from the router bit. These two extremes, therefore, dictate the spread between the two slots in the router table and the length of the adjustment slot in the fence arm. With the setup shown here, the work should be rotated counterclockwise, into the bit's rotation.
—*Robert Warren, Camarillo, Calif.*

Variable-width dado fixture

Clamp fence to workpiece.

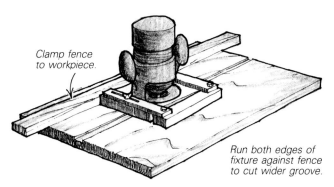

Run both edges of fixture against fence to cut wider groove.

This variable dado fixture will allow fine adjustment of the dado width from bit diameter to double the bit diameter. The fixture works on the principle that one edge of the router base is farther from the bit than the other. To use, clamp a fence in place on the workpiece and make one pass with the wide side of the fixture against the fence. Turn the router around (narrow side to the fence) and make a second pass.

To make the fixture, cut a 9-in. square from ¾-in. hardwood plywood and rout a ½-in. deep recess in the center to receive the router base. Rip one edge off the fixture and reattach it with two cleats. Slot one cleat to allow adjustment. The other cleat is fixed, and the adjustable edge is pinned to it so that the edge can pivot. You will have to trim the corner of the base outside the pivot point so that the adjustable edge won't bind. After the fixture is attached to the router, check to be sure that the distance from the bit to the adjustable edge is slightly (¹⁄₁₆ in.) less than the distance to the fixed edge. If it isn't, saw a little off. Otherwise, slight adjustments over bit size are impossible. —*Jere Cary, Edmonds, Wash.*

Making Wooden Beehives
Precision homes for the honeycombs

by Kevin Kelly

Within the woods where we gather and saw fine lumber, a few trees conceal, under their bark, hollows stuffed with honeycomb. This is winter food, to sustain a colony of bees while the flowers are gone. But it's a rare tree that has a perfectly shaped cavity to hold all the honey the bees could make. By taking lumber and constructing an ideal beehouse, the craftsman encourages the bees to gather more honey than they'll need for winter, and he pockets the surplus as his rent. The woodworker who ordinarily builds to close tolerances, but is the only one to know it, will find bees to be appreciative guests, for bees care about even a sixteenth of an inch. Mistakes slim to our eyes can cause the bees to construct an unworkable mess inside their hives, to the woe of the keeper.

In the past, bees were kept in all kinds of things, but prin-

Not only must the separate stories of a beehive stack neatly and tightly (left), but such interior spaces as the gap between two frames (right) must be scaled to the bees themselves. Otherwise, the disconcerted insects will glue the parts together, locking up the honey.

cipally, in old Europe, in the dome-like straw "skep" so often pictured on honey jars. In that primitive method both the skep and the bees were destroyed when the honey was harvested. About a century ago an ingenious hive system, made completely of wood, started beekeeping along its modern practice of conserving both hive and bees. Wooden stuff has worked so well with beekeeping that even today, despite the unbalanced tilt toward a world of plastic, most beehives are still made of wood. You can get people to live in plastic houses, but bees, so far, rebel.

The contemporary beehive is a stack of boxes piled up as high as needed and able to be taken down easily. The lowest box is the hive proper, where the bees live and raise their young. The upper boxes, properly called "supers," are where the honey is stored. There are no tops or bottoms inside the stack, but each story is divided within by ten intricate frames, arrayed like slices in a loaf of bread. Hives and supers must stack neatly, and supers should be interchangeable—they will be removed and replaced as they fill. Their outside dimensions are standard throughout the United States, with the inevitable exceptions here and there. Heights, however, can vary, although two sizes, "shallow" and "deep," are most common. Any woodworker making bee equipment should resist the temptation, no matter how compelling, to produce equipment not to standard size.

The side pieces of the box-like super are plain rectangles that fit into rabbets cut on the end pieces. Measurements for the cuts have been planned to form a box with inside dimensions of 18¼ in. by 14⅝ in. (figure 1), which allows a constant space between the edges of the frames and the inside wall. This gap is called the "bee space," and its discovery and application by the Reverend Langstroth in 1851 was the key to modern beekeeping. He measured the natural space maintained between combs built by bees in the wild and found it to be exactly ⁵⁄₁₆ in. ± ¹⁄₃₂ in. Any gap less, even ¹⁄₃₂ in. less, had been caulked by bees with a secretion called "bee glue," and any void wider had been filled with honeycomb. Bees are slightly more tolerant when it comes to the built-in spaces in a wooden hive, but the hive maker, by aiming to construct a consistent ⁵⁄₁₆-in. gap between movable parts of the hive, ensures that the bees will leave the gaps unfilled. Thus, each internal piece will be able to be lifted out, emptied of honey and returned.

Super construction—The sides of the supers are traditionally joined with a finger joint, erroneously called a dovetail joint in bee craft. Finger-jointed hives are strong and durable. By using multiple blades, this is also a quick cut for commercial manufacturers, and this style is childishly simple to assemble—an important feature, since most beehives are sold "flat," to be put together by the buyer. An easier joint to make on small runs is the half-lap joint, secured with 8d nails, which is adequately strong, and more weather-resistant besides. It has two clear advantages: it creates a windproof corner and it uses shorter sections of boards. If laid out carefully, a 6-ft. board—too short for a finger-jointed super—will conveniently build a half-lap super.

We began building our own hives because we had access to about 1,000 bd. ft. of small but well-proportioned white pine scraps that would otherwise have become winter heat. For half-lap supers, the longest piece need be only 19¼ in., with a width of about 5⅞ in. for the shallow supers and 9⅝ in. for the deep. Small knots, cracks and other minor defects in the wood are for once usable, because the bees will repair them by chinking them with their bee glue, called propolis, a sticky resinous all-round filler, glue and varnish that they apply to interior parts. So ubiquitous is this propolis that one of the very few vital beekeeping tools is a flat prybar, which is used to separate the supers in a stack—the bees automatically glue them together. Don't go overboard with nasty wood, however, because bees have two character traits that will work to your eventual disadvantage. First, they are fussy craftspeople themselves—they will waste much time smoothing rough wood and repairing cracks, instead of going outdoors to

Fig. 1: A modern beehive

Parts must stack neatly—any gaps will be invaded by other bees seeking to rob the honey store. This shopmade hive features windproof, lap-joined corners instead of a commercially made hive's finger joints, but the dimensions are compatible with beekeeping's standard sizes.

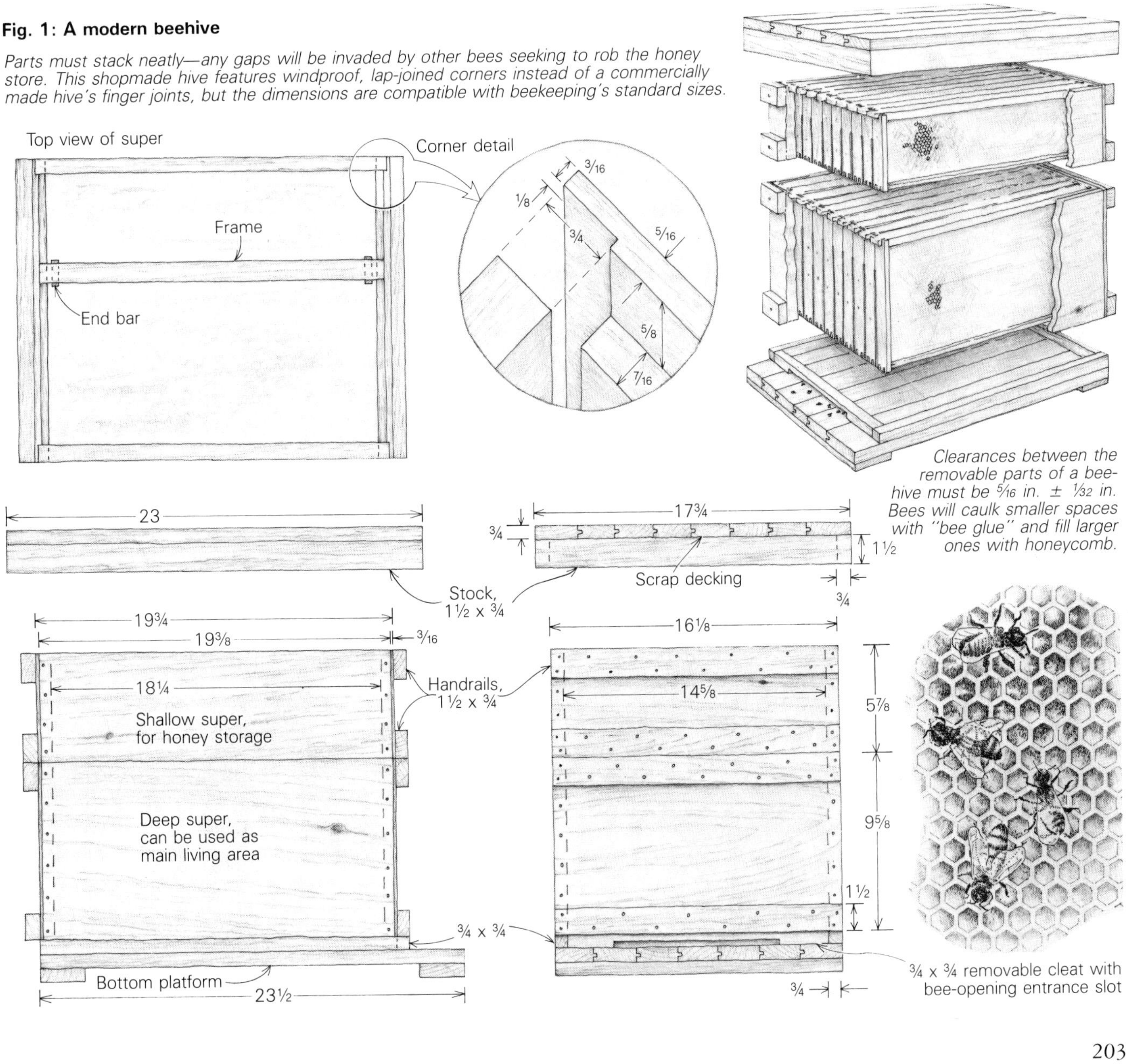

Clearances between the removable parts of a beehive must be ⁵⁄₁₆ in. ± ¹⁄₃₂ in. Bees will caulk smaller spaces with "bee glue" and fill larger ones with honeycomb.

¾ x ¾ removable cleat with bee-opening entrance slot

Drawings: Christopher Clapp

Fig. 2: Cutting sequence for top bars

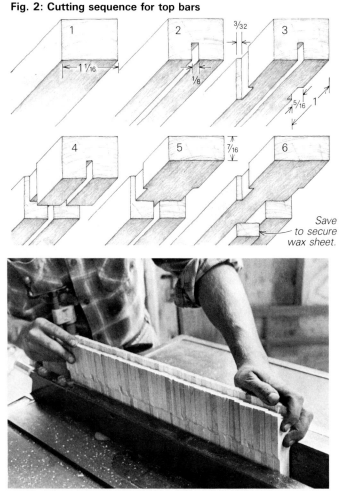

Stacks of parts are dadoed in a 'chute' composed of the tablesaw fence and a length of wood clamped to the table.

Fig. 3: Making the end bars

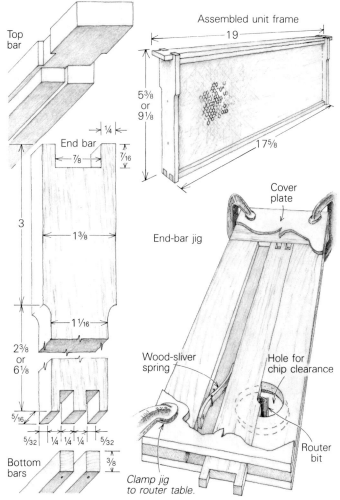

gather nectar. Second, while not exactly what anyone could call lazy, they will take the path of least resistance in their search for sweetness—bees will steal honey from a neighboring hive flawed by an unrepaired bee-sized chink in its armor.

The unit frames, as shown in figures 2 and 3, are a critical construction. Each consists of four parts: two vertical end bars, a horizontal top bar bridging the length of the box, and a bottom bar (which is most easily made from two pieces). The top bar extends beyond the two end pieces to form tabs from which the frame hangs in the super. The bottom bar has a ¼-in. wide slot down its length to hold a sheet of beeswax, the base on which the bees will build honeycomb.

The beeswax sheet is inserted into the slot of the bottom bar, and is supported at the top in a rabbet, secured by the thin wood strip that was cut out when the rabbet was made. Most wax foundation is sold with stiff wire embedded in it so that it does not balloon like a sail and sag into its neighbor. The sides can also be supported with thin wires through holes in the end bars. Once in the hive, all the edges will soon be secured by propolis or by wax comb.

The end bars, by placement and shape, set the proper ⁵⁄₁₆-in. bee space throughout the entire hive. When the frames are placed in the hive, the end bars are recessed from the walls to give the bee space. The end bars are wider than the top bars they hold, so that on adjacent frames the shoulders of the end bars touch, while the top bars have a bee space between them. The length of the end bars is calculated so that they hang exactly ⁵⁄₁₆ in. above the set of frames in the

super below. And the lower half of each end bar is routed on both sides to a narrower width, so that when they are placed side by side there is a passage of ⁵⁄₁₆ in. between frames.

The top bars are easily cut from ¾-in. stock in a sequence of cuts shown in figure 2. The bottom bars are also simple to cut. But because the end bars must measure ⁵⁄₁₆ in. by 1⅜ in., if they are cut from ¾-in. stock, the stock should first be resawn to ⁵⁄₁₆ in. thick and then 1⅜-in. wide blanks cut. The blanks are next arranged face to face in a long train and fed through a chute formed by the tablesaw fence and a board clamped to the table. As the blanks go through the chute, a ⅞-in. dado blade cuts the top notch. With the pieces flipped over and the blade set to take a narrower ¼-in. kerf, two subsequent passes slice the lower notches for the bottom bar.

To rout the contour of the end bars—half a bee space—we devised a simple jig placed on a router table. The jig has a stop and a wood sliver as a spring to keep the piece in place, as shown in figure 3. Routing these pieces is the most tedious task of the run, but when the chips settle, you should harvest a uniform pile of accurately sized end bars.

The assembled parts ought to hug each other snugly. We marry them with Weldwood plastic resin glue. Ordinary carpenters' glue will fail, quickly deteriorating in the tropical conditions inside the hive. Resin glue is waterproof and insectproof, yet seems agreeable to chemically finicky honeybees. The frames will have to undergo a strain of several "g"s while spinning in the centrifuge that whirls the honey from the comb, and they will be battered by tools prying apart

Photos by the author

propolized pieces, so the units must be rigid. We reinforce each glued joint with 1-in., 18-ga. brads.

The new, cleanly cut frames and inside walls of the hive gradually become stained with a glossy yellow-orange color as the bees use their home, even during the first season. In time the interior collects a lacquer of uneven amber glaze from the thin layer of propolis painted by the bees. I enjoy opening an older hive and inspecting the mellow shellac that's been literally rubbed into the wood by millions of tiny bee feet. This natural finish must have intrigued earlier woodworkers, because Stradivarius and other famous violin makers of old Cremona, Italy, used propolis as a principal component in their varnish.

A beekeeper always finds more propolis than he wants. The stuff is compounded of 30% waxes, 55% resins, and 15% oils and oddments, and it readily dissolves in acetone or ethyl alcohol. Someone with an experimental bent may someday rediscover how to apply this as a radiant wood finish.

To complete the hive, some sort of handhold is needed on each super to enable you to move it around. Full of honey, a deep super weighs 60 lb., and even a healthy farmhand will have to grunt to set it gently on top of a chest-high stack. The shallower, and thus lighter, size is still surprisingly heavy. Customarily, a scalloped handhold is routed into each side of the box. Ormond Aebi, however, who earned the world's production record for extracting 33½ *gallons* of wildflower honey from one hive, finds that the routed handhold cools the hive at that spot, diminishing yields. Instead, he attaches two wooden rails on each opposite end, which also enables the super to stand on end, taking less ground room when a tall hive full of bees is being dismantled. We now do the same.

Early in this century, hives often sported peaked roofs, shingled like tiny cottages. They were picturesque but uneconomical. Flat roofs can be made of plywood, covered with sheet metal. But both roof cover and the bottom platform are best made of odd pieces of hardwood flooring or softwood decking. For the top, narrow strips should be splined together—it is best not to use wide pieces because they will cup from the rain and sun, even if thoroughly nailed down with 8d galvanized box nails, as we do. For the bottom, join the boards with tongue and groove so that rain water and melting snow can drain out.

Ignoring tradition, we leave our hives completely unpainted. The primary reasons beekeepers paint hives white are to keep them groomed and to prolong the life of the wood. The hives may or may not do better, but the bees inside do not. More often than not, when a colony of bees dies over winter, wet is to blame rather than cold. Cold weather condenses the moisture in the hive onto the comb and walls. This film of pooled water breeds mold and crippling bee diseases. Wood can breathe the wetness out, even as it sheds rain and snow. Paint hinders this respiration. But, even if it made no difference to the bees, and the hives were painted just to keep things tidy, we'd still not lift our brushes. Wood has a grace in weathering, and the natural graying of the pine is genuinely attractive—much like an old barn or a dock. There are other benefits: In remote apiaries, vandals and beehive rustlers may overlook unpainted hives. In towns, neighbors who might protest against bees may never notice them. We once kept an unpainted beehive on a porch roof in the middle of a village—no one realized it was full of bees and honey, because it looked like a collection of old boxes, and as everyone knows, beehives are painted white.

Fitted with sheets of wax foundation and arrayed like slices of bread in a loaf, the precisely fitting frames in each super can be lifted out for inspection or honey extraction.

If one is not careful and lets it, the paraphernalia in any craft will overcome its practitioner. We have deliberately kept our bee supplies to a spartan minimum: a smoker, bee veil and pry tool. The only purchases we must regularly make are wax sheets. These will last for ten years or so, and then can be melted by the sun's heat, sent away as wax lumps to a bee supplier and, for a small fee, "worked" into new foundation sheets. There are a dozen major suppliers and scores of smaller ones, all shipping wax sheets, tools, books, and cages of live bees (sold by the pound!) through the mail. Our favorite for price, variety and service is the Walter T. Kelley Company, Clarkson, Ky. 42726. The bulk of trade for all the suppliers is selling wooden hive parts to be assembled by the buyer. One sample set could be bought to use as a template for building others.

The best time to start a hive and fill it with bees is in the spring, about the time the dandelions bloom. Hopefully you'll need lots of supers—a good colony in peak season can produce 20 lb. of honey a day. Cutting heaps of hand rails, stockpiling rows of end bars, and gluing up frames to be fitted with wax sheets a little later is the kind of relaxing woodwork we fit around the edges of the day's chores. It's best done anytime but summer, when the bees are returning in haste, heavily laden with sweet nectar, unable to wait. What is not stored is lost. What is kept is shared. ☐

Kevin Kelly keeps bees, travels, and publishes Walking Journal, *Box 454, Athens, Ga. 30603. For more about beekeeping, read* First Lessons in Beekeeping, *Dadant and Sons, Hamilton, Ill. 62341, 1980, $1.40, 144 pp.*

An Adaptable Instrument Form

Bob Mattingly's straightforward route to a musical box

by Jim Cummins

I'd had in mind building a vielle, a sort of modern medieval fiddle, ever since I traced and sketched one about six years ago, but the project kept stalling. I'd done enough repair work to know that the intimidating complexity of most musical instruments is an illusion—that instrument building is basically simple, depending more on common sense and sharp tools than on magic and secrets. I already knew something about the separate procedures involved—bending the sides, thicknessing the back and top, what woods instru-

ment makers use. What I lacked was a straightforward way to fit all the procedures together.

Then, at the 1982 Guild of American Luthiers Convention in Colorado (*FWW* #37, pp. 80-81), I met Bob Mattingly, a guitar maker from Long Beach, Calif., who has developed a course aimed at non-woodworkers who want to make guitars. His best trick is two clever forms built up from layers of plywood and/or particleboard. When the stack is bandsawn, it yields both a bending form for the instrument's sides and an assembly form—an outside mold the exact size and shape of the instrument—that will hold the pieces of the project for clamping. The bending form comes out of the center waste from the assembly form, so both are economical and quick to make. They allow for shortcuts, ingenuity, and whatever tools or clamps you may have around your shop, even rubber bands. The principle can be applied to making any hollow shape with top, bottom and curved sides: ukuleles, dulcimers, guitars of all styles and sizes—any curved box (such as the one on p. 209), whether or not it's

intended to make music. The whole process seemed so accessible that I dug out my old drawings and cleared my workbench. With help from my wife, Karen, I got the fiddle ready for pegs and strings over a three-day weekend.

Figure 1 shows how simple the basic construction is. The instrument has a flat top and back, bent sides reinforced by strips called linings, and blocks inside the body at the neck and tail for strength. Guitars and other modern instruments have a series of internal cross-braces to stiffen the back and the top. The vielle, with its relatively heavy, ⅛-in. thick pieces, needs none.

Template—Whatever your project, draw or trace its outline, and make an exact template of half its top—mine was of plexiglass. If the box is not symmetrical, make a full template. Determine the depth of the finished box, and pile up enough plywood or particleboard to match, with the pieces at least 1 in. larger all around than the body of the instrument. The middle sheet in the stack should be thick and sturdy, and about 3 in. larger. This sheet will act as

Fig. 1: Parts of a vielle

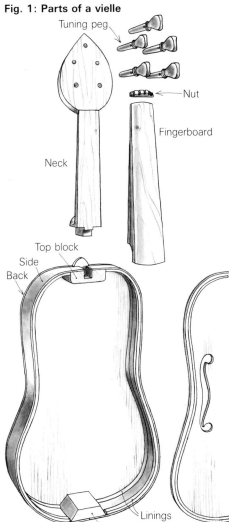

Tuning peg
Nut
Fingerboard
Neck
Top block
Side
Back
Top
Purfling
F hole
Bridge
Tail piece
Linings
Tail block
String loop
Tail peg
Oak bow

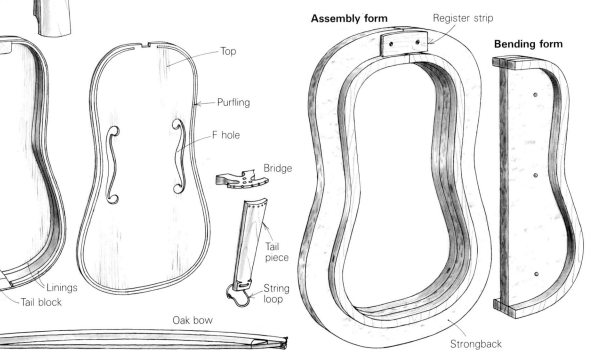

Assembly form
Register strip
Bending form
Strongback

a strongback, an oversize, wider lamination that will make the thin walls more rigid. I used particleboard for the strongback, but something as large as a guitar needs ¾-in. plywood instead. The stack should be at least the height of the deepest part of the instrument; later the box's walls can be trimmed down to exactly the right height or even tapered. Figure 2 shows the steps that get you both forms from the stack.

Register strip—As seen in steps 4 and 5, a register strip placed over the entrance kerf solidifies the assembly form and compensates for the sawkerf, keeping the form the exact size of the template. The shape of a vielle is a straightforward curve that can be made with one continuous bandsaw cut. For more difficult shapes, including those with right-angle corners or other tight spots that require you to back up the blade and reapproach from another direction, you can design various inserts, held in place by additional register strips, that will restore the assembly form to one piece, as shown in figure 3. Thus you can adapt the form to other methods of attaching the neck, as well as to cutaway guitar styles.

Sanding—The assembly form is so accurate that it exactly reproduces any error. Take care to sand the bandsaw marks away without distorting the shape or flaring the walls. If you want the instrument to be tapered in depth (many guitars are deeper at the tail than at the neck), be sure to taper the bottom side of the assembly form rather than the top, otherwise the neck's top surface won't lie in the right plane. Mattingly's students make an extra-long sanding block to help them keep the mold's top and bottom surfaces flat and even. Shellac and wax the form so it will resist glue.

Using the forms—I'll move quickly through the following steps to show how the forms are used. Rather than attempting to give a crash course in luthiery, I've put a list of references on p. 209. The basics of instrument making are simple enough to cover here, although the fine points can be argued forever.

Bending wood—You have to prebend the instrument's sides and the linings in order to be sure of a tight glue joint when you clamp them in the assembly form. I made a steamer from a

Fig. 2: Making the forms

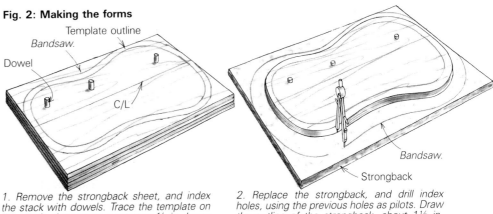

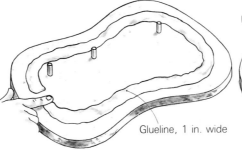

1. Remove the strongback sheet, and index the stack with dowels. Trace the template on the stack, then trace a contour ½ in. larger than the template. Bandsaw the outside line.

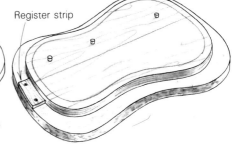

2. Replace the strongback, and drill index holes, using the previous holes as pilots. Draw the outline of the strongback, about 1½ in. wider than the previous cut. Bandsaw.

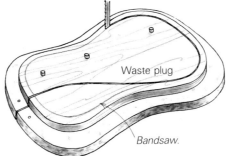

3. Use the dowels to glue the layers to the strongback one at a time. Spread a 1-in. wide band of glue around the edge of each layer. Clamp up.

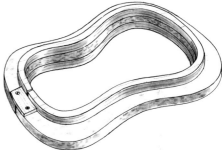

4. Screw a register strip across the top of the strongback, then remove it. Later on the strip will hold the mold at its original dimensions and strengthen it.

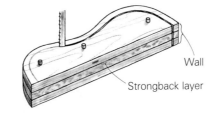

5. Beginning the cut at the top, bandsaw around the template outline.

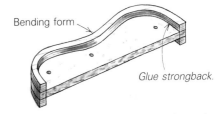

6. Reattach the register strip. This completes the assembly form.

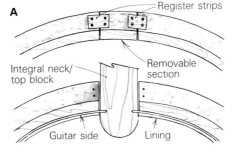

7. Saw the waste plug down the centerline, and scribe a line ½ in. from its edge. Bandsaw to make the wall of the bending form.

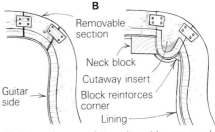

8. Split the waste layers away from the strongback, then glue it back to the wall to complete the bending form.

Fig. 3: Variations   *A shows the Spanish method of attaching neck to body, with a removable, neck-size section in the mold. B shows a cutaway guitar.*

After the linings have been glued to the bent sides, remove the section and install the neck.

Build up the complete guitar sides as usual. Then remove the section where the cutaway will fit, miter the sides, install the cutaway insert and complete the shape.

hot pot and a rolled-up-cardboard tube (photo, below), and steamed a single 1½-in. strip of dogwood (it was handy, though maple would have done fine) to make the linings. They will eventually be glued around the inside of the sides, as shown at right, to provide more gluing surface for attaching the top and bottom. Don't slice and taper the linings before you bend them, or they'll twist. In the bending-form photo below, the wood is being heated with an industrial hot-air gun to set the bend. After the bend had set, I bandsawed the piece into four narrow strips (about ¼ in. wide), and then tapered them so they would blend smoothly into the instrument's sides.

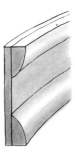

Mattingly bends guitar sides on the bending form, too, using a natural-gas flame to steam up the damp wood as he clamps along. But a vielle's sides are thicker than a guitar's. It turned out that my clamps were not strong enough to hold the sides on the form. So I prebent mine around a bending iron I rigged up—the hot-air gun held in my vise, shown in the photo, below left.

Clamping the sides in the mold—
The sides are butt-joined and glued at the bottom of the instrument, but at the top, at this stage, they just float free. Figure 1 shows the maple tail block, which strengthens the joint and will later be drilled to hold the peg to which the tail piece is tied. The linings butt against it, and I clamped and glued them one at a time to the sides as shown

below. The tail block could be smaller in an instrument with less string tension, or it could be replaced by another lamination if you were building a box. In fact, for a box, you could dispense with linings entirely by double-laminating the sides, perhaps with one lamination narrower than the other to form a rabbet for the box's top.

After the glue had dried, I removed the sides from the assembly form to check that I hadn't glued them in, and I found that there was little springback.

Fitting the neck, top and back—I
shaped the maple neck with bandsaw, jointer and belt sander, then cut its tenon on the tablesaw. Next I made a top block with a matching mortise and glued it in place in the assembly form. The tenon is stepped down so the top

The bending form: Linings are first steamed, then clamped and heated with a hot-air gun or a gas flame to set the bends. Guitar sides can be bent the same way.

An improvised bending setup: An industrial hot-air gun can plasticize the wood as it is levered around the vise's tommy bar. The steamer in the background is a cardboard tube in an electric hot pot.

The assembly form: Pre-bent sides and linings are laminated with spring clamps, while the handscrew secures the tail block. The top block will be glued in last.

can overlap it, but I left a little of the tenon showing as a clue to anybody who might ever try to remove the neck. I made the back from bookmatched maple and the top from bookmatched spruce. I know people who've made instrument tops by quartersawing red cedar construction lumber, but it makes a quieter instrument.

The next step was to plane the linings, sides and blocks to make a good glue joint with the top and back. Most of the truing-up can be done with the sides in the assembly form, which provides stability and reference points.

I clamped the neck to the top block with the instrument outside the mold, as shown below. While the glue dried, I cut the F holes in the top with a knife. Since spruce grain is alternately hard and soft, which makes for a jumpy cut,

The neck can be clamped to the top block outside the assembly form. For an alternative neck joint, see figure 3.

Further reading:

"Appalacian Dulcimer," *FWW* #33.
"Binding and Purfling," *FWW* #28.
"Guitar Joinery," *FWW* #5.
"Hot Pipe Bending," *FWW* #10.
"The Shape of a Violin," *FWW* #15.
Data sheets from the Guild of American Luthiers, 822 South Park Ave., Tacoma, Wash. 98408.

I made a light cut around the outline, and gradually deepened the cut by making wider and wider Vs until it went through. I'm tempted to try some filigree the same way.

I clamped the back and top to the instrument using rubber bands for tension around the sides and Jorgensen handscrews over the blocks.

Odds and ends—Figure 1 shows the other parts needed to complete the vielle. The relationships between the tail piece, bridge, fingerboard and nut are interdependent, and determine how easily the instrument will play. The player must be able to bow each string separately and to fret the strings on the fingerboard easily. I made my vielle wider than the one I'd traced because I thought it looked better, but this meant that I had to change the height of the strings at the bridge. The dimensions and curves of the parts I'd traced six years before no longer worked. It was late Monday before I finally got most of the pieces roughed out.

I spent the next Saturday chiseling out a groove for the dogwood and poplar purfling, which I first laminated on the bending form. Then I experimented with a series of maple bridges until the arc and the height worked out right. Eventually, I raised the fingerboard by putting a full-length wedge between it and the neck. I bought viol strings from an early-music store, and a neighboring luthier turned me a nicer set of tuning pegs than I could have managed. Then I varnished the vielle.

While the varnish was drying, I made a crude bow from some synthetic horse-

hair I'd stashed away. I rosined the bow, touched it expectantly to the strings, and was rewarded with an intermittent squeaking wail that sounded like a dried-out bearing sounding its death rattle. I didn't find out until weeks later that the sound was all my fault and not the instrument's. In the hands of a string player, it sounded fine. Making the box was the easy part. Now I have to learn how to play it. ☐

Jim Cummins usually makes and plays flutes. He is an associate editor at FWW.

The finished vielle next to another shape that can be made by adapting Mattingly's assembly form, a little dogwood-and-ash box.

Bookmatched doors hinged on concealed hardware make for clean, uninterrupted kitchen cabinets.

European-Style Cabinets
Frameless carcases, hidden hinges and continuous veneers

by Bill Pfeiffer

About four years ago, I happened upon a dazzling maple kitchen in a New York loft that changed the way I look at kitchen cabinets. The kitchen's sleek, seamless doors and drawer fronts and clever concealed hardware gave it an uncluttered appeal that I'd never seen. When I looked closer, I discovered yet more refinement beneath the pretty shell—the cabinets were of a remarkably simple, direct construction that squeezed the most out of materials and space, both in short supply in the small rooms that become today's kitchens.

The cabinets were built in what has come to be called the European style, a no-nonsense construction that's gaining favor on this side of the Atlantic. Euro cabinets evolved in postwar Germany as tradesmen, strapped by materials shortages, struggled to restore bombed-out housing. To save wood, they turned to man-made materials, often attractively veneered

plywood and particleboard trimmed with thin strips of solid wood instead of a bulky face frame. And by joining panels with knockdown fasteners, cabinetmakers catered to the European custom of bringing the kitchen along when moving the rest of the furniture from one home to another.

In the United States, we don't take our kitchens with us when we move. Nonetheless, I find European-style cabinets appealing because of the sophisticated result I get without having to resort to long-winded joinery. You need only master a simple corner joint to build cabinets elegant enough to be adapted as built-in furniture for the living room, or even freestanding pieces for other rooms in the house.

Bill Pfeiffer makes cabinets and architectural millwork in New York City.

Layout and construction—In a nutshell, Euro-style cabinets are simple boxes made of ¾-in. plywood, banded on their front edges with ½-in. by ¾-in. solid wood strips. This banding replaces the wide, solid wood frame that trims traditional cabinets (figure 1). There are two advantages to frameless construction: you can bypass the tiresome job of mortising or doweling the face frame together and, once done, the cabinets are more spacious because there's no frame to encroach. As figure 2 shows, each base cabinet consists of two sides, a bottom, and a ¼-in. back let into grooves. A doweled or mortised frame holds the top of the cabinet square and serves as a mounting surface for counters. Wall cabinets are similarly constructed, but have a plywood top instead of a frame top.

Before I explain construction details, I need to say a word about design. If a kitchen is to be functional as well as attractive, cabinets must be sized and located to encourage an economic work flow. This is a complex subject that's beyond the scope of this article, so I refer you to three books for help: Terrance Conran's *The Kitchen Book* (Crown Publishers), Sam Clark's *Rethinking the Kitchen* (Houghton Mifflin) and Jere Cary's *Building Your Own Kitchen Cabinets* (Taunton Press). I suggest you start your design by selecting appliances, favoring ones whose proportions will relate to the width of the cabinet doors—which, along with drawer fronts, are the single most important visual element. Once you've decided what will go where, draw cabinet and appliance locations on a scale floor plan.

As figure 3 on p. 213 shows, wall (upper) and base (lower) cabinets should conform to some standard depths and heights, but the width of each cabinet will be set by the appliances and room size. The 36-in. standard countertop height seems to be comfortable for most people. You can vary it to suit, but don't make it too low, else dishwashers and other under-the-counter appliances might not fit. Positioning the lowest shelf of the upper cabinets 52 in. above the floor, with 16 in. between countertop and cabinet, is the best compromise between working room and comfortable access to the upper cabinets.

I try to work out the width of my cabinets so that all the doors will be between 14 in. and 19 in. wide. These dimensions produce the most pleasingly

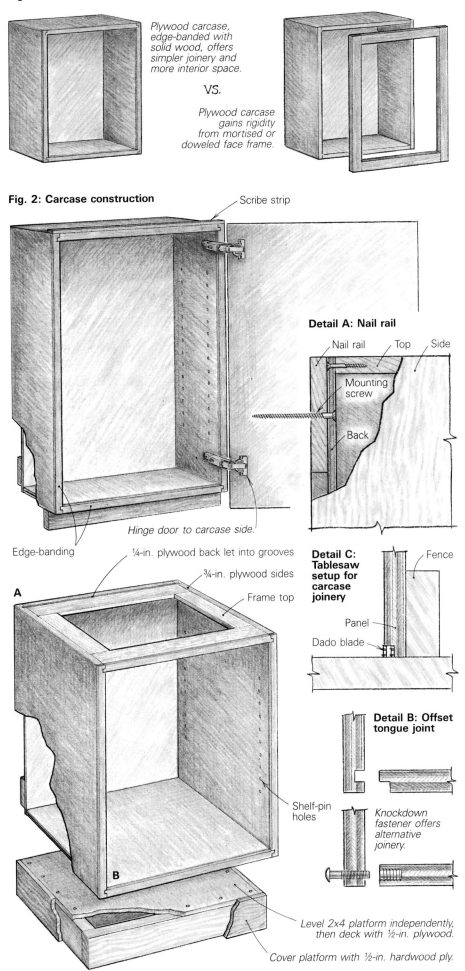

Fig. 1: Euro-cabinet vs. face-frame construction

Plywood carcase, edge-banded with solid wood, offers simpler joinery and more interior space.

VS.

Plywood carcase gains rigidity from mortised or doweled face frame.

Fig. 2: Carcase construction

Scribe strip

Detail A: Nail rail

Nail rail   Top   Side

Mounting screw

Back

Hinge door to carcase side.

Edge-banding

¼-in. plywood back let into grooves

¾-in. plywood sides

Frame top

A

B

Shelf-pin holes

Detail C: Tablesaw setup for carcase joinery

Fence

Panel

Dado blade

Detail B: Offset tongue joint

Knockdown fastener offers alternative joinery.

Level 2x4 platform independently, then deck with ½-in. plywood.

Cover platform with ½-in. hardwood ply.

Scribe strip fits bumpy walls

In a new house, kitchen cabinets may be ready to hang as soon as they're finished. But in an older home where extensive renovation is contemplated, wall framing, rough electrical and plumbing work, and drywalling must be done first. Some makers install the cabinets before the walls are painted, but I prefer to wait until afterward, so there's no chance of paint spatters ruining the finish.

If I can offer any cardinal rule of cabinet installation, it's take your time and get at least one other person to help you. Even carefully crafted cabinets will look awful if sloppily hung.

So I won't have to clamber over the base units, possibly damaging them in the process, I install the wall cabinets first, beginning in the corners and working out. They're screwed directly to the wall studs with 3-in. No. 8 screws passed through the nail rails.

Begin by marking out stud centers on the walls. Measure and transfer these marks to the cabinets so you can predrill and countersink the screw holes. Taping two levels to the carcase—one vertically and one horizontally—will free up your hands for scribing, as shown in the drawing. Knock together a 2x4 T-brace to help support the load. The scribe should be trimmed to fit the wall as neatly as possible, but minute gaps, say, 1⁄8 in. or so, can be filled with a bead of latex caulk and painted over.

A screw at each corner is plenty to hold a small carcase, but a larger one needs fastening in the middle of the cabinet's length. A shim between the nail rail and wall keeps the carcase from bowing back. Base and wall cabinets can be screwed together by driving extra-long screws through the hinge mounting plates.

Screw the base cabinets to a platform made of 2x4s decked over with 1⁄2-in. plywood. The platform, which forms the cabinet's toespace, is leveled independently with shims before it's screwed to the floor. Bolts passed through brackets fabricated from angle iron and into lead anchors will fasten the platform to a concrete or masonry tile floor. Once the platform is in place, the base cabinets need be scribed only where their back vertical edges contact the wall.

Setting the countertop completes the job. Plastic laminate is the most popular counter material, although wood, tile, marble, slate and granite are attractive, if expensive, alternatives. After they're scribed to the wall, the laminate, wood and the plywood ground for tile counters are anchored by screws driven up through the base cabinet top frames. Gravity and a bead of mastic will hold stone counters in place.   —*B.P.*

rectangular proportions. Also, plywood shelves tend to sag if asked to span more than about 38 in. Carcases can be wider and have three or more doors, but you'll need to install partitions on which to mount shelves and doors. Bigger carcases are hard to keep square during assembly and installation.

As you build a kitchen, you'll discover that square cabinets won't fit into the room as readily as a drawer might fit into a carcase. This is because walls, floors and ceilings, no matter how carefully constructed, are rarely plumb, level and square with each other. The sagging foundation of an older home makes this problem particularly troublesome, so you need a way to fit the cabinets.

Adding a scribe—a small strip of wood attached to the carcase to extend its overall dimensions—is the simplest way to do this. The scribe strip is first marked with a compass, then trimmed to match the contour of the wall or ceiling (see box at left). Usually a 3⁄8-in. by 1-in. scribe strip screwed to the carcase is enough, but badly out-of-plumb walls may need more. Before you calculate precise carcase sizes, check the walls and ceilings with a level, then decrease the overall carcase sizes to fit the minimum distances and allow for the scribe you need (*FWW* #41, pp. 42-45). For base cabinets, the 2x4 platform serves as a leveling device. It can later be covered by cabinet-grade plywood or by flooring material (figure 2).

With scribe accounted for, you can calculate the size of each carcase and the parts needed to make it. In figuring the size of each part, don't forget to allow for the solid wood edge-banding when you work up your cutting list. Plywood components for base cabinets, for example, can be rough-cut slightly narrower than their finished sizes, since gluing on the solid wood edge-banding will bring them to the finished width. Wall cabinet sides, which usually get edge-banded on both their front and bottom edges, can be sawn a bit undersize in both width and length.

For an economical plywood cutting list, keep two things in mind: first, figure from large pieces to small, and second, to ensure uniformity, cut all similarly sized pieces at one saw setting. For most kitchens, expect to get six base cabinet sides or twelve wall cabinet sides from a 4x8 sheet of plywood.

I use 3⁄4-in. lumber-core red birch plywood made in Japan. This material is

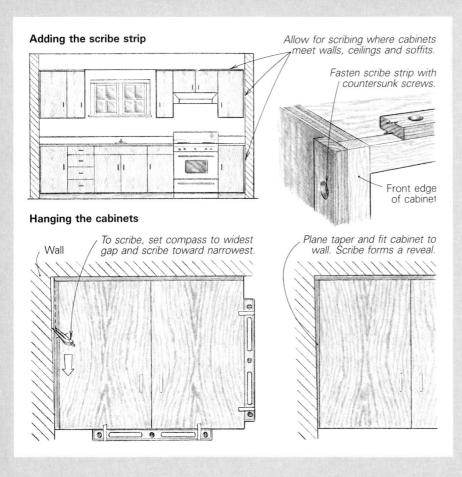

Adding the scribe strip

Allow for scribing where cabinets meet walls, ceilings and soffits.

Fasten scribe strip with countersunk screws.

Front edge of cabinet

Hanging the cabinets

Wall

To scribe, set compass to widest gap and scribe toward narrowest.

Plane taper and fit cabinet to wall. Scribe forms a reveal.

not only cheaper than its American counterpart, it's also of more uniform thickness, thus making for more precise joinery. Cabinet-grade plywoods may be hard to find, but I recommend this material, even if you have to special-order it through a commercial cabinet shop. Interply voids in fir structural plywood make it troublesome to join, and its wild grain is unattractive, even if painted. Cabinet-grade plywoods are sold in dozens of species and several grade ranges. For kitchens, an A-1 or A-2 grade with a lumber, veneer or fiberboard core is suitable.

Fig. 3: Cabinet dimensions

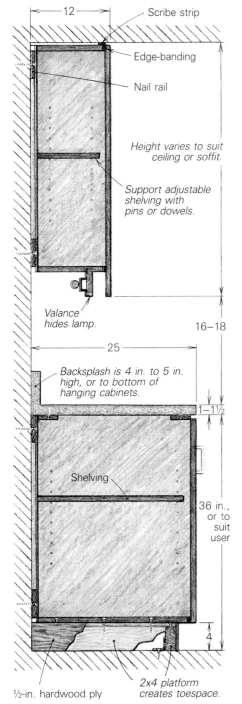

½-in. hardwood ply

2x4 platform creates toespace.

Carcase joinery—Begin construction by cutting the plywood, labeling and stacking each piece as it comes off the saw. Next, glue on ¾-in. thick by $^{13}/_{16}$-in. wide edge-banding, which will later be ripped down to about ½ in. wide when the plywood parts are trimmed to final size. Wall cabinet sides get bands on their front and bottom edges. So end grain won't show at the front of the cabinet, do the bottom edge first, trim a bit off the width of the panel to flush up the joint, and then band the front edge. Once the plywood parts have been banded, trimmed to size (including the top frame for base cabinets) and carefully checked for square, you're ready to cut joints.

Plywood lends itself to production machine joinery. I cut most of the joints on my shaper, but the only essential tools are a tablesaw, a router and the usual hand tools. For lumber-core and veneer-core plywood, the offset tongue joint shown in figure 2, detail B, is strong and quick. Plate joints (*FWW* #34, pp. 95-97) or dowels are better for particleboard and fiberboard. Knockdown fasteners are suitable for either material, if you prefer that method.

Whether you machine the offset tongue on a tablesaw fitted with a dado blade or on a router table, plywood that varies in thickness will cause some joints to be loose. One remedy is to machine the tongue slightly oversize and then hand-plane it to a good fit. A second, as shown in detail C of figure 2, is to feed the plywood vertically between the fence and the dado head, with the tongue against the fence. Most ¼-in. plywood seems particularly scanty these days, being only 0.220 in. thick. If you don't have a 0.220-in. cutter but still want the backs of your cabinets to fit snugly, try cutting the groove in two passes with a ⅛-in. wide blade in the tablesaw. Move the fence slightly to widen the groove for the second pass.

With machining complete, you can sand the carcase parts before assembly. Glue-up is straightforward, but check carefully that everything is square, to avoid trouble when fitting the doors and drawers later.

After assembly, clean up the carcases with a hand plane and/or a finish sander and ease the edges with sandpaper. Before you begin drawer and door construction, drill holes for the shelf pins using the template shown in the photo, above right. I use 5mm brass shelf pins,

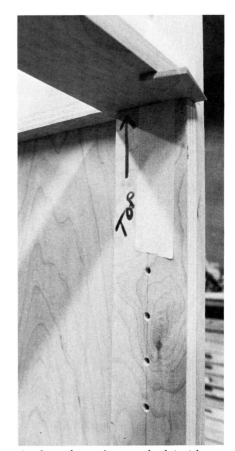

A plywood template, wedged inside assembled carcases, speeds boring of shelf-pin holes, which should be spaced about 1½ in. apart.

but dowels will also work, or, if you prefer, metal or plastic shelf standards. On narrow carcases, you may want to drill the shelf-pin holes before assembly.

Doors and drawers—I figure door and drawer face sizes at the same time I calculate case dimensions, but if you're uncertain about these sizes, wait until you've completed the cases. If you're using full-overlay doors and drawer fronts, size them so that they will completely overlap the front edge of the carcases. I leave about $^{3}/_{32}$ in. between two doors or between a door and a drawer front. This clearance is fine-tuned later by planing the doors and/or adjusting the hinges.

Concealed hinges work with plywood or solid panel doors, but they're also fine on frame-and-panel doors, provided that the hinge stile is wide enough for the cup flange, usually a 2¼-in. minimum. I make my doors of ¾-in. fiberboard edge-banded with solid wood and veneered on both sides. To allow for trimming later, I make the edge-banding ½ in. wide.

Choosing the veneer with the customer is the highlight of the job for

213

After glue-up, the fiberboard and edge-banding assembly shown above will be veneered then crosscut to yield a cabinet door and drawer front with continuous grain. Figure 4, below, shows a similar setup for a bank of drawers.

Fig. 4: Drawer face cores

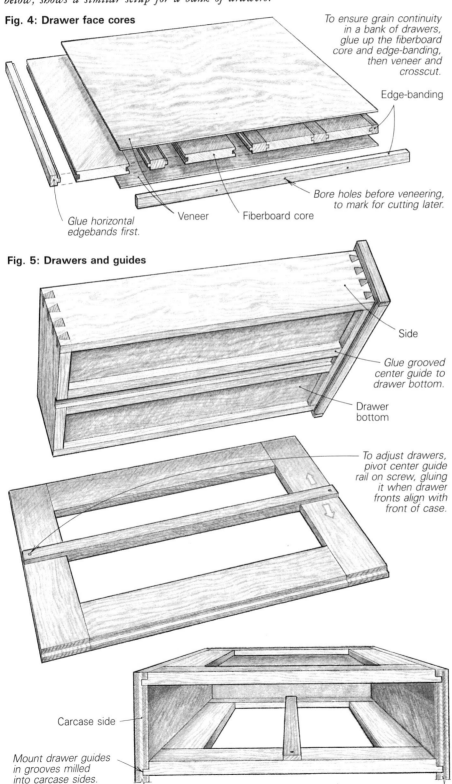

To ensure grain continuity in a bank of drawers, glue up the fiberboard core and edge-banding, then veneer and crosscut.

Edge-banding

Bore holes before veneering, to mark for cutting later.

Glue horizontal edgebands first.

Veneer

Fiberboard core

Fig. 5: Drawers and guides

Side

Glue grooved center guide to drawer bottom.

Drawer bottom

To adjust drawers, pivot center guide rail on screw, gluing it when drawer fronts align with front of case.

Carcase side

Mount drawer guides in grooves milled into carcase sides.

me. We usually pick veneers from the same flitch, and it's fun to flip through the stack, envisioning how the raw log was sliced into so many thin sheets. We organize the veneers to be bookmatched or slip-matched in sequence for each door and drawer face. To assure grain continuity between a drawer face situated above a door or in a bank of drawer faces, I glue up a sandwich core (figure 4 and photo at left) which is then cut into components after it's veneered.

If I've got only a few doors to make, I veneer them myself on a shopmade press. Otherwise, I job out the work, sending the matched, taped veneers and cores to a local architectural millwork house, preferably one equipped with hot presses. If you don't want to bother with veneered or frame-and-panel doors, fiber-core hardwood plywood edged with solid wood is a stable alternative. To hang the doors, refer to the box on the facing page.

I like the whisper of a well-fitted wooden drawer sliding on a wooden track, so I use the drawer scheme shown in figure 5. The drawers slide on bearing rails grooved into the sides of the carcase. A grooved member glued to the drawer bottom slides on a center guide rail, making for smooth, accurate travel. But practically any method for hanging drawers is okay for kitchen cabinets, including metal ball-bearing slides, which are quicker to install than wooden tracks. Most metal slides require at least ½ in. of clearance between the inside of the carcase and each side of the drawer, so be sure to allow for it.

Honduras mahogany router-dovetailed together makes strong, attractive drawers, but poplar, maple and Baltic birch plywood are excellent, less expensive alternatives. In fact, I recommend making drawers deeper than 10 in. out of plywood—they'll be less likely to warp. Once I've hung and fit the drawers to my satisfaction, I install the drawer fronts with screws driven in from the inside of the drawer. Make sure the edges of the drawer fronts align with each other and with the doors.

With all the doors and drawers in place, and before I apply the finish, I make any final adjustments that require planing or cutting. I coat the carcases, doors and drawers with nitrocellulose vinyl sanding sealer, followed by a fine sanding two to three hours later. A coat or two of Flecto Varathane completes the finish. □

Hanging doors on concealed hinges

The trouble with a lot of cabinet hinges—including some expensive ones—is that you can't adjust the doors once they're hung. Some hinges permit a smidgen of adjustability through slotted mounting holes, but these are awkward and liable to work loose in service.

Concealed hinges made by several European firms solve these problems cleverly. Though formidably complicated in design, these hinges are simple to install. Besides remaining out of sight when the doors are shut, they are adjustable in three planes, by as much as $\frac{3}{16}$ in. for some models. You need only locate mortises to within a fraction of an inch—you can fine-tune *after* the door is hung. Euro hinges work with an elbow action that throws the door's hinged edge slightly sideways, keeping it from banging into the adjacent door. Though invisible when the doors are closed, concealed hinges are big and mechanical-looking when the doors are open.

Most concealed hinges consist of two parts: a baseplate which you screw to the inside of the cabinet carcase, and a metal arm that pivots on a cup-shaped flange which you let into a round mortise in the door, as shown in the top photo at right. To hang a door, mark out and bore the hinge mortises. With a fence clamped to the drill press, use a $1\frac{3}{8}$-in. (35mm) Forstner bit (available from hinge suppliers) to bore a $\frac{9}{16}$-in. deep mortise for each hinge. The edges of the mortises should be about $\frac{5}{32}$ in. in from the edge of the door. Push the hinge temporarily into place. Locate the baseplate by holding the door in the position it will be when open, and transfer the center marks. A jig like the one shown in the photo, far right, will speed the mounting of baseplates. Screw the hinge cup into the mortise, then hang the door by sliding the hinge arms onto the baseplates.

Once the door is hung, you adjust it by turning screws in the hinge arm to move the door vertically, horizontally, or toward or away from the carcase.

You can buy spring-loaded, self-closing hinges or else use nylon roller catches to hold the doors closed. I find an Austrian brand of hinge called Grass to be the strongest and most adjustable. Grass hinges are sold wholesale by Kessler Inc. (229 Grand St., New York, N.Y. 10013), and are available retail (about $9 a pair) from Woodcraft Supply; you can get a complete list of local distributors from the importer, Grass America (1377 S. Park Dr., Kernersville, N.C. 27284).   —B.P.

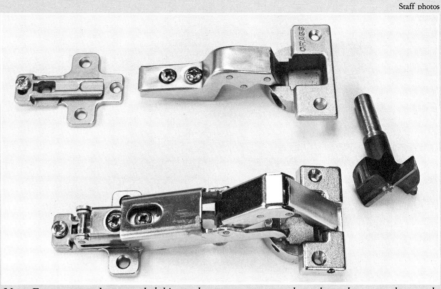

Most European-style concealed hinges have two parts—a baseplate that attaches to the inside of the carcase, and an arm-on-flange that fits into a round mortise in the door. The top hinge opens about 100°; the lower, 176°. Made by Grass, both self-close, and are available for either inset or overlay doors. The bit bores a 35mm round mortise.

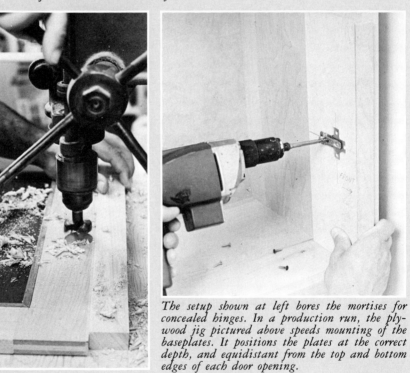

The setup shown at left bores the mortises for concealed hinges. In a production run, the plywood jig pictured above speeds mounting of the baseplates. It positions the plates at the correct depth, and equidistant from the top and bottom edges of each door opening.

In the arm of this hinge, the screw at the right controls the door's lateral position; the middle screw, its distance from the front edge of the carcase. The third screw, when loosened, allows the door to be moved up or down in the vertical plane.

Drawing an ellipse

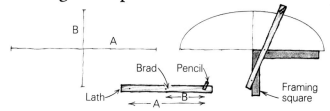

Here's how to draw all or part of an ellipse with a lath and a framing square. First, lay out the major and minor diameters of the ellipse on the workpiece, and clamp a framing square on these lines with its outside corner at the center. Install a pencil in a hole near one end of the lath, and measuring from the pencil, drive two brads through the lath, one at distance A from the pencil, the other at distance B. Clip off the brads so that they don't protrude more than the thickness of the square. If you swing the lath, keeping one brad riding the top edge of the square and the other brad riding the side edge, you will scribe one-quarter of the ellipse. Complete it the same way. —*Frank Grant, Round Pond, Maine, and Matt Longenbaugh, Darrington, Wash.*

Splint joint

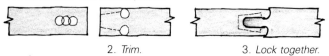

To splice pieces of ash splints for chair seats, first soak the splints to make them pliable. Then, with a leather punch, punch holes in the splints and trim the ends to the shape shown in the sketch. This procedure achieves the same result as the traditional method (knife and chisel), but it's faster, easier, and handier in tight places. And the rounded edges resist splitting while the seat dries and tightens.
—*Bruce Herron, Ganges, Mich.*

Sliding dovetail fixture

While attempting to rout long sliding dovetails on the end of shelving joints, I found it impossible to keep the over-wide and long shelves perpendicular to my router table. This fixture brings the table to the work. It's a platform with a slot in the middle and two perpendiculars for sandwiching the work. To rout the dovetail, I clamp the work in the jig flush with the top of the platform. Two fences, attached at the proper spacing, guide the router. —*Victor Gaines, Glenside, Pa.*

Flip-up router fence

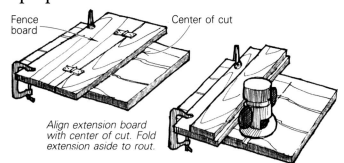

When routing grooves, some people draw a line on the work where the groove will be, then calculate where to clamp the fence. Others draw the line where the fence will be. Both methods have obvious drawbacks. But if you make a router fence with a hinged extension, you can mark the center of the actual groove on the work, line up the extension with the mark, then flip it out of the way to rout the groove. Make the fence out of a straight, flat 1x4. Now rip another board half the diameter of your router base (measure from the center of the bit to the edge of the base) and hinge it to the fence. As shown in the drawing, offset the hinges so they won't protrude when the extension board is swung up out of the way. —*James F. Dupler, Jamestown, N.Y.*

Shaping with pencil-sharpener cutter

In my woodworking classes, I have been using an old spiral cutter from a pencil sharpener, chucked in the drill press, for smoothing small-radius internal curves. The cutter works very well, and saves the time and tedium of sanding or filing.

To make the tool, simply hacksaw one of the two cutters free of the mechanism. Replace the pin with a short length of $\frac{3}{16}$-in. cold-rolled steel rod. For the correct cutting action, make sure the drive gear is on the bottom. Hammer the bar a bit so that it will wedge tight in the spiral cutter. To use, chuck the cutter and lock the quill.
—*David Glen Whitling, Bolivar, Ohio*

Dressing thin stock

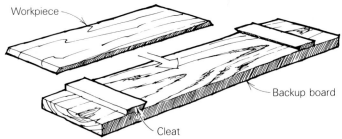

This jig allows you to dress stock to thinner than $\frac{1}{8}$ in. on a conventional thickness planer. Without it the thin workpiece will vibrate and often splinter on the ends. To make the jig, glue 45° beveled hardwood cleats to a length of lumber as wide as and slightly longer than the wood to be dressed.

To use, bevel the ends of the workpiece so that it fits snugly under the cleats. Wax the back of the jig, slip the stock in the jig and run the jig through the planer, taking light cuts down to the desired thickness. Push the jig into the planer, then pull it through from the other side to prevent the feed rollers from pushing the workpiece out of its cleats.
—*John S. Pratt, Avondale Estates, Ga.*

Making Your Own Hardware
Hand-worked brass beats the store-bought stuff

by David Sloan

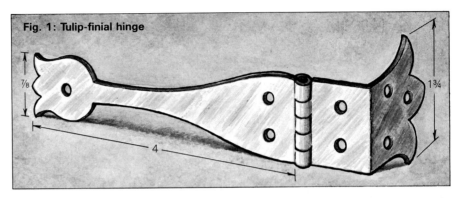

Fig. 1: Tulip-finial hinge

Why let a limited selection of brass hinges force you to compromise the design of a project? You can have any style hinge you like if you make it yourself. The work is not difficult, even if you have no metalworking experience. All you need, in addition to regular woodworking tools, are a jewelers' saw and blades, a set of needle files, a propane or an acetylene torch, silver solder and flux.

The example here is a simple brass strap hinge with tulip finials, but the techniques I'll describe apply to any kind of brass hardware. Hinges can be constructed with a pin inserted through looped knuckles, or with a simple pivot pin. You can devise all manner of hinges, locks, pulls and handles, each tailored to your project.

The color and workability of brass make it the right metal for hardware making, though copper, silver, aluminum and steel are certainly acceptable. Brass is sold in dozens of different alloys, but one called CA-260, which is 70% copper and 30% zinc, offers the combination of strength and workability demanded for hand-working. It buffs to a rich, yellow luster. Brass comes in five hardness ranges: dead-soft, quarter-hard, half-hard, hard, and spring. Like most metals, brass work-hardens, that is, it gets tougher as you bend and hammer its crystalline structure into smaller, tighter patterns. To soften it again, you anneal it by heating it to a cherry-red

Sources of Supply

Cardinal Engineering Inc., RR 1, Box 163-2, Knoxville, Ill. 61448. Brass, steel and aluminum sheet; rod and bar stock.

Paul H. Gesswein & Co., 255 Hancock Ave., Bridgeport, Conn. 06605. Jewelers' tools and supplies, including saws, files, scribers, solder, and polishing material.

Kitts Industrial Tools, 22384 Grand River Ave., Detroit, Mich. 48219. Metalworking tools, including taps and dies, measuring and marking instruments, and drills.

Small Parts Inc., PO Box 381736, Miami, Fla. 33138. Brass sheet; rod and bar stock; small fasteners.

glow with a torch, followed by a quick quenching in cool water. Picking a hardness range depends on how much cutting and shaping your design requires. Quarter-hard is a good grade to start with, since you can anneal it or work-harden it as required, but don't hesitate to use any available piece of brass whose hardness is unknown.

Brass sheet stock comes in various sizes, and in thicknesses measured by gauge numbers:

$$24 \text{ ga.} = 0.020 \text{ in.}$$
$$20 \text{ ga.} = 0.032 \text{ in.}$$
$$16 \text{ ga.} = 0.051 \text{ in.}$$
$$11 \text{ ga.} = 0.091 \text{ in.}$$

Rod, tube and bar stock are available in all sizes and shapes as well, usually in increments of $\frac{1}{16}$ in. or $\frac{1}{8}$ in. See the supplies box at left for mail-order sources.

I start my hinges by transferring a drawing of the shape to a piece of annealed 16-ga. sheet stock, allowing about $\frac{5}{16}$ in. extra length for the fingers, which later will be looped into the knuckles of the hinge. Draw the fingers directly on the metal with a jewelers' or machinists' scriber and square. It's important that the fingers be square and accurate, or gaps between the knuckles will result.

A jewelers' saw—a small, adjustable-frame saw similar to a fretsaw—is used to saw out the hinges. Jewelers' blades are very fine and easily broken, but they're cheap and sold by the dozen, so it's best to purchase at least that many for one job. For cutting sheet brass, a fine-tooth No. 2 blade is good to start

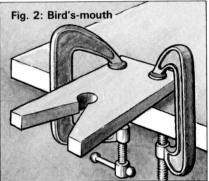

Fig. 2: Bird's-mouth

with. The saw should cut on the pull stroke, so when you insert the blade, make sure that the teeth are pointed toward the handle. The blade needs plenty of tension, too. To accomplish this, adjust the frame's blade opening so it's $\frac{1}{4}$ in. to $\frac{1}{2}$ in. larger than the length of the blade or piece of blade (broken blades of sufficient length may be reused). With the blade mounted in the front clamp, press the front end of the frame against the bench, bending it toward the handle enough to catch the blade in the rear clamp. When you release the pressure, the frame will spring back, tensioning the blade. A properly tensioned blade responds with a clear, musical "ping" when plucked.

Clamp the work to the benchtop so that the section being sawn projects over the edge, or else make a bird's-mouth, as shown in figure 2, to better support the work. This makes cutting somewhat easier, particularly with thin stock or where a piercing cut is made in the middle of a piece. When sawing, keep the blade perpendicular to the surface of the

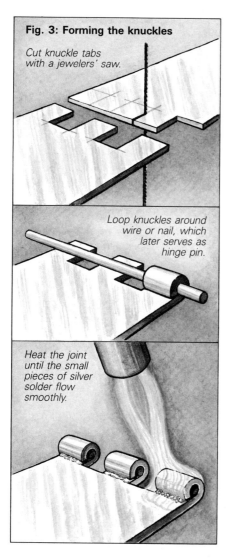

Fig. 3: Forming the knuckles

Cut knuckle tabs with a jewelers' saw.

Loop knuckles around wire or nail, which later serves as hinge pin.

Heat the joint until the small pieces of silver solder flow smoothly.

ing the part and melting the solder into the joint. Soldered joints are well up to the loads most furniture hardware must bear, and you can solder small pieces together to form whatever shapes you want. First, clean the parts thoroughly with fine steel wool. On the hinge shown here, I held the knuckle ends in the right position for soldering by simply bending the metal into place. If you are soldering separate parts together, clamp or wire them in position. Then brush on silver-solder flux—usually a borax compound that chemically cleans the metal and promotes adhesion and flow—being careful to wet only the parts of the joint that you want to solder. Cut the silver solder into tiny pieces and arrange them along the joint, as close to the mating surfaces as possible. Play your torch quickly over the joint at first, until the parts heat up. Then concentrate the flame right on the joint. When it reaches the melting point, the solder will flow all at once, and you're done. When the solder has cooled, a drill passed through the knuckles will clear the pin hole of excess solder.

Next, true up the soldered hinge halves with files and fit them together. This is a trial-and-error procedure and it helps to hold the two pieces up to a light to see where material must be removed. Once the pieces fit, you may still have to drill or bend the knuckles slightly to get the pin in. Oiling the pin helps. Once you've inserted the pin, you can close up slight gaps between the knuckles by gently tapping at either end with a small mallet.

When the two halves fit satisfactorily, use a fine file to smooth out the knuckles, and make sure that the outer surfaces are parallel. Make any additional bends your special hinge may require, but keep in mind that you can't anneal after soldering, so don't overwork the metal. Cut the hinge pin to length and peen the ends slightly to hold it in place. Finally, drill and countersink holes for the mounting screws.

To clean away the residue left from annealing and soldering, polish up your work with progressively finer grits of wet sandpaper and steel wool, and, if you want a high polish, finish up with rouge on a buffing wheel. But use a light touch, else you'll dub over your carefully filed edges. □

─────────

David Sloan is an associate editor at Fine Woodworking.

stock. After sawing, clean up the hinge with files, checking the fingers carefully for square.

I bend each finger separately to form the knuckles. A nail or a wire about $\frac{1}{16}$ in. in diameter makes a good bending form. This will later become the hinge pin. Start each bend with a pair of pliers, wrapping the finger around the pin (figure 3), completing the bend by squeezing the knuckle in a vise whose jaws have been covered with wood or aluminum to protect the brass from marring. You should be able to make all these bends without having to anneal the brass again. When all the fingers are bent around the pin, a final clamping of all knuckles in the vise at once draws them up tight.

With the knuckles bent, I remove the pin and then silver-solder the ends of the knuckles to the back of the hinge, for appearance and strength. Silver-soldering differs from soft-soldering in that the solder has a much higher melting point. You also heat the part and the solder at the same time, instead of heat-

A catch, three hinges and a lock

Door catch: This spring-loaded catch, which I smithed for a fall-flap door, is essentially a three-sided box soldered to a flat mounting plate. I made the box by engraving V-grooves in flat brass stock and then folding the metal along the mitered grooves. A bead of silver solder reinforces the miter joint. The catch bolt is soldered to a piece of brass rod drilled to accept the steel pivot pin, which fits loosely so that it can be driven out for disassembly. I soldered a pin to the bottom of the box to anchor the spring; the top of the spring nestles in a dimple drilled in the underside of the catch bolt. The wooden activating button, which slides in a mortise, is beveled for leverage on the catch bolt. The strike plate is sawn from the same stock as the mounting plate.

—*Ian J. Kirby, Bennington, Vt.*

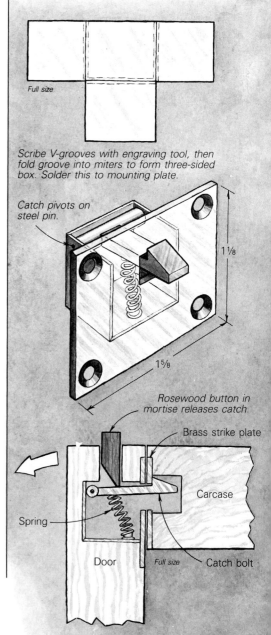

Full size

Scribe V-grooves with engraving tool, then fold groove into miters to form three-sided box. Solder this to mounting plate.

Catch pivots on steel pin.

1⅛

1⅝

Rosewood button in mortise releases catch.

Brass strike plate

Carcase

Spring

Door

Full size

Catch bolt

Knife hinges: These knife hinges, which I made for a drop-front desk, can be tailored to fit any door where a small, unobtrusive hinge is wanted. I start with ⅛-in. thick, rough brass blanks slightly larger than the finished size of the hinges. I locate the holes in one knife with a scriber and center punch, drill the holes and then use this as a master template to transfer hole locations to the other knives. A #2/0 steel taper pin, available from industrial supply houses, serves as the pivot. Once I've drilled all the holes, I clamp the knives together, using 4d finish nails as locators, and then file the hinge to its final shape.
—*Tim Simonds, Chico, Calif.*

Fall-flap hinge: Good fall-flap hardware is always hard to find, so I made a pair of these hinges for a desk I designed. I sawed the hinge parts out of ³⁄₁₆-in. by 1½-in. brass bar stock, cutting, fitting and test-pinning the angled knuckles before shaping the rest of the hinge. The 55° angle on the flap-side knuckle is critical, to keep the hinge from binding when the flap is closed. I encountered one problem in soldering: small parts, the pivot brackets for example, floated out of position on a river of molten solder. When clamping isn't possible, I just tack the parts in place with brass pins and then solder the joint.
—*Randall Torrey, Scottsville, N.Y.*

Cam lock: When I built grandfather clocks for each of my 12 grandchildren, I designed this cam lock to hold the pendulum door closed. The parts can be of brass or steel, silver-soldered together. I turned the shank on a lathe and cobbled the bearing block from a single piece of metal. The lock is operated from the side rather than the front of the case. I made my own brass key, but you can size the square part of the shank to fit the same key that winds the clock. A small section of brass tubing driven into the keyhole serves as an escutcheon. —*Raymond H. Haserodt, Lyndhurst, Ohio*

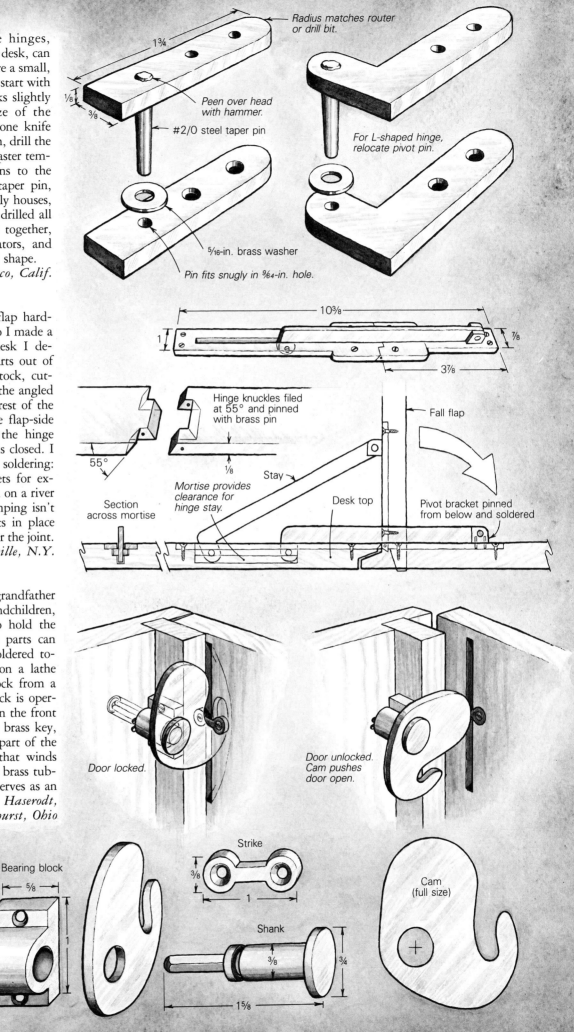

Radius matches router or drill bit.

1¾

⅛

⅜

Peen over head with hammer.

#2/0 steel taper pin

For L-shaped hinge, relocate pivot pin.

5⁄16-in. brass washer

Pin fits snugly in 9⁄64-in. hole.

10⅜

1

⅞

3⅞

Hinge knuckles filed at 55° and pinned with brass pin

Fall flap

55°

⅛

Mortise provides clearance for hinge stay.

Stay

Section across mortise

Desk top

Pivot bracket pinned from below and soldered

Door locked.

Door unlocked. Cam pushes door open.

Strike

⅜

1

Bearing block

⅝

Snap ring holds shank in bearing block.

Brass tube escutcheon

1

Shank

⅜

¾

1⅝

Cam (full size)

Methods of Work

Table design converts to desk

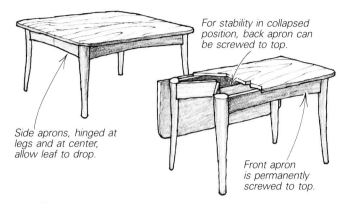

For stability in collapsed position, back apron can be screwed to top.

Side aprons, hinged at legs and at center, allow leaf to drop.

Front apron is permanently screwed to top.

This table design folds in to convert to a more compact side-table or a desk. It has been quite convenient during my frequent Navy transfers, where my furniture has had to adapt to various household settings.

The two table sections are fastened together at the center by a piano hinge. The front section of the top is permanently attached to the apron along the front edge. The two side aprons are hinged to fold in, allowing the rear legs to move forward. At its folded-in position, the rear apron can be screwed to the tabletop for stability. The entire conversion takes just a few minutes. *—Andrew J. Pitts, Orlando, Fla.*

Chamfering tambour strips

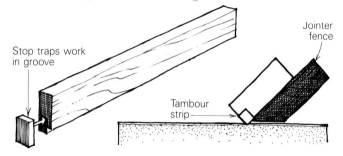

Stop traps work in groove

Jointer fence

Tambour strip

Here's a jig I developed to safely chamfer the edges of narrow strips, such as tambours. It consists of a straight piece of scrap as long as the strips and wide enough to be handled safely. Rabbet the bottom edge of the jig a fraction narrower and shallower than the strip, and attach a stop to one end of the rabbet. Now set your jointer fence to the desired angle, place a strip in the rabbet, and run the jig across the jointer. The depth of cut determines how wide the chamfer will be.
—Greg Forney, Gilcrest, Colo.

Enlarging flute bores

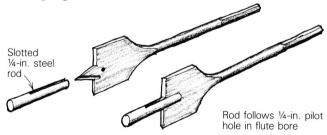

Slotted ¼-in. steel rod

Rod follows ¼-in. pilot hole in flute bore

To drill long, straight holes of various diameters, first drill a pilot hole through the blank with a ¼-in. shell auger. Then construct a follower bit by cutting a slot in a short length of ¼-in. rod and slipping it over the tip of a spade bit. The rod will follow the pilot hole and the spade bit will self-center.
—Bob Vernon, Keuka Park, N.Y.

Sawing and assembly work station

24

30

36

Here's a shop aid that let me put three different sets of saw-horses out to pasture. It makes a strong, portable work station for sawing, sanding, assembly and other operations. Simply flop the box to position the work 24 in., 30 in. or 36 in. off the floor. Construct the unit by screwing together six dowel-joined frames. *—Bill Nolan, Munising, Mich.*

Picture-frame clamp

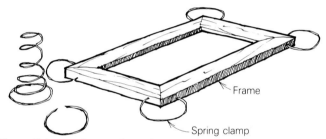

Frame

Spring clamp

These light-tension spring clamps are made by cutting up coils from an old bedspring. Sharpen the ends to needle points, then bend the circle so that the points are aligned, leaving a ⅜-in. gap. To use, simply place the frame to be glued on a flat work surface and use one of the spring clamps at each corner to clamp the frame. The points leave pinholes in the frame, but if care is taken, damage is minimal.
—H. Hugh Miller, LaHabra, Calif.

Producing dollhouse siding

Here's how to produce simulated clapboard siding for doll-houses with a router and an easy-to-make subbase. First, to make the subbase, bevel a ¾-in. thick, 6x10 block on the tablesaw in much the same fashion as you would cut a raised panel. Be sure to leave a ¹⁄₁₆-in. or so fillet, as shown. Now bore a hole through the block, and mount the router so that a ¾-in. straight bit chucked in it is tangent to the fillet of the base. After experimenting with the bit depth, you should be able to rout multiple beveled cuts across the workpiece, indexing each cut in the previous cut. For narrower siding, relocate the subbase on the router and use either the same or a smaller bit. *—Jim and Dan Fortner, Newport, Ind.*

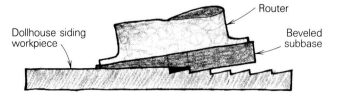

Router

Dollhouse siding workpiece

Beveled subbase

Making Wooden Buckets
White cooperage, the Swiss way

by Drew Langsner

Swiss-style buckets of close-grained pine, with maple hoops. Traditionally used in small dairies, these liquid-tight containers are known as 'white' cooperage. The sculpted bucket, right, is carved from extra-thick staves after the staves have been glued together.

Coopered containers range in volume from huge wine vats to pint-size beer steins. Whatever their size, they are all basically tapered cylinders made of vertically arranged wooden staves with mitered edges. The staves are held tight by two or more hoops made from wood or metal. Bottoms consist of one or more boards which fit into a groove cut into the staves. Because of their cylindrical shape and the compression/tension relationship among staves, bottom and hooping, coopered containers are remarkably strong and durable.

As a trade and technique, cooperage may be divided into four overlapping areas: Wet cooperage is for holding liquids. Dry (or "slack") cooperage is for such less demanding needs as transporting or storing grains, fruits or nails. Of greater importance to woodworkers is the distinction between single-bottom and double-bottom cooperage. Double-bottom containers have bowed staves whose mitered edges are curved. Whiskey barrels are typical. In single-bottom cooperage—called "white cooperage" because the buckets are traditionally used to hold milk in small dairies—the staves are straight, as are the mitered edges.

The methods for single-bottom cooperage described in this article were taught to me by Rudolf Kohler, an 83-year-old cooper who lives and works in the Swiss Alps. I met Kohler in 1972, while I was searching for a traditional Swiss milking bucket to purchase as a souvenir. I'd not done much woodworking, but I became so fascinated with his work (and his beautiful shop) that I asked if it would be possible to study with him. He agreed and we managed well, even though I speak little German and Kohler knows no English; we put a great deal of positive energy into the relationship. Ten weeks later I wasn't a cooper, but I had become a wood-worm. In 1980 I returned to Switzerland and worked with

Ruedi Kohler again, this time for three fast-moving, hard-learning weeks.

Cooperage in the Swiss Alps was traditionally a winter trade practiced by farmers who were occupied with outdoor work from spring to fall. When Kohler was 22, having practiced alpine farming and cheesemaking with his father, he paid an old cooper fifty Swiss francs for four months of winter training. At the time (1923) the wage for a day's work was three francs. The next winter Kohler returned for another session. This time his usefulness earned back the fifty francs, and he was presented with a set of coopers' tools, which he still uses. Kohler says that when he got into cooperage the craft was in its decline. New factory-made metal containers were cheaper than coopers' woodenware, and modern health regulations gradually prohibited using old dairy vessels except high in the Alps. World War II was a good time for coopers, because metal was scarce. But after the war cheap plastics were introduced, and cooperage almost died out. During the last 15 years, interest in traditional crafts has renewed the demand for woodenware. In 1967 Kohler retired from farm-

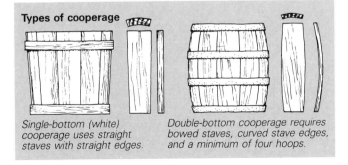

Types of cooperage

Single-bottom (white) cooperage uses straight staves with straight edges.

Double-bottom cooperage requires bowed staves, curved stave edges, and a minimum of four hoops.

ing and cheesemaking to become a full-time cooper. He still makes a few coopered vessels for farm use, but the greater part of his output goes to the tourist trade: milk buckets, bowls and butter churns that will never be put to work.

Cooperage techniques are closely related to those of many other traditional woodcrafts. Most of the work is done at a shaving horse, although a workbench with a vise and bench dogs is also useful. Many cooperage tools are shared by other crafts—hewing hatchets, froes, carving knives, drawknives, spokeshaves, planes, saws, drills, etc. Coopers also use several specialized tools—curved (hollowing) drawknives, convex-soled planes, and a device called a *croze,* which cuts a groove for the bottom board inside the assembled staves. I'll discuss each as it comes to hand when making a typical, single-bottom, staved container, 220mm (8⅝ in.) in diameter and 120mm (4¾ in.) high.

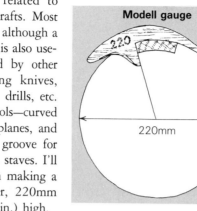

Modell gauge

220mm

Wood selection—Many woods can be used for cooperage, but there are definite qualities that all coopers look for. The wood must be straight-grained and must work easily with hand tools. Cooperage requires well-seasoned wood, because shrinking staves leak and loosen the hoops. Double-bottom cooperage requires wood that bends easily; the best is white oak. For single-bottom cooperage, the favored wood in Switzerland is arve (*Pinus cembra*), known in English as Swiss stone pine. It is a slow-growing conifer found at altitudes generally above 3,300 ft. Arve growth rings average about 1mm (¹⁄₂₅ in.) per year. The fibers are extremely small, and the wood works easily, even across end grain and through knots. Arve does grow in the United States (it's planted as an ornamental), but any straight-grained softwood will do: pine, cedar, redwood, Douglas fir. Linden (basswood) can also be used. One of the appeals of cooperage is that the wood is readily available, and you need only a few board feet to make a bucket.

Traditionally, coopers buy wood as bucked logs, either round or split. A neighbor tells Kohler about some pine firewood of extra-fine quality, or a local sawmill puts aside an arve log. Kohler used to begin with a crosscut saw, but today he bucks out sections with a chainsaw, working around major knots, sawing suitable stave lengths. Staves for our 120mm high bowl are initially cut 150mm (6 in.) long. These rounds are then radially split into pie-shaped billets, which are air-seasoned in a drafty hayloft for at least a year.

Kohler sometimes buys wood that has been plain-sawn into thick, unedged planks. Sawmill edging often wastes much wood. The advantage of lumber is that it is easy to handle. The disadvantage is that some staves will not be quarter-grained, which is never the case with split-out stock. After air-seasoning, the wood is roughed into stave blanks—split along a radial plane using a small froe and a maul. Stave width varies. For our small container, widths can range from 35mm (1⅜ in.) to 80mm (3 in.). Kohler uses a broad hatchet for trimming and roughly tapering the sides, perhaps 3mm to 6mm (¾₆ in.) wider at the top than at the bottom. This produces a taper in the finished bucket such that the diameter of the bottom is about 10% less than that of the top.

Kohler next stacks the blanks against a south-facing outdoor wall for further air-drying. Then a few days before he needs them, he takes the staves indoors for a final drying on a

rack above the stove. He often groups stave blanks in bunches according to length, for single projects. At this stage the aggregate width of the staves should be about four times the bowl's diameter—in this case about 880mm (35 in.).

Shaping the staves—Swiss coopers find the correct edge angle of a stave with a simple gauge called a *modell.* The modell is a thin crescent-shaped piece of wood whose inner contour matches the exterior curve of the container. The perpendicular edge guide at one end of the modell represents the radius line of the curve.

Staves are shaped at a shaving horse, using a flat drawknife, a hollowing drawknife, a long jointer plane and an appropriate modell. Shaping begins with drawknife work on the exterior face. Hold the modell across the top end of the blank to gauge the curvature, then with the blank in the shaving horse, shave the top third of the stave to fit the modell. You could pencil in the shape on the end grain, but Kohler just judges by eye. The first cuts should be light, to verify grain direction and irregularities. Block out the curve from the sides toward the center, keeping the stave as thick as possible. Turn the blank end for end and drawknife the rest of the outside face. The curve for the bottom end is gauged by eye to match that of the top end. The modell is not used at the bottom end because stave taper results in a tighter curve there. Fair the whole outside face. If necessary, use the drawknife in reverse, as a push tool, to handle grain that runs into the wood. Or reposition the stave in the shaving horse, to get the most from your pull stroke. Then turn the stave over.

Rough out the inside face with a hollowing drawknife. This is a deeply curved coopers' drawknife with an exterior bevel. Shave from both ends, to approximately 18mm (¹¹⁄₁₆-in.) thickness. Do not attempt to cut thinner walls at this stage. If you don't have a hollowing drawknife, you can use either a scorp or a narrow inshave ground with an outside bevel. Or you can reshape (and retemper) a flat drawknife to an appropriate curvature, about 35mm (1⅛-in.) depth across a circular arc that spans about 120mm (4¾ in.). Another method (which Kohler uses for the inside of his oval milking buckets) is to dog individual staves to the workbench and hollow them with a convex-soled plane.

Edge angles are roughed out with a flat drawknife and the modell, which is always gauged at the upper rim. To hold the stave and have tool access along the full length of the edge, Kohler sets one end against a rabbet cut across the near end of the work ledge on his shaving horse. He holds the other end tight against a breast bib, a small flat board that hangs by a string around his neck. Stave edges must be flat, not twisted or curved. Any container has to be tapered so that the hoops can be driven tight, but more than an 8mm (⁵⁄₁₆-in.) taper for a 150mm (6-in.) long stave results in a container with too much taper, which won't hold its hoops.

Stave edges are finished with a jointer plane set upside down on the edge of the shaving horse, or secured in a vise. Run the stave over the plane, checking the angle between passes. For safety, grip the staves well above the plane sole, and spit on your fingertips to increase your hold. Besides the

Drawings: Christopher Clapp

correct angle, check for flatness. Hold pairs of staves side by side and look for uniform contact. Try wiggling them back and forth, making sure they don't wobble or roll.

Once the staves are jointed, lay them out side by side in a flat shallow arc to check for correct circumference (3.14 times intended diameter). The proper length, measured with a tape or a folding rule, which can follow the arc, should be the circumference you are aiming for, plus or minus 2%. If the series is too long, drawknife and plane one or more staves down to size. If too short, substitute a slightly larger stave.

Test assembly—Two wooden hoops will hold the completed container together. To position the staves for setting the hoops, Kohler drills mating holes and inserts small hardwood pegs into the sides of each stave. The pegged staves won't shift while the hoops are hammered tight.

Two temporary metal hoops are used in an initial test assembly, and to hold the staves in place for further shaping before the wooden hoops are fitted. Kohler makes his own metal hoops (see drawing, below right), and keeps a large collection of them in various diameters. To test-assemble, peg the staves together and place the cylinder on a workbench, bottom rim facing up. Fit the larger metal hoop onto the assembled staves first, and drive it tightly in place with a square-headed hammer or a coopers' hoop driver. A hoop driver looks like a blacksmiths' hammer with a notch ground along the peening edge. I made one by taking a small rock-climbing hammer and filing a groove into the face of its pick end. Set the groove over the hoop edge and hit the head of the driver with a second hammer. Work round and round until the hoop stops moving downward. The correct test-fit should be about one-fourth from the top rim of the container. When the first hoop is in position, fit the second, smaller hoop.

Although the staves are pegged, they can pivot in and out on those pegs. If a stave protrudes, hammer it in—but place a second hammer inside to dampen the blows, and vice versa—until you have averaged out the differences.

Check the container for roundness by measuring across the upper rim from two perpendicular locations. You can live with a discrepancy up to 5mm (³⁄₁₆ in.). Look for openings between staves. If you find any, knock off the temporary hoop and check all edge angles against the modell. Reassemble. If there are still spaces on the inside, disassemble and plane one stave narrower. If gaps show on the outside, remove a stave (save it for your next container) and substitute a new one that's wider. This is your last chance to be sure that the staves fit together perfectly.

Dressing the assembled staves—Once you have the stave edges flush, you can dress the rims and the interior surface. Slightly moisten the end grain of the upper rim with a wet sponge, to soften the wood. Then plane the rim flat. A block plane works nicely. Check by eye or by placing the container upside down on a flat surface.

The lower rim of the assembled staves generally requires sawing before planing. Pencil a series of marks measuring from the (now flat) upper rim, in this case at 120mm (4¾ in.). Set the container on its side and begin a shallow sawcut aimed from one pencil mark to the next. Kohler uses a small backsaw. Make a series of shallow passes around the container. For a flat cut, hold the saw parallel to the plane of the rim, not perpendicular to the side of the staves. With the

The outside curve and edge bevel of a bucket stave are checked with a gauge called a modell, *drawn on facing page.*

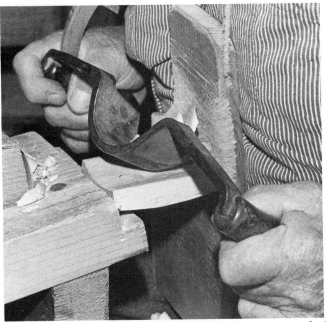

To shave short staves, cooper Ruedi Kohler supports one end of the blank in a rabbet on the front of his shaving-horse ledge, the other against a wooden bib.

Making metal hoops *1. Lay out and drill rivet holes in ¹⁄₁₆-in. thick strap iron or galvanized steel.*

10mm (³⁄₈ in.)

Circumference minus 8mm (⁵⁄₁₆ in.)

A B   C

35mm (1³⁄₈ in.)   26mm (1 in.)

2. Hammer one edge of strap to induce curve. Leave overlap area unhammered.

50mm (2 in.)   50mm (2 in.)

3. Attach rivet through holes A and C, then crease end of overlap on a small anvil. Test-fit hoop on container, re-rivet if necessary. When hoop fits, drill and fix second rivet through hole B.

223

The staves are test-assembled and temporarily held in place with two metal hoops, so that the inside of the cylinder can be smoothed either with a convex-soled plane, or with a Surform, as shown above.

This croze *is like a marking gauge with teeth. Instead of merely scribing the groove for the bottom, it cuts it directly into the assembled staves.*

Shaping bottom board

1. Use a marking gauge to scribe the edge of the bottom board, and drawknife to this shape.

4.5mm (³⁄₁₆ in.)
5.5mm (¼ in.)
8mm (⁵⁄₁₆ in.)

2. Use a slotted hardwood stick (called a fümel) to compress the edge to 4.5mm.

4.5mm

Fümel

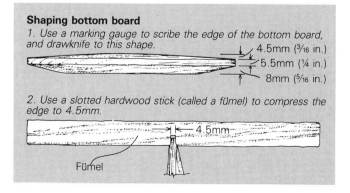

waste sawn away, plane the lower rim smooth.

At this point the staves are still of various thicknesses. To indicate their dressed thickness, bevel the rims inside and out, leaving the upper rim 15mm (⅝ in.) thick and the lower rim 17mm (¹¹⁄₁₆ in.) thick, to accommodate the groove for the bottom of the container. For the outside bevel, use a spokeshave held about 30° from the staves and produce a rim line as close to a circle as possible. Gauge the proper thickness and bevel the inside, using a sharp carving knife, held point down in your fist like a dagger.

Some white coopers dress the inside with a scorp, but Kohler uses small wooden planes with convex soles and irons. He planes along the length of the staves, first from the upper rim, then from the lower, until the inside surface is worked down to the rim guidelines. Difficult grain can be shaped with a convex Surform. Sand the inside with 80-grit, then 120-grit paper, working across the grain. The outside of the container will be dressed later.

The bottom—Kohler's croze, the tool that cuts the bottom groove in the assembled staves, resembles an enlarged marking gauge with a row of coarse teeth in place of the scriber (photo, below left). This cutter is held by a setscrew or a wedge in the sliding arm. The cutter's teeth are filed much like coarse crosscut-saw teeth, having 5 points to the inch. Kohler made his from an old plane iron. The groove can be cut in a number of other ways, including scribing the edges with a marking gauge and excavating it with a chisel.

On our container, the groove is 13mm (½ in.) above the lower rim, 5mm (³⁄₁₆ in.) wide and 5mm deep. Set the assembled staves bottom up on the shaving-horse bench, secure between your thighs and against a block between the container and the upright supporting the shaving-horse work ledge. Be sure to hold the croze flat against the bottom rim. Press down hard to avoid chatter (and scratching the dressed staves) and take a series of shallow passes around the rim. The 5mm width of the groove requires resetting the distance between cutter and fence for a second round of passes.

Bottoms can be split from a wide straight-grained billet, taken from a clear sawn board, or glued up from narrower stock. The bottom wood is planed smooth on one side, scribed with a marking gauge to 18mm (¹¹⁄₁₆ in.) thick and planed to thickness.

You can find the radius for the bottom with straight-leg dividers. Open them to the approximate radius, judged by eye. Place one leg in the bottom of the groove and walk the dividers around the groove. By trial and error, readjust the dividers until you can walk off six equal divisions. The dividers are now set for the exact radius of the bottom.

Scribe the circumference on one face of the bottom and saw it out just outside the scribed line. Put the bottom in a vise, and spokeshave the rim to just inside the scribed line, rotating the wood in order to spokeshave with the grain. The bottom should be 0.5mm (0.02 in.) undersize.

With your marking gauge, scribe two lines 5.5mm (¼ in.) apart on the edge of the bottom board, and then drawknife the board to the shape shown in the drawing at left. With the board still in the vise, use a hardwood stick with a 4.5mm (³⁄₁₆-in.) slot and compress the rim to 4.5mm thickness. Then sand the bottom board across the grain.

With the bottom shaped, you are ready to glue up. Knock off the metal hoops and disassemble the staves, laying them on the workbench in order. Spread a thin coat of white glue on both edges of each stave. Glue is used so that the exterior can be dressed with the hoops removed. Do not use yellow glue. It sets too fast and complicates knocking the staves apart again if you run into trouble fitting the bottom. Reassemble the staves with glue and pegs, and lower the bottom board (chamfered edge down) into the container from the top. Spread the lower rim until the bottom board snaps into its groove. Hold the staves in place with a loose-fitting, temporary upper hoop. Tap the staves around the bottom, replace the lower metal hoop, and tighten it with hammer and hoop driver. Hammer the staves in or out as necessary. Then tighten the upper hoop. Allow the glue to set at least one hour before you remove the metal hooping, so you can spokeshave the exterior of the staves to the beveled upper and lower edges. Sand the outside of the container.

Wooden hoops—The most distinctive feature of Swiss milk buckets is their beautiful wooden hoops. The design is a refined variation of the so-called arrow-lock pattern. Hoops can be made from maple, walnut, oak, even pine limbs. Traditionally, hooping stock comes from the trunk of a choice young maple, 120mm (4¾ in.) to 200mm (8 in.) in diameter at the butt. A tree that is growing in an open area is preferred because its limbs grow outward, perpendicular to the stem, yielding minimal grain deformity around knots. In thick woods, tree limbs reach up to the light, causing irregular stem grain.

Buck the bole to a length at least 200mm longer than the circumference you will need. The bottom hoop will fit flush with the container's bottom, and the top hoop will be about a hoop's width below the rim. Hoop length includes an overlap of some 160mm (6⅜ in.), plus about 50mm (2 in.) for waste and end-cuts. Each bole length will yield 20 to 40 hoop blanks, and it may be possible to take two clear lengths from a single tree. Seal the end grain, and split the bole in half and then into eighths as wood is needed. Green wood is easiest to work and to bend, but air-dried wood can be used. Maple splits easily, but its grain is rarely straight, so bandsaw two radial strips 8mm to 10mm (about ⅜ in.) thick, and 30mm to 35mm (about 1⅜ in.) wide; the growth rings will cross the thickness of the strips. Blanks from ring-porous hardwoods can be split to size. Drawknife the bark side to a smooth and straight, or slightly bowed, edge. You will have to support the hoop wood on an extension stick sandwiched between shaving-horse ledge and jaw.

Next, decide which will be the outside face of the hoop. This can be either side of the blank, but the wood often takes a natural bow. Drawknife the outside face smooth, then scribe a line 26mm (1 in.) from the dressed edge and drawknife the blank to width.

To fit the tapering shape of the container, the hoop in section must be thicker at the bottom than at the top. Mark and then drawknife the hoop 7mm (¼ in.) thick at its top edge, 9mm (⅜ in.) thick at its bottom edge.

The next step is to measure the exact length of the hoop. Wrap a piece of stout string around the container where the center of the hoop will lie. Add 8mm (⁵⁄₁₆ in.). Transfer this length to the hoop blank, leaving room for the 80mm (3-in.) overlap at each end. The drawings at right detail the steps for first shaping the same side profile at each end of the hoop, and then shaping the female and male pattern in plan view.

Assemble and fit the longer upper hoop first. Ladle boiling

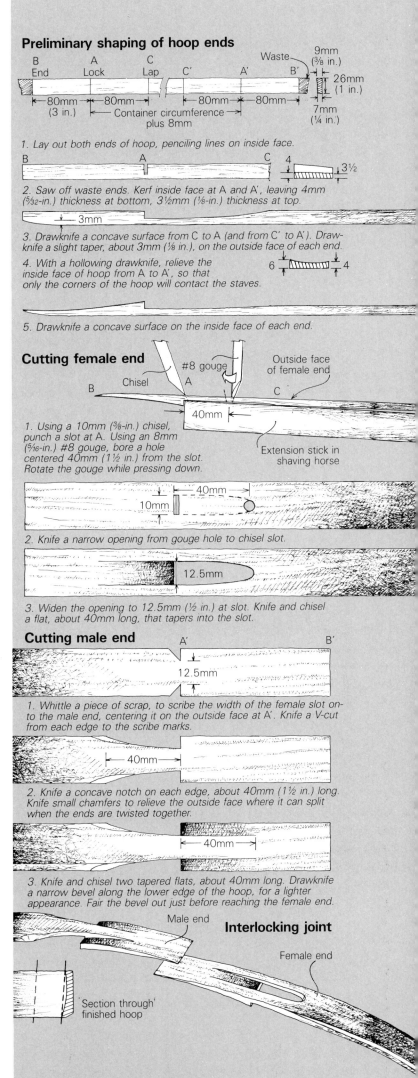

Preliminary shaping of hoop ends

1. Lay out both ends of hoop, penciling lines on inside face.

2. Saw off waste ends. Kerf inside face at A and A', leaving 4mm (⁵⁄₃₂-in.) thickness at bottom, 3½mm (⅛-in.) thickness at top.

3. Drawknife a concave surface from C to A (and from C' to A'). Drawknife a slight taper, about 3mm (⅛ in.), on the outside face of each end.

4. With a hollowing drawknife, relieve the inside face of hoop from A to A', so that only the corners of the hoop will contact the staves.

5. Drawknife a concave surface on the inside face of each end.

Cutting female end

1. Using a 10mm (⅜-in.) chisel, punch a slot at A. Using an 8mm (⁵⁄₁₆-in.) #8 gouge, bore a hole centered 40mm (1½ in.) from the slot. Rotate the gouge while pressing down.

2. Knife a narrow opening from gouge hole to chisel slot.

3. Widen the opening to 12.5mm (½ in.) at slot. Knife and chisel a flat, about 40mm long, that tapers into the slot.

Cutting male end

1. Whittle a piece of scrap, to scribe the width of the female slot onto the male end, centering it on the outside face at A'. Knife a V-cut from each edge to the scribe marks.

2. Knife a concave notch on each edge, about 40mm (1½ in.) long. Knife small chamfers to relieve the outside face where it can split when the ends are twisted together.

3. Knife and chisel two tapered flats, about 40mm long. Drawknife a narrow bevel along the lower edge of the hoop, for a lighter appearance. Fair the bevel out just before reaching the female end.

Interlocking joint

Ladling hot water over the hoop blank, above, limbers it for bending. The blank must be twisted, below, in order to fit one end through the other.

A knife sizes the rim line by beveling the waste away. Both the inside and the outside of the container will be thinned to meet these top and bottom rim lines.

water over the hoop for about one minute. Limber the hoop by flexing it. Limber the joint ends by inserting them in a vise opened about 10mm (³⁄₈ in.); bend toward the interior face. Reheat the hoop by ladling more boiling water. Bend the hoop into a circle and twist the ends to insert the tab through the outside face of the slot. Any small splits should be immediately pared off with a knife so they don't run into the hoop.

With your container upside down on the bench, fit the hoop. Drive it into place by hammering on a small hardwood block. The hoop should become tight 25mm to 30mm (about an inch) from the upper rim. If the hoop is too tight (short), remove it from the container, and with the joint still assembled, saw 2mm to 3mm (up to ⅛ in.) from one of the locking edges of the tab. An alternative is to thin the overlapping section by paring the inside faces with a knife. If the hoop is loose (too long), add a thin spacer between the male and female locking edges.

Now heat, limber and lock the lower hoop. Fit it so that the bottom of the hoop is flush with the bottom of the container. With a knife, trim the edges of the overlapping ends. Nail or peg both hoops in place. For pegs, drill 3mm (⅛-in.) diameter holes through the hoops and into, but not through, the staves. Locate one peg on each side of the lock joint, plus two evenly spaced pegs on the opposite side of the hoop. Nails are generally brass with round heads.

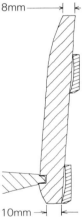

After the wooden hoops have been fitted, the inside face of the rims can be dressed with a knife for a lighter, more finished look. Take long, smooth slices, beveling them about 65mm (2½ in.) from the top rim. The final thickness at the rim should be 8mm (⁵⁄₁₆ in.). Make a similar bevel around the interior of the bottom rim.

A handle is optional. If you want one, make it from maple and secure it with wooden pegs. Note Kohler's clever arrangement in the photo on p. 221: the two extra-long staves are relieved, so the handle moves freely and doesn't bind against the rim. This photo also shows how the sides of a bucket are sometimes sculpted. While the effect is decorative, the purpose is really practical—it allows the bucket to be made more tapered, while still using a basically circular hoop of minimum inside taper. Kohler begins such a bucket with thicker, more tapered staves, gluing up the bucket as usual. Where the top of each of the two wooden hoops will be, he makes a sawcut about 3mm (⅛ in.) deep. With a skew chisel, he carves flat the area where each hoop will land. Above the area for the top hoop, he drawknifes the outside of the bucket concave. Above the area for the bottom hoop, he drawknifes the bucket convex. He then fits the wooden hoops as usual.

For farm use, staved containers are not given any surface treatment. The hoops of bowls and buckets sold as gifts or prizes are often chip-carved, and the whole is given a coat of quick-dry semigloss lacquer. Lacquered ware is easy to keep clean, but it is decorative, never used on the farm. Under continuous wetting and drying, it would soon deteriorate. □

Drew Langsner teaches courses in chairmaking and other woodworking skills every summer. For details on his latest offerings, write Country Workshops, Rt. 3, Box 262, Marshall, N.C. 28753. Photos by the author.

Splitting Out a Firewood Tote

This project gets you started with green wood

by Wayne Ladd

The first time I met Vermont chairmaker Dave Sawyer, he was sitting on a shaving horse making a pitchfork. The only sounds were the creaking of the horse and the hiss of his drawknife. Having played at woodworking myself, I looked around the shop for the familiar router, bench saw and jointer, but saw only bits, braces, hand planes and, against one wall, a fine bench. Sawyer asked if I knew of any ash trees for sale. As it turned out, a huge, straight ash had blown over on my land. The following week, wedges in hand, Sawyer came over to split the trunk. We carried the splits to my car, then to his shop. The next day, I was amazed to find that he had a pitchfork made from my tree.

I was so impressed with Sawyer's skill and practiced eye for simple, sturdy woodworking that I spent the following year as his part-time apprentice. One of the first projects I learned was the log carrier shown here. Though the graceful bow gives the tote a fragile look, I've discovered that it can carry more wood than I care to heft at one time. And you can wrap twine around the foot rails and hang it from a rafter to make a wonderfully sturdy indoor child's swing.

Splitting green wood—Making the log carrier from riven green wood affords some important advantages over sawn, kiln-dried wood. First, you can go straight to your woodlot, fell a tree, and then split, shave and assemble it into a finished product, all in a matter of hours. Split along the grain instead of being sawn across it, riven wood is stronger than sawn wood, and satisfyingly easy to cut, bend and shape while green. You don't have to glue your projects together, either. Whittled tenons, dried over the woodstove, slip into mortises bored in wet wood, where they swell and lock the joint. For working green wood, you'll need two steel wedges, a mallet and a froe for splitting. A drawknife, spokeshave, brace and bit, and shaving horse complete the toolkit. For a shaving horse design, see the box on p. 229.

Green-wood tote holds all the wood you want to carry.

I use white ash for my carriers because it's the best bending wood that grows on my land. Hickory and oak also bend well. Whatever wood you choose, it should be straight-grained. Read the bark. If it's free of swirls and scars, chances are the wood will be the same. A 5-ft. log, 6 in. in diameter, will provide enough wood for a dozen carriers.

Quarter your log by first driving a wedge into one end and then leapfrogging the wedges up the side. If you've got a big log, split it into eighths. I use wedges only to get the log into manageable splits or bolts, which I then carry to the shop, where I split the parts closer to the final size with a froe. You'll need a brake—a mechanism that props the bolts at about 35° from the vertical for froeing. The crotch of a fallen tree or two heavy logs adjacent to each other make a suitable brake. Work with the bolt angled toward you.

Learning to froe is easy if you remember that this tool doesn't cut the wood, but rives or splits it along the material's natural fibers. Start the froe with a wack or two from the mallet. Then set the mallet aside, and continue the split by alternately levering the fibers apart and advancing the tool into the split. Split the unusable heartwood off the point of the quarter first. Then follow the sequence shown in figure 1, splitting in halves so that an equal amount of wood on each side of the froe will keep the cleave going straight down the length of the bolt instead of running off and exiting where you don't want it to. If the split does run out, put the heavy side down, and with the heel of your hand, put weight on this side of the split only. This will make the heavier half "give up" its grain. You can tell by the sound whether you

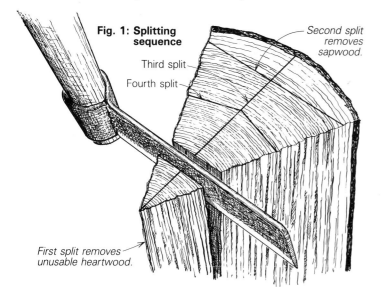

Fig. 1: Splitting sequence

Second split removes sapwood.

Third split

Fourth split

First split removes unusable heartwood.

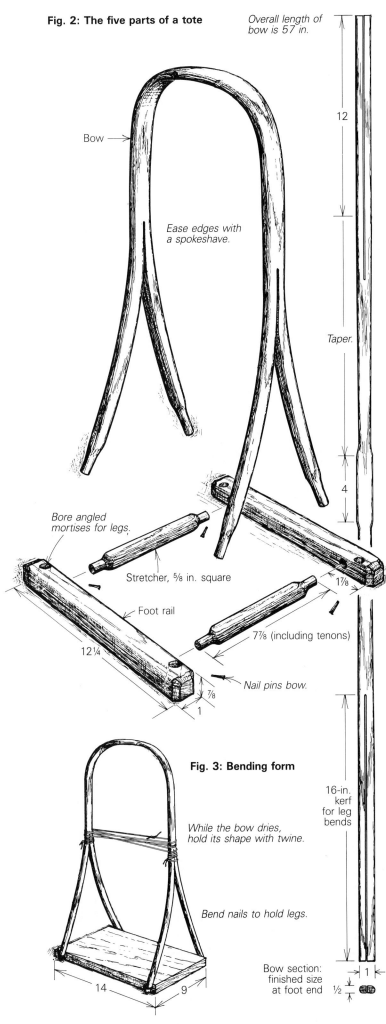

Fig. 2: The five parts of a tote

Bow

Ease edges with a spokeshave.

Bore angled mortises for legs.

Stretcher, ⅝ in. square

Foot rail

12¼

7/8

1

Nail pins bow.

7⅞ (including tenons)

1⅞

Overall length of bow is 57 in.

12

Taper.

4

16-in. kerf for leg bends

Bow section: finished size at foot end

1

½

Fig. 3: Bending form

While the bow dries, hold its shape with twine.

Bend nails to hold legs.

14   9

are following the grain. If it goes *tic, tic* and gives a little at a time, you're on. When it sounds like a branch breaking, it's jumping the grain and you need to straighten it out.

Make your rough splits ¼ in. oversize in section; you'll be shaving them down to finished dimensions with the drawknife. The bow will be steam-bent later, so keep grain direction in mind. Whether the growth rings are radial or tangential to the bend is up to you. I prefer a tangential split—it looks nicer and it makes it easier to follow the grain.

Drawknifing to size—Now the pleasant work can begin. Clamp the bow in your horse and shave one face smooth with the drawknife. Shave with the grain as much as you can and watch for tearing. You may not be able to read the grain, but your drawknife will. Downhill, the cut will be deliciously smooth; uphill, the knife will dig in. Pull in long, even strokes, sliding the drawknife sideways as you go. If you're doing it right, the slicing motion will peel off long shavings of even thickness. On each piece, smooth one face first, then square up an adjacent edge and shave the opposite face and edge to yield the finished dimensions. It's the same order of cuts you'd follow using a jointer, tablesaw and thickness planer. Keep the rails in a cool, damp spot so that they'll retain enough moisture to swell the tenons later. Dry the stretchers and the bow over a woodstove.

Define the handle's shape with graceful, ⅛-in. radius scallops on each side. By using the drawknife with the bevel down, you can control the depth and the shape of the scallop. Otherwise, the knife will want to dig in. Starting about 12 in. from each end of the bow, drawknife a taper toward the handle, as shown in figure 2. Also, hollow the inside (compression side) of the bow a little, maybe 1/16 in. at the handle tapering to zero about 19 in. from each end.

Shape the handle to your liking, then ease the edges of the bow, rails and stretchers with your spokeshave. Finally, with a handsaw or bandsaw, rip 16-in. long kerfs at each end of the bow so that it can be wishboned into the rails after steaming.

My steamer is a stainless steel tube capped at one end, half filled with water and placed in the firebox of my woodstove. Any steel pipe or even an old steel drum will work. While the bow steams, make up the simple bending form shown in figure 3. It should be constructed to overbend the leg splits a little so that they'll have to be sprung back in to fit into the rails. This tension will stop the legs from splitting further.

With gloved hands, remove the bow from the steamer and limber up the bends by forming them over your knee. First put bends on each side of the handle about 4 in. from the center. This creates a bow with two "shoulders" rather than one that's a perfect half-circle. After you've defined the shoulders, bend the bow like Superman would bend a bar of steel. Make adjustments where needed—the handle has to look right, and you can't change the bend when it's in the form.

To keep the wood from splitting as you limber the leg bends, clamp the top of the kerf in your shaving horse and flex the legs into a graceful sweep from a point 1½ in. below the end of the kerf. Watch for kinks. A couple of turns of twine at the end of the kerf will keep the split from advancing when you release it from the shaving horse. Put the bow in the form and pull its sides in with a twine wrap.

Assembling the carrier—I assemble the stretchers to the rails after first whittling ⅝-in. long by 7/16-in. diameter tenons at the ends of the stretchers. Trim the tenons for a squeaky-tight fit in a test mortise bored into scrap. To avoid splitting out the mortises, flatten the top and bottom of the tenon with your knife, bore the mortises in the rails and then tap the pieces together. The dry tenons swell, so I don't use glue, but if you feel that this is tempting fate, use some.

The legs fit into angled mortises bored through the rails. I eyeball the angle by clamping the base assembly in my vise, boring $\frac{7}{16}$-in. mortises from the top inside corner of each rail with a brace and bit. The mortises should be located about $\frac{7}{8}$ in. in from the end of each rail. I angle the brace so that the edge of the mortise will exit about $\frac{3}{16}$ in. from the outside bottom edge of each rail. Just as the point of the bit breaks through, I withdraw it and complete boring from the bottom up. This eliminates splintering.

Before you whittle the tenons on the bow, it needs to be cleaned up with a scraper. Any splinters or hairline cracks in the bends will show up when you put a finish on, so examine the bow closely. To trim it, I stand it on the bench between two sticks clamped $8\frac{1}{4}$ in. apart. Nails driven into the sticks stay the bow while I stand back and take a look. If the bow

appears crooked, I raise one leg or the other until it looks good. Then, using a compass to scribe them, I trim the ends of the long legs at an angle that will sit them flat on the bench.

The leg tenons should be 1 in. long. I shape the leg to taper right into the tenon. Shoved home at assembly, the joint fits tightly without fussing. Since these joints carry most of the stress, I glue them and drive a cut-nail pin from the inside of the foot perpendicular to the bow. Before pinning the joints, though, turn the carrier upside down and sight the legs. Align them by pushing one or the other beyond its mortise.

The final step is to trim the projecting leg tenons flush and to flatten the bottom, which always twists a little from the tension of the bow. I shave the feet with my drawknife, testing for flatness on the benchtop. When the carrier sits right, I sand out any dirty marks and put an oil finish on it. I mix a little stain in the oil to bring out the grain of the ash. □

Wayne Ladd turns trees into totes, treen and chairs at his home in East Calais, Vt. For more on the green woodworkers' art, see FWW #12, pp. 46-48 and pp. 64-67; #25, pp. 92-94; and #33, pp. 50-56.

Plans for a Swiss shaving horse

by Drew Langsner

These plans are adapted from the shaving horse used every day for the past 60 years by Swiss cooper Ruedi Kohler (see pp. 221-226). It has several advantages over other shaving horses. The position of the pivoting arm provides great leverage. The treadle extends forward for a comfortable reach, the bridge extends a generous 4 in. past where the head contacts it, and the angle of the head provides direct downward pressure, important because draw-

knifing tends to pull the stock forward. With the pivot holes at the front of the arm, the head swings open automatically when you release the treadle, so that it's easy to reposition stock. The central arm with the head open on both sides is a pleasure when turning long stock end-for-end.

Keep in mind that the shaving horse is a folk tool, and lots of variations are possible. Bridge height, for instance, can range from 7 in. to 11 in., depending on

your own height (I'm 5 ft. 8 in., and the height as drawn is good for me). The head and treadle are held by tusk tenons, which I find easy to construct, but I've bolted and face-glued heads to arms. All versions work well. One advantage of tusk-tenoning the parts is that it makes the arm easy to detach for transportation. □

Drew Langsner operates Country Workshops in Marshall, N.C.

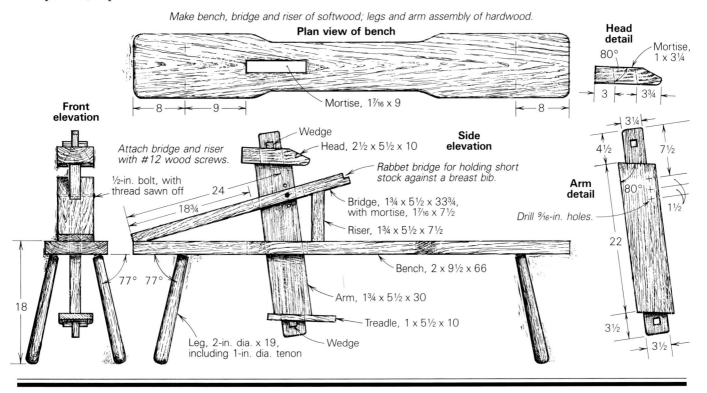

Make bench, bridge and riser of softwood; legs and arm assembly of hardwood.

INDEX

230